The United Nations
at Work in Asia

The United Nations at Work in Asia

An Envoy's Account of Development in China, Vietnam, Thailand and the South Pacific

Roy D. Morey

McFarland & Company, Inc., Publishers

Jefferson, North Carolina

LIBRARY OF CONGRESS CATALOGUING-IN-PUBLICATION DATA

Morey, Roy D.
The United Nations at work in Asia : an envoy's account of development
in China, Vietnam, Thailand and the South Pacific / Roy D. Morey.
p.   cm.
Includes bibliographical references and index.

ISBN 978-0-7864-7871-2
softcover : acid free paper ∞

1. United Nations—Asia.   2. Economic assistance—Asia.
3. Humanitarian assistance—Asia.   4. Morey, Roy D.   I. Title.
JZ4972.M67 2014   338.91095—dc23   2013041290

BRITISH LIBRARY CATALOGUING DATA ARE AVAILABLE

On the cover: Cambodians returning from refugee camps in
Thailand aboard a United Nations High Commissioner for Refugees
train as it approaches Phnom Penh (UN Photo/Pernaca Sudhakaran)

Manufactured in the United States of America

*McFarland & Company, Inc., Publishers
Box 611, Jefferson, North Carolina 28640
www.mcfarlandpub.com*

To the three ladies of my life,
Delores, Diana and Carolyn

Contents

Good governance is perhaps the single most important factor
in eradicating poverty and promoting development.
— Kofi Annan, United Nations Secretary-General, 1997–2006

Preface

The groundwork for the Asian economic miracle was established in the last quarter century, the period covered in this book. With China's Mao Zedong's death in 1976 and the death of Vietnamese Communist Party Secretary Le Duan ten years later, China and Vietnam decided to start substituting pragmatism for communist ideology and Thailand started on a path toward great political stability. The timing was perfect for an American United Nations representative to arrive in the two communist countries because, for the first time, both placed a premium on improved relations with the United States and both were moving toward a market economy. The major policy reforms started changing the political and economic landscape, thus providing an opportunity for the United Nations Development Programme to engage the governments in undertaking sensible and sustainable development projects.

The first purpose of the book is to acquaint the reader with the evolving political, economic and social conditions in these countries prior to their rise as important emerging economies. The chapter on Samoa and the South Pacific is included to apprise the reader of a little-known part of the world and the challenges of providing appropriate and useful development assistance in small, isolated countries.

The second purpose is to reveal a hidden side of the United Nations. When the average American thinks about the United Nations, a thirty-eight story rectangular tower on the East River in midtown Manhattan comes to mind. The tower houses the offices of the secretary general and the secretariat. Attached to the tower is a building complex which houses the Security Council and General Assembly. What this picture omits is the larger UN system composed of more than thirty agencies, funds and programs, only some of which are headquartered in New York. If the truth were known, there are funds and programs in this group which do more to improve the lives of people throughout the world every day than one could ever imagine.

These thirty-plus agencies, funds and programs constitute the hidden side of the United Nations because their contribution to humankind is rarely covered in the popular press. The leading development fund within the group is the United Nations Development Programme, headquartered in New York with field offices in 135 developing countries. The UNDP is rarely mentioned in the popular press unless it is associated with a political controversy. Hence, there is a need for a book which describes and analyzes the development role of the UN. The truth needs to be known that at least in Asia and the Pacific, where the political and economic center of gravity has shifted, the UN has an enviable development record. An additional purpose of the book is to contravene ill-informed charges made against the UN. The United Nations has a serious image problem on Capitol Hill, especially among Republicans. For example, in May 2012 a key House appropriations subcommittee cut more than $400 million in contributions to the UN international organizations and peacekeeping. In addition, funding was eliminated for the UN Population Fund (UNFPA) and the UN Educational, Scientific and Cultural Organization (UNESCO). Many members harbor a distorted image of the UN. They see a Security Council stymied by vetoes or threat of vetoes by Russia and China and a General Assembly dominated by developing countries heaping abuse on the United States and Israel. Moreover, they imagine a bloated UN bureaucracy which is inefficient and ineffective in administering aid to a collection of corrupt and ungrateful developing countries. The book will show that this view of the UN is distorted and ill-informed.

My first inclination was to write an academic treatise on international development based upon twenty-two years of experience with UNDP. But I encountered considerable resistance when I discussed this approach with my wife, family and friends. They argued such a book would appeal to a small audience and would minimize special qualities I could bring to the topic. They contended that there is a plethora of books on the UN and international development written by scholars, but very few by practitioners especially with the career background of a college professor, White House staffer and senior officer in the U.S. State Department and the UN Development Programme. The advice was accepted and the result is a book which provides an insider's view of the development process, within an Asian context, with political and economic analysis and observations on cultural adjustments required to work and enjoy life in a fascinating set of countries large and small.

In his best selling book *Outliers*, Malcolm Gladwell explodes the myth of the "self-made man" and reminds us that in any of our accomplishments, we stand on the shoulders of our contemporaries and those who came before. Any book represents the contributions of many who in the past have provided wisdom, inspiration, guidance and advice. My father, Douglas, kindled my interest in Asia, and my mother, Lucretia, inspired my commitment to social justice.

My most imposing debt is to my wife and high school sweetheart, Delores, who served as editor, advisor and typist. Our lives have been linked for sixty years and the story could never have been written without her. There are others to whom I am deeply grateful who read and made extensive comments on the entire manuscript, including Professor Craig Murphy who wrote the definitive work on UNDP, my friend of fifty years Bruce Ladd and my esteemed UNDP colleague Robert England. I was fortunate to have a distinguished group who read and commented on parts of the manuscript including Ambassador Winston Lord, Professor Charles O. Jones, Ambassador Earl Drake, former UNDP administrators William Draper and James Gustave Speth, Professor Emmett Buell and Douglas Haaland. A special thanks goes to my nephew Mark Aitken for his technical support and advice in preparing the manuscript for publication. I also wish to thank Bruce Marcotte for his technical support. Special thanks also goes to Tim Weber for giving me permission to publish a vignette on his experience during the Cultural Revolution.

Over many years numerous friends and family members were of immense benefit to me in providing support and encouragement including Teall and Carolyn Edds, Leonard and Diana Ditmanson, Tim and Sandy Brancheau, Chuck and Linda Pilon, Richard and Donna Webb, Bill and Cathy Westwood, Joe and Darlean Worischeck, Ed and Polly Renwick, Marilyn Dresser, Wilfred Declercq, Jeffrey Aitken, Bob and Eileen Thompson,

Mary Anne Fay, Pat Roberts, Bill Foster, David Fennell, Bob Henze, James Akre, Peter Tomsen, Jonathan Pincus, Mike Gonzales and Audrey Morey Gonzales. UNDP colleagues who made such a difference for me include Andrew Joseph, Adriano Garcia, Winston Prattley, David Lockwood, Herb Behrstock, Denis Halliday, Nguyen Xuan Thuan, Long Yongtu, Jordan Ryan, Jan Mattson, Romy Garcia, Liuga Faumui, Elena Martinez, Robert Glofchesky, Nay Htun, Shunichi Murata, Setsuko Yamazaki, Sarah Burns and Tom Cox.

Abbreviations

ASEAN —Association of Southeast Asian Nations

DPRK —Democratic People's Republic of Korea

ECOSOC —Economic and Social Council (UN)

ESCAP —UN Economic and Social Commission for Asia and the Pacific

EU —European Union

FAO —Food and Agriculture Organization of the UN

GFATM —Global Fund for AIDS, Tuberculosis and Malaria

G77 —Group of 77 Developing Countries and China

HDI —Human Development Index

HDR —Human Development Report

IBRD —International Bank for Reconstruction and Development, also known as the World Bank (UN)

ICAO —International Civil Aviation Organization

IFAD —International Fund for Agricultural Development (UN)

ILO —International Labor Organization

IMF —International Monetary Fund

ITU —International Telecommunications Union

LDC —least developed country

MDGs —millennium development goals

NGO —non-governmental organization

OECD —Organization for Economic Cooperation and Development

ROK —Republic of Korea

SUNFED —Special UN Fund for Economic Development

TA —technical assistance

TCDC —technical cooperation among developing countries

UN —United Nations

UNAIDS —Joint UN Program on HIV/AIDS

UNCDC —UN Capital Development Fund

UNCTAD —UN Conference on Trade and Development

UNDG —UN Development Group

UNDP —UN Development Programme

UNDRO —UN Disaster Relief Organization

UNEP —UN Environment Programme

UNESCO —UN Educational, Scientific and Cultural Organization

UNFPA —UN Population Fund (formerly UN Fund for Population Activity)

UNHCR —UN High Commissioner for Refugees

UNICEF —UN Children's Fund

UNIDO —UN Industrial Development Organization

UNODC —UN Office on Drugs and Crime (formerly UNFDAC — UN Fund for Drug Abuse Control)

UNRRA —UN Relief and Rehabilitation Administration

UNV —UN volunteers

UPU —Universal Postal Union

WFP —World Food Programme (UN)

WHO —World Health Organization

WIPO —World Intellectual Properties Organization

WTO —World Trade Organization

1

Creation of the United Nations System

The term United Nations was first used to describe a group of nations opposed to the Axis powers (Germany, Japan and Italy) in World War II. The term was coined by U.S. President Franklin D. Roosevelt on New Year's Day 1942. U.K. Prime Minister Winston Churchill was spending the holidays with Roosevelt. After a long discussion the night before and no doubt martinis, which both of them savored, Roosevelt went to the guest bathroom in the East Wing of the White House, knocked on the door, wheeled himself into the room and tried the term on Churchill while he was still sitting in the bathtub! Churchill immediately embraced the term and was reminded of lines from Byron's *Childe Harold:*

> *Here, where the sword United Nations drew,*
> *Our countrymen were warring on that day!*
> *And this is much—and all—which will not pass away.*[1]

These were the two titans of history who were the main architects of the western world in the post–World War II period. They were also very human, smart, witty, and loved each other's company. One reason they both liked the term United Nations was because neither wanted to use the term alliance for fear the collective agreement they had in mind would be considered a formal treaty thus requiring U.S. Senate approval. That afternoon the two of them joined representatives from twenty-six allied nations, including those from the Soviet Union and China, in a formal ceremony to sign the Declaration by United Nations. By signing this pact, the countries pledged to fight against the Axis powers and not to make a separate peace with any of them.

Building on this January 1942 declaration, another document was signed in October 1943 in which the United States, United Kingdom, Soviet Union and China agreed to establish an international organization to maintain peace and security in the world after the end of World War II. Roosevelt, Churchill and Joseph Stalin reaffirmed this pledge at the Teheran Conference in December 1943.

The next step in creating the United Nations was at a conference held at the Dumbarton Oaks mansion in Washington in September and early October 1944. The first outline of the aims, functions and structure of the proposed new world body was drafted in this conference and received the agreement of the United States, United Kingdom, Soviet Union and China. The desire to create a new international organization was reaffirmed at the Yalta Conference in 1945.

The efforts leading toward the creation of the United Nations culminated in the Conference on International Organization. This conference was opened by President Harry Truman on April 25, 1945, in San Francisco — just thirteen days after the death of Franklin Roosevelt in Warm Springs, Georgia. In a stirring speech, Truman paid tribute to Roosevelt and reminded the delegates that, "the conference owes its existence to the vision, foresight and determination of Franklin Roosevelt."

The U.S. delegation to the San Francisco conference had been selected by Roosevelt shortly before his death and was led by Secretary of State Edward Stettinius. It included several members of Congress, most notably the Republican senator from Michigan, Arthur Vandenberg. For years Vandenberg had been a member of a conservative coalition in the Senate which opposed the New Deal, and Vandenberg was one of the president's most outspoken critics. However, in January, 1945 Vandenberg had an epiphany, took the Senate floor and announced to the nation that he was converting from isolationism to internationalism. Roosevelt knew he would need Vandenberg's support to gain Senate approval of the treaty establishing U.S. membership in the UN. In selecting Vandenberg, Roosevelt was following the age-old practice of co-opting one's detractors by engaging them in a common effort. This practice was carried to a fine art when Lyndon Johnson was Senate majority leader. His colleagues were astounded when he selected the acerbic and vocal Wayne Morse of Oregon to become a member of the prestigious Democratic Policy Committee. Johnson did this despite the fact that Morse was a turn-coat Republican and had only been a Democrat for a short while. When Johnson was asked why he made this unusual decision, he replied, "It's better to have Wayne inside the tent pissing out than outside the tent pissing in!"[2] The use of this approach, and other maneuvers too numerous to mention, distinguish Roosevelt and Johnson as two of America's most skilled politicians.

Arthur Vandenberg was an active member of the delegation in San Francisco and soon became a staunch supporter of the United Nations. After many late-night working sessions, the Charter of the United Nations was adopted unanimously two months later on June 25, 1945. In accordance with Article 10 of the Charter, it did not enter into force until it was ratified by the five permanent members of the Security Council (U.K., U.S., USSR, France and China) and a majority of the other signatories. This was accomplished on October 24, 1945, which forever after has been celebrated as United Nations Day.

In recent years there has been a sizeable group of conservative Republicans in the U.S. House of Representatives who have signed onto a resolution calling for the removal of the United States from the UN and the removal of the UN from the United States. My, how times change. In 1945, less than two months after the UN Charter came into force, both houses of the U.S. Congress, by unanimous vote, requested that the headquarters of the United Nations be located in the United States. After considering several sites, the UN accepted this request. The first meeting of the United Nations was held in London and the still grieving widow, Eleanor Roosevelt, was chosen by President Truman to be a member of the U.S. delegation. This was the beginning of Eleanor Roosevelt's deep involvement in the United Nations. She was later elected Chairperson of the UN Commission on Human Rights. She directed the drafting of the Universal Declaration of Human Rights which she considered her greatest accomplishment.

For several years the temporary home of the UN was Lake Success, New York — a village twenty-six miles from New York City located on Long Island. At this location, the UN set up shop in a building which had been occupied by the Sperry Gyroscope Company. This was not a very auspicious start for the world's most important international organization. But help was on the way. In 1946, John D. Rockefeller, Jr., had his young son, Nelson (forty-first U.S. vice president), negotiate the sale of a parcel of land along the East River in mid-town Manhattan valued at $8.4 million. This land was then donated to the United Nations. Construction started in 1949 and the UN headquarters officially opened on January 9, 1951.

Planning in the Midst of War

As early as August 1941, Winston Churchill and Franklin Roosevelt agreed to meet to chart a course for the world after the end of World War II. At the time, Britain had just gone through the blitzkrieg which lasted from September 14 until May 1941. During this period the German Luftwaffe bombed Britain for seventy-six consecutive nights killing more than 20,000 civilians and destroying or damaging more than a million homes in London alone. The Americans had been in the war for only nine months and Japan was still ruling the sea in Asia. The two leaders were reading war reports one minute and plotting the course of history the next.

They met on British and American warships anchored in Ship Harbor, Newfoundland. On one occasion when Churchill boarded the American ship, a band played "God Save the King," the British national anthem. When Roosevelt embraced Churchill, he smiled and said, "Winston, that was the best rendition of 'My Country Tis of Thee' I have heard in years."[3] On August 14, 1941, Churchill and Roosevelt announced the eight-point Atlantic Charter as a blueprint for the post-war world. Among the points, the two pledged their countries support for the right of all people to self-determination, freedom from want and fear, global economic cooperation and the advancement of social welfare. Today, we have the United Nations and all of its funds and agencies, the independence of former French, British and Portuguese colonies, World Trade Organization (WTO) and the General Agreement on Tariffs and Trade (GATT). What vision and courage these two friends had.

Aside from the points covered in the Atlantic Charter, Roosevelt and Churchill both agreed that refugees of war must be cared for and Europe must be rebuilt. To address these two needs, there were three United Nations organizations created in 1943 and 1944, more than a year before the Charter of the United Nations came into force.

In June 1943, Roosevelt proposed to the U.S. Congress the creation of an international organization to provide relief to persons living in areas liberated from the Axis powers. He informed Congress that he already had the U.K., USSR and China on board and would seek the agreement of forty other governments. In November, 1943, Roosevelt received delegates from forty-four countries at the White House to sign the foundation document creating the United Nations Relief and Rehabilitation Administration (UNRRA). The headquarters for UNRRA was established in Washington. Before the end of the war, UNRRA was providing food, shelter and medical supplies to 74,000 refugees throughout the Middle East, North Africa and the Mediterranean. But that was just the beginning. When the war ended in Europe, there were millions of displaced persons and refugees who required immediate attention. Within a few months, UNRRA was running full speed and by the end of 1945, two-thirds of the transit centers and refugee camps in West Germany were managed by UNRRA. By the time UNRRA ceased operations, eight million people had received assistance from the organization. UNRRA also operated in China and Taiwan from 1945 until the Communist Revolution in 1949. In 1947, UNRRA was replaced by another UN entity called the International Refugee Organization (IRO), which was then replaced in 1950 by the United Nations High Commissioner for Refugees (UNHCR). Since

1950, UNHCR has continued to play a vital role in the world and in any recent year, about forty million persons are uprooted for political reasons. UNHCR help a large portion of these — living outside their country or those who are internally displaced. At least seventeen percent of UNHCR's work force (1,000) are now United Nations Volunteers (UNV)— an organization which operates under the aegis of UNDP.

Meanwhile, in 1943, economists in the U.S., U.K. and elsewhere were starting discussions on the global organizations required to address the monumental task of rebuilding Europe. This was not an easy undertaking, especially for the British, because it was clear, even in 1943, that the center of gravity of the world economic and financial system was rapidly crossing the Atlantic from Europe to the United States. This meant that whatever would emerge, the United States would have the dominant role. That proved to be the case and still is to this day.

A month after the troops stormed the beaches of Normandy on D-Day (June 6, 1944), 730 delegates (mostly economists) from forty-four allied nations assembled at the Mount Washington Hotel in Bretton Woods, New Hampshire, for the United Nations Monetary and Financial Conference. Three weeks later, documents emerged creating two organizations that would eventually become UN specialized agencies — the International Bank for Reconstruction and Development (IBRD, now called the World Bank) and the International Monetary Fund (IMF). The first was designed to provide loans to rebuild countries after the war (primarily in Europe) and the IMF was designed to provide enough liquidity to these countries to ensure they could meet their balance of payments requirements. Both are still headquartered in Washington and the World Bank has always had an American as its president. A European has usually headed the IMF. The first World Bank loan in the amount of $987 million was provided to the new French government. Today, both institutions continue to be a major positive force with billions of dollars in loans to countries throughout the world

Another UN organization which emerged to promote what Roosevelt and Churchill described in the Atlantic Charter as the freedom from want and fear for the children in war torn Europe is UNICEF (United Nations International Children's Emergency Fund). Created by the UN General Assembly in 1946, its original purpose was to provide clothing, food and health care to the millions of European children in need. Under a General Assembly resolution adopted in 1953, UNICEF became a permanent part of the UN. It has kept the acronym, but now calls itself the UN Children's Fund. In recognition of its enormous contribution, it was awarded the Nobel Peace Prize in 1965. Over the years it has broadened its mandate to cover both humanitarian relief and development. In 150 countries throughout the world it provides children with clean water, education, protection, improved health and emergency relief. It has become the world's best known UN organization and has always been headed by an American.

In the immediate post-war period there were numerous Americans doing yeoman service on behalf of humankind. One was a quiet spoken peacemaker. Then, as now, a major focus of the UN's attention was peacekeeping. Also, then as now, the most explosive conflict was between the new state of Israel and the Arab states. The UN envoy to be selected for this challenging assignment had to be knowledgeable of the area, highly intelligent and a skilled negotiator with an ego under control. The Secretary-General turned to an African American by the name of Ralph Bunche. Bunche received a doctorate from Harvard in 1934 and became Chairman of the Political Science Department at Howard University — a university for black students located in Washington, D.C. During World War II, Bunche was a senior officer in the Office of Strategic Services (the precursor of the CIA). He was an advisor to the U.S. delegation to the San Francisco Conference and played an active role in drafting the UN Charter. He also assisted Eleanor Roosevelt in drafting the UN Declaration of Human Rights.

After many months of patience, perseverance and perspicacity, Dr. Bunche secured a cease-fire between the warring parties in 1949. Another major event in 1949 was the creation of the United Nations Relief and Works Agency (UNRWA) to care for the Palestinians displaced by the fighting. In 1950, there were 914,000 Palestinians registered in the UNRWA camps. As this conflict has continued over the decades, today there are 4.3 million Palestinians under the care and protection of UNRWA in camps located in Gaza, the West Bank, Lebanon, Syria and Jordan. These people will continue to rely on UNRWA until a permanent Middle East settlement is achieved.

For his efforts on behalf of the United Nations, Ralph Bunche was awarded the Nobel Peace Prize in 1950. He was the first person of color to ever win a Nobel Prize in the history of the program. He was awarded the Medal of Freedom, the highest U.S. award for a civilian, by President John F. Kennedy in 1963. Ralph Bunche died at the age of 68 in 1971.

There are volumes written on the role of Franklin Roosevelt and Harry Truman in shaping the course of the United Nations. Yet, very little has been written on the enormous impact on the United Nations by President Dwight D. Eisenhower. Eisenhower was not a gifted speaker and public communicator in the style of John Kennedy and Ronald Reagan. Ike, as everyone affectionately called him, was a quiet person. While he was a boy living in a modest house in the middle of Kansas, his parents taught him to demonstrate his worth in deeds and not words. The record will show that this beloved warrior-statesman was responsible for the creation of two of the most important organizations in UN history.

After the U.S. dropped atomic bombs on Hiroshima and Nagasaki to end World War II, there was enormous global concern in the post-war period over limiting the spread and harnessing of nuclear energy to benefit all humankind. In 1953 Dwight Eisenhower delivered his Atoms for Peace address to the General Assembly in which he called for the creation of an international organization to promote the peaceful use of atomic energy and provide international safeguards against the misuse of nuclear technology. As a result of his initiative, the International Atomic Energy Agency (IAEA) was created for this purpose. In 2005 the IAEA and its Director General Mohammed El Baradei were awarded the Nobel Peace Prize. The IAEA is an important instrument through which a resolution of the conflict over Iran's nuclear program might be achieved.

In 1954, Eisenhower asked the Congress to consider a plan that would utilize surplus food produced in the United States for the benefit of the rest of the world. Later in the year he signed Public Law 480. The President said that the purpose of this legislation was to "lay the basis for a permanent expansion of our exports of agricultural products with lasting benefits to ourselves and peoples of other lands." In his last address to the UN General Assembly in 1960, Eisenhower proposed that "a workable scheme should be devised for providing food aid through the UN system." In 1961, the UN Food and Agricultural Organization (FAO) and the UN General Assembly approved parallel resolutions establishing the World Food Programme (WFP).

Like the United Nations High Commissioner for Refugees (UNHCR), it's difficult to imagine what the world would do without the World Food Programme (WFP). The WFP helps feed over 45 million people per annum, including half of the world's refugees and internally displaced persons. WFP cares for those who would starve to death without its help. But there are those who are hungry, but not starving, and this group (the majority of them women and children) number 800 million. The organization carries out its work with great efficiency and it only costs a quarter ($.25) a day to feed a refugee.

By the time the United Nations Charter went into force in October, 1945, there was one UN organization already in operation — the United Nations Relief and Rehabilitation Administration (UNRRA) and two that were created and ready for operation (World Bank and International Monetary Fund [IMF]). In addition, there were three organizations which predate the UN — International Labor Organization (ILO, 1919), the International Telecommunications Union (ITU, 1865) and the Universal Postal Union (UPU, 1874). All three were subsequently incorporated into the UN system.

The UN Charter provides for six entities:

The General Assembly (GA) started with 51 members and now has 193, two-thirds of which are developing countries. The GA approves the annual budget, formulates recommendations and creates organizations and is involved in approving the membership of other main UN organs including the ten non-permanent members of the Security Council.

The Security Council started with eleven members and now has fifteen including the five permanent members with right of veto (U.S., U.K., France, Russia, China). The Security Council is responsible for maintaining international peace and security. It is empowered to approve the mobilization and deployment of peace keeping forces. It can also sanction the use of armed forces against a country as it did in the Korean War and the 1991 Gulf War.

The Economic and Social Council (ECOSOC) is a 54-member body which organizes the work of the UN in all economic and social matters and promotes human rights.

The Trustee Council was created to assist the process of converting non-sovereign territories into sovereign and independent states. It played an important role in the de-colonization of former British and French possessions. It suspended operations in 1994 for lack of requests for its assistance.

The International Court of Justice is located in The Hague, Netherlands, and is composed of fifteen judges selected jointly by the Security Council and the General Assembly. It settles legal disputes submitted by member countries and issues advisory opinions on legal questions submitted by the GA and other international organizations.

The Secretariat is the administrative arm of the organization and is headed by the Secretary-General who is appointed by the GA upon the recommendation of the Security Council for a five year renewable term.

There are 16,000 people employed by the UN Secretariat. Most are located in New York, but they also work in UN installations in Geneva, Vienna, Nairobi and the five regional commissions. There are 64,500 employed throughout the entire UN system including the Secretariat. This is a remarkably small number for those who staff a collection of 14 funds and programs (UNDP and UNICEF, etc.) 16 specialized agencies (ILO, FAO, World Health Organization, etc.) To show just how small this number is, it can be compared with the Coca Cola Company which has 74,000 employees and the U.S. Department of Education which has 71,000 employees. If the United Nations civil service fails to deliver required goods and services in an effective and efficient (which is sometimes the case), it is not because of a bloated bureaucracy. It is more likely the result of not having enough staff. Stories about the ever expanding UN behemoth are simply not true. All UN organizations have faced a serious financial squeeze in the past decade and for many, staff size has been reduced and not expanded.

UN detractors have long argued that the UN has an inefficient, ineffective and bloated bureaucracy. It is true that certain governments have used the UN as a dumping ground for their political friends and supporters. While this practice still exists to a limited extent, there is far less of it since the collapse of communism. Moreover in the past twenty-five years, many UN organizations (especially UNDP) have adopted a more transparent and professional approach to recruitment. If the United States ever asked the United Nations to leave, a lot of money would be lost. Each year the U.S. makes over a billion dollars out of UN procurement awards to U.S. companies and hosting the United Nations in New York.

Especially in the past twenty years, being a UN staff member serving in the field has become a very dangerous occupation. The most vicious attack against UN staff was the 2003 bombing of UN headquarters in Baghdad. There were more than 150 injured and 22 killed including the Head of Mission Sergio Vieira de Mello, who was a friend. Since 1992, 230 UN civilian staff members have been killed while serving in the line of duty. In addition, there have been 10 cases of sexual assault, 17 kidnappings, 119 armed robberies and 220 incidences of physical assault at check points or road blocks.

Since 1945, the Secretary-General, a UN employee, a UN agency or a committee has won the Nobel Peace Prize nine times. The most recent was in 1997 when the award was given to the UN Inter-governmental Panel on Climate Change — not a bad record for an organization some people feel is no longer useful!

International Development and the Creation of UNDP

Normally when the term 'international development' is used, one thinks of a relationship between developed and developing countries. Some have described it as a relationship between the industrialized and non-industrialized countries. But given the growth of industrialization throughout the world in the past 50 years, especially in countries like China, India and Brazil, this latter distinction has become blurred. In this relationship there is a transfer of resources (financial, physical and human) from developed to developing countries. Development is a transformational process intended to improve the quality of life. It involves economic, social and political change and has occurred in all countries over many centuries. The term international development is used when an outside party (like UNDP) provides assistance to accelerate the transformational process.

However one defines development, most agree that it is a practice which has gained popularity since the end of World War II. In the last twenty years, UNDP and the World Bank have led the way in defining development. This was not the case at the end of the war. The most ambitious development program in history actually involved the transfer of resources from the United States to the countries in Europe devastated by the war. This program was outlined by Secretary of State (General) George Marshall in a speech delivered at Harvard University in June 1947. Forever after, it has been called the Marshall Plan. His remarks sparked a new feeling of hope around the globe. When Marshall delivered his remarks, the United States was truly the colossus of the world. It could either reach out to the rest of the world or retreat into a shell as a strategy for protecting its unchallenged position. Thankfully, isolationism was not gripping the minds of American leaders in 1946, as was the case previously. Marshall and Truman had an internationalist vision and they knew that putting Europe back on its feet would benefit the whole world including the United States. They also had a moral compass and, who knows, perhaps they both wished to follow the advice found in Ecclesiastes to cast one's bread upon the water. No one was surprised in 1953 when George Marshall was awarded the Nobel Peace Prize.

In 1948, the Economic Cooperation Administration (ECA) was established to administer the Marshall Plan. The Administrator of the ECA was Paul G. Hoffman, a Republican appointed by Democratic President Harry Truman. Throughout the war and after, there were numerous titans of industry pressed into national service to deal with the war and its aftermath. Hoffman became one of the major players in the new world of international development and was truly a remarkable person. He dropped out of college at age eighteen to start selling Studebaker cars in Los Angeles and ten years later, he was president of the company. He took a two-year leave of absence from Studebaker to direct the ECA. By the time he took the job, the president of the IBRD (World Bank) was John McCloy, an internationally known figure and a close acquaintance of Hoffman. Both had offices in close proximity in downtown Washington and both shared the same mission to reconstruct the sixteen countries in Europe destroyed by the war. These two friends had frequent meetings and long lunches. Hoffman developed a great admiration for the work of the Bank and eighteen years later, he became the first Administrator of the United Nations Development Programme (UNDP). After Hoffman went to UNDP, he still had a high regard for the institution which by then was called the World Bank. At times, UNDP has found itself at odds with the World Bank. But it is worth noting that throughout its history, UNDP has always had a close relationship with the Bank. This relationship was never closer than when Hoffman was serving as Administrator. It has always been a win-win situation. By 1966, the focus of the World Bank was on the same developing countries in which UNDP was working. It was a very straightforward partnership — the Bank would provide the loan and UNDP would provide the grant assistance to train the locals to eventually manage the projects. In the first fifteen years, most of these partnership projects were either for infrastructure (dams, irrigation systems, roads and ports) or agriculture.

In the immediate post-war period, major western governments were not prepared to create a development agency within the United Nations. In any event, it was clear that nothing would happen without the United States taking the initiative. For the first few years after the war, President Truman was intent on helping Europe first and was, therefore, resistant to creating a multilateral aid program. But as he saw the Soviet Union starting to gain friends and influence people, especially in developing countries in Asia and Africa, he knew the United States should show the same generosity to the rest of the world as it was showing toward Europe. As freedom, hunger and human rights were seriously under threat in many corners of the world, Truman used the occasion of his January 20 Inaugural Address in 1949 to reach out to the developing world. His address became known as his Four Points Speech. In these points, Truman pledged the "unfaltering support to the United Nations and related agencies," confirmation of "our programs for world economic recovery," to "strengthen freedom-loving nations against the dangers of aggression," and "embark on a bold new program for making the benefits of our scientific advances and industrial progress available for the improvement and growth of under-developed areas." Harry Truman was no development scholar, but this Four Point Speech is as good a definition of development one will ever find.

Truman's Four Points Speech gave a new lease on life to UN staff member, David Owen. The United States had a major role in shaping the architecture of the UN, but the British had a bigger role in staffing the UN and establishing its administrative structure and procedures. Owen, a Welshman, was one of the first employees hired at a senior level, and less than a year after the UN started operations, he was appointed Assistant Secretary-General for Economic Affairs. From his first day on the job, Owen envisaged the establishment of a UN development program to aid what Truman called, the "underdeveloped areas." After reading Truman's address, David Owen now knew the United States would support such a program and he put his ideas on paper. What emerged was a voluntary fund, located within the Secretariat, which would be used to hire technical assistance consultants. These consultants would go to developing countries to share their knowledge and expertise in various fields including health, education and especially agriculture. A small amount of funding would also be for equipment required in the projects. Consultants would be drawn from the specialized agencies and a group of technical advisors from the Secretariat. In those countries receiving assistance, there would be a resident UN representative to manage and coordinate the program. The fund would be called the Expanded Program of Technical Assistance (EPTA). One year after Truman's speech, the EPTA became operational after unanimous approval of the General Assembly. Most important, the United States agreed to provide more than half of the funding. Owen became the Executive Chairman of the Technical Assistance Board — EPTA's governing board. The fund never grew as large as Owen had hoped, but it gave a whole new dimension to the role of the United Nations in the world.

The issue of inadequate funding for development was debated in the UN for the next decade. Those concerned with the issue eventually agreed that no matter how large the EPTA could grow, the grant assistance it provided would still only constitute a small portion of the development assistance required. Clearly the bulk of the assistance needed would come in the form of loans. Paul Hoffman joined the debate and argued that "investment, public or private, will not venture into the unknown." He pressed for the creation of a new program which would fund and mobilize teams of experts drawn mainly from the specialized agencies to conduct pre-investment studies in various project fields including transport, communications, irrigation and agriculture. Hoffman's argument was simple — there was the need to increase the flow of both private and public loans to the developing world and this pump would be primed by undertaking pre-investment studies. The General Assembly's response to Hoffman's suggestion was the creation of the Special Fund which became operational in January, 1959 with Paul Hoffman as its Director. There were now two UN programs running on separate tracks and both dealing with development assistance. During the five year existence of the Special Fund, 1,500 experts were sent to the field who undertook pre-investment analysis and provided advanced training to more than 50,000 developing country recipients.

It would come as no surprise that the next issue to be debated focused on the alleged waste and duplication resulting from operating two separate programs. In 1965, Secretary-General U Thant and the General Assembly agreed to a merger of the two programs which resulted in the launching of the United Nations Development Programme (UNDP) on New Year's Day 1966.[4] Paul Hoffman was nominated by the Secretary-General and approved by the General Assembly to head this new development agency. Hoffman chose the title administrator because that was his title while directing the Marshall Plan. David Owen became Hoffman's deputy, but as a consolation prize for not getting the top job he was given the title co-administrator. Owen left the UN three years later and died in 1970. Today the UNDP Administrator is the third highest ranking officer in the UN system after the Secretary General and the Deputy Secretary General. Until 1999, an American always held the position of UNDP Administrator, but this changed when the American contribution continued to slide and the contribution of other countries continued to increase.

It took three years for UNDP to integrate the role and responsibilities of the EPTA with those of the special fund. Once integration was completed, Hoffman realized that a new structure and procedures would be required for the new organization. A major study and set of recommendations was needed and Hoffman turned to his old friend and confidant, Sir Robert Jackson, to undertake the work. Jackson agreed to take the job and he then turned to old friend and confidant, Margaret Joan Anstee, to become his "chief of staff" for the study. One could not have found a pair of UN professionals who had a better knowledge and understanding of the UN system. Jackson, an Australian, started his career as Director of the Relief Operations of UNRRA in Europe and part of Asia and Africa. Throughout his career he held a number of diverse senior level posts in the UN reaching the rank of Under Secretary-General. Joan Anstee (U.K.) also rose to the rank of Under Secretary-General and spent most of her career as a senior officer in UNDP.

Their undertaking soon became known as the Capacity Study. Originally it was to be limited to the UNDP. But the UNDP Governing Council composed of member states, including the five permanent members of the Security Council, wanted the focus expanded to cover the entire UN development system. There has never been a UN study before or since of the magnitude of the Capacity Study.[5]

After thirteen months of exhaustive work, including interviews with government leaders all over the world, the report was ready for presentation to Paul Hoffman. His initial reaction to the report was positive. But as several of his trusted colleagues expressed their concerns about various parts of the report, Hoffman's attitude turned from warm to decidedly cool. For some odd reason he became more and more convinced that parts of the report were designed to undercut his authority and reputation. Hoffman's reaction was strange because the recommendations were designed to enhance the authority of the Administrator and make him *primus interpares* (first among equals) in the whole UN development system. Obviously, Hoffman had a much better feel for American politics and congressional attitudes than either Jackson or Anstee. No doubt a major reason for his coolness toward some of the recommendations was because he knew they would not fly with the U.S. government. For example, he knew that UNDP couldn't plan its finances with certainty for more than one year at a time because the U.S. Congress will always reserve its right to change the value of an appropriation item from one year to the next — including the annual U.S. contribution to UNDP.

Jackson and Anstee had in mind the establishment of a global indicative planning figure (IPF) from which each country would draw its prescribed share, thus constituting its country IPF. According to Anstee, the IPFs "were to be projected ahead, on a rolling basis, for five-year periods and would serve as a pointer to contributing governments as to the scale of resources required." If one were teaching a course on development planning, the notion of rolling IPFs with projections would be regarded as a sensible idea. But if one were teaching a course on American legislative behavior (as I once did at Denison University in Granville, Ohio), both professor and students would know that regardless of its merits, the proposal would not receive congressional approval. The U.S. congressional appropriators would say, "We don't need any pointers and no one should ever make even tentative projections five years in advance on what the U.S. contribution is likely to be. Come to us on a yearly basis and we will let you know." Planning for any voluntarily funded organization (UNDP, UNICEF, UN Population Fund — UNFPA) is at the whim of the major donors and this funding conundrum is not likely to change.

As one might expect in any political body, a compromise (consensus) was finally reached on the Capacity Study. The most important recommendations that were approved included:

- making the recipient governments responsible for determining their own development priorities
- decentralizing significant authority over projects to the resident representatives in the field
- establishing regional bureaus at New York headquarters
- establishing a global IPF and country IPFs for five-year planning purposes, but not on a rolling basis with projections of ever-increasing amounts.

The specialized agencies saw the Capacity Study as a threat to their funding pipeline from UNDP and we shall soon see that their fear was well-founded. Because of specialized agency opposition, the major recommendation to amalgamate the various governing bodies was never adopted. As we shall also soon see, separate governing bodies for each organization makes aid coordination among the UN organizations a difficult, if not impossible, task.

Joining the Fray

When I joined UNDP in January 1978 and was assigned to Thailand as Deputy Resident Representative six months later, many of the recommendations from the Capacity Study were firmly in place. The authority of the resident representative was enhanced in project formulation and approval. Backstopping and policy guidance in New York headquarters reached the field offices via the newly created regional bureaus. The office in the Thai government responsible for aid coordination knew that the government was responsible for prioritizing its own development objectives which would shape the UNDP Thai country program. The government would do so in consultation with the resident representative.

Joan Anstee tells us that when this country-centered approach to development was discussed in the UNDP Governing Council, U.S. Ambassador Arthur ("Tex") Goldsmith used an expression taken from a popular American song entitled, "Whatever Lola Wants" and exclaimed, "Does this mean that Lola gets whatever Lola wants?" One can appreciate Goldsmith's humor, but his concern completely missed the point. There was never any intention in the Capacity Study to give governments anything they wanted. First, field offices are forbidden by the Governing Council to partner with the police or military. Second, project requests would have to fit into UNDP's mandate, policy goals and procedures. It is true that project formulation was always a bargaining process. Often government departments would start the negotiation by requesting too much money, too much equipment and clever ways to subsidize their departments' budget. Some UN detractors argue that organizations like UNDP simply pass the money onto the recipient government to be spent as the government sees fit. If this were ever done, it would certainly be in violation of UNDP rules and procedures.

There was one practice Jackson and Anstee wished to abolish, but continued for years after the approval of the modified Capacity Study. The practice centered on the issue of who was responsible for executing the project. For the first decade of my twenty-two years with UNDP, we operated with a tripartite arrangement. UNDP funded the project, a UN specialized agency executed the project and the third leg of the stool were those receiving project benefits from government departments and the private sector in the form of training and advisory services. For example, one of the most successful projects in the Vietnam country program during my tenure as resident representative was an aquaculture project started back in the tripartite era. UNDP provided the funding; FAO executed the project and mobilized the advisors and training experts. By starting with small ponds on land held by individual farmers in the dirt-poor hills of northern Vietnam, the project revolutionized the raising of fresh water fish in ponds and rice paddies. Throughout Vietnam today, the poorest of the poor receive their protein from fresh water fish and it all started with a UNDP/FAO project.

Throughout the world, specialized agency executed projects were successful and produced enormous benefits for the poor living in developing countries. The problem was that the agency/UNDP arrangement put the specialized agency in the driver's seat rather than UNDP which, at the end of the day, had to be held accountable for the use of every cent spent by the project. Based on years of personal experience, here's how the agency-led process worked. The director of one of the agency departments at headquarters would fly into town, land, jump into a cab and make a beeline for the office of his government counterpart. FAO officers would head for the Ministry of Agriculture; ILO types would go to the Ministry of Labor; WHO officers would go to the Ministry of Health, and so on. A meeting would be scheduled and the agency rep would say, "My friend, do you know that your government's aid coordinating office and UNDP are putting together a new country program? I bet the two of us can come up with some good project ideas to be included in the program?" After deciding on some possibilities, the officer from the ministry would ask his colleagues in the government's aid coordination office to include the proposals in the new program. Before leaving town, the agency rep would drop by the UNDP office meeting with either the resident representative or deputy resident representative and say, "It is my impression that such and such ministry has several project proposals they would like to see included in your new UNDP country program. Thanks, and please excuse me, I have a plane to catch."

True, there were a number of excellent proposals which emerged through this process. But it was a hell of a way to formulate a country program and here's why:

(1) Government aid offices were able to shirk their responsibility of consulting the various ministries to prioritize the country's most pressing needs. Rather, they simply collected proposals which came in over the transom from the various ministries and chose those which were most strongly pushed by the ministries.
(2) The agency-led process did not lead to good programs. A good program is more than a collection of projects grouped in substantive categories — agriculture, transport, health, education and so on. A good program should have a sharp focus, a unifying theme and projects grouped in components which share a common focus on a common problem.

In the first decade of my UNDP experience, we wound up with programs resembling a laundry list. I must admit that I was just as involved in producing such lists as were all the rest of my colleagues. Given the nature of the process, we didn't have much choice.

The Quiet Side of the UN

I take the agencies to task for their involvement in a dysfunctional programming process which thankfully was abandoned years ago. In no way have I ever questioned their competence and dedication in improving the lives of billions of people, many of whom live in the industrialized countries of Western Europe and North America. This is the quiet side of the UN because most people are uninformed about the contributions these organizations make for a better world. Unfortunately, most people do not even recognize the names of many of these agencies.

Since 1847, the Universal Postal Union (UPU) has been quietly carrying out its duties in negotiating and implementing international postal agreements. Tomorrow, one can mail a package from Tucson to somewhere in Angola. The post office will know the postage required and the sender will have a 99.9 percent assurance the package will be delivered to the intended recipient. While all the developing countries were going through the process of de-colonization, their postal systems were built or improved with technical assistance provided by UPU, funding from the UNDP and a construction loan from the World Bank. Should you find yourself in the quaint and quiet Swiss city of Bern, you can stop by and thank the folks at the UPU headquarters.

A year after moving to Bangkok I was sitting next to a well groomed, trim, middle-aged Filipino on a flight to Manila. As the plane was preparing to land, we struck up a conversation and the man asked about my occupation. When I told him I was with UNDP, he shook my hand and said, "thank you." When I asked the reason for this unexpected expression of gratitude, he replied, "I am an air traffic controller and I was trained at a center in Bangkok established by the International Civil Aviation Organization [ICAO, Montreal 1947], and funded by UNDP. By the way, I am sure you know that most of the air traffic controllers in Asia have been trained at the Bangkok ICAO center." Just as we were ready to touch the ground, he turned to me and said, "Don't worry about a thing, the guy in the tower is my friend and he is also a Bangkok boy."

Now for a very obscure organization established after the war with headquarters in Geneva. It is small, but highly valuable to the world. It is the World Meteorological Organization (WMO). It established and currently operates the World Weather Watch which provides weather forecasting for land and sea and covers the globe. The WMO also manages the International Panel on Climate Change which won the Nobel Peace Prize in 2007.

On 24 May 1844, Samuel Morris sent the world's first telegraphic message from a room in the U.S. Capitol to the city of Baltimore — thirty-three miles away. Ten years later the International Telegraph Union (ITU) was established in Geneva with twenty founding members. Today it is called the International Telecommunications Union and its membership includes virtually every country in the world. Through the administration of various international agreements, ITU sets the standards and regulates all forms of international communications including the assignment of radio frequencies.

One of my favorite UN organizations is the World Intellectual Property Organization (WIPO) headquartered in Geneva. This organization administers the world's most important international agreements protecting intellectual property including The Patent Cooperation Treaty adopted in 1970 and is considered to be the closest thing in existence to a truly global patent treaty. Over the years WIPO and UNDP have partnered in numerous countries to establish or strengthen copyright, trademark and patent offices. Nothing is more important to business and the science and technology community than intellectual property protection that spans the globe. Intellectual property protection is what propels innovation and creativity.

Two UN specialized agencies deserve special mention — the World Health Organization (WHO) and the UN Food and Agriculture Organization (FAO). Throughout history, smallpox was one of the most deadly communicable diseases. Between 1914 and 1977, experts estimate that 300–500 million people died of smallpox just during that time span. In 1967, WHO announced a global campaign to eliminate smallpox through a massive vaccination program. In 1979, WHO documented the last case of smallpox and announced that smallpox was eliminated from the world. Thirty years after the eradication of smallpox, FAO announced in October, 2010, the extermination of rinderpest, the most devastating viral disease in the world affecting livestock. Throughout history the ancient disease of rinderpest destroyed billions of cows, buffalo and yaks. FAO succeeded in erasing rinderpest from the world through use of diagnostic tests and vaccination. In the western world, few people will have ever heard of the rinderpest, but if one were a Masai herdsman in Kenya, one would have always known of this disease. Equally impressive work is carried out everyday by all the other UN specialized agencies. It is difficult to imagine how the world can get along without them. Unfortunately, these "quiet" UN agencies have a very poor public education outreach and most people don't even know they exist.

UNDP Administrators and the Mark They Made

When I first joined UNDP in 1978, the Administrator was Bradford Morse, who had assumed his post two years earlier. Brad was a large bear of a man — gregarious, wise, witty and full of life. He was a politician in the best sense of the term because he kept his ego under control (very difficult for most politicians) and saw politics as the art of the possible.

I first met Brad in 1964 when he was a member of the U.S. House of Representatives representing a district in the Boston area. I was a member of the Congressional Fellowship Program supported by the American Political Science Association working as an intern for a year on Capitol Hill. I was serving as legislative assistant to Congressman Robert Griffin of Michigan. When I began my assignment in November 1964, the House Republicans were morose and licking their wounds from the drubbing they received in the Goldwater debacle on Election Day earlier in the month. Most felt a new image was required and therefore, Minority House Leader Charles Halleck would have to go. The malcontents settled on Gerald Ford as the alternative. The congressional districts of Ford and Griffin shared a common boundary and they were the best of friends. Griffin became Ford's campaign manager and Brad Morse became one of Ford's staunchest supporters and helped elect him Minority Leader.

The next time I saw Brad was in 1973 while he was serving as UN Undersecretary-General for Political and General Assembly Affairs. In 1976, Brad was elevated from that position when he was approved by the General Assembly to become UNDP Administrator. Brad was responsible for recruiting me into UNDP and years later he was responsible for reassigning me from the field (Samoa) to headquarters. I wasn't anxious to be reassigned to New York, but I knew better than to resist a promotion recommended by the Administrator and the regional director. Like the U.S. Foreign Service, most people who join UNDP want to serve in the field. The brass ring in the Foreign Service is to be appointed ambassador. In UNDP, it is to become a resident representative.

Prior to his election to Congress in 1960, Morse had served as Deputy Administrator of Veterans Affairs. It was here that Brad honed his management skills and learned that the most precious resource of any organization is its staff. Brad took this lesson with him to UNDP and spent more of his time on personnel decisions than any administrator before or since. He made many contributions during his tenure. But his most lasting legacy was the improvements in human resource recruitment and deployment. To cite an ancient expression of someone who knows how to select the right person — Brad was an excellent judge of horseflesh.

The Administrator with whom I worked most closely was James G. (Gus) Speth. Both Brad Morse and Gus Speth served in a day when the U.S. ruled the roost and it would have been unthinkable for the Secretary-General to nominate anyone but an American as Administrator. The reason was simple: the U.S. was the biggest donor and played a more important role than any other country in guiding the work of UNDP. Brad was put forward by the Nixon administration and Gus Speth by President Bill Clinton.

Speth served as Administrator from 1993 to 1999. I first became acquainted with him while serving in Vietnam. Speth decided Vietnam would be his first country visit after taking his post. Speth had truly a dream career. He was a Rhodes Scholar from Yale and received a Master's Degree in Economics at Oxford. He returned to Yale for a law degree. In 1970 he became one of the founding fathers of the National Resources Defense Fund, a non-profit legal organization to defend the environment. He was appointed by President Jimmy Carter to serve on the Council on Environmental Quality, a part of the Executive Office of the President. In this role he became Vice-President Al Gore's mentor on the environment. In 1982, Speth founded the World Resources Institute — an environmental think tank in Washington.

When Speth became head of UNDP in 1993, he was recognized as America's leading environmentalist. His most important contribution to UNDP was his effort to make energy and environment one of UNDP's major areas of focus. He also insisted that all UNDP projects be evaluated for their sustainability — not just environmental sustainability, but also financial, political and cultural sustainability.

The last administrator with whom I worked was the first non-American to head UNDP, Mark Malloch Brown of the U.K. I only overlapped with Mark for a few months, but I thought he was a good choice. He gained UN field experience in Thailand working in the office of UNHCR serving as field director for Cambodian refugees. Before joining UNDP, Malloch Brown was World Bank Vice President for External Affairs and UN Affairs. He left UNDP in 2005 to become the Secretary-General's Chef de Cabinet and the next year was appointed Deputy Secretary-General — the UN's second highest position. Mark was just starting as Administrator when I was in the process of stepping down as the Director of the UNDP office in Washington. While I didn't know him as well as the others, I feel his greatest contribution to the organization was his advocacy of democratic governance and his efforts to promote it as the most important focal point of the program.

The Legacy of William H. Draper III

When William (Bill) Draper became the UNDP Administrator in 1986, some of the old hands at headquarters thought he was a most unlikely choice.[6] In the first few months of his tenure, they learned that he liked to receive his information verbally not in written form. Moreover, he was not a gifted speaker. Most people knew that he had served as President and Chairman of the U.S. Export-Import Bank and therefore, his skeptics assumed he knew something about international trade. But what, they asked; does he know about international development?

Draper was recommended to the Secretary-General by President Ronald Reagan. Later we learned that it was really Vice President George H.W. Bush who pushed his candidacy. Not only were Bush and Draper school mates at Yale, they were also both members of the prestigious secret society, Skull and Bones.

Draper has an M.B.A. from the Harvard Business School. Midway in his career, he left Chicago and his job at Inland Steel Company. He and his wife, Phyllis, moved to northern California and in 1965, he founded Sutter Hill Ventures which remains one of America's top venture capital firms. During the 1980 Republican presidential primary, Bush decided to challenge Reagan for the nomination and Draper was asked by Bush to be his campaign finance co-chairman. Reagan eventually asked Bush to be his vice presidential running mate and the rest is history. As a result of the 1980 presidential election Jimmy Carter was driven from the White House, Reagan became President, Bush ascended to Vice President and Draper moved to Washington to join the staff of the White House personnel office. It was from that position that Draper moved to the Export-Import Bank and eventually to UNDP in 1986. Bush, of course, replaced Reagan as President in 1988.

I first saw Draper in action in the senior staff meetings he chaired. I soon became very impressed with him because he had such self-confidence that he invited the staff to disagree with him. He loved a lively discussion and would smile and listen to the debate. If he thought a better idea than his own had emerged from the discussion, he would grab it and run. I thought that he really did learn something about good management practices at the Harvard Business School. I didn't go to a business school, but all the years I was with UNDP, if a trade-off was required between having management skills or knowledge of development, I would opt for management skills every time.

Draper was a major mover and shaker in American business and politics, but he was never a name dropper. For example, he was chairing a senior staff meeting one morning when his secretary came into the room and told him the President was on the phone. After he excused himself and left the room, a colleague sitting next to me whispered, "President — president of what?" I replied. "Oh, it's just his closest friend, George H.W. Bush, President of the United States of America." My colleague's jaw dropped in disbelief.

Changes in project execution preceded Draper, but it took his intervention to launch the organization in a new direction. One of his early contributions was his decision to break, once and for all, the stranglehold of the specialized agencies in the execution of UNDP funded projects. A few months after taking office, he made his first visit to several program countries. After returning to New York, he shared his observations at a senior staff meeting. He said that one morning he and the resident representative were en route to visit a project when they passed a jeep with the FAO logo on the door. This was not the first FAO logo he had seen and he commented that he didn't know that FAO had a fleet of vehicles in the country. The resident representative told him that it was a project vehicle from a FAO executed project with money provided by UNDP. Draper was dumbfounded and exclaimed, "What kind of a system is this? If UNDP is footing the bill, the vehicle should carry the UNDP logo. No wonder, no one knows who we are." In that meeting Draper was told that in a number of countries a government agency executed the projects and these projects in turn are monitored and audited by UNDP. Under this "government execution" arrangement, agencies like FAO could still play a role by providing training and advisory services, but they would not be the executing agency. Draper thought government execution made eminent good sense. Today, all UNDP funded projects are government executed.

Not everything Bill Draper tried was successful, but I admired his determination to try. Usually he had the right problem in mind. He just did not always have the right remedy. Draper had a rapid learning curve and the longer he served as Administrator, the more impressed he was with the organization and the work it does in the world. But like all the rest of us, he was frustrated by the fact that most Americans know nothing about UNDP. He said that everyone knows the World Bank, but not UNDP. To remedy this situation, he suggested that perhaps UNDP's name should be changed to World Development. A number of us strenuously objected to the suggestion because we felt that especially in developing countries, if we lost the United Nations part of our name, nobody would know who we are. In all the developing countries, UNDP is still synonymous with the United Nations. Bill did not think the less of us for disagreeing with him. After many discussions, he settled for having World Development printed below our name and logo on our official stationery.

Draper was only the second businessman (Hoffman was the other) to serve as administrator and he used his background and experience to make UNDP a better organization. He and I had a few disagreements, but never about the direction he wanted to take UNDP. We were both Republicans (perhaps a bit different breed than what you find today). We both were private sector and market economy types. We both saw the value in democratic institutions and the importance of the non-governmental sector. We also both agreed that investments in UNDP projects should be monitored and assessed as carefully as one would do in business.

Draper and Denis Halliday, our Director of Human Resources at the time, changed the culture of the organization by emphasizing the importance of sound management practices. Management training was expanded and required. Management skills became paramount in the recruitment, evaluation and promotion of staff.

Bill Draper was a good entrepreneur before and after he joined UNDP. He would look at development and human needs in the world and then ask the question, "Are the needs being addressed adequately and if not, should UNDP expand its role to cover these needs?" For example, Draper started looking at countries in crisis and concluded that their needs were not being met adequately, and he was determined to do something about it. At any point in time in the twenty-first century, there will always be 25 or 30 failed states racked by political violence such as Somalia, Sudan, Afghanistan and Iraq. In addition, there will be several countries in crisis caused by a natural disaster such as the tsunami in the Indian Ocean and the massive flooding in Pakistan. These countries need help, but a different development approach is required once the immediate relief needs of shelter, food and medical care are met. Programs of disarmament, demobilization and reintegration are needed in the countries disintegrated by political violence, but what they really need is the type of program UNDP undertook in El Salvador a number of years ago. When political stability is achieved, it is then possible to move onto projects promoting state-building, economic reform and rule off law. Since Draper started the ball rolling, UNDP has since assumed the lead role within the UN system in this area. There is now a major unit at headquarters called the Bureau for Crisis Prevention and Recovery which works in partnership with numerous donor governments to help the crisis countries located throughout the world.

The UNDP Human Development Report

Draper saw himself as a doer and certainly not as an intellectual. Yet his most important contribution of all derived from the fact that he was the Administrator who put UNDP on the path to becoming the world's most important intellectual leader in the theory and practice of international development. He did so by hiring a Pakistani intellectual by the name of Mahbub ul Haq to formulate a definitive report on international development. Dr. Haq was the perfect choice to move UNDP to the front of the line as the world's best source of knowledge of development theory and practice. Before joining UNDP in 1989, as Special Advisor to the Administrator, he was the World Bank's Director of Policy Planning and later served six years as Pakistan's Minister of Finance. Dr. Haq traveled in an elite circle of international economists which became his advisory team in drafting the first Human Development Report. This team included Amartya Sen, an Indian school mate and Nobel Laureate in Economics at Harvard. Midway through the drafting process, Draper was warned that the Report would be controversial because it would include a statistical index which would rank the world's countries from first to last in human development. These countries would fall into three categories — high, medium and low. He was also told that UNDP would be seen as a major advocate for political freedom and human rights. Draper's attitude was that just as long as the report was based on sound, objective data and scholarship, then let the chips fall where they may. He added that UNDP had already passed the threshold as an advocate for democratic governance, market economics, political freedom and human rights. Besides, these values should not be too controversial to be embraced by a UN organization because, with the exception of market economics, they were all clearly spelled out in the UN Charter and Declaration on Human Rights.

To this day, what sets the Human Development Report apart from other studies on international development is that human well being is calculated by analyzing factors well beyond income levels and a country's gross domestic product. Additional factors include political freedom, human rights, infant mortality, access to education and health care, life expectancy, access to safe water, nutrition and caloric intake, population growth, levels of indebtedness, social versus military public spending and many more. The Report still has sweeping concepts and highly sophisticated statistical analysis.

As the name of the Report indicates, the focus of development should be human centered and is defined as follows in the introduction of the first report:

> Human development is the process of enlarging people's choices. The most critical ones are to lead a long and happy life, to be educated and to enjoy a decent standing of living. Additional choices include political freedom, guaranteed human rights and self-respect — what Adam Smith calls, the ability to mix with others without being "ashamed to appear in public."

The Report makes clear that the major determinants of a person's well being are social, economic and political. Development concerns both a process and outcomes — the process of widening peoples' choices and the level of their achieved well-being.

Draper was both wise and courageous. He knew he would catch flak from various quarters once the report was released. He, therefore, made the following disclaimer in his forward of the report, "The views expressed in this Report are those of the team and not necessarily shared by UNDP or its Governing Council or the member governments of UNDP. The essence of any such report must be its independence and its intellectual integrity."

In his quest to heighten the profile of UNDP, Draper struck out with his idea to change the name. But he hit a home run with the Human Development Report. When it was released in May 1990, it received instant massive media coverage throughout the world. Not surprisingly, the governments of the countries ranked in the top twenty in the high human development category congratulated the organization on a job well done. Thankfully, UNDP's major donors were at the top of the index which was dominated by North America, Western Europe, Japan and Australia. Canada was ranked first, the United States was second, Iceland was third, Japan was fourth and Switzerland was fifth. Yemen was at the bottom of the index along with Nigeria, Tanzania, Bangladesh and Nepal.

The political right-wing in America, ever skeptical of the United Nations, were disappointed that the communist countries were not clumped at the bottom of the list. Had they read the report more carefully they would have found that political and economic variables were factored into a mix with many other variables.

I was serving as resident representative in China when the Report was released. It came just a few weeks before the first anniversary of the Tiananmen crisis and the hard-liners were firmly in control at the senior most levels of the party and government. I knew the Report was not likely to go over well, but I didn't know how strong the reaction would be. When I received my copies to distribute to the UN agencies, I had a discussion with my two deputies (Herb Behrstock and David Lockwood) on what we thought the government's reaction would be. One deputy said that for a country with such immense poverty, the government should take heart in the fact that China is ranked midway in the index — quite far from the bottom. I said that I agreed with his point, but I feared the government would have a political aversion to the Report when party officials read the introduction which clearly states the importance of political freedom and guaranteed human rights. Sure enough, I soon received a phone call from my friend and government counterpart, Long Yongtu (all foreigners called him YT Long). In a friendly, but emphatic tone, YT said his government was very unhappy with the Report and added that I could distribute my copies to whomever I pleased, but he was under strict instructions not to distribute his copies within the government.

On several occasions like this, the Chinese government (and if we really knew, probably the Communist Party) felt compelled to state an objection. But once it was stated, we went on with business as usual. There were no threats, no retribution, no hard feelings and no lingering discussion on the issue. YT and I never discussed the report again. As time went on, the Report was received, distributed, read and discussed within the government. A practice then started for a joint meeting to be held with UNDP to discuss the Report.

Emergence of a New Development Model

By the time the Human Development Report was published in 1990, improvements had been made in both the UNDP country programming process and the country program document itself. Certainly the programs were several notches above what I found when I was assigned to Thailand in 1978. Government execution of projects had replaced agency execution and the laundry lists of agency-inspired projects were fading into history. Moreover, as government execution took hold, the aid coordination offices in the recipient countries became proactive and started playing a more constructive role in consulting the ministries and sorting out their country's priority development needs. While the programs were better, they still lacked several key features:

(1) They lacked an over-arching concept which would illustrate that the projects all shared a common purpose or goal.

(2) It was not always clear who the intended project beneficiaries were.

(3) There was not a clear connection between the lofty development goals stated in the introduction of the program document and the proposed projects that followed.

(4) Poverty reduction was always mentioned as a key development goal, but there was no clear linkage between how this goal would be attained by undertaking the proposed projects.

What was needed was not a better program framework, but rather a whole new concept of development. The Human Development Report was the catalyst that started development economists to search for a new approach to development, not just in UNDP, but throughout the development community.

UNDP Today

UNDP has an annual budget of approximately $1.5 billion. It has field offices in 77 countries which manage over 10,000 separate projects. The total workforce including head-quarters and all field offices is 8.500 which indeed is modest given the size of its operation. UNDP is funded entirely by voluntary contributions. The top 10 donors (in U.S. dollar millions) to the regular resources of the organization in 2010 were:

1. Netherlands: 121.46
2. Norway: 117.67
3. United States: 100.50
4. Sweden: 85.99
5. United Kingdom: 85.36
6. Japan: 73.32
7. Denmark: 57.95
8. Switzerland: 55.33
9. Canada: 48.26
10. Spain: 40.82

To put these figures in perspective, it is worth noting that the Netherlands, the top donor, has a population (16.6 million) roughly the size of the U.S. state of Florida. Norway in second place has a population of 5.5 million which is smaller than New York City with a population of 8 million. The fourth place is Sweden with a population of 9.8 million. The United States in third place has a population of 312 million.

Today the global focus of UNDP is to assist countries to achieve positive change in the following five major policy areas:

• Democratic governance
• Poverty reduction
• Crisis prevention and recovery
• Environment and energy
• HIV/AIDS

The most challenging and important of these policy areas is democratic governance because it covers a multitude of sub-areas including: (1) justice and rule of law; (2) anti-corruption; (3) civil engagement; (4) election systems and processes; (5) human rights; (6)

local government; (7) parliamentary development; (8) public administration; (9) gender equity. During the nine years I served in China and Vietnam, our UNDP country programs had projects in all nine of these sub-areas. Not a bad record for doing development in the two remaining most important communist countries in the world.

In addition to the normal program activities in the policy area stated above, UNDP has been given the added responsibility of assisting countries to meet the Millennium Development Goals (MDGs). The MDGs are a set of eight international development goals endorsed by all 192 UN member states at the Millennium Summit in New York in 2000. All countries (developing and developed) agreed to achieve the goals by 2015. The eight MDGs are:

- Eradicate extreme poverty and hunger
- Achieve universal primary education
- Promote gender equality and empower women
- Reduce child mortality rate
- Improve maternal health
- Combat HIV/AIDS, malaria and other diseases
- Ensure environmental sustainability
- Develop a global partnership for development (with the private sector, foundations and non-governmental organizations)

Each goal contains targets to be achieved — such as reducing under-five child mortality rates by two-thirds between 1990 and 2015. Another target is to halt the spread of HIV/AIDS by 2015 and start reversing the spread. UNDP field offices are assisting governments in measuring progress in meeting the goals and publishing progress reports. Some countries like China have been successful in achieving several of the goals. For example, China's poverty population (using $1 per day per person) has been reduced from 452 million to 278 million. The countries most likely to miss the 2015 targets are in Sub-Saharan Africa, many of which have been beset by natural disasters and political violence.

Reconciling Unity and Diversity

In any organization which purports to be a global institution such as UNDP, or the Roman Catholic Church, there will always be tension between headquarters and the representatives in the countries in which it serves. This stems from the fact that the Administrator in New York and the Pope in Rome are committed to the principle that if policy or church doctrine is not carried out in a consistent and transparent manner throughout the entire system, the global institution will lose its integrity and support. The argument is that the global institution becomes meaningless when 160 resident representatives (or priests and bishops) throughout the world are doing their own thing. The resident representatives (or priests and bishops) counter this argument by saying that senior staff in headquarters or the Vatican must be sensitive to the social, economic and political culture of each country. A policy edict will have one meaning in headquarters and quite another in the field. In a world so diverse, headquarters should not take a "one size fits all" attitude and should keep in mind that Tuvalu, a collection of small islands in the South Pacific with a population of 15,000, has a UNDP program of assistance as does China with a population of 1.3 billion.

The resident representatives recognize that there are universal principles like human rights that must be advocated worldwide. They argue that they should use their own judgment, timing and approach in advocating such principles and carrying out certain policies. For example, after Gus Speth replaced Bill Draper, he instructed every field office to engage the government and other UN organizations in preparing a country Human Development Report. Had Draper issued the same instruction when the first Human Development Report was published in 1990, I would have been hesitant to ask the Chinese government to engage in such an exercise because the government made clear to me that it rejected the whole notion of a Human Development Report. But time changes things and my successor did not encounter the same obstacle.

On one occasion, I raised the unity versus diversity issue at a global meeting attended by senior staff throughout the world. Draper ended the discussion when he took the microphone and said, "Roy, your problem is that you just don't want to have a boss!" Some of my colleagues looked at me and thought, "Wow, Roy, you are going to be in trouble this time." I didn't worry because I knew that Bill respected my work and I was certain that he was not going to become angry and ship my off to Ouagadougou. We joked about it after the meeting, and I told Bill that communicating on this issue between headquarters and the field is like when two people in bed get their electric blanket controls switched. They irritate each other all night long because they can't get comfortable as one makes the other too warm which is countered by making the first person too cold. When one looks at UNDP today, it seems that the headquarters side eventually won the argument because the resident representatives are far less autonomous than they were in my day. But the tide could turn back to the field in the future; however, it is highly unlikely.

The thirty-six member Executive Board sets policy for UNDP. Headquarters is directly under the guidance of the Board. But the field offices are remote and only indirectly under the influence of the Board. The more specific the Board is in providing policy guidance, the more specific headquarters is in providing policy guidance to the field. Hence the natural tension between headquarters and the field is a permanent attribute of any global organization whether it be the Vatican in Rome or UNDP headquarters in New York.

Herding Cats

In most countries throughout the world, the UNDP resident representative also serves as the UN resident coordinator.[7] The resident coordinator appointment is made by the UN Secretary-General based on the recommendation by the UNDP Administrator. The resident coordinator is the designated representative of the Secretary-General for all development operations and the leader of the UN country team. The resident coordinator tries to insure a multi-disciplinary dimension in the various UN programs within the country. The idea is to avoid duplication and increase coordination and collaboration among all UN funds and agencies. The ultimate objective is to have a single integrated program with various parts of the program funded and implemented by the appropriate UN agency. This integrated (One UN) approach has been launched in a few select pilot countries.

In 1997, the Secretary-General established the United Nations Development Group (UNDG) at headquarters level to "deliver more coherent, effective and efficient support to countries seeking to attain internationally agreed development goals." There are now thirty-two funds and agencies that are members of this coordinating body and it is chaired by the Administrator of UNDP. Normally meetings are held in New York.

In theory the integrated approach is appealing. In practice it is very difficult to achieve. Like many vicissitudes in life, the difficulty of improving UN agency coordination comes down to a question of money. It is especially difficult to integrate the programs of those organizations funded by voluntary contributions; the most important of which are UNDP, UNICEF, WFP and UNFPA. Their contributions come to them separately and they must account for the use of their funds separately. Moreover, each year the advocates for these organizations go to the parliaments of the major developed countries with hat in hand requesting funding. Each organization feels that it must maintain its separate identity as it competes with sister organizations to gain the favor of highly opinionated committee chairs and members.

I can speak with some experience on this matter as I spent the last three years of my career with UNDP serving as the Director of the UNDP Office in Washington. I had the unenviable task of trying to convince members of Congress that UNDP plays a positive and important role in the world and, therefore, it is in the interest of the U.S. government to support it. I started the job in the fall of 1996, and it was like stepping into the eye of a hurricane. In 1994, Republicans gained control of both houses of Congress for the first time since 1946. President Clinton's effort to maintain a Democratic majority failed and the hard-charging Newt Gingrich became Speaker of the House — the most powerful position on Capitol Hill. By the time I arrived on the scene, Congress had already slashed the UNDP appropriation to the lowest level in decades ($85 million) and for the first time ever, UNICEF was given more money than UNDP. Did I every have my work cut out for me! Fortunately, I had a very effective deputy and during my three years in the position we were able to restore some of the funding, but never to the glory days of the past. It is interesting to note that the highest annual contribution to UNDP ($135 million) occurred under the conservative Republican administration of President Reagan and Vice President Bush. We can assume that this was due to the fact that one of Vice President Bush's closest friends was serving at the time as the Administrator of UNDP.

For the voluntary funded UN organizations, the two power points on Capitol Hill are the House and Senate Appropriations Sub-committees on Foreign Operations. During my tenure, the chairs of these sub-committees were not hostile. Rather it was the professional staff appointed to the sub-committees who were bellicose; and one should never underestimate the importance of committee staff. Fortunately, there were two Democratic House sub-committee members (Nita Lowey and Nancy Pelosi, who later served as Speaker of the House from 2007 to 2011) and one House Republican (John Porter) who knew UNDP and appreciated its work. There was considerable hostility in Congress at the time toward the entire UN system. Congressional leaders were basically negative and a surprisingly large number of House Republicans (including 2008 and 2012 presidential candidate Ron Paul) supported a resolution calling for the withdrawal of the United States from the United Nations. I sometimes wondered if I should purchase a fire retardant suit of chain mail to wear to meetings with some of these characters.

My impression was that the Republicans on the two Appropriations Sub-committees decided that they should find at least one UN organization they could support. They decided on UNICEF. There are several reasons for their choice:

- It has a universally recognized focus. Everyone knows that UNICEF focuses its attention on children and mothers. It is difficult for even the most anti-UN member of Congress to come out four-square against women and children.

- It has a strong and committed lobby. Since the inception of UNICEF in 1947, highly effective non-governmental support groups were established in the U.S. and other major donor countries.
- UNICEF has a huge, obvious constituency. There are thousands of non-governmental groups and governmental agencies that focus on the needs of mothers and children. Such groups have a natural affinity for an international organization like UNICEF that shares their same concerns.
- UNICEF, among all United Nations organizations, has always had the most effective public relations capability. It was the first to have Ambassadors of Good Will; the first to have children collect contributions at Halloween; the first to establish gift shops; and the first to have its logo painted on the fleet of a Japanese airline.

Of course, I would have preferred that the Republicans shower their good will on both UNDP and UNICEF. But there are several reasons why that didn't happen. Especially in the last twenty years, UNDP has taken a deeper and more systemic approach to development than has UNICEF. UNICEF has gained its fame by undertaking projects which promote the immunization of children, the use of re-hydration salts to treat diarrhea, breast feeding of infants and digging wells for safe water. These are basic, easy to understand projects that are vital to the health and nutrition of children. Conversely, UNDP has moved to a higher branch of the development tree by undertaking projects that promote civil service reform, clean and fair elections, the management of environmental pollution, new management structures for combating HIV/AIDS, and training for improved macro economic policy. These projects are complex and often take years to show any results, but are fundamental in promoting a more open society and reducing the gap between wealth and poverty.

By addressing problems at a systemic level, UNDP is able to better leverage its investment — to get more bang for the buck. Most UNDP projects are designed to enhance the capacity of nationals in their own countries to solve their own problems. But when one briefs members of the U.S. Congress, it would be highly counterproductive to get into a discourse on the development theory behind these projects. Written material must be limited to a single sheet (front and back) and no more. What the members really want to know is: (1) Whom are you helping? (2) Why are you helping them? (3) What results do you have to show for your efforts? If I am a representative of UNICEF, I can summarize the achievements of the organization in two simple sentences by saying, "Diarrhea is the third largest cause of childhood deaths in the world. UNICEF is the world's leading organization that assists countries in treating the disease through the use of re-hydration salts and we have saved the lives of millions of children." In a similar fashion the United Nations High Commissioner for Refugees (UNHCR) could easily win over members of Congress by simply saying, "There are currently millions of refugees living in camps throughout the world administered by UNHCR and if we did not have these camps, a large percentage of these refugees would perish." The representative for the World Food Programme (WFP) could go to the same meeting and add, "The daily food ration for these millions of refugees is provided by WFP." I could walk into these offices (which I have done many times) and say, "I represent UNDP in Vietnam and I am pleased to tell you that we have launched a major project to reform the judicial system to make it more independent and professional." The reaction would be, "Well, Mr. Morey, we are talking about a communist country and, therefore, I will be greatly surprised if this project achieves any success. Of course, we won't know the lasting results for years to come, but good luck and thanks for dropping by."

The UNDP projects are just as worthy of support as the UNICEF projects, but they lack the sentimentality of UNCEF and are more esoteric and can neither be reduced to a sentence nor condensed on a bumper strip. In addition, it is difficult to pull the heart strings by describing to a congressman how UNDP has helped a country improve its macro-economic framework. As mentioned earlier, UNICEF has a natural constituency as do many other UN agencies. WHO has the vast health community; ILO has organized labor; UNESCO has the academic community; FAO and WFP have the powerful agriculture lobby. Because of its systemic approach to development, plus its multi-disciplinary focus, UNDP does not have an identifiable constituency — at least one with any political clout. While UNICEF has always had strong non-profit support groups, UNDP has been very late getting into the game. During my tenure in Washington (1996–1999), the Administrator finally succeeded in receiving non-profit tax status for the new United States Committee for the United Nations Development Programme. In addition, my colleague, Tom Cox, and I succeeded in negotiating cooperation agreements with the American Bar Association and the National Democratic Institute (NDI) to collaborate on legal and governance projects in various countries throughout the world. NDI is a non-profit organization funded by the U.S. government to support democratic institutions in developing countries. All three of these entities now support UNDP through disseminating public information and meeting with key members of Congress and State Department officials. Kenneth Wollack, President of NDI, also serves as chair of the Board of Directors of the U.S. Committee for UNDP.

When the Capacity Study was being debated by the UNDP Governing Council, Robert Jackson and Joan Anstee pressed hard for the adoption of their recommendation to amalgamate the various executive boards of UN funds and agencies involved in development. Not surprisingly, this recommendation was rejected. As mentioned before, each UN organization has its own political constituency. For example, the U.S. Department of Agriculture wanted to continue its guidance of FAO; the Department of Labor and the AFL/CIO wanted to continue its guidance of the ILO and so on. As a resident coordinator trying to "herd the cats," I regret the recommendation failed. Had it been adopted, all organizations around the table would be receiving common guidance and, therefore, it would be easier to reconcile the differences and prevent inefficiency caused by competition among support groups.

A decision by UNDP that caused antipathy toward the organization by some of the specialized agency representatives (especially FAO) was the switch from agency to government project execution. The specialized agencies lost appeal to their counterpart ministries when they could no longer promise UNDP funded projects.

Another development that made the resident coordinator's job more difficult was the approval of their respective governing bodies to allow UN organizations to demonstrate their independence from UNDP by establishing their own offices headed by their own representatives. When I was serving in the U.S. State Department before joining UNDP, I was guilty of approving this unwise trend. During the early days of UNDP, FAO appointed a senior agriculture advisor who was located in the UNDP field office. After Edouard Saouma was elected Director-General of FAO, he made a visit to Washington to seek U.S. government approval to establish a new position with the title of FAO Representative who would be housed in a separate FAO field office. The U.S. Department of Agriculture enthusiastically endorsed the proposed change of field representation. In a weak moment, I was swayed by their enthusiasm and went along with the change. Years later, I learned to regret the decision when I received my first appointment as UN Resident Coordinator. The cats were out of the UNDP office and on the loose!

For many years, WFP and UNFPA had senior officers located in the UNDP field offices and the UNDP resident representative served as representative for both organizations. Today both organizations have their own representatives and field offices. I should add that these independent representatives are pleased to arrive at a diplomatic reception in their sedans flying the UN flag. It's a case of overkill — the parking lots at such receptions are full of vehicles all displaying the same UN flag.

Many of my UN colleagues shared the same office building in Washington. We had periodic meetings to discuss what each was doing and we maintained a congenial atmosphere, but especially with UNICEF (and to a certain degree UNFPA) it was a zero sum game. When the final foreign operations bill was approved, if UNICEF funding went up, UNDP would go down proportionately. It is said that all is fair in love and war. I would like to add that so is fighting for appropriations from the U.S. Congress. On one occasion, Carol Bellamy, then Executive Director of UNICEF, traveled to Washington to discuss the newly established UN Development Group (UNDG) with the chair and staff of the House Appropriations Sub-committee on Foreign Operations. Bellamy was a formidable woman who had honed her political skills in the jungle of New York City politics. She expressed a concern about the UNDG because it is chaired by the Administrator of UNDP and, therefore, she feared UNDP might attempt to control UNICEF, diminish its autonomy and make it a less effective organization. Bellamy's meeting prompted the sub-committee chair to send a strongly worded letter to Gus Speth who was serving at the time as UNDP Administrator. Naturally, Gus wanted my office to do the draft reply. As you can imagine, our reply categorically denied any intention "to control" UNICEF and the letter went on to explain the purpose of the UNDG. Apparently the reply did little to diffuse the issue. Subsequently, the chief staffer for the sub-committee laced into me one day on the same topic and concluded his remarks by saying, "UNDP had better not touch a hair on the head of UNICEF."

It is my impression that the UNDG in New York now conducts its business in a more harmonious fashion than at its inception. The UNDG was the brain child of Secretary-General Kofi Annan and UNDP Administrator Gus Speth. Annan was required to expend considerable effort using his conciliatory skills to keep the UN cats from clawing each other. Here again, finding common ground among such a diverse collection of funds and agencies, each with its own governing body, is no mean feat. While coordination is important, it should not be carried to the fourth decimal point. It would not be desirable for all UN organizations to march lockstep within the same program framework. Diversity in the UN system is natural because each organization performs different functions and has its own focus and goals. Moreover, forcing the UN cats to all behave the same way would require suffocating centralization which would stunt initiative and creativity.

It is also my impression that a degree of progress has been made at the field level in coordinating the work of the UN family of organizations. At least now there is general agreement among the UN organizations that the ultimate purpose of any development program is poverty alleviation. This agreement allows the resident coordinator a small piece of common ground as a starting point. Based on my subsequent experience serving as resident coordinator in Vietnam, I found that the most critical factor required to enhance coordination and cooperation is the attitude of the government. The Vietnamese Ministry of

Planning and Investment made it clear to all concerned that UNDP was the lead organization in the country to coordinate technical assistance (grant development assistance). At the time, UNDP had a major project assisting the Ministry of Planning and Investment to better manage development assistance within the government.

The Vietnam experience also showed that the most difficult UN cat of them all to bring into the herd is the World Bank. The World Bank is a specialized agency of the United Nations, but one would never know it from the way it operates. It has been a special breed of cat from the beginning. When it was founded in 1944, there was a specific purpose for naming it the International Bank for Reconstruction and Development (IBRD). It was designed as an international loan agency to help Europe recover from the destruction of World War II. The original intent was for the IBRD to provide loans to industrialized and middle income countries. Some years later, the International Development Agency was added to the Bank to provide interest free loans to impoverished countries. More recently the World Bank started providing grant assistance in some of the poorest countries and some argue that the World Bank wants to eclipse UNDP as the world's largest provider of grant development assistance. We shall see.

Joining UNDP in Mid-Career

In my graduate program in political science at the University of Arizona in the early '60s, my primary focus was on American politics. After receiving my PhD in 1964, I had every intention of finding a congenial department of political science in a recognized college or university and start a career of teaching and research. Living abroad, joining the U.S. Foreign Service or becoming a professional staff member of a UN organization never entered my mind. You will find in the next chapter that I did start my career in academia, but the lure of Washington was simply too strong to resist and my life changed forever. My career path to UNDP was indeed circuitous.

2

U.S./UN: Sitting on the
Other Side of the Desk

Last Days at the White House

It was a cold morning and a steel gray sky in Washington in mid–November 1972. I was then a member of President Richard Nixon's White House staff. I was sitting in my office in the Old Executive Office Building next to the West Wing of the White House. I arrived early that day because I had an important meeting scheduled with my boss, John Ehrlichman. I was a member of Ehrlichman's Domestic Council staff serving as Staff Assistant to the President. I had been informed a few days earlier by Kenneth Cole, Deputy Director of the Domestic Council staff, that President Nixon was going to request the resignation of everyone in the Administration including the Cabinet. In fact, staff chief H.R. (Bob) Haldeman had already informed Cabinet members that their resignations were requested.

There was a chilly breeze blowing off the Potomac River that morning. Because of my scheduled meeting with Ehrlichman, I felt the atmosphere within the White House complex was chilly as well. I had finished my usual morning reading (*New York Times, Washington Post, Wall Street Journal*) and I still had an hour before the meeting. I leaned back in my chair and started to ruminate on my situation — how did I get into this predicament and where would I wind up?

As a Ph.D. candidate in the Department of Government at the University of Arizona in 1964, I desperately wanted to go to Washington and immerse myself in the political scene. I was amazed to find that I would have just such an opportunity when I received a telegram from the headquarters of the American Political Science Association (APSA) informing me that I was one of sixteen applicants in the country to receive the APSA Congressional Fellowship. As a congressional fellow, I was to serve on the staff of a member of the House for half the year and as a Senate staffer for the other half.

After arriving in Washington, my first stop on Capitol Hill was the office of my Congressman, Morris (Mo) Udall, Democrat of Arizona. I had met Udall in Tucson while I was a graduate student and he knew that I was a Republican. In an era (which now seems eons ago) when members of Congress easily sought friendship with those in the opposite party, Mo told me some of the best members were Republicans and proceeded to give me a list of twelve House members I should interview. Moreover, he told me to use the fellowship to learn something about the country. Since I had lived my life in the west, he urged me to work for a member from a state east of the Mississippi River. For the first half year I worked for Congressman Robert Griffin, Republican of Michigan. The second-half of the year I worked for Senator Norris Cotton, Republican of New Hampshire. For a kid out of an Arizona mining camp (Silver Bell), the year in Washington changed my life. It also changed the life of Delores, my wife and high school sweetheart. I now had Washington political experience and, more importantly, I made many new friends.

Despite the excitement of Washington, I had my eye firmly fixed on cloistering myself in the ivy-covered walls of academia. I found the perfect place. After the year in Washington, Delores, daughter Diana and I packed our 1957 Chevy and drove to Granville, Ohio, where I joined the political science faculty at Denison University. To this day, the village of Granville is a gem plucked from the nineteenth century. The picture-perfect Denison campus would cause one to fantasize a scene of Ronald Reagan in a cardigan letter sweater sitting on a window sill strumming a ukulele. I liked the students and I liked my colleagues. We enjoyed roaming the Welsh Hills of central Ohio on a fall day in Kodachrome color in search of the nearest tree to pick apples.

While it was a wonderful life in what some of the locals called "Happy Valley," I started to grow weary of my job and especially some of my academic colleagues. It was the 1960s and all that went with it. The Vietnam War was coming to a boil and both students and faculty wanted to vacate the classroom and travel twenty-eight miles into Columbus to demonstrate against the war. Over my objection, the Convocation Committee invited Dr. Timothy Leary, the Harvard counterculture psychologist and psychedelic guru, to lecture to the students on the wonders of hallucinogenic drugs. Students went on strike and boycotted classes. I opposed the war as much as anyone on the faculty, but I was paid to do a job, and, by God, I planned to be in the classroom every day and I told my students that they had better be in class as well if they expected a passing grade.

In the midst of this nonsense, I was invited to Washington in 1970 to participate in the White House Conference on Children and Youth because I had co-authored a book the year before on education policy. I was delighted to be away from the campus so I spent two days in Washington after the conference to visit friends and soak up Washington gossip. A dear friend of mine and former congressional fellow, Bruce Ladd, who was serving at the time as White House staff assistant for personnel asked if I was still enjoying my life in academia. When I responded that I was enjoying it less and less, he suggested that I consider a policy position in the Nixon Administration. He mentioned that former Congressman Donald Rumsfeld was serving as Director of the Office of Economic Opportunity (OEO) and Richard Cheney was serving as a key deputy. Bruce had served in Rumsfeld's congressional office and we both knew Dick Cheney. I had been on the national selection board of the Congressional Fellowship Program when Cheney was selected as a fellow. (Of course, I never let him forget that I was involved in his selection!) Under Rumsfeld's direction, OEO was a very exciting place for a social scientist because it served as an experimental domestic policy laboratory. I had an excellent meeting with Cheney that afternoon and he thought OEO would be a good fit for me because of the book I had written earlier. Bruce Ladd also suggested that I meet with David Lissy, Executive Assistant to Secretary of State William Rogers. I had a good meeting with Lissy who was seeking someone to fill the position of Director of the Foreign Service Institute — the training center for the Foreign Service. He liked my academic background and the fact that I had spent a year and a half in Japan directing a student program.

I flew back home and discussed these new exciting possibilities with Delores. She agreed that there was a big world beyond Granville, Ohio, and felt Washington would be a good move. A few weeks later the secretary of the Denison political science department burst into my office and exclaimed, "Someone from the White House is on the line." Naturally I wondered, "Who in the White House would be calling me?" I soon learned that it was Edwin Harper, a senior member of the White House Domestic Council staff. He said that John Ehrlichman would like for me to visit Washington to interview for a position on the Domestic Council staff and, would I be interested? I expressed an interest and added that I was surprised by the call because I had never applied for a position at the White House. He replied that we could discuss that and other matters in a personal interview. I later learned that Bruce Ladd had sent my resume to John Ehrlichman as had the personnel director of OEO.

I packed my bag and drove to Columbus and flew to Washington. I stayed with Bruce and his wife, Dolly, which was convenient and helpful because Bruce briefed me on the do's and don'ts of interviewing at the White House. I had interviews with Ehrlichman, Cole and Harper. The final interview was with a formidable staff member of the White House personnel office by the name of Frederic V. Malek. Somehow, I impressed all concerned and I gladly accepted the job offer which included a considerable increase in salary. I negotiated a two-year leave of absence with the Provost of Denison: the Morey family took up residence in Bethesda, Maryland (a Washington suburb) in early June and, just like that, I became a player on President Richard Nixon's team.

So here I sat with a half hour to go before my meeting with Ehrlichman. I started reflecting on the previous eighteen months on the White House staff. It was like running a DVD on fast forward. In a sense, I became involved in Nixon's reelection campaign immediately after taking the job, yet the election was a year and a half away. When I arrived, Ehrlichman had just charged Ed Harper with the task of developing a domestic policy presentation for the President. He wanted the presentation to be used to shape the State of the Union Address to Congress in January 1972 and the Republican Party platform at the convention in August. It would also serve as a policy framework for the campaign. I joined Harper's team and my assignment was agricultural policy.

We started the process by choosing the eleven states with a combined total of electoral votes needed to win the presidency. We examined domestic policy issues in each state that we thought would be important in November 1972. The list of issues included everything from busing students to achieve racial balance in schools to the allocation of defense contracts. The object was to show the President what the domestic problems were and we also used data from public opinion polls to show him how the voter perceived problems — both national and personal problems. Vietnam, crime in the streets, and the budget topped the list of national problems. The top personal problems were mainly economic plus school busing. The busing issue was red hot because a huge number of white parents living in the suburbs did not want their kids bused into inter-city black schools. Caspar Weinberger, Deputy Director of the Office of Management and Budget (OMB), made a comment about the presentation that would be just as applicable to American voters today as it was in 1971. "There was an inconsistency in the results," said Weinberger, "They all wanted the government to spend less, but they wanted more services for themselves."[1] The data were presented on transparent overlays for use on an overhead projector plus flip charts — there were no PowerPoint presentations in those days. Ehrlichman reserved the Cabinet Room and arranged a two-hour presentation for the President which included Nixon's most trusted political counselors: John Connally, Secretary of the Treasury; John Mitchell, Attorney General; Bob Haldeman, John Ehrlichman, Charles Colson; George Shultz and Caspar Weinberger,

Director and Deputy Director of the Budget. We staff sat in chairs along the wall. Fortunately, the President and his advisors were pleased with the presentation which we then condensed into a booklet providing a useful reference for the next fifteen months.

As we started to prepare for the campaign in the spring of 1972, I became Ehrlichman's chief public opinion polling officer. At first, we contracted our polling with firms such as Louis Harris. After the President's campaign committee was established a few blocks from the White House, Robert Teeter (later Gerald Ford's campaign manager) did all our polling. Ehrlichman, Harper and I would formulate domestic issues to be included in the polls and Henry Kissinger and his staff chose the foreign policy issues. My job was to analyze the polling data and condense my analysis into a memorandum which I sent to Ehrlichman, some of which were forwarded on to the President.

When George McGovern, Senator of South Dakota, was nominated as the Democratic Party's candidate for the presidency, I hosted an office party to celebrate his nomination. We knew he would run an anti–Vietnam War campaign. By mid–July our opinion polling data clearly indicated that the vast majority of potential voters agreed with the Nixon policy to withdraw from Vietnam with honor and turn the fighting over to the South Vietnamese. In fact, as the campaign progressed, Nixon's lead on the Vietnam issue continued to increase. Bob Teeter and I would scratch our heads and say, "We just don't get it. Pat Caddell [McGovern's chief pollster] must be reading the same data we are and if so, why in the hell does McGovern keep harping on Vietnam because it is clearly a losing issue for him."

By the time Nixon was nominated at the Republican National Convention in Miami Beach, Florida on August 23, the poll data indicated that he was unstoppable in his race for a second term. Most people knew this and, therefore, the convention was a very relaxed affair. Two of my colleagues and I were given a few days off to attend the convention and we had a ball. One evening we flashed our White House security cards to gain entrance to an exclusive party hosted by Frank Sinatra. The next evening we were hobnobbing with Governor Ronald Reagan and the California delegation. But we ran into a snag when we attempted to fly back to Washington the day after the President was nominated. We panicked when we found that every flight to Washington was fully booked. As a last resort, one of my colleagues mentioned that he was the White House liaison with the Civil Aeronautics Board (CAB) and he would call his friend at the CAB and see if he could finagle a way to free up three seats on one of the flights. It's amazing what can be done when one works at the White House. That afternoon we received word that we had three seats on a late flight to Washington. When we entered the plane, we found the seats were scattered throughout the cabin. I took my window seat and started reading a book. After take-off, the man sitting next to me seemed agitated and anxious to talk. After exchanging a few pleasantries, he blurted out, "Boy, am I pissed off." When I asked him why he was unhappy, he replied, "I am going to a conference in Washington with three other friends and they were bumped off this flight. We think there were some damned political bigwigs who got the seats." He then asked me what kind of work I did, and I calmly replied, "Oh, I'm a dentist." I disappeared into the night as soon as I got off the plane.

In mid–September John Ehrlichman provided a special treat for the staff. We boarded a bus in front of the White House that took us to Camp David, the presidential retreat in the Catoctin Mountains of Maryland. After a tour of the facilities (no photos allowed), we went to the Aspen Lodge and met in the President's conference room. John called on several staff members to make comments. When he got to me, he said, "Roy, the diviner of tea leaves and chicken entrails, tell us about the polls you have been analyzing." I provided the latest results on a variety of domestic issues and closed with the following comment:

> John, I have no idea who was involved in the Watergate break-in, but it is an issue which will continue to loom larger and larger. I think the President should go on television and inform the public that anyone on the staff or associated with the campaign committee who are involved should face the consequences for their actions. If he made a clean breast of it, any suspicion of his involvement would be cleared. His standing in the polls is so strong that nothing short of being accused of a capital offense could derail his reelection.

John replied that my suggestion was interesting and that he would take it under advisement. Ehrlichman later wrote that indeed he had made a similar proposal to Nixon and other advisors but to no avail.[2] We will never know whether coming clean from the very beginning would have saved Nixon's presidency.

Well, I still had a few minutes before my meeting and I thought once again that after Nixon's landslide election victory of historic proportions only a few weeks before, why was the White House atmosphere so glum. Obviously, it was that 500 pound gorilla with Watergate tattooed on its forehead sitting in the room. Everyone knew it was there, but most refused to recognize it.

The image of John Ehrlichman among his staff was 180 degrees different from the way he was described in the press and the image he presented on television during the Senate Watergate Hearings. The press referred to Ehrlichman and Haldeman as the Berlin Wall. Many thought John was cold, calculating and arrogant. He may have been calculating, but certainly neither cold nor arrogant. In fact, John was a first-rate boss. He was smart, open-minded and willing to listen. Even if we did not see him everyday, he knew exactly what we were working on. He had an excellent sense of humor and did not take himself too seriously. Like any good boss, he gave credit where credit was due. For example, after the major presentation in the Cabinet Room in 1971, the President thanked him for a job well done. John immediately turned to us sitting on the back row and said, "Mr. President, you are only as good as your staff." He then encouraged those sitting with the President at the table to give us a round of applause. I never forgot that moment and I used John's comment for the rest of my career.

Ehrlichman's office was located on the second floor of the East Wing of the White House and a short walk from mine. When I entered the room, John greeted me warmly as was his custom. He told me that he and Bob Haldeman had been discussing with the President plans to reorganize the Executive Branch for the new term. He said that everyone's resignation was being requested because the President wanted to start his second term with a new slate. He assured me that the request for my resignation was in no way a reflection on my work. He mentioned that those leaving the staff had two choices. They could either enter the private sector or continue serving the President in a federal department or agency. He said, "Roy, if you would like to serve in the new Administration, I suggest that you go to a department or agency of your choice and if there is an opening at an appropriate rank, you will have my full support. Just give me a call when that time comes." I was delighted to be given this assurance, and the melancholy attitude I had the previous week vanished.

When I started my job search, I went in opposite policy directions. I first called my two main contacts at the Department of Health, Education and Welfare (HEW), Lawrence Lynn and Michael Timpane. They both had read my book on education policy and liked it. After leaving HEW, they both became internationally recognized academicians. Larry Lynn became the country's foremost authority on public management and held posts at several of the top universities in the country. Mike Timpane became President of Teachers College of Columbia University and Director of the National Institute of Education. Both of them suggested that I meet with Sidney Marland, U.S. Commissioner of Education, to discuss a slot that was open at the Assistant Commissioner level. I knew and respected Marland who had come out of public school administration to become Commissioner. He was smart, innovative and not in the pocket of the teachers' unions. I first met him when he went to Denison to deliver the commencement address in 1971. I also had contact with him during my time at the White House. I think it is likely I would have been offered the job and it would have been great fun to work with Lynn and Timpane.

I would have taken the job had I planned to return to the academic world. But at this point in my life I came to realize that I was not cut out to be an academician. I found the university no longer to be the market place of ideas. Rather, I realized that because of the university's pursuit to find the purest form of political correctness I would always be stepping in front or behind the line. There were several reasons for this. First, I am a Republican and Republican political scientists are scarce as hen's teeth. Second, I have always seen politics as the art of the possible and I am a pragmatist. I found too many of my colleagues in the profession to be ideologues. Third, I grew tired of academic politics which someone once aptly described as being so predatory because the stakes are so low. My political orientation was best described by the eminent historian and political scientist, Clinton Rossiter, who said that he was the most liberal of conservatives and the most conservative of liberals. In the final analysis, I wanted to be a practitioner in politics and public policy rather than teaching and writing about it.

My next move was to call David Lissy in Secretary William Rogers' office at the Department of State. David was smart and clear-headed. In our meeting he described two openings at the deputy assistant secretary level. One was in the Bureau of International Organization Affairs (IO) and the other in the Bureau of Economic and Business Affairs (EB). In IO I would be dealing with all United Nations organizations involved in social and economic policy. The EB bureau deals with matters such as international trade and transport, commercial affairs and intellectual property. As an elementary school student after the end of World War II, I learned about the United Nations and I continued my interest in it throughout college and graduate school. Therefore, applying for the position in the IO bureau was an easy choice.

My first interview was with one of the grand lions of the Foreign Service, William J. Macomber, Jr., Under Secretary for Management at the time. Bill had given his all to his country — in combat during World War II as a U.S. Marine, as a CIA officer before joining the Foreign Service in 1953, and as ambassador to Jordan and Turkey. Small wonder that the career service held him in high regard. The interview proceeded swimmingly until I posed a very presumptuous question. I asked him if there was anything open at the assistant secretary level (one level above deputy assistant secretary). He looked at me quizzically and said,

> Dr. Morey, your resume indicates that you are 36 years old. No career officer is ever elevated to the assistant secretary level at the age of 36. In fact, if you were to take the IO position, you would have officers ten to fifteen years older reporting to you. I don't know what the deputy assistant secretary level amounts to in other departments, but in the Department of State, you would be the equivalent of an ambassador. I think you would be fortunate indeed to get such a position.

We ended the meeting on a positive note and I thought to myself as I walked down the corridor from his office, "Just because you have been serving on the White House staff, you shouldn't get too big for your britches." Bill Macomber did a good job of bringing me down to earth.

My last interview at the State Department was with another highly respected senior officer, but this one was not a career officer. His name was Kenneth Rush and he was Deputy Secretary of State. Several years before, he was asked to join the administration because he was a close friend of the President. Rush was an Assistant Professor of Law at Duke University Law School when Nixon was a first-year student. Rush left academia after one year and joined the Union Carbide and Carbon Corporation and became corporate president in 1966. He had served with distinction as U.S. Ambassador to West Germany (Federal Republic of Germany) before going to the State Department. In the interview we had a broad-ranging discussion on international relations and foreign policy. It was like two college professors having a discussion over lunch. It must have gone well because a few days later I was notified by Secretary Rogers' office that I had been hired. William Rogers would be replaced by Henry Kissinger six months later. I somehow knew that it would lead to a whole new life. Delores and I would return to Granville to visit Denison friends, but never to live there again.

Joining the IO Bureau

When I joined the Department of State in March 1973, there were five regional bureaus and several functional bureaus including the Bureau of International Organization Affairs (IO). Each bureau is headed by an assistant secretary who is nominated by the President, confirmed by the Senate, and who reports to the Secretary. Each bureau has one or more deputy assistant secretaries who are appointed by the Secretary and report directly to the assistant secretary. When I served as Deputy Assistant Secretary of State in the IO Bureau, there was one other deputy who looked after political affairs which primarily concerned the UN Security Council. My job was to pay attention to all organizations reporting to the UN Economic and Social Council (ECOSOC). These included all voluntary funds such as:

> United Nations Development Programme (UNDP)
> United Nations International Children's Emergency Fund (UNICEF)
> United Nations Population Fund (UNFPA)

All specialized agencies of the United Nations including:

> United Nations Education, Cultural and Scientific Organization (UNESCO)
> Food and Agriculture Organization (FAO)
> World Food Programme (WFP)
> International Labor Organization (ILO)
> International Atomic Energy Agency (IAEA)
> United Nations High Commissioner for Refugees (UNHCR)
> World Health Organization (WHO)
> International Civil Aviation Organization (ICAO)
> United Nations Industrial Organization (UNIDO)
> United Nations Environment Programme (UNEP)
> World Meteorological Organization (WMO)

In addition, I reported to the assistant secretary on all administrative and budgetary issues for the United Nations and all affiliated organizations. It is not surprising that today the IO Bureau has four deputy assistant secretaries with three of them covering the job I used to have. It was a very demanding job, but as John Ehrlichman said, "You are only as good as your staff" and I was blessed with a superb team of career foreign service officers.

There were at least forty officers who worked under my direction. One section focused on budgetary and administrative matters and the others were clustered into substantive areas such as food and agriculture, labor, health, education, culture and science, industry, environment, meteorology and air transport. Perhaps I had the largest number of personnel evaluation reports to prepare each year of anyone in the Department.

A Visit to the Missions

Just as the regional bureaus have embassies in various countries reporting to them, IO has several missions which report to it. The most important is the U.S. Mission to the United Nations in New York which is headed by a cabinet-level ambassador. The next largest mission is in Geneva where numerous UN entities are located. In addition, there is a mission in Vienna focusing on industry and atomic energy. A mission in Paris to cover UNESCO and another in Rome to monitor the FAO, WFP and the International Fund for Agricultural Development (IFAD). There is now a mission in Nairobi to keep track of UNEP, but in my day it was covered by someone on the staff in the U.S. Embassy in Kenya.

A month or so after my arrival at State, the assistant secretary suggested that I travel to Europe to meet the chief officers of our U.S. missions and also to have an introductory meeting with the directors general of the UN specialized agencies. Flights to Europe from Washington are often late afternoon departures and early morning arrivals. The day of my departure was hectic because I did not count on last-minute meetings. At my level I was entitled to top security clearance. Periodically, I would read intelligence reports mainly from telecommunication intercepts. A federal employee would arrive at my office with a brief case chained to her wrist. She would unlock the chain, hand me a packet of reports, and remain in the room until I finished reading. She would then carefully stash the packet in her brief case, reattach the chain and continue her appointed rounds. Unfortunately, I had forgotten this appointment and I ran behind in my schedule for the remainder of the day until I was driven to Dulles Airport for my flight to Paris.

Government regulations specify that foreign service officers are required to fly on American carriers whenever possible and my ticket was always for an economy class seat. After we achieved cruising altitude over the Atlantic, I retrieved a copy of the *Washington Post* I had been saving for my evening reading. I will never forget the day — April 30, 1973. The headlines announced the resignations of John Ehrlichman and H.R. (Bob) Haldeman. This was the biggest news in the country and perhaps the world, but I was running so hard that day that I was unaware of this momentous event until that evening. I thanked the Lord that the President had requested my resignation thus prompting my departure from the White House just before the ceiling collapsed. I escaped without a scratch and I was on my way to Europe for only the second time in my life. During the next four years I would spend at least twenty percent of my time in Europe, mainly in Rome and Geneva.

My first stop was Paris where I had a meeting with Rene Maheu, the Director General of UNESCO. He was a French national and had been in office for fourteen years. He was prepared to step down the following year and somehow I felt he had already started his retirement. He was previously a professor of philosophy and was a bit stiff and taciturn. I was told that he had been a close friend of Jean-Paul Sartre and somehow I could picture Maheu more comfortable huddled with Sartre in a deep discussion of existentialism than in managing UNESCO. My other meeting was more lively and informative. It was with the Deputy Director General John (Jack) Fobes. He was an American of many talents especially in management and administration. No wonder Maheu cherished this American as his deputy. Jack brought to the table precisely what the Director General lacked and they complemented each other beautifully.

In Geneva I had meetings with the Directors General of WHO and ILO and then I was off to Vienna for meetings with heads of the IAEA and UNIDO. I was exhausted by the time I reached Rome and when I arrived at my hotel, I was given a note instructing me to call the American Embassy immediately. My call was answered by a marine guard who informed me in an excited voice that I had received a call from Secretary of State Rogers. His call was made on a secure line and the guard suggested I return the call using a secure line at the embassy. Fortunately my hotel was only a ten minute walk from the embassy. I left my luggage with the concierge, set out for the embassy like a bat out of hell and kept asking myself, "Why in the world is the Secretary calling me — it can't be good." The guard placed the call and the Secretary's executive assistant, David Lissy answered. David informed me that the Secretary was not available and I exclaimed, "David, why in the world did the Secretary call me?" David replied, "Roy, I am sure you are aware of the fact that the President has fired Ehrlichman and Haldeman and the Secretary wants to know whether or not you were involved in any illegal activities while working for Ehrlichman." I shot back my answer, "No, I was not involved in any illegal or questionable activities while working at the White House." David had a simple response, "Fine, Roy, I will inform the Secretary of our conversation and I will see you when you return."

I knew that Lissy would convey the message, but I still felt uneasy when I returned to work, so I requested a meeting with Secretary Rogers and was given a half hour time slot the following day. Rogers was a man of grace and charm and he warmly welcomed me and ordered coffee. He then asked, "Roy, how can I help you?" Wound up like a top, my denials of any wrongdoing at the White House came spewing out fast and furious. After a minute or so, Rogers held up his hand for silence and simply asked, "Roy, are you an honorable man?" I replied, "Why, of course I am." He then said, "You have already told David that you were not involved in any illegal or questionable activities at the White House. I consider you an honorable man, and I take you at your word. Let's talk about something else." That was vintage William Rogers — a gentleman in the full sense of the word.

Going to Capitol Hill

Aside from my active participation in numerous international conferences, perhaps the most demanding part of my job was testifying before a variety of congressional committees, thereby getting a real feel for the impact of the principle of separation of powers in the U.S. Constitution. As a senior officer in the executive branch, I was treated with respect, but committee chairmen made it clear I was on their turf and I was expected to play by their rules and they, not I, were the ultimate guardians of the American taxpayers' pocketbook. After being given an opportunity to make a short presentation, I was expected to keep my mouth shut unless I was asked to respond to a question. Moreover, I was expected to give concise answers, and if I did not, I would be cut off in mid-sentence. A member of my staff could sit in the audience, but I was alone once the interrogation started. Like most young men in a high pressure job, I was fearless and convinced I could beat the world. Twenty years later, with much more experience and maturity, I would have been shaking in my boots facing the committee. I was expected to have at least some knowledge of a vast array of foreign policy issues and, as Secretary Kissinger's representative, I was expected to support the administration's position. During most of my years at State, I was representing a Republican administration facing two houses of Congress dominated by the Democratic Party. It was not my role to make partisan comments, but the members of Congress could be as partisan as they wished. Fortunately, I did not receive many partisan invectives.

Despite extensive preparations, I occasionally got a policy question which was not in my briefing book. Unless the question involved specific facts and figures, I could not very well say, "Well, Senator, I will take your question under advisement and get back to you later." For example, I was asked to testify before the Senate Foreign Relations Committee on the outcome of the World Food Conference. Charles Percy of Illinois was the ranking Republican on the committee and he asked me point blank, "Does this administration favor withholding food aid for those in need as a political weapon?" I replied, "No, the administration does not favor using food aid as a political weapon." The Senator then retorted, "For example, does the administration favor giving food aid to Uganda which is ruled with an iron fist by President Idi Amin?" I replied, "The U.S. is a major contributor of food to the World Food Programme and I believe WFP does indeed provide food to those in need in Uganda." When the hearing was over, I dashed back to the office and within an hour a member of my staff reported that I had given the correct answer on this politically sensitive issue. I breathed a sigh of relief.

Most of my work on Capitol Hill entailed testifying on the administration's appropriations requests for voluntary contributions to UN funding agencies such as UNDP, UNICEF and UNFPA. In the vernacular of Washington this would be considered a job that involved "heavy lifting" because the combined total of these requests exceeded $300 million. The request process ended on Capitol Hill, but it started with briefing sessions with my staff. When I thought I was ready to take the show on the road, my staff would organize a "murder session." In this final warm-up session, the staff would pretend to be members of Congress and would spend hours peppering me with the most difficult questions imaginable. Eventually I would decide on the level of funding to be requested for each organization and my recommendations were then presented to the assistant secretary for his approval.

The U.S. Agency for International Development (USAID) had their own budget requests, but since their requests fell into the same appropriations category as the voluntary requests for UN agencies, the first step in my annual run through the appropriations maze was with USAID. My interlocutors at AID were friendly but tough. In addition, they were knowledgeable because they were professional foreign assistance experts. It was a good place to start because I knew I would be exposed to tough questions before I ever went to Congress. My next stop was at the Office of Management and Budget (OMB) because my requests were incorporated into the annual budget submitted by the President. Of course, both USAID and OMB had a good idea of the size of my requests before meeting with them. It was in these informal discussions prior to my formal presentation that the real horse trading was done. It was highly unlikely that my figures would ever exceed what OMB had in mind. When there is a serious conflict between a department and OMB, the Secretary is occasionally forced to get involved in the negotiations. But this never happened with my requests. Because we all knew the rough magnitude of the size of the requests, the sessions with USAID and OMB focused more on why the funding was required and how it would be spent rather than its size.

My congressional testimony each year was before the House and Senate Appropriations Subcommittees on Foreign Operations, Export Financing and related programs (the scope of these subcommittees has been changed since 2008). The contrast between the chairmen of these two subcommittees could not have been greater. The Senate Chairman was Daniel Inouye of Hawaii who subsequently chaired the full committee. Inouye was a smart, soft spoken, highly respected Japanese-American. He was a hero in World War II and received the nation's highest military award, the Medal of Honor. Daniel Inouye died at the age of eighty-eight in December 2012. On the House side sat Otto Passman, the son of a dirt poor sharecropper from Monroe, Louisiana. To say the least, Passman did not share Inouye's soft-spoken demeanor. Passman was blunt and aggressive in his questioning. While Inouye saw value in the United Nations and foreign assistance, Passman made his reputation as the most implacable foe of foreign aid in the entire Congress. He even hated the Peace Corps and was once quoted saying, "If I had three minutes left to live, I'd kill the Peace Corps."[3] Fortunately there were plenty of supporters from both parties on the full House committee to protect the size of our requests and I do not recall a single instance when the requests were diminished by congressional action. But Passman greatly enjoyed his role as inquisitor.

I got off on the wrong foot with Passman, but it wasn't my fault. Several weeks before I was scheduled to testify, I received a call from Passman's chief staffer who informed me that the chairman wanted me to send to the committee all UNDP project documents which had been approved during the previous year. I was so incredulous that I asked him to repeat his request which he did. I then said, "Sir, you cannot imagine the volume of paper that will be involved in your request; it will be enormous." For fear of offending him, I didn't dare ask what in the hell the chairman planned to do with several thousand project documents. The staffer ended the conversation by saying, "The chairman wants these documents and he wants them before your committee appearance." I immediately called Charles (Pete) Perry who was then Director of the UNDP office in Washington. When I informed him of Chairman Passman's request, he pretended to drop the phone in disbelief and started laughing uproariously. When he finally calmed down, he said, "There are more than a thousand documents approved last year and I will need a U-Haul trailer to transport them to Washington from New York." As it turned out, that is exactly what Pete was required to do.

When I entered the small ornate conference room in the Capitol Building, there were cardboard boxes of documents stacked half way to the ceiling throughout the room. When the chairman took his seat, he looked me in the eye and said, "Mr. Morey, do you think this is funny?" I replied, "Mr. Chairman, what do you mean?" He shouted, "All these boxes covering most of this room, that's what I mean." I quietly said, "Mr. Chairman, you requested all UNDP project documents approved the previous year to be delivered to the committee and I have complied with your request thanks to the efforts of UNDP in New York and Washington." He bellowed, "You wait just a minute." Passman left his chair, grabbed his chief staffer by the arm, and the two vanished into an ante room for a little *tête-à-tête*. When he returned five minutes later, he said in a stern voice, "Mr. Morey, I sure hope you don't waste any more of my time this afternoon." And with that, he asked me to submit my prepared statement for the record — all in a day's work!

The World Food Conference and Its Aftermath

Each year the UN General Assembly (GA) opens its regular session in September. It is truly a global event because it results in gathering the largest group of heads of government and foreign ministers that will occur in any one year. Henry Kissinger or President Ford headed the U.S. delegation to the GA during my years at the State Department. In 1973, Kissinger had only assumed his position as Secretary in early September — 10 days or so before the opening of the GA. Nonetheless, work was required on his speech weeks before he assumed office. Kissinger made it clear that he wanted to include at least one item in the address that would appeal to the developing countries. He also made it clear that food security should be the major item.

In 1973, there was serious concern about the supply and affordability of food in developing countries in general and Africa in particular. This concern was recognized by leaders of the Non-Aligned Movement (NAM) who met in early September in Algiers and called for a global meeting to focus on food shortages and prices. Given the anti–American track record of the NAM, we quickly agreed that the Secretary certainly would not want the NAM to take the lead in organizing a global meeting on food. Kissinger agreed with this view and was determined that the U.S. should take the lead in calling for such a meeting. Kissinger had a knack for grabbing the headlines and the attention of world leaders. In his GA address on September 24, he did so by proposing that, "A World Food Conference be organized under UN auspices in 1974 to discuss ways to maintain adequate food supplies, and to harness the efforts of all nations to meet the hunger and malnutrition resulting from natural disasters; that nations in a position to do so offer technical assistance in the conservation of food."

The GA endorsed the Kissinger proposal by adopting a resolution drafted by the U.S. which specified that the principle task of the conference was to develop "ways and means whereby the international community as a whole could take specific action to resolve the world food problem." The resolution also asked the UN Secretary General to organize a food conference in consultation with the heads of the Food and Agriculture Organization (FAO) and the UN Conference on Trade and Development (UNCTAD). It was envisaged that the conference would last approximately two weeks and would be held in Rome. Director General Boerma of the FAO was incensed that the conference was not being organized by the FAO. But the general feeling in the GA was that the proposed conference would be one of the most important conferences ever assembled and was too big a job for a single specialized agency. The U.S. and other countries did not want the FAO to run away with the show. In addition, we had no idea what would emerge from the conference and whatever it may be, we did not want it to be under the thumb of the FAO. We learned early on that it was very important to have an independently organized conference. The FAO did provide $500,000 in support of the conference and offered the services of one of its most senior officers, Sartaj Aziz, who became one of the deputy secretaries general of the conference.

After consulting the U.S. and other major countries, the UN Secretary General selected a former Egyptian Minister of Agriculture, Sayed Marei, as conference secretary general. He, in turn, appointed two deputies, one from the Soviet Union and John Hannah of the U.S. Hannah was an excellent choice and played an important role in the conference. He was an agriculturist by background and the former President of Michigan State University. Hannah had served four years as Administrator of the U.S. Agency for International Development (USAID). It didn't hurt that President Gerald Ford regarded him as a personal friend.

Kissinger was willing to give a role to the Department of Agriculture in planning for the conference, but he wanted the State Department to maintain the lead role. He appointed Ambassador Edwin Martin to take charge of conference preparations and gave him the title, Senior Advisor to the Secretary. Martin was a seasoned diplomat with a solid background in economics. He was congenial company, but our meetings were strictly business. (He is the first lunch partner I ever had who presented me with a typed agenda when we sat down to eat!). I had several luncheon meetings with Martin and he would use these occasions to brief me on preparations within the U.S. government and the three international preparatory conferences held in New York, Geneva and Rome.[4]

Located within the IO Bureau is the Office of International Conferences which provides administrative backstopping for all U.S. delegations attending international conferences. It was headed by Murray Jackson, a no nonsense officer with excellent political skills. Murray reported though me to Assistant Secretary William Buffum. Murray and I spent a lot of time together during my years at State and I learned that the most difficult part of multilateral diplomacy is assembling a delegation for an international conference. First, there are disagreements over which departments and agencies should be represented. Second, there are always problems keeping the delegation to a manageable size. Third, there are occasional disputes over the pecking order — who heads the delegation, who is second in command, and so on. For example, I was personally involved in two pecking order disputes when I appointed myself as head of delegation to FAO and World Food Programme (WFP) conferences. I did so because budgetary and political issues were going to be discussed and these were issues of prime concern to the Department of State. I healed the wounds with a senior officer in USAID concerning the WFP conference, but my relationship with my counterpart in the Department of Agriculture was never the same after I assumed command of the delegation to the FAO conference.

Assembling the delegation for the World Food Conference was most challenging. In addition to executive branch officials, a large number of members of Congress requested to be included. It's worth noting that the conference was held in mid–November after the 1974 elections and the Congress was in recess. We knew that at least one member of the White House staff would be on the list and there were numerous requests for delegation membership by agricultural organizations, agro businesses, and non-governmental organizations. Of course, we were in close consultation with Ed Martin in compiling our suggested list for the delegation, but we knew that ultimately the list would require the approval of Secretary Kissinger. The political wheeling and dealing was so intense that cabinet secretaries were phoning their demands to the White House. Martin tried hard to exclude all non-governmental representatives by arguing that it would be unseemly to have an enormous number of delegates in Rome gorging themselves at evening receptions while attending a conference held to address the food needs of the malnourished in developing countries. His efforts were successful with the exception of a last minute request from the White House to add Joseph E. Lonning, chairman of the board of the Kellogg Corporation, from President Ford's home state of Michigan. Lonning, of course, was a friend of the President and proved to be an excellent addition to the delegation. Finally, Kissinger announced a list of 47 members of the U.S. delegation — one of the largest ever. It included 11 Senators, 9 Congressmen, and 26 from the Executive Branch including Special Assistant to the President, Ann Armstrong. Everyone would question a delegation list compiled by Murray Jackson and me, but no one questioned the decision of Henry Kissinger.

The opening day of the conference required careful planning, and, fortunately Murray

Jackson was on the delegation to do the choreography. Kissinger and his entourage were on their way to yet another session of mid–East peace talks and landed only a few hours before the opening ceremony. Since the Secretary had suggested the conference, there was no trouble scheduling him as the first speaker after the welcoming remarks of the Italian Prime Minister. Agriculture Secretary Earl Butz was on hand to lead the delegation after Kissinger's departure. There was more media coverage of the conference than any other international conference up to that time. It was in full force the afternoon Kissinger delivered his address. The maestro electrified the audience when he declared in his statement, "Within ten years no child will go to bed hungry." Unfortunately that has never been achieved, but it was a noble goal and caught the attention of the world. Coming from the U.S. Secretary of State at that moment, and perhaps still today, the United States was the hope of the world. A country only gains this status through generosity, and there has been no country in history that has done more to feed the hungry of the world and improve agriculture in developing countries than the United States. I was especially proud to be an American that afternoon sitting among representatives from 135 countries.

The morning of the second day, Ed Martin approached me and said that conference Secretary General Sayed Marei proposed that someone from the U.S. should chair the second committee of the conference. Martin told me,

> Roy, this is the most important committee because it will be the most politically charged. It is the committee that will handle the creation of follow-up institutions which undoubtedly will be recommended by the conference. As you know, our current delegation position paper flatly states that no new institutions are needed and hence, this will put the U.S. in a difficult spot. These are matters that squarely fall within the purview of the IO Bureau, and besides, you are just below me in delegation rank. It is certainly not a chore we should hand over to Agriculture, Commerce, Treasury or any other department.

I accepted this charge nervously because of my limited experience at State and my relative youth at 37. In short order, however, 135 country representatives approved. The job was mine for the next two weeks.

As a former professor of political science, I found doing politics much more challenging than teaching it. As chairman of the most volatile and important committee at the conference, I had to give all appearances of being impartial. But I could not forget that I was a senior American policymaker and I was under strict instructions to carry out the policies of the U.S. government. The conference also elected two vice-chairmen for Committee II, but it was my decision as to when they would assume the chair and how long they would preside. I felt it was important to take the chair most of the time, but it meant that I was stuck in one place every day while the political wheeling and dealing was taking place elsewhere. With my approval, a twenty-two country Contact Group was established to hammer out resolutions to be considered by the committee and the plenary, the session involving all delegates. Ed Martin spent most of his time representing the U.S. at this Contact Group.

When the delegation was being assembled, I insisted that two of my closest associates be included — Paul Brynes, director of the unit on food and agriculture in the IO Bureau and Robert (Bob) Kitchen, a senior officer in the U.S. Mission in New York. While I sat in the chair and listened to country representatives drone on, Paul and Bob were my eyes and ears and they would regularly report to me. Most of the time Paul occupied the U.S. seat in Committee II and he also would sit in on Contact Group meetings where the main negotiations were taking place. Bob was the U.S. representative on the Credentials Committee which decided on the seating of delegates. The fact that Bob was an African American helped the U.S. cause greatly because he was skilled in establishing a rapport with developing country representatives especially the Africans. He was smart, tough and had years of political experience. We knew in advance that the Credentials Committee could be a political nightmare because the credentials of Israel would be challenged (which they were, but unsuccessfully) and every political liberation organization on the planet was seeking admission to the conference. Our strategy was to keep the Credentials Committee in session throughout the conference by using every delaying tactic in the book and Bob knew them all. Each day Bob would have stories about verbal combat and shouting matches, but he held the flood gates as best he could. Eventually six liberation movements were seated including the Palestinian Liberation Organization. If it weren't for Bob, who knows how many more of these groups would have gained admission.

Fortunately I had been to Rome on several previous occasions and I knew that I would not be going out in the evening to toss a coin in the Trevi Fountain or dine at a favorite restaurant. We worked sixteen-hour days because most evenings Ed Martin would organize a meeting of the delegation which sometimes would have more than sixty people involved because the congressional contingent insisted on bringing along their staff. Congressional members on a delegation require deft handling. This was especially true of a delegation that included twenty congressional members including Hubert Humphrey, former Vice President and presidential candidate in 1968, and Robert Dole, Senate Republican leader and presidential candidate in 1996. Most members of Congress do not deliberately undermine executive branch foreign policy positions, but, in fact, they are free agents from a separate branch and they are accustomed to taking their own positions on any issue foreign or domestic.

This is best illustrated by a delegation problem that occurred concerning the question of increasing U.S. food assistance. Kissinger wanted it increased to strengthen the U.S. position at the conference. But the Treasury Department, Office of Management and Budget and others were opposed to an increase because they feared it would inflate U.S. food prices. They succeeded in convincing President Ford to oppose an increase. Secretary Butz agreed to Martin's suggestion to send an urgent cable to the White House arguing that U.S. food aid would be increased in any event in the near future, and that Butz shared the view that a fifty percent increase in food shipments would have little effect on domestic prices. Unfortunately three senators led by Hubert Humphrey couldn't wait for a reply from Washington and called a press conference immediately after the meeting and announced to the world that they would take the initiative in increasing U.S. food aid. This was major news the following morning in Washington. It put the President in a box. He did not want to appear to be knuckling under to Hubert Humphrey and his friends and, therefore, would not change his position. As a result the U.S. missed an opportunity to pull off a major public relations coup at the conference. I made it a point to keep members of Congress briefed on the ever changing conference political scene. My favorite was Republican Congressman (later Senator) Mark Andrews of North Dakota who became very engaged and was helpful in promoting the U.S. position. Midway through the conference he gave me a card I prized for many years. The card read, "I am a member of the Mushroom Club — everyone keeps me in the dark and feeds me a bunch of shit." I tried not to keep him in the dark, but Mark would be the best judge as to whether or not I met the second criterion for membership.

There are very few activities which are more important in promoting a positive image of America throughout the world than assisting foreign students to come to the U.S. for higher education. Many of the foreign students return to their home countries to rise to positions of high prominence in government, law, medicine and business. I was reminded of this when I attended one of the few receptions held during the World Food Conference. The reception was hosted by the government of Sudan. I was chatting with a senior member of the Sudanese delegation who asked me what I considered to be my home state and I replied, "Arizona." He exclaimed, "Arizona is my state also because I received my Ph.D. in agriculture from the University of Arizona." I informed him that I received my Ph.D. from the same institution. He immediately embraced me and said, "Dr. Morey, we are fellow Wildcats!" He then inquired where I went to high school and I brushed off his question by saying that it was a small school I was sure he had never heard of. He kept pressing me, and I finally said, "Marana High School." His face lit up and he bellowed, "Why didn't you tell me that in the first place. I spent months in the Marana area doing research on long staple cotton for my dissertation." He then grabbed one of his colleagues and mumbled something to him. Soon at least half the delegation rushed to surround me and I was informed that they too had done their graduate work at Arizona. We concluded the mini reunion by joining hands and singing the Arizona fight song — "Bear Down Arizona." For the remainder of the conference I was considered an honorary member of the Sudanese delegation.

The first day I assumed the conference committee chairmanship, I was introduced to the committee secretary whose sole job was to assist me in conducting the meetings. He would compile a running list of those seeking the floor; his knowledge of parliamentary procedure was encyclopedic. I could not have managed without him. Within the UN system, a select number of officers receive conference secretary training. The numerous international conferences held throughout the world each year could not function without them.

In all the conferences I attended during my years at State, I noticed that Japan, Australia, New Zealand and the Western European countries tended to reserve their positions on issues until the U.S. showed its hand. This was never more pronounced than at the World Food Conference. In Committee II, clear instructions to the U.S. delegation was, "The creation of no new institutions is needed." Hence, for the first dozen days of the conference, I had no substantive issues to bring before the committee because no initiatives were emerging on institutional follow-up. Time was filled each day with country representatives presenting prepared statements to the few who were willing to listen. There was the occasional exciting moment when a delegate would veer off into a political screed. On such occasions, I would remind committee members that we were involved in an important conference where political posturing was to be avoided.

The U.S. had an aversion to the creation of new entities because we didn't want to pay 25 percent of a new organization's budget. However, even before the conference started, Kissinger wanted at least one new UN organization to emerge. He saw the conference as his initiative and he wanted it to produce something tangible, useful and lasting. But he was so busy traveling during the time of the conference that he had little time to convince the White House and other major players that such follow-up was in the U.S. interest.

Another reason why institutional follow-up proposals were stymied was because of a disagreement among delegations both large and small on the role that should be played by FAO in any follow-up institutions. From the beginning, the U.S. did not envision a significant role for FAO in any follow-up efforts, but this was not shared by some of our closest Western allies. The first of two major proposals being discussed was establishing a World Food Council (composed of perhaps 15 to 20 members) which would meet periodically to focus the international community's attention on food problems. The other proposal under consideration was the creation of some type of a fund to assist developing countries to increase food production. In order to encourage the Western countries (particularly the U.S.) to support such a fund, the Egyptian Secretary General of the conference, Sayed Marei, promised to convince members of the Organization of Petroleum Exporting Countries (OPEC) to co-finance the new fund. Kissinger knew and respected Marei from his mid–East negotiations. Only four days before the conference was scheduled to end, the log jam on institutional arrangements started to break when a proposal purported to have developing country support was introduced in the Contact Group. The proposal called for the creation of a World Food Council to be located in Rome. After intense negotiations with the Western countries, it was agreed that the new body would be independent from FAO, but would receive administrative support from it.

Marei continued negotiations on a proposal to create a fund while discussions on the World Food Council were under way. On the final day of the conference when negotiations ran into the wee hours of the morning, the conferees finally agreed on a draft resolution creating the International Fund for Agricultural Development (IFAD). It envisioned a tripartite structure composed of developed (Western) countries, OPEC member states and developing countries. To obtain U.S. support for the resolution, the following concessions were made:

- An exact figure was not specified for the amount of funding needed to start the fund.
- An exact figure was not given on the proportion of contributions by developed as opposed to OPEC countries, but the general assumption was that each category would provide 50 percent of the funds required.
- Most important, the UN Secretary General was given the authority to call for the creation of the fund if "it holds promise of generating substantial additional resources for assistance to developing countries," and if, "its operations have a reasonable prospect for continuity."

With these two loopholes in place through which the U.S. could extricate itself from the creation of the new body, Ed Martin succeeded in obtaining Washington's approval to support the resolution.

With the need for the two most important resolutions to be debated and approved before the conference ended, as chairman of Committee II, I was under enormous pressure. I could not cut off discussion without causing a ruckus. Yet, I could not let the delegates drone on endlessly. Hence, I made an announcement at the beginning of the last day that I needed the approval of the committee for these two important resolutions by 8:00 P.M. that evening because a minimum of two hours would be required for final approval and a closing ceremony in the plenary session. I told the committee that the interpreters had informed me that they would conclude their services promptly at 10:00 P.M. Discussion on the World Food Council did not conclude until mid-afternoon at which time I announced that the committee would work through the dinner hour to insure that business would be concluded in time for the delegates to attend the plenary session.

That evening the delegates were tired, hungry and cranky and the atmosphere was tense as we raced to a close. With an end to the debate in sight, there were several hundred delegates quietly listening to the discussion wearing head phones. The quiet was shattered and the deliberations thrown into pandemonium when the head of the Soviet delegation started banging his country's nameplate on the table. Of course my immediate thought was of another Soviet official who caused tumult in a conference setting when Nikita Khrushchev allegedly banged his shoe on the table during a debate in the UN General Assembly in 1960. I handed the gavel to my secretary, leapt from the dais and ran to the location of the Soviet delegation. After a few unintelligible exchanges in Russian and English, I learned that the wires in the main delegate's headset had become crossed and the static was drowning out the interpretation. On behalf of the Secretariat, I expressed my most profound apologies and provided a new headset. Thankfully the problem was mechanical and not substantive. At 8:15 P.M. Committee II concluded its business and I joined the rest of the delegates in a mad dash for the main conference hall for the plenary session. The resolutions were approved and Secretary General Marei concluded the conference just as the interpreters were fleeing their booths.

A month after the conclusion of the World Food Conference, a UN General Assembly resolution called for the creation of a thirty-six member World Food Council to be located in Rome. Egypt became a member of the council and Sayed Marei was elected council president. Dr. John Hannah was appointed the executive director. The World Food Council provided a platform for Marei and Hannah to continue their quiet lobbying for the creation of the International Fund for Agricultural Development (IFAD). It was a perfect team. Marei worked on the OPEC countries and Hannah worked on the Western countries.

A few months after his appointment as executive director, Hannah met with President Ford, Kissinger and Butz in Washington. At the time of his arrival, the U.S. had a noncommittal position on IFAD. Our strategy was to lie low and wait and see how much money the OPEC countries were willing to contribute. Hannah knew the U.S. position and naturally he thought it should be changed. In his meeting with Kissinger (which I attended), Hannah said that the U.S. position would lead to a stalemate because the OPEC and other developed countries were also playing a waiting game for the U.S. to make the first move. Kissinger concluded the meeting by saying, "John, I think the creation of IFAD would support U.S. foreign policy goals, but OMB and Treasury are opposed. The only person who can break the deadlock is your friend, President Ford." The following day, Hannah met with the President and shortly thereafter, it was announced that the U.S. was willing to contribute $200 million to create IFAD provided at least $1 billion was mobilized and that the contribution by the OPEC countries would be roughly equivalent to the contribution by the developed Western countries.

In 1976, I attended two UN conferences in Rome which were held to hammer out an agreement creating IFAD. It was an arduous task made even more difficult because Ibrahim Shihata of Kuwait, who served as spokesman for OPEC, had difficulty in making a clear and unequivocal statement on the size of the OPEC contribution. Of much greater concern however, was determining the country category for Israel. The Israeli ambassador made it clear to me that his country wished to be included in category C (developing countries). When I mentioned this to Sartaj Aziz, the senior FAO officer deeply involved in IFAD negotiations, he said the Arab countries and OPEC would never accept Israel in the developing country category because it would make Israel eligible for assistance which was totally unacceptable. Neither side would budge and for a while it appeared that this issue would be the deal breaker for the whole conference. The night the conference was scheduled to close, Aziz and I came up with a formula which is now enshrined in the international agreement establishing IFAD. In the agreement Israel is listed as a category C developing country. It is the only country with an asterisk and footnote which reads, "This country will not seek nor receive financing from the fund." IFAD would never have come into existence without that footnote. Despite John Hannah's best efforts, the World Food Council got off

As an elected officer of the World Food Conference, the author had an audience with Pope Paul VI in Rome in 1974.

to a rocky start and never generated much enthusiasm among either developed or developing countries. As a result, in 1996 its members voted to have it abolished. It isn't often that an intergovernmental body passes into extinction.

IFAD, on the other hand, developed into a thriving and well managed organization and remains so today. Like all UN organizations, it receives an external and internal audit and it has a good evaluation department to assess the effectiveness of its projects. Over the years it has met its funding targets and since its inception in 1978, it has invested $12 billion in 860 projects which have reached over 300 million impoverished farmers throughout the world. It provides assistance in both grants and loans. One of the main reasons for its success is that IFAD operates on the basis of weighted voting which gives the larger contributors a larger say in running the organization. The larger contributors have the most at stake to make certain that they get a good return on their investment. IFAD has the distinction of being the first UN institution with weighted voting since the creation of the World Bank in 1944.

The last night I was in office, the IO Bureau staff organized a farewell party and award ceremony. Much to my surprise, I was presented the Department of State's Superior Honor Award which is granted by an awards committee for special acts of individuals or groups "which substantially contribute to the advancement of U.S. Government interests." I received the award for the role I played in the World Food Conference and in the creation of IFAD.

A Gathering Storm

For the first two decades after the creation of the United Nations in 1945, there was enormous support for it within the U.S. Children learned about the UN in school and there were UN stories in the *Weekly Reader*—a classroom magazine. After all, the United States played a major role in the creation of the UN and the U.S. government assumed that the whole world should be grateful for it having done so. There was nary a proposal sponsored by the U.S. that did not receive strong support in the General Assembly and the Security Council. Beginning in 1945 there were two factors at work which would drastically alter this record of success. One was the growing hostility of the Soviet Union toward the West and especially the United States. The other was the changing dynamic of the UN General Assembly with the addition of a large number of newly independent African and Asian countries In reality, communism was a totalitarian menace that reeked death and destruction. Nonetheless, it was a creed that would resonate in vast regions of the non–Western world after World War II.

The Cold War was a struggle between the West and the Soviet Union to win the hearts and minds of those living in developing countries. Once the Chinese communists overthrew the Nationalist government, the race was on to convert the rest of the world. Soviet agents could go to newly independent country leaders and tell them that the USSR understood their problems better than any other country. They could point out that Russia had been invaded several times by Western countries including the Germans in 1941. These agents could argue that the Soviet Union abandoned capitalism in favor of communism because it wanted to eliminate the greed, avarice, income disparity, and lack of equality found in Western countries. They could argue that the West had colonized most of the non–Western world and the Western countries treated those in the colonies like second class humans. The Soviets could end their spiel by adding that the West had plundered the Third World's natural resources and established a trading system which was loaded against them. For many of them there was enough truth in the argument to make it plausible.

It became clear to the leaders of the developing countries that they would never have a voice in world affairs unless they became organized. In 1961, the Non-Aligned Movement (NAM) was established primarily through the efforts of Yugoslavia's first President Josip Tito, Indonesia's first President Sukarno, Egypt's President Gamal Abdel Nasser and India's first Prime Minister Jawaharlal Nehru. In theory the NAM was intended to reduce the tensions of the Cold War by steering a course between the West and the Soviet bloc. Hence, grew the notion of Third World countries — neither West nor East. In practice the organization included countries friendly with both blocs, but with a definite tilt toward the Soviet Union because of vocal and active members who were Soviet allies such as Cuba — both Fidel and Raul Castro have served as Secretary General of the organization. Since its inception, the NAM has attacked the United States. For example, despite the fact that there have been several plebiscites on the issue, to this day the NAM continues to insist on self-determination for Puerto Rico. In more recent years, the NAM has denounced the U.S. invasion of Iraq, the war on terrorism and U.S. efforts to restrain the nuclear activities of Iran and North Korea. Of course, these latter two beacons of freedom and international responsibility are members of the organization. Since the collapse of the Soviet Union, the Non-Aligned Movement has lost its *raison d'être,* but continues to issue the occasional diatribe to satisfy its more totalitarian membership including Iran and North Korea. The NAM is not only a misnomer, it is a perfect example of "doublespeak."[5]

In 1964, the representatives of seventy-seven developing countries attending a meeting of the United Nations Conference on Trade and Development (UNCTAD) signed a joint declaration establishing what has become known as the Group of 77. The organization continues to exist with the same name, but there are now 130 developing country members. The expressed aim of the group is to promote the collective economic interests of developing countries. Its crowning achievement was the adoption of a UN General Assembly resolution in 1974 declaring the establishment of a New International Economic Order (NIEO). The NIEO condemned "the remaining vestiges of alien and colonial domination, foreign occupation, racial discrimination, apartheid and neo-colonialism." The key word is neo-colonialism, a Marxist concept which describes the continued economic dominance of developing countries by capitalist countries (the West) after political independence has been achieved. To alleviate this struggle between developing countries and the West, the declaration calls for preferential and non-reciprocal trade arrangements for developing countries, the nationalization of foreign assets, international regulation of transnational corporations, and an increase of assistance from the West without any strings attached.

When I joined the State Department in 1973, I had no idea that I would soon be seen as a purveyor of neo-colonialism as I represented the United States in various international conferences. In the 1970s there were several factors which elevated tensions in the world:

- The Cold War was at its height and there was a fear that the Soviet Union was more successful than the West in winning the support of the developing world
- The United States finally pulled its troops out of Vietnam in 1973, but not before tarnishing the image of America in the eyes of most of the world especially the developing world. The communist countries (notably Cuba) used the War as a metaphor of the rapacious and predatory behavior of a major Western power toward a developing country.
- On October 6, 1973, as Israel was observing the start of Yom Kippur (the day of atonement and one of the holiest days on the Jewish calendar), Egypt and Syria launched a surprise attack against it. The U.S. came to the aid of Israel and a truce was achieved nineteen days later. While the war was still in progress, the Arab members of the Organization of the Petroleum Exporting Countries (OPEC) decided to boycott all oil shipments to the U.S. and curb shipments to Western Europe and Japan. Simultaneously, the price of oil rose by 70 percent. The embargo was in effect until March 1974.

Despite deleterious effects to their own economies, the Group of 77 supported the actions taken by OPEC and its Arab members. On the agendas of the Group of 77 and the Non-Aligned Movement, economic grievances were now wed with grievances against Israel and its supporters — an explosive combination.

Withdrawal Pains — UNESCO

In December 1973, I met with David Newson, the Assistant Secretary of State for African Affairs. He asked me if I was aware of Amadoe-Mahtar M'Bow's interest in replacing Rene Maheu as Director General (DG) of UNESCO the following year. I replied in the affirmative and Newson went on the say that the government of Senegal was giving him strong support and added that since M'Bow was from a francophone country, he would receive the support of the former French colonies and even the support of the anglophone African countries as well. I responded by saying, "If all the black African countries are backing M'Bow, his election is essentially wrapped up because I think the prevailing view of most member states is that the next DG should come from a developing country. Since Maheu has already indicated his intention to retire, I think the French government would like to see a French national replaced by a French speaking African." Most importantly, M'Bow was already serving with UNESCO as Assistant Director General for Education and had been campaigning for months. Newson concluded by saying that if it is inevitable that M'Bow would be elected, the African Bureau thought the U.S. should get on the band wagon sooner rather than later. This act would be noted and appreciated by the African countries.

I reported to my boss, Assistant Secretary Bill Buffum on the Newson meeting and he felt we should have our U.S. representative to UNESCO in Paris check out the attitude of the Western European members. I asked that this be done and the report I received back confirmed what I told Newson — it seems certain that a developing country person would be elected and M'Bow was clearly the frontrunner. Some weeks later I informed Buffum I would like to be a part of the U.S. delegation to the General Conference of the newly created United Nations Environment Programme in Nairobi, Kenya. He agreed and suggested that I travel to East Africa (Nairobi) via West Africa (Senegal) and stop in Dakar to get the U.S. Ambassador's opinion of M'Bow and what he thought of the pending election. I took his advice. It was my first visit to Africa and the most tiring trip I had ever made. It is an eight hour flight and a distance of more than 3800 miles (6100 km) from New York to Dakar, but that was just the beginning. Two days later I realized the immense size of Africa when I flew almost 4000 miles from Dakar to Nairobi via Lagos, Nigeria. Counting a miserable layover in Lagos, I was in transit for fourteen hours — but it was worth it. There was important work to be done and I had so much to learn about Africa.

In Dakar I stayed at the ambassador's residence. The U.S. ambassador at the time was an outstanding African American by the name of Orison Rudolph (Rudy) Aggrey. He was smart and was comfortable living in a French speaking country because he had lived in Paris for years. The first day I spent with members of his staff and that evening he held a dinner in my honor and invited the Senegalese Foreign Minister. Most of the conversation was in French, but the Foreign Minister had a chat with me in English to make certain I fully understood the importance the government of Senegal placed on the election of Mr. M'Bow. The next morning I met with Aggrey on this topic and he made a strong recommendation that we endorse M'Bow as soon as possible.

That afternoon he took me to one of the most visited sites on the west coast of Africa — the small island of Goree in Dakar Harbor. The island has a museum on the site of what was once called the House of Slaves. Starting in the late eighteenth century, Goree was a shipping point of slaves bound for America. The visit brought me to tears and on the ferry ride back to Dakar, Aggrey told me about his most amazing father. His father, James Emman Kwegyir Aggrey, was born in the West African country of Ghana. In 1898 at the age of 23, he was selected by the Methodist Church for missionary training at Livingston College in Salisbury, North Carolina. He graduated with three academic degrees, spoke five languages, received a Doctorate in Theology, joined the faculty of Livingston College and became one of America's most prominent black educators. He returned to Africa for several years and had an impact on numerous West African leaders including Kwame Nkrumah, the first President of Ghana. The ambassador said, "It is a privilege to represent the U.S. in West

Africa because the name Aggrey is golden." Here was an African American going full circle and returning to his roots. Ambassador Aggrey and the memory of his father made me proud to be an American on that first visit to an African country.

That fall M'Bow was elected unanimously to become the first black African to head a United Nations organization. Unfortunately, the U.S. government's satisfaction with his performance was short-lived. I had barely unpacked my suitcase after arriving home from the World Food Conference in November 1974, when Bill Buffum called me to his office to inform me that I must leave at once to fly to Paris. He said the general conference of UNESCO would end within a week and there was a resolution on the agenda which Secretary Kissinger wanted the United States to oppose in a strong and resolute manner.

Still smarting over the Yom Kippur War, the Arab group sought revenge via a UN resolution punishing Israel. The resolution accused Israel of ignoring Security Council and General Assembly resolutions calling for the preservation of the status of Jerusalem. It ordered Israel to desist from archaeological excavations in the city that would alter the cultural and historical character of Jerusalem especially regarding Christian and Islamic religious sites. The resolution also charged Israel with violations of UNESCO resolutions and condemned its conduct and attitude toward the organization.

Buffum said that our first line of defense was to seek a withdrawal of the resolution. If that was unsuccessful, then I was to make a strongly worded statement of opposition when the vote was taken in the plenary session. Both Kissinger and Buffum felt there should be a higher level of involvement and that is why I was being asked to undertake the emergency mission. The head of the U.S. delegation was Dr. Miller Upton, President of Beloit (Wisconsin) College, who was well prepared to coordinate agenda items related to normal UNESCO educational, scientific and cultural activities, but certainly not an explosive political issue involving Israel.

Fortunately, the meeting with Buffum was in the morning which allowed enough time for my secretary to secure air tickets from the travel office. That afternoon I rushed home, packed my bag and Delores drove me to Dulles Airport in time for the evening flight to Paris via London. I spent most of the night pouring over briefing notes and jotting down talking points. The plane landed at Heathrow in the early morning for a two-hour layover. In the terminal I found a row of seats with enough room to stretch out and I fell fast asleep. I awoke with a start upon hearing the final boarding call for my flight. I checked to make certain my wallet had not been stolen, grabbed my briefcase and was the last to board the plane. It was fortunate I made the flight because I did not have a minute to spare once I reached Paris.

The U.S. representative to UNESCO was at Charles De Gaulle Airport to meet me. He informed me that the conference was in session and that we would drive straight to UNESCO headquarters where he had reserved a room for me to meet with all the Arab country representatives. Within an hour I was ushered into a crowded room. The Arab representatives were seated in several rows of chairs. At the front of the room was a small table with two chairs—one for me and one for a French interpreter. Like a scene from an old French Foreign Legion film, I could see myself being blindfolded, led to the front of the room with the Arabs rising with rifles in hand ready to fire! There weren't any rifles, but the group was in a surly mood and there were plenty of epithets and brickbats hurled in my direction. I started by introducing myself, but it was clear they knew who I was and why I was there. I first let the delegates state their positions. I then took the floor to make a response on behalf of the United States government.

The session went on for more than an hour and the first speaker made clear that the resolution in question had the full support of the Group of 77, the Non-Aligned Movement and all Arab states. Some simply attacked Israel without any reference to Jerusalem and the alleged violation of UN resolutions. Others dwelled on previous UN and UNESCO resolutions in a didactic and legalistic manner. When I finally had my say, I made the following three points: 1) Your complaints about Israel should be raised directly with Israel in a forum specifically designed to discuss such issues, 2) Your resolution distorts the very purpose for which UNESCO was founded and the resolution is inappropriate and destructive; and, 3) Your action to politicize UNESCO will undercut American support, not only for UNESCO, but for the rest of the UN system. Moreover, it could well encourage the U.S. Congress to call for the withdrawal of the U.S. from UNESCO which will cost the organization 25 percent of its funding.

After meeting with the Arab representatives, I met with the new director general. I reminded M'Bow of the early support of the U.S. for his candidacy because we believed he would be fair and even-handed in his actions. He ignored this comment and proceeded to lecture me on conference procedures emphasizing the fact that delegations have every right to introduce and sponsor resolutions as they wish. The resolution under discussion, he said, would be decided by a majority of the members, and, as director general, he would abide by whatever decision was made. He concluded by mentioning that the resolution was supported by the African countries, including his own. Of course, the resolution was adopted later that afternoon over the objection of the United States and a handful of other countries.

Within two weeks after my return to Washington from the conference, it was clear that the pro–Israeli lobby was highly successful because numerous members of Congress started calling for the withdrawal of the U.S. from UNESCO. The pressure, of course, was strongest from those senators representing large states with a significant Jewish vote such as New York, New Jersey, California and Florida. I made many trips to Capitol Hill to meet with those senators in an effort to calm their fears. I seemed to be making some headway in this effort until I received a call one day from Undersecretary Joseph Sisco, who requested that I stop my lobbying. He reminded me that there was a bureau in charge of legislative relations and I should leave the job up to them. I will never know why Sisco told me to cease and desist — was it a call he received from the Israeli lobby? Or did Sisco want me to stop meddling in the Israeli-Arab conflict which he saw as his exclusive purview? I will never know.

Clearly, I could be accused of making a questionable decision in the selection of M'Bow, but there were plenty of others to share the blame. I took some comfort in knowing that he would have been elected with or without the support of the United States. Kissinger was unhappy with the politicization of UNESCO, but believed we could be more successful in promoting American values and interests by continuing our membership rather than withdrawing. This was precisely the argument I had been using on Capitol Hill.

The unhappiness of the U.S. government toward M'Bow continued after the Ford Administration left office in 1973. As time went on, it became clear that not only was M'Bow in the pocket of the Non-Aligned Movement, the Group of 77 and the Arab states, he actually advanced their cause and saw UNESCO on the vanguard of promoting political change in aiding the developing countries in their neo-colonial struggle with the West. By the time the Reagan Administration entered office in 1981, UNESCO was involved in one controversy after another.

Finally in 1984, one of UNESCO's constituencies (the press) felt it was under attack within the organization by Soviet bloc and developing country members. Secretary of State George Shultz decided enough was enough and issued the order for the withdrawal of the U.S. which cost UNESCO 25 percent of its budget. The final straw was UNESCO's adoption of the New World Information and Communication Order (NWICO). In a sense this was the application of the New Economic Order (NEO) to the world media. Like the NEO, the NWICO was an anti neo-colonial dictum which denounced the media in the West for distorting news and events in developing countries. According to the NWICO, this occurred because the developed countries (especially the U.S.) dominated all communications, including satellites and mainframe computers. In the view of the U.S., this new order questioned the role of the private sector in the role of communications and favored state-run organizations. Especially troubling was a provision proposing the licensing of journalists in developing countries. Such licenses could be revoked if the journalist wrote stories considered by the government to be unfair to the country. The American press saw this as a call for government control of the global media which would lead to censorship.

In addition to the NWICO, the U.S. and several of its Western European allies charged M'Bow with the misuse of funds. When the U.S. withdrew in 1984, the U.K. and Singapore followed suit. A former Minister of Education of Spain, Frederico Mayor Zaragosa, finally defeated M'Bow for the position of Director General in 1987. Under Mayor, the organization began a slow and steady effort to extricate itself from being used as a political instrument. The U.K. rejoined in 1997. In September 2002, President George W. Bush announced the United States' intention to rejoin UNESCO because the organization had been reformed and America intended to "participate fully in its mission to advance human rights and tolerance and learning." Singapore rejoined in 2007.

Withdrawal Pains—International Labor Organization (ILO)

The ILO is an unusual specialized agency of the UN. First, it was established in 1919 under the same Peace Treaty of Versailles that established the League of Nations. Second, unlike any other UN organization, it has a tri-partite membership composed of workers (organized labor), employers and government. The United States joined in 1934 and American presence in the organization soon rose to prominence. The Soviet Union was expelled from the ILO in 1939 because of its attack against Finland. It rejoined in 1954 and soon started challenging policy positions taken by the U.S. and Western Europe. As was the case in other UN organizations, the Soviet Union became quite successful in wooing the newly independent countries. Membership of communist countries caused a fundamental problem in ILO because the tri-partite structure became a sham. There are not three parties in communist countries because the labor organizations and employers are the creatures of the government and the Communist Party.

The American Federation of Labor and Congress of Industrial Organizations (AFL-CIO) still maintain the U.S. labor membership and the U.S. Chamber of Commerce determines the employer membership. Within the U.S. government there are three departments involved — State, Labor and Commerce. State takes the lead in all matters involving politics, the budget and membership. Of all the ILO's constituent groups, the AFL-CIO has always been the most important.

George Meany was a high school drop-out who got his start as a journeyman plumber. He was intelligent and had exceptional organizational skills. He experienced a rapid rise as a labor leader and by 1939 was the secretary of the country's largest labor federation. He became president of the AFL-CIO after the two organizations merged in 1955. The public image of George Meany was of a rotund, cigar chomping, hard as nails labor leader who knew what he wanted and how to get it. Meany was on a first name basis with every President from Franklin Roosevelt to Jimmy Carter. Above all, he was a genuine American patriot and an implacable foe of communism. For decades he worked diligently to keep communists from gaining a foothold in American labor unions. He worried greatly about communism taking over the international labor movement. In 1944, Meany created the Free Trade Union Committee to foster foreign trade unions, especially those in Europe. At the end of World War II, Meany and his friend, Jay Lovestone, sent Irving Brown to Europe to help non-communist unions. Brown worked closely with the State Department and the CIA and was highly successful in his fight against communists gaining control of labor unions in France, Greece, West Germany and Italy. He held this covert assignment over a 20 year period. For his efforts, Brown was awarded the Presidential Medal of Freedom (the nation's highest civilian honor) by President Ronald Reagan. Meany had received the same award from President Lyndon Johnson in 1963.

Although a staunch Democrat most of his life, Meany supported the war in Vietnam and also endorsed Richard Nixon in 1972. As a potent force in American and international politics, Henry Kissinger made it a point to cultivate Meany. Periodically Meany would lunch with the Secretary at the State Department and they were frequently on the telephone with each other. Fortunately, Bill Buffum and I knew about this relationship and that is why Buffum listened very carefully in a phone call he received from Kissinger in September 1975. Buffum was informed that George Meany was organizing a meeting to discuss U.S. membership in the ILO and Kissinger wanted the IO Bureau to represent him. Since the ILO was a part of my work mandate, Buffum asked me to join him in the meeting. Our instructions were to listen to what Meany had to say, and, if asked about the Department's position on withdrawal from the ILO, we were told to say that the Secretary was still studying the matter.

The meeting was held in the main conference room of the AFL-CIO headquarters. Aside from the State Department, senior representatives from the U.S. Chamber of Commerce and Department of Labor were in attendance. Representing the Commerce Department was a young and impressive James A. Baker, the nation's future Secretary of State. Meany started the meeting with a fifteen minute monologue. He knew the ILO and its history better than anyone sitting at the table. He reminded us that the ILO was founded two years after the Bolshevik Revolution to protect free and democratic trade unions from state controlled communist unions. He said that starting with the appointment of a Soviet as an ILO Assistant Director-General in1970, the Soviet Union steadily gained influence in the organization thus causing an erosion of the fundamental right of freedom of association and the right to organize. In his view, the ILO had been completely politicized by a coalition of the communist bloc and developing countries. He said that this unholy alliance is running rough-shod over basic rules and procedures of the organization, and he cited the resolution condemning Israel for violating trade union freedoms and racial discrimination without the matter ever being reviewed by an expert body as specified in the rules governing the ILO. He concluded his presentation by proposing that the U.S. detractors be put on notice that the U.S. will withdraw from the organization unless significant changes are made.

When we returned to the office, Buffum asked that I prepare a memorandum for the Secretary. I knew that I had to follow a prescribed format. As soon as Henry Kissinger assumed office, he let us all know that once a professor, always a professor. His appetite for work was astounding. Aside from a select number of cables received overnight, he read every memo sent to him and, in most cases, they would be returned with comments. A memo was required to be clear, concise and conclude with three options for the Secretary to consider. The memo was to include a recommendation attached to one of the options. He cautioned us that he could spot a "straw man" option a mile away and also warned us not to postulate an option at one pole and another at the opposite pole with a recommended middle course that would split the difference. I wouldn't have been surprised if he marked every memo just as he used to grade student papers at Harvard. We recommended that as a first step our ambassador in Geneva should warn ILO Director-General Francis Blanchard that if changes were not made, the U.S. would announce its withdrawal and thereby jeopardize 25 percent of the organization's budget. This was the option Kissinger chose, but frankly, very little happened because Blanchard simply replied that he had no effective control over the actions of member states. Meany kept pressing his point, and in early November, 1975, Kissinger requested the IO Bureau prepare a letter giving the required two-year notice that the U.S. intended to withdraw its membership from the ILO unless changes were made. Most of Meany's concerns found their way into the letter.

Two years later the Carter Administration was in office. Despite appeals from Western Europe and the Roman Catholic Pope, plus a recommendation by Secretary of State Cyrus Vance to extend the deadline by one year, President Carter made the decision to withdraw. According to press reports, domestic politics swayed his decision. Aside from the AFL-CIO, business and the pro–Israeli lobby favored withdrawal and Carter needed support from all three groups for other legislative priorities he had on his agenda. In 1979, George Meany decided to retire and his deputy Lane Kirkland became president of the AFL-CIO. Meany died in January 1980 and it is more than coincidental that one month later Secretary of State Cyrus Vance issued a letter announcing the U.S. would rejoin the ILO. The king of labor was dead and the Carter Administration was prepared to reverse course.

Both UNESCO and ILO were being politicized by the Soviet Bloc, Arab states and the Group of 77 during the same period of time. In fact, the rhetoric contained in draft resolutions promoted by these groups was similar in both organizations. One may ask why it took ten years and three administrations to finally withdraw from UNESCO and only two years to withdraw from ILO. The answer lies in the position taken by domestic constituencies served by each organization. The academic, scientific and cultural communities never clamored to withdraw from UNESCO. Eventually the American press was aroused and a willing Reagan Administration was prepared to withdraw. No doubt, this was a decision Reagan and his colleagues were more than happy to make when they first took control of the executive branch three years earlier. But it didn't happen until an incensed constituency called for withdrawal.

Daniel Patrick Moynihan — Rebel with a Cause

When I entered the IO conference room one morning in March 1975 to attend the senior staff meeting, I noticed a stack of papers at the end of the table. When Assistant Secretary Buffum took the chair, he announced that we would each receive a copy of an article written by Daniel Patrick Moynihan entitled, "The United States in Opposition," published in the magazine *Commentary*. Buffum learned of the article at the Secretary's staff meeting and said that Kissinger liked the piece and thought we should take it into account in plotting strategy in the United Nations. We were all aware that Kissinger and Moynihan were Harvard friends and had served together in the Nixon White House. We also assumed that Kissinger played a role in Moynihan's appointment as U.S. Ambassador to India in 1973. Moynihan had just returned from India when the article was published.

The Moynihan piece was not required reading, but it was strongly recommended. Its main thesis was that at the end of World War II, Britain had a socialist government and the basic tenets of socialism were adopted by the leadership of the newly independent countries which were formerly British colonies. Many of these leaders attended the London School of Economics, the leading faculty of which had a decided socialist bent. The former French colonies also adopted a socialist orientation. While most of these new states were not communist, their economic thinking was much closer to the Soviet Union and China and at odds with the fundamental American belief in free enterprise and the market economy. These newly independent states swelled UN membership from 51 to 138 which constitutes an overwhelming majority of developing countries in the UN General Assembly. This new majority was now well organized in the Group of 77 and the Non-Aligned Movement. The article contended that with the encouragement and support from the communist bloc, these two organizations were used to express the demands and grievances of the developing world against the West and the United States in particular. As the volume and decibel level of vitriolic statements from Third World countries increased between 1971 and 1975, Moynihan argues that the United States should not meekly sit and listen to the abuse, but rather should counter these fallacious attacks. Moreover, the article maintains that the U.S. should start keeping score of the developing countries opposing the U.S. position in various UN fora, and then reduce foreign assistance to those who hurl the most abuse.

Frankly, I thought then, and still believe, that the Moynihan *Commentary* article is excellent. By the time Moynihan had spoken out in 1975, I had represented the United States in numerous international conferences and General Assembly sessions, and I also resented the aggressive tactics and anti–American diatribes of many of the developing countries. But the reaction to the article by my career foreign service colleagues was decidedly mixed. While all of them shared Moynihan's frustration with the negativism displayed by certain developing countries, many of them felt quiet diplomacy would be more effective than confrontation in dealing with them.

Of course, once the Moynihan article was published, rumors immediately began to circulate that he would become the U.S. Ambassador to the UN replacing John Scalie. The formal announcement of his nomination was made by President Gerald Ford in May 1975. Shortly thereafter, Moynihan was given an office in the IO Bureau, and we started conducting a series of briefings to prepare him for his confirmation hearing before the Senate Foreign Relations Committee. At the time the committee was chaired by Republican Charles Percy of Illinois who was a strong Moynihan supporter. In all, I spent a day and a half briefing Moynihan on U.S. relations with all the major social and economic UN organizations, and their administrative and budgetary issues. He was most interested in my experience in presenting and defending UN appropriation requests on Capitol Hill. He was confirmed without a dissenting vote.[6]

After Moynihan settled into his new job in August 1975, he invited me to New York to have a chat and go to lunch. This was the first of several occasions I had to spend time with him, and my admiration increased each time we met. We lunched at Billy's on First Avenue, one of the oldest restaurants in New York and one of his favorite haunts. We started our conversation by focusing on New York. Above all, Moynihan was a proud New Yorker and was delighted to be back in Manhattan. He admitted that living in the UN Ambassador's suite in the Waldorf Towers gave him a different perspective of New York from the shabby apartment in Hell's Kitchen he occupied with his mother and two siblings when he was a young boy. Moynihan reveled in his poor Irish Catholic origin and was proud of his enrollment in City College for a year before joining the navy in 1944. His naval service led him to Tufts University where he eventually received a Ph.D. He was interested in the fact that we were both out of academia and asked me if my focus was on international relations. When I told him that my main interest had been American politics, he said that he had done extensive work in international relations and his Ph.D. dissertation was on the ILO. He added that his new appointment brought him full circle back to international organizations.

Pat Moynihan was a larger than life character. He was tall, slender, gregarious, loquacious, and loved to impress everyone with his comprehensive intellectual interests in everything from classical European literature to the social and economic behavior of American working families. He had an excellent sense of humor. He was often described as the ultimate scholar/statesman. He dabbled in Democratic Party politics most of his life. On a university campus he would have been at home in several different departments in the social and behavioral sciences. He enjoyed having this dual persona and never let his public service duties stifle his academic pursuits. When he ended his 24 years of service in the U.S. Senate in 2000, his friend and syndicated columnist, George Will, said that Moynihan had written more books than most of his Senate colleagues had ever read. I am not certain Henry Kissinger fully realized what was in store when he recommended Moynihan's appointment as UN Ambassador. Of course, he knew Moynihan's point of view because he read and enjoyed his piece in *Commentary*. Yet I doubt he realized that he would be releasing an angry rottweiler on unsuspecting representatives to the United Nations in New York.

During our second luncheon meeting, Moynihan and I discussed the upcoming General Assembly session and what he intended to accomplish. He said that he was not spoiling for a fight. But if others picked a fight by proposing measures that were antithetical to basic American principles of freedom, democracy, justice and human rights, he was prepared to take off his jacket, roll up his sleeves and counter attack with all the force he could muster. Reverting to the main thesis of his *Commentary* article, he said that those representing the U.S. at international conferences had been far too timid in countering the attacks made on the United States and its basic values. The role of a great power, he contended, was not simply to vote against an offensive resolution and then make nice at a diplomatic reception later in the evening. He said that our actions should go beyond rhetoric. The developing countries should know that they cannot attack us in a UN forum one day and receive U.S. foreign assistance on the next. We should put them on notice that we will keep score and act accordingly.

Our conversation then turned to the career foreign service. Moynihan said that he had immense respect for the high level of competence, professionalism and dedication of the career Foreign Service officers with whom he had worked especially in the American Embassy in New Delhi. But he found them overly cautious and unwilling to state their point of view publicly including those occasions when basic American values were being questioned. Since we were both non-career outsiders, he asked for my views on his more pugnacious style and the resistance of the career officers to join his camp. I told him that I agreed that there should be consequences for those countries making attacks on the United States.

I added that the two of us were not only representing the U.S. government, but in a broader sense the American people. We both knew that "the man on the street" would think it ridiculous for the United States to give aid and comfort to those who were willing to undercut us at every turn. I cautioned, however, that these were views of an outsider and that I could also appreciate the different orientation of a career foreign service officer. I said that as non-career officers, we would be in the diplomatic service for a few years and then we would be on to something else. Conversely, career officers decide to devote their lives to the diplomatic service and are devoted to diplomacy in the full sense of the word. Diplomacy, after all, is the art and practice of negotiation. For this process to be successful, it must be done out of public view. It is certainly not done by venting one's spleen to an assembled mass. Therefore, I concluded that we should let the career officers do what they do best. I joined the diplomatic service from the world of practical politics and, as a result, I felt that I was more knowledgeable and sensitive to this outside world than most career officers. I added that he too came from this political world and therefore, I was certain that the Congress, press and the voting public would see his more confrontational style as a breath of fresh air. In short, both career and non-career officers are needed for an effective foreign policy.

During the ensuing activities in New York during the fall of 1975, Pat Moynihan did exactly what he said he would do. A special session of the General Assembly was held just before the regular session to discuss the global economy. He knew that a creative effort was required to avert a confrontation with the Group of 77 over the New International Economic Order and all of the neo-colonial claptrap that went along with it. He decided that a good offense was the best defense. With the help of Thomas Enders, the Assistant Secretary for Economic and Business Affairs, he proposed a set of economic policies which would benefit developing countries. After much travail, a resolution was adopted which received support from both developing and developed countries.

Moynihan was jubilant over the outcome of the special session. A clash with the developing countries had been avoided and he hoped that a more positive and non-confrontational spirit would carry over into the regular session scheduled to convene the following week. Regrettably, this hope was soon shattered when a coalition of Islamic and Soviet bloc countries introduced an anti–Israel resolution which declared that Zionism is a form of racism and racial discrimination. Moynihan made a concerted effort to dissuade developing countries from supporting this resolution. He reminded them that Zionism was the nationalist political movement that led to the creation of the state of Israel just as these countries had their own political movements that led to the creation of independent states throughout Africa and Asia after the end of World War II. When the final vote was taken on November 10, 1975, many of the developing countries abstained or voted "no." But there were still many members of the Non-Aligned Movement joining the Soviet bloc and Arab states to ensure adoption of the resolution by a vote of 67 to 55 with 15 abstentions.

Moynihan was outraged by the vote and he was forceful and eloquent in stating his case. In his view, not only was the resolution a vicious and unwarranted attack on the honor and legitimacy of Israel, but more importantly, it made the United Nations a party to a blatant lie. Moreover, it destroyed the credibility of the United Nations in promoting human rights. He told the rest of the delegates that the outside world would see this resolution as a perversion of the UN's role and that it would result in the erosion of trust and support for an institution that the United States played a major role in creating.

Refurbishing the Image of the United Nations

Paraphrasing Franklin Roosevelt, Moynihan said that November 10, 1975, would be a day that would live in infamy. Unfortunately he was correct in his prognosticating that the adoption of the anti–Israel resolution would despoil the image of the United Nations. The resolution itself was bad, but more importantly, it was the culmination of a period of history in the United Nations when the West in general, and the United States in particular, were under attack. Its adoption triggered a negative reaction toward the UN that still exists in certain circles of American politics; however, most of this discountenance was misplaced. One should distinguish between the behavior of certain member states of the United Nations from the UN itself. It was not the Secretary General nor the Secretariat attacking Israel. In fact it was less than a majority of the members of the General Assembly. One could argue that once adopted, the resolution becomes a policy position of the General Assembly which is an important part of the United Nations. While this may be true, the resolution did not bind any member state to such a policy because it was only a resolution and not a law. The General Assembly was never intended to be a global law-making body and resolutions it adopts can be ignored by member states with impunity. The only decision made by the General Assembly that affects member states is the adoption of the budget. The U.S. and other permanent members of the Security Council are assured a seat on the committee that formulates the budget. The Security Council, on the other hand, is empowered to make decisions which can have a major impact on member states such as the decision to make an armed intervention in Korea. But as a permanent member, the United States has the right of veto.

Whether or not the disfavor of members of Congress and the voting U.S. public toward the UN is misplaced does not alter the fact that such attitudes still exist. The acrimonious decade of the 1970s was the nadir in a history of the UN. Fortunately in the past quarter century, there has been a gradual change in the political atmosphere of the UN General Assembly. Compromise is now more prevalent than confrontation and the United States and the West are no longer the object of attack. The General Assembly is a microcosm of the world and there were enormous alterations in the global political landscape starting in the 1980s which have changed the agenda and the atmosphere of the General Assembly.

In 1985 Mikhail Gorbachev became General Secretary of the Communist Party of the Soviet Union and started undertaking domestic and foreign policy reforms that eventually led to the collapse of the Soviet Union in December 1991. During this period it was clear to most of the world that history was on the side of democracy and market economics and not totalitarianism and state-driven economics. Gorbachev improved relations with the west, and the Soviet Union ceased playing the role of provocateur among the developing countries in their "neo-colonial" struggle with the west. In China, Deng Xioping emerged as the country's paramount leader after the death of Mao Zedong in 1976. As a result, China started moving closer to the West and commenced instituting market economic principles. In UN circles, China never played the same role as agitator against the West as was played by the Soviet Union. But many developing countries looked to China as a model for social and economic development and they were eventually impressed with China's new economic reforms that caused them to question the by-gone days of socialist solidarity. The developing world started to look for improved trade with the West and improved capital flows from the developed world. Multinational corporations were welcomed rather than vilified.

In short, globalization started to replace developed-developing country confrontation. This trend is especially evident in the evolution of policy concerns of the UN Conference on Trade and Development (UNCTAD) established in Geneva in 1964 to assist developing countries in their economic struggles with the West. The Group of 77 still exists, but it has lost much of its vitriol. Of much greater importance to developing countries is the Group of Twenty composed of the finance ministers and central bank governors of nineteen countries and the European Union. The Group represents 85 percent of gross national product, 80 percent of world trade and two-thirds of the world's population. In addition to the major countries of Western Europe, North America and Japan, there are ten developing country members including China, India, South Africa, Indonesia and Brazil. During the 1970s in various UN venues, the socialist government of India was one of the most vocal opponents of the United States. Today India and the U.S. are close allies and trading partners. The U.S. now supports a permanent seat on the UN Security Council for India. (My, how times have changed!) If Pat Moynihan were still alive and returned to New York as U.S. Ambassador to the UN, the Sheriff of Tombstone would have to put away his gun and enjoy afternoon tea in the Delegate's Dining Room with his new-found developing country friends.

"Turn Out the Lights, the Party's Over"

The week after Jimmy Carter defeated Gerald Ford for the presidency in November 1976, Delores and I drove to Granville to visit Denison faculty friends. One of my former colleagues from the Political Science Department asked me if I planned to continue on at the State Department. I said, "There is not a chance in hell of staying on because we have a new administration which will clean house of all political appointees." My friend (a staunch Democrat which is a redundancy when speaking of American political scientists) replied, "Roy, Jimmy Carter is not going to be like Nixon and the rest. He is not a hard-ball player and good people like you will be kept on based on merit and not partisanship." I retorted, "Fred, you are a damned good political scientist, but you are a bit naïve about Mr. Carter. Every new administration since the birth of the Republic has cleaned house and the Carter Administration will be no different."

After returning to Washington, I received a call from my friend, Bruce Ladd, a fellow Republican who knew Washington better than most, who said, "Roy, I hope you have been exploring alternative employment opportunities because a new team will soon arrive and you don't want to spend your last night at State taking down your art work from the walls of your office." I told him that I had started looking for alternative employment at least a month before the Ford defeat because the polls indicated that I would soon be relinquishing my State Department security pass. Like most of my friends, Bruce asked if I would like to stay in Washington. I replied, "I don't really want to stay within the Beltway because Washington is a company town. You either work for the company and have something to offer, or you hang around trying to get something from the company. We all know it is more fun being inside the company and I would really like to find something with an international dimension."

Soon Cyrus Vance arrived to replace Henry Kissinger as Secretary of State and a week later, Charles William Maynes arrived to assume the position of Assistant Secretary for the IO Bureau. Not long after he was confirmed by the Senate, Maynes informed me that I would be replaced, but asked me to stay on for a few months to help with the briefing of the new U.S. Ambassador to the UN, Andrew Young, and to testify before the House and Senate Appropriation Committees to justify executive branch funding requests for UN organizations.

One of my colleagues suggested that I convert my status to that of a career foreign service officer. But another trusted member of my staff, Richard Hennes, thought a conversion was a bad idea. He said, "Even if the conversion is successful, you will never be fully accepted into the fraternity of career officers because you were not recruited as a career officer. Therefore, your chances of ever receiving an ambassadorial appointment would be slim." Hennes suggested that I should consider joining the UNDP. I discussed his suggestion with Delores and we were both positive about the idea because it would provide an opportunity to live and work abroad.

Because of the work load the last two months I was at State, I did not take the initiative in probing employment opportunities with UNDP. Rather, the initiative was taken by a career officer, Chester (Chet) Norris. Chet knew I needed a job and he thought I would be a good fit for an international organization. In mid–March 1977, Chet arranged a meeting with UNDP Administrator Bradford Morse to discuss the annual U.S. contribution to UNDP. The morning of the meeting, Chet suggested that he meet Morse at the airport and escort him to my office. I didn't see the necessity for such an elaborate arrangement, but I gladly agreed. I later learned that Chet really wanted to get Morse alone for an hour to cook up a scheme which would allow me to get a foot in the door of UNDP.

After discussing the U.S. contribution to UNDP, Brad floored me when he said, "Roy, Chet tells me you may be interested in doing some work for UNDP. Is that correct?" After representing the U.S. at numerous international conferences, I had learned to be quick on the uptake. I calmly replied to Brad, "Well, I have several possibilities I am exploring [ha ha ha]. What kind of time frame do you have in mind and what type of work would be involved?" Brad was quick to respond, "At the moment, I don't have in mind a regular long-term position, but rather, a consultancy for three or four months." Without a job in sight, I was pleased to take anything—even a short-term assignment. But I was careful to contain my enthusiasm. I told Brad the offer sounded interesting and I would like to accept. We agreed it would start in May and continue through the summer. I was told to contact Eugene Youkel, the personnel director of UNDP in New York, to work out the details. As he was escorting Brad out of my office, Chet winked at me and I realized that not only was he an excellent colleague, but also a friend, and he remained so after I joined UNDP.

3

Thailand: Land of Smiles and Instability

Checking My Pedigree

At the suggestion of the Administrator of UNDP, Bradford (Brad) Morse, I flew to New York in April 1977 to meet with Eugene Youkel, UNDP Director of Personnel. The purpose of the meeting was to work out the details of a four-month consultancy which the Administrator had offered me the previous month. I was pleased to take the consultancy because I was in hopes it would lead to a long term assignment.

After working out the details of my consultancy, I met with the Director of the Bureau for Development Policy and was given an assignment to prepare a study on how UNDP would go about promoting appropriate technology. Fortunately the Bureau Director and her colleagues were pleased with my report as was the Administrator.

Toward the end of my assignment, I finally had my "big meeting" with Brad. Since we were friends, we could communicate in a direct unvarnished fashion. He made the following points:

- Those who have reviewed your report are pleased with the results.
- You may make a good UNDP officer, but you can not expect to start in this organization at the same senior level you were in the State Department — you are still young (40 yrs old) and have plenty of time to grow.
- I know that you would like to be assigned to the field and that is fine, but you will go as a deputy resident representative and not a resident representative. Because of political pressure, I have made several appointments from the outside directly to the resident representative level and these have not always worked out very well, and you are a bit young for that level.
- I will not appoint you directly. If I were to do so, you would always be regarded as my fair haired boy and your colleagues would never accept you as a full member of the fraternity. If you are interested in UNDP, I will ask Gene Youkel to put your name forward to the Appointments and Promotion Board composed of staff members. They can review your background which I think they will find very impressive. But it is their decision to make and my putting in a good word for you would be totally counterproductive.
- You would receive a two year contract with no guarantee of renewal. In two years,

you can decide if UNDP is right for you and we can decide if you are right for UNDP.

- Finally, and most importantly, no one is assigned to the field without the approval of the appropriate regional director. So to get this process started, you will first meet with one of the regional directors who has a field opening.

After receiving the approval of the Appointment and Promotion Board, I met with the Director of the Regional Bureau for Asia and the Pacific who was willing to find a suitable slot for me. I was assigned as deputy resident representative in Thailand.

Arrival in Krung Thep (Bangkok)

Delores, daughter Carolyn and I arrived in Bangkok in late August 1978. Shortly after arriving at the hotel, I received a phone call from Adriano Garcia, the Resident Representative. He asked if I would drop by his office for a chat. I was pleased he called and was at the United Nations building in less than an hour.

Adriano was within a year of retirement and he seemed at peace with himself. By the time I met him, he was perhaps the most respected senior officer in the field and was completing a remarkable career. Like many Filipinos educated during the 1930s, Adriana was fluent in Tagalog (language of the Philippines), Spanish and English. In his early professional life he was a journalist and worked with a fellow journalist by the name of Carlos Romulo. Romulo became aide-de-camp to General Douglas Mac Arthur during World War II. Later Romulo served as Secretary of Foreign Affairs for the country. Adriano named his son Romulo after his dear friend.

Because of his fluency in Spanish, Adriano served most of his career in Latin America and was one of the first resident representatives in UNDP's history. He later joined the Regional Bureau for Asia and the Pacific and served as resident representative in Indonesia before taking his post in Thailand. Adriano and I bonded as soon as we met and I became his deputy and close friend. Down deep, Adriana was a scholar, and after his retirement, he had several books published on development issues. He much appreciated my academic background and we would spend hours in the evening discussing international politics and development theory.

The UN Presence in Thailand

On October 24, 1945 the United Nations was established at the conclusion of the San Francisco International Conference. Thailand joined the UN the following year and the Thai government has placed great value on the country's membership. The government and his Majesty the King also place great value on the large presence of the UN in the country. The clearest indication of this support occurred on October 24, 2009 when HRH Princess Maha Chakri Sirindhorn and Prime Minister Abhisit Vejjaijiva addressed UN staff and their guests to celebrate the sixtieth anniversary of the founding of the UN.

The UN had a large presence when I arrived in 1978 and it is much larger today. The UN complex of buildings is the third largest piece of real estate owned by the UN in the world (after New York and Geneva). The complex is like a mini city. Aside from offices and a major conference center, there is a dining area and cafeteria, a branch of a major Thai bank, a post office where both UN and Thai stamps are available, a medical center with a full-time physician and registered nurse in attendance, gift shop and an American Express travel agency.

There are thirty-two UN agency offices in the UN system in Thailand and the largest is the UN Economic and Social Commission for Asia and the Pacific (ESCAP) with a staff of over 600. ESCAP is the largest of five UN regional commissions spread in various regions in the world. It was established in Shanghai in 1947 and has sixty-two members. Its membership outside Asia includes the United Statres, United Kingdom, France and the Netherlands. ESCAP is a combination think tank and forum for discussing and negotiating inter-country programs and agreements. For example, ESCAP assisted in standardizing and modernizing Asian railroads and highways under the Asian Land Transport Infrastructure Development Program. Areas of inter-country cooperation include environment, trade and investment, transport, statistics and social development.

When I joined the UNDP office in 1978, it had a staff of approximately forty. Then, as now, most staff members are Thai nationals. During my time, the international staff was quite small — resident representative, two deputy resident representatives and two assistant resident representatives. There were also UN agency representatives who reported to the resident representative. These included the UN Industrial Organization (UNIDO), World Food Programme (WFP) and the UN Fund for Drug Abuse Control (now called the UN Office on Drugs and Crime). The other deputy resident representative was a prickly character, but it was easy for me to avoid conflict because my job was to look after the country program and his was to serve as the main liaison officer with ESCAP. I had two talented assistant resident representatives reporting to me and he was on his own.

Orientation

It is impossible to be effective in any country without some knowledge of the country's history and culture. In the case of Thailand, one must start with the monarch. For 800 years Thailand has always been a kingdom and will always be a kingdom. The monarch symbolizes the unity of the Thai people. He must preserve and represent all that is good in Thai history, tradition and the two most important components of Thai culture — the language and Theravada Buddhism. Thais consider the King to be sacred and one must always show respect for him.

Starting with the King and the royal family, Thailand is a very hierarchical society. The Thai social structure was actually captured very well by the noted American newscaster, Eric Sevareid, when describing those assembled to hear President Lyndon Johnson's 1965 inaugural address as "the great, the near great and the near." In Thai society the King, Queen and royal family are the "great." The extended royal family of uncles, aunts, cousins and in-laws are the "near great." Moreover, they would have titles attached to their name which every Thai would recognize as having a link to the royal family either current or past. The "near" are those who curry favor with the royal family by contributing to royal charities, foundations and projects and receive some type of honorific recognition in return.

Thais seek to learn their relative status with others in any social situation. Normally in any group (the family, at work, at play) someone will be seen to have higher status than others, and when one is meeting someone for the first time, it is useful to know this as soon as possible. Social rank is determined by age, occupation, wealth and governmental position — civilian or military. If one is a parent, political figure or factory boss, one is considered a senior person, and the rest are considered junior persons. Social obligations run both ways between a boss and a subordinate. Without even trying, I was given considerable status just for representing the United Nations.

Thais are private about their person and their life. They do not care to be touched. When one meets a Thai, one doesn't shake hands, hug them, or heaven forbid, slap them on the back. Rather, you bring your hands to your chest as though praying. This greeting is called the "wai" and it is both a graceful and submissive gesture. There is a suffix for all occasions. For example, the honorific suffix for all names, male or female, is "Khun" followed by the first name. Among Thais who knew me well, I was often called Khun Roy. For centuries Thais had only one name and even in the modern era, the first name is most important. This is a great blessing for foreigners because once one gets into second Thai names, the spelling and pronunciation becomes very difficult.

The Thais share some social graces with other Asians. Tone of voice is important and speaking in a loud and aggressive manner anywhere in Asia is a complete turnoff. Being boastful and full of one's self is another major turnoff. Like most Asians, losing face for a Thai is the ultimate humiliation and reprimanding someone in public is simply not acceptable. As I learned to negotiate with my Thai counterparts in the government, I had to make certain I always allowed them a way out. Forcing a Thai into a corner will kill the negotiation. Also, like other Asians (especially the Japanese), one must know when a Thai is silently signaling a "no" because they are loath to utter the word "no." Doing so is regarded as being confrontational and at all cost one should not engage in confrontation. If you want something to be done by a Thai, and somehow you have missed the body language telling you "no," what ever you wanted done will simply not happen. Nonetheless, your counterpart who didn't fulfill your wish will have a smile on his face and will be genuinely pleased to see you at your next meeting.

When communicating with Thais, it is important to ask the right question to get the right answer. They are very parsimonious with gratuitous information. I told my colleague, Robert England, a story which captures this Thai trait precisely. It is the story of a New York tourist traveling in the state of Maine. The tourist encounters a flinty old man sitting in a rocking chair on the front porch of a general store with a dog lying nearby. The tourist cautiously approaches the store steps and asks the old man, "Say, does your dog bite?" The old man says, "Nope." When the tourist reaches the porch, the dog jumps up, rips his pants and bites his leg. As the tourist is writhing in pain and grasping his leg, he yells to the old man, "I asked you if your dog bites, and you said, no, and now look what has happened." The old man calmly replies, "He ain't my dog." It seems folks from Maine have something in common with Thais. As we went about our duties working with Thais inside and outside the office, Robert and I were always happy to swap new "Ain't my dog" stories.

The King and I

His Majesty, Bhumibol Adulyadej, King of Thailand, would be considered a truly remarkable man even if he were not the King. Let me be more specific. He received his education in Switzerland, and is fluent in Thai, English and French. He studied Latin and Greek in secondary school and science at the University of Lausanne. He is an accomplished artist, musician, cartographer and boat designer. In his prime, the King had a remarkable grasp of the development issues facing the country. Since taking the throne in 1950, the King has witnessed fifteen coups, sixteen constitutions, several elections and a revolving door through which twenty-eight prime ministers have passed. Under the law, the King is a constitutional monarch and is not to be directly involved in Thai politics. However, some would argue that has not always been the case.

His Majesty refused to endorse military coups on two occasions—1981 and 1985. We were living in Thailand in 1981 and we were grateful that the King did not sit on the sidelines and allow the coup to develop into a violent and bloody armed conflict. On March 31, I flew to Chiang Mai with two of my colleagues to review a UNDP project. The next morning, on a VOA news broadcast, there was an announcement that a military coup was underway in Bangkok. The rebel forces had gained control of the international airport and were fanning out along several major thoroughfares in the city. I immediately notified my two colleagues. We placed a call to the UNDP office and were informed that we could not return to Bangkok later that day because the rebels were not allowing arrivals or departures at the airport. The three of us were facing the same troubling reality. Our wives and children were in Bangkok and we were stranded in northern Thailand 700 kilometers (435 miles) away. We were wondering how long we would be separated from our families and we were concerned about their personal safety. After considerable effort, I finally got a phone call through to Delores and I was relieved to know that both Delores and Carolyn were safely locked in our apartment with our Thai helper. I was assured there was plenty of food in the pantry and our Thai helper heard on Thai radio that everyone was advised to stay home and off the streets. We cooled our heels the remainder of the day in Chiang Mai. Fortunately the next day the Bangkok airport was open and we took the first available flight to return home.

I went to work the following day and learned that the "April Fools" coup was initiated by a group of young officers known as the Young Turks. Initially this group supported General Prem Tinsulanonda who was serving as Prime Minister. But they became disgruntled over several of his military appointments. The Young Turks also felt they did not have the favor of the King and Queen which proved to be the case. In the initial stages of the coup, the Prime Minister evacuated the entire Royal Family by helicopter to a friendly military base 300 kilometers from Bangkok. The whole country soon learned which side was favored by the Royal Family when the Queen broadcast a statement castigating the Young Turks and asking the country to return to calm under the leadership of Prime Minister Prem.

It took Prem several days to solidify his support within the military. During this period, we did not accomplish much in the office because we were distracted by the coup. We had an excellent vantage point to view the coup unfold because Government House, where the Prime Minister's office is located, is visible from the upper floors of the UN Building. It was like watching a silent menacing ballet. The rebels would roll up the street in tanks and face off against the troops loyal to Prem located within the compound. Both sides moved carefully because everyone knew that the slightest misstep in the choreography could trigger a conflagration. Both sides were disciplined and well trained and with good reason. Thailand is the best training ground in the world to learn the art of staging or countering a coup. Thankfully, the April Fools' Coup turned out to be bloodless due to the intercession of the Her Majesty. The UN Building could have been reduced to rubble had a fight to the death occurred.

There are certain kings in Thai history who are regarded as great kings. Most Thai historians believe that Bhumibol Adulyadej will be remembered as a great king. Aside from his numerous personal accomplishments, he will probably be remembered as the "Development King" because of his efforts to undertake royal projects in social and economic development throughout the country. The focus of most of these projects has been the rural poor. During my time in Thailand, the King was especially concerned with poverty and agricultural development in northern Thailand including the ethnic minorities living in the hills. Royal projects have been funded by private contributions, the government and occasionally an international organization like UNDP.

During my first year in Thailand, UNDP agreed to provide funding for a royal project to undertake an aerial survey of the north. Like many of the King's projects, the project manager was the King's cousin and sailing buddy, Prince Bhisadej Rajini. On one occasion the Prince and I were co-chairing a workshop on the aerial survey project in Chiang Mai and at the end of the morning session, the Prince announced that His Majesty would grace the workshop with his presence in the afternoon. During lunch the Prince and I discussed royal etiquette. I was informed that Thais will receive the King in a crouching position near the floor, but such prostrating is not required of a foreigner. However, I should remember that no one's head should be above the King's and therefore, since I am tall, I should bow when approaching him. A simple wai would be appropriate rather than shaking hands. I was further informed that it was likely that HRH Princess Maha Chakri Sirindhorn would accompany her father to the workshop. The Prince added that of all the children in the Royal Family, Princess Sirindhorn was the most interested in development issues and her father's royal projects. All I needed to remember was to address the King as Your Majesty and the Princess as Your Royal Highness. Above all, I was told, just relax and be yourself and let His Majesty take the lead in initiating the conversation.

That afternoon the King and the Princess arrived at precisely the appointed time. All the Thais assumed a prostrated position and I became nervous as the two of them started walking directly toward me. I bowed, waid and whispered, "Your Majesty, Your Royal Highness." Obviously the King had been well briefed by Prince Bhisadej because he greeted me by saying, "Are you Dr. Morey of UNDP?" After replying in the affirmative, he floored me by saying in perfect English, "Dr. Morey, would you like to join us this evening for dinner at the Palace?" I told him I would be honored to accept his invitation. His Majesty then addressed the workshop participants (mainly in English) for thirty minutes. It was like a well-prepared lecture, but without the use of notes.

The main palace in Thailand is the Grand Palace in Bangkok. But I learned that afternoon that the Royal Family has palaces located in all major regions of the country. Today, the King is in frail health and doesn't stray very far from the Grand Palace. But in the 1970s and 1980s, the King was quite peripatetic and spent at least a week in each of the palaces. His two favorite palaces were Chiang Mai and Hua Hin which is a beach town on the Gulf of Thailand 200 kilometers (124 miles) south of Bangkok.

When I reached the dining room of the palace that evening, I was escorted to the head table (which accommodated approximately twelve persons) with His Majesty seated at one end and Her Majesty at the other. I was amazed to find that I was given a seat next to the King. I allowed the King to lead the conversation. We started by discussing the workshop. He thanked me for giving him the opportunity to address the group. He expressed his gratitude for the contribution that UNDP was making to the project. He especially appreciated the foreign technical consultants supported by UNDP who were expert in analyzing the results of aerial survey data. The King saw two main uses for the survey data: (1) a reading on the degree of deforestation that was taking place; and (2) a picture of the size of the total area under cultivation of the ethnic minorities especially the opium poppy fields. He was well-briefed on a UNDP project that was underway designed to encourage the hill tribes to shift from opium poppies to other crops. It was his view that crop substitution would take many years and finding the correct approach would be a matter of trial and error. He said that the government was under considerable pressure (both domestic and foreign) to start the suppression process of destroying the opium crop. But he added that if suppression were started too soon, it would be counterproductive and could alienate the ethnic minorities and make them enemies of the country. He would not recommend suppression until there were clear economic opportunities for the hill tribe people. History proved the King was correct on all his observations.

In June 1979 (almost a year after my arrival), the UNDP Resident Representative, Adriano Garcia, made a formal announcement that he planned to retire and take up residence in Canada. A week or so before his departure, His Majesty hosted a dinner at the palace in Hua Hin and I was also invited. We drove the 200 kilometers and later that evening when we reached the palace we found that it was to be an intimate dinner. The only other guest was the King's close friend, and at the time, Minister of Defense Prem Tinsulanonda who became prime minister the next year (1980). The initial conversation was small talk between His Majesty and Adriano — thanks for helping in Thailand, would he enjoy his new life in Vancouver, and so on. During the dinner, discussion shifted to the King's favorite topic — development. In order to make sure the Defense Minister was brought into the conversation, the King asked General Prem to give some of his thoughts on the new strategy of the Internal Security Operational Command (ISOC) which operated under Prem's direction. The ISOC was established to suppress the spread of communism in the kingdom.

By way of background, it should be noted that in the early 1960s communist insurgents started receiving support from China and Vietnam in the form of money, weapons and guerrilla training. The insurgents were especially active in the northeast, north and the far south. There was even a clandestine Thai language radio station established in Kunming, Yunan Province, China — the Voice of the People in Thailand. The station transmitted propaganda encouraging the Thais to overthrow their government.

During the 1960s and early 1970s a counter-insurgency program was launched by the government, but it was heavy on the military component, violent, not well-organized nor well-funded. The program was reorganized in 1974 with the creation of the ISOC designed to consolidate the efforts of various military and non military agencies and departments.

The mid–1970s in Southeast Asia was a period of immense political turmoil. The communists had captured control of Vietnam in 1975, communist forces took control of Laos the same year and the dreaded Khmer Rouge controlled Cambodia. Many Thais, especially those in the military, feared that the domino theory would become reality and all of Southeast Asia would fall to the communists including Thailand. During this time, students and labor unions started staging mass demonstrations out of fear that the weak civilian government would be toppled by a military coup, which eventually was the case. The police and military feared that mass demonstrations would destabilize the country and make it easy prey for the communists. Bangkok was primed to explode and the fuse was lit on October 6, 1976, when police and a para-military organization opened fire on thousands of demonstrators who had barricaded themselves within the ground of Thammasat University. More than 75 demonstrators were killed, 167 wounded and at least 1,000 were arrested. Perhaps as many as 5,000 of the demonstrators fled the city and went to northeastern Thailand to join the Communist Party of Thailand (CPT). That evening in 1979, while we were having dinner, there were at least 12,000 members of the CPT active in the country.

General Prem said that previous attempts to suppress communist insurgents were unsuccessful and a new approach was needed to bring these people back into Thai society. His Majesty said that you cannot change the situation through the use of force and violence. Those who are alienated must be welcomed back and treated with respect. He said that they must be given access to health care and education. Moreover, projects must be undertaken to improve their standard of living by enlarging economic opportunities. At the conclusion of the dinner, we all agreed that a new approach was required to bring the insurgents back into the fold.

Once again, His Majesty's advice was sound, and Prem and his colleagues took it to heart. In 1982, the Prem government issued an executive order offering amnesty to the insurgents. During the first ten months of the amnesty, more than 2,000 surrendered, followed by thousands more in the next few years. During this same period, the government launched projects to improve the socio-economic condition of the former guerrillas. Concurrently, the Thai military destroyed the remaining guerrilla bases. Despite a more positive approach by the national government, for many years there has been a sizeable disaffected rural population, especially in the northeast and far south. Until the national election in 2011, these alienated Thais opposed the central government, but few would support the CPT which is now essentially defunct.

In 1979, the Director of the UNDP Regional Bureau for Asia and the Pacific, Andrew Joseph, made a country visit. Because of His Majesty's admiration for the organization, it was not difficult to arrange an audience. We were well received in the Grand Palace and we spent a full hour discussing the development needs of the kingdom. Before the substantive discussion got underway, there was the usual introductory exchange of remarks. The King started by saying that he understood Andrew Joseph was a Sri Lankan. After Andrew replied in the affirmative, His Majesty said, "Mr. Joseph, our two countries have at least two things in common — Theravada Buddhism and the roots of the ancient Pali language. Some say that with my full title, I have the longest name in the world. But my main name is Bhumibol." He then asked Andrew, "What meaning does the word bhumibol have in Sri Lanka?" Andrew answered, "of the earth." The King replied, "It is very similar in Thai — strength of the land. When I was a young boy, I was walking with my mother one day and she said to me, 'Why do you think I gave you the name Bhumibol?' I could not answer her and she said, 'I gave you that name because I want you to have your feet on the ground and not your head in the clouds.' I have tried to follow my mother's advice ever since." Indeed he has.

Rubber Replanting Project

During my tenure in Thailand UNDP jointly funded a major project with the World Bank on replanting rubber trees. The project headquarters were located in Hat Yai near the Malaysian border. In the summer of 1979 I visited the project.

The Thai Rubber Replanting Research, Development and Training Center is still in existence and operates under the authority of the Office of the Rubber Replanting Aid Fund (ORRAF). At the time, UNDP was funding a team of advisors, one each from the U.K., France and Malaysia. My guide that day was a French expert who had extensive experience with every phase of the rubber process. He had worked in the Michelin plantation south of Saigon which before its decline during the Vietnam War was the largest Michelin rubber tree holding in the world. He was also involved in rubber in Cambodia, but fled the country with his family after the rise of the Khmer Rouge. He told us that he would first take us through every phase of rubber cultivation and processing and then follow with a discussion of the role of ORRAF and the UNDP and World Bank project. There was an initial 160,000 hectares (395,200 acres) which would eventually be replanted. He said that in Thailand, or any other rubber producing country, all rubber trees must be replaced because they have a productive life of only sixty years before they become (like humans) "senile." Most of the original rubber tree seedlings in southern Thailand came over the border from Malaysia and were planted during the first two decades of the twentieth century. Hence, it was time to start felling the old trees and planting new ones.

He accompanied us to the nursery where we saw thousands of small saplings (2 1/2 ft tall) which had rubber tree "buds" grafted to their tops. We then went to inspect a field where holes had been dug and the saplings planted. Since this process had been underway for several years, we found trees in various stages of growth. We were told that the young trees must have a growing period of at least seven years before they are sufficiently mature to start producing.

We went to several fields where mature trees had been tapped and the milky raw latex was running down several spiral grooves cut in the base of the tree. The latex is collected in a cup attached to the tree. It is a labor intensive exercise because the farmers collect the latex twice a day. The latex is then congealed by adding water and acid and this substance is then rolled into thin sheets. The farmers hang the sheets on a line next to the road. A middle man comes by on a motorbike, collects the sheets and transports them to a local processing plant. We were then taken to the Teck Bee Hang Plant and greeted by the owner, a Thai-Chinese man, who was very pleased to welcome a representative from UNDP. In the plant the latex sheets were cleansed of impurities and then pressed into large dense blocks ready for export.

We returned to the center for the final stage of the briefing. I was told that during the British control of Malaysia, the rubber industry was established by planting trees on large plantations. Thailand is different because more than 90 percent of the rubber trees are planted on smallholder farms. These farmers knew that someday they would need to replace their trees, but wondered how they would feed their families during the seven-year period required for the new trees to start producing. ORRAF was established in 1960 to provide training and low interest loans to sustain the farmers and their families. Under the project the World Bank substantially augmented the loan fund and UNDP financed all the experts and training. The experts were identified and hired by the UN Food and Agriculture Organization (FAO).

Today Thailand produces three million tons of rubber annually. It is the world's largest producer followed by Indonesia and Malaysia. Some of the raw rubber is exported to Europe, but the largest destinations are China, the United States and Japan. Years ago when Robert McNamara was serving as President of the World Bank, he described the joint World Bank–UNDP rubber replanting project as one of the most successful in the Bank's history.

The Geopolitics of the Golden Triangle

The golden triangle is the tri-lateral border area of Thailand, Burma (now called Myanmar) and Laos. The common border line is the Mekong River. It is a beautiful highland

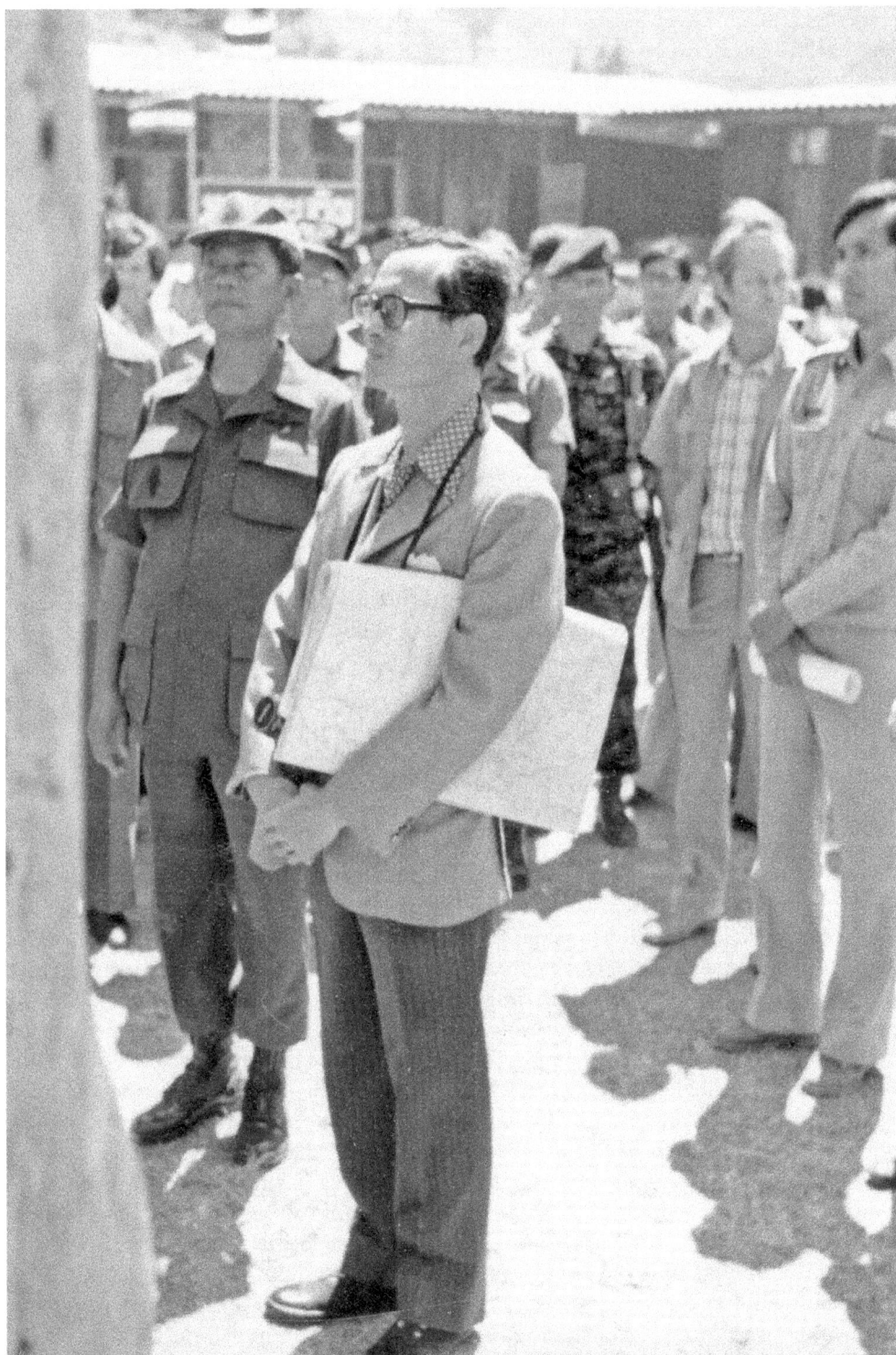

His Majesty Bhumibol Adulyadej, King of Thailand, on a project visit in Northern Thailand, 1979.

rain forest area. However, because of legal and illegal logging and slash-and-burn agricultural practices, the forest cover has continued to shrink. For centuries, this area has been so remote and isolated from the political capitals of the three countries that it was virtually beyond the control of government. There is a bit more government control today. The area is known throughout the world for two reasons: (1) it is heavily populated by ethnic minorities known as the hill tribes; and (2) until a few years ago it was the world's largest source of opium — a dubious distinction now claimed by Afghanistan. In our analysis of the golden triangle, let's start with a couple of definitions.

When I was a graduate student at the University of Arizona during the 1960s, the most renowned American political scientist was Harold Lasswell of Yale University. Among political science graduate students, Lasswell was considered the "guru." He was considered a pioneer because he shifted the focus of political inquiry from governmental institutions to social behavior. I was especially taken by his seminal work, *Politics: Who Gets What, When, How*, first published in 1935, and reprinted by Literary Licensing in 2011. The title captures the main argument of the book — the study of politics is the study of influence and the influential. In the words of Lasswell, "Influence is gained by claims over values like deference, income and safety." Geopolitics is the art and practice of using political power over a given area. The area under review is the golden triangle. But the politics is not that which is related to established governmental institutions and practices. Rather it is the politics of an underworld where Lasswell's value of safety is paramount and political decisions were implemented through the threat or use of force and violence.

Until the turn of the twenty-first century, the political game in the triangle revolved around opium and a score card and a roster of the players was essential to understand relationships and outcomes. On the production side the main players were several hill tribes especially the Hmong. The purchase, transport and refining of raw opium was done by a group of middlemen. Finally those in charge of distribution were the drug lords in cities like New York, Chicago and Detroit.

Let's start with the middlemen. One of the best known American drug smugglers was already behind bars by the time I started making frequent trips to northern Thailand to monitor the UNDP Crop Replacement Project. His name is Leslie "Ike" Atkinson. Atkinson moved to Bangkok in the 1960s and ran a bar. He went into the drug trade with his Chinese Thai business partner in 1968. During the Vietnam War, Atkinson was a U.S. Army sergeant and eventually became known among drug enforcement officials as Sergeant Smack. During his time in Thailand, there were numerous mobile refineries close to the source that produced heroin from raw opium (it takes 10 kilograms of raw opium to produce 1 kilogram of heroin). Atkinson bought the heroin for U.S. $4,000 per kilogram; he would put the heroin in quarter kilogram packets and using a network of military friends, the heroin was stashed on U.S. Air Force planes. Eventually it would be off loaded at Ft. Bragg, North Carolina or other military installations. It was sold to the drug lords (distributors) for U.S. $25,000 a quarter kg for a tidy profit of $96,000 per kilogram. Of course, he would have to share some of this profit with his partner and the military personnel in his drug ring.

Shortly after entering the drug trade, Atkinson began supplying heroin to one of the most notorious drug lords in the annals of New York City crime — Frank Lucas of Harlem. Both Atkinson and Lucas grew up in poor African American families in North Carolina and Lucas is married to a cousin of Atkinson. In his heyday, in the early 1970s, Lucas claims he could make $1million in street sales per day and he amassed a fortune of $52 million. Both Atkinson and Lucas were convicted on drug charges in 1975. Lucas claims the heroin was stashed in the false bottoms of coffins of dead servicemen being transported from Southeast Asia to the United States. Atkinson vehemently denies this claim. Both men are still alive and out of prison. The career of Frank Lucas was dramatized in the 2007 feature film *American Gangster* staring Denzel Washington.

No one denies that Atkinson had an amazing and ingenious operation and the street value of the heroin he smuggled out of Thailand is estimated to be at least U.S. $400 million. But the real opium king of the golden triangle during my tenure in Thailand was a Burmese war lord with a *nom de guerre* of Khun Sa. I never met the illusive Khun Sa, but I certainly saw numerous fields from which he got his opium. He was born in Burma to an ethnic minority Shan mother and a Chinese father. In 1963 he convinced the Burmese government that he had formed a small army to counter the insurgents who were fighting the government to gain Shan autonomy. In return, he received from the government weapons, uniforms and money. He soon expanded his army to 800 men, broke his ties with the Burmese government, and took control over large areas of the Wa and Shan states. The Shan state is on the border with Thailand. In the 1960s and '70s the golden triangle was a no-man's land. The Thai and Burmese authorities had no control over immigration and people crossed the border at will. Khun Sa entered the drug trade to support his private army. His smuggling business was going swimmingly until he ran afoul of another set of drug traders — remnants of the Kuomintang (KMT) Army.

In 1942, Chiang Kai-shek gained approval of the allied forces to transfer a division of the KMT Army from Yunnan Province, China to the Shan State of Burma to help insure that the Japanese forces occupying Burma would not interfere with the supply route between India and the Yunnan capital of Kunming. Many of these Chinese soldiers married Shan women and when Chiang Kai-shek and his Nationalist followers were defeated by the Communists in 1949, a large number of KMT troops decided to remain in Burma rather than retreating to Taiwan. Moreover, additional KMT troops became permanent residents in northern Thailand. These KMT holdovers established an effective drug ring and entered the opium and heroin trade in competition with Khun Sa.

In 1967, Khun Sa's army clashed with the Kuomintang and were defeated. Khun Sa was captured by the Burmese government in 1969 and imprisoned in Rangoon. He was released in a hostage swap in 1973 and set up a new base camp in Thailand. He returned to smuggling opium by 1976. At the insistence of the U.S. Drug Enforcement Agency, he was constantly pursued by Thai police and military and was forced to move back into Burma. It actually didn't matter whether he operated in either Burma or Thailand because the drug trade covered the entire triangle. In 1985, he formed an alliance with a Thai revolutionary force which enabled him to dominate the drug trade like no one else before or since. During the twenty year (1974–1994) reign of "King" Khun Sa, the global volume of street heroin from his golden triangle kingdom rose to 80 percent and was reputed to be the purest "smack" on the planet. To avoid extradition to the U.S. on drug charges, Khun Sa agreed with the Burmese government to retire in Rangoon where he died in 2007 at the age of 73.

An additional dimension on the drug wars in the Golden Triangle can be found in *The Politics of Heroin in Southeast Asia* by Alfred W. McCoy with Cathleen B. Reed and Leonard P. Adams. The main thesis of the book is that the CIA was deeply involved in the drug trade by supporting the Hmong farmers who raised the opium as well as the drug lords who sold the opium. The dubious rationale for this nefarious operation was to keep the farmers and dealers from becoming communist supporters. Moreover, the book claims that senior government officials in South Vietnam and Thailand were also involved in the drug trade, and large quantities of heroin refined from opium produced in Thailand was used by U.S. servicemen during the Vietnam War.

I mentioned that a score card and a roster of the players are essential to understand the geopolitics of the golden triangle, but there is more. So far we have only covered Lasswell's influential elite who mold the behavior of others through money or the barrel of a gun. We now turn to the most important players of all — the producers who are the dispossessed hill tribes. For Lasswell, the hill tribes are those who are influenced and certainly not a part of the influential elite.

For more than a millennium the hill tribe people lived in splendid isolation in the upland areas of Yunnan and Sichuan provinces of southern China. Traditionally they engaged in subsistence agriculture and were left to their own devices. The physical features and cultures of the hill tribes are different from the Chinese. The Chinese lumped the tribes into two groups — Miao and Yao. Of those who eventually immigrated into Thailand, the Hmong are the best known of the Miao group and the Mien are the best known of the Yao group. When the migration took place, the Hmong and Mien were joined by members of other hill tribes which originated closer to the golden triangle. These latter minority groups include the Lisu, Lahu and Akha. Each minority group has its distinct culture including language, religious beliefs and social norms. The hill tribes are also noted for their distinctive and colorful clothing and jewelry.

Especially after the British started importing large quantities of opium into China from India in the nineteenth century, the recreational use of opium became very popular. By the middle of the nineteenth century, 4,500 tons of opium were imported into China annually. By the end of the century, this figure was enormous (50,000 tons) because it included domestic production especially in the highlands of Yunnan and Sichuan. At the time, opium cultivation and use was legal in China. Because of their traditional agricultural skills, the hill tribes were well positioned to cash in on the rush of those seeking a "rush." They soon became China's most efficient opium farmers, but their success and security became increasingly threatened by warlords and bandits at the dawn of the twentieth century. It was a time of growing political instability as the Ching Dynasty started to fade into history. At the time, population density in the golden triangle was relatively light. There was plenty of forest covered land above 1,000 meters (3280 feet) which is an altitude favored by the hill tribes. The Hmong and Mien could avoid the turmoil in southern China, move to Thailand, join some other friendly minority groups and start a new life. As an added bonus, cultivation and the use of opium was legal in Thailand and there was a good market for their crop.

The hill tribes continued life in peaceful seclusion in Thailand planting their food crops in the warm months and making a little cash on opium in the winter. In fact, by the mid–1950s opium prices in Thailand increased after the new communist government in China cracked down on its use and cultivation. But it was also in the mid–1950s that the quiet unfettered lives of the hill tribes started to become complicated. There were several reasons:

- Prime Minister Sarit Tanarat declared that all use, sale and production of opiates was banned as of January 1956.
- There was a growing fear of insurgency in Thailand, especially communist insurgency. Since the hill tribes were living in the country illegally, and because

A hill tribe woman gathering opium tar in Northern Thailand, 1979.

of their distinctive non–Thai cultures, leaders in Bangkok started to worry about their loyalty.

- The hill tribes engaged in a slash and burn type of agriculture. They felled the trees in a given area and then burned the remaining vegetation to enrich the soil with nutrients before planting a new crop of fruits, vegetables, opium or whatever. Despite studies which have found this agricultural approach to be sound and has contributed little to the destruction of the forest compared to logging, slash and burn became the battle cry of the Royal Forest Department which announced that it simply would not be tolerated.
- Various governmental departments and agencies finally started to "discover" the hill tribes and they formulated policies and launched projects which were often in conflict with each other.

In 1959, the National Tribal Welfare Committee was established under the authority of the Ministry of Interior to coordinate the government's efforts. But the committee did not have the political clout to make a difference. Fortunately His Majesty could operate above the din and back-biting of the Thai bureaucracy and he started launching his own projects to help the hill tribes. Being well-versed in the literature of international development, the King knew from the start that one gains the confidence and support of people more easily by listening rather than lecturing, and he followed this philosophy in his projects. With the help of Prince Bhisadej Rajani serving as his project manager, the King undertook a number of small scale projects following development principles belatedly adopted by government departments and bilateral and multilateral aid agencies in subsequent projects.

As indicated in a report prepared for the UN International Drug Control Program, there were three major phases of project work in the golden triangle over a thirty year period.[1] Aside from small royal projects started in the late 1960s, the most significant work was launched in the 1970s.

As a part of President Nixon's "War on Drugs," John Ehrlichman, Director of the Domestic Council staff at the White House (and my boss at the time), sent Egil (Bud) Krogh, one of my colleagues, to Thailand in 1971 to examine how the U.S. could help stem the drug flow. As a result of his visit, the United States decided to fund a $3.4 million, seven-year project implemented by the UN Fund for Drug Abuse Control (UNFDAC). This was very much a donor driven project because Krogh (speaking on behalf of the U.S. government) made it clear that funds were to be used only for a new crop replacement scheme. Funds were not to be used for other purposes such as community development, roads, education, developing community forests, health care or drug use rehabilitation. History would prove that crop replacement was actually a good idea. But no one in Thailand had any experience with such an undertaking and no one realized how the conflicting demands and policies of the various parts of the national bureaucracy would retard progress. Moreover, it is only natural that any donor government wants to see tangible results in the first few years of a project especially to placate an impatient congress or parliament responsible for allocating the taxpayers' money. Had the key appropriators in Congress realized that it would take thirty years (and not seven) to gain success in opium poppy crop replacement, it is doubtful the appropriation would have been made. The international development community would have a more realistic view on the time required to see tangible results, but it is doubtful that most of the experts thought it would take thirty years since they had no experience with such a project. This UN project was the first crop replacement project undertaken anywhere in the world. The only expert at the time who knew that it would take at least thirty years was the King.

UN organizations like UNDP and UNFDAC are not naïve about the long term nature of development. But if there is widespread agreement that a problem exists, then these organizations must start somewhere, sometime to find a solution. In doing so, and like the Hippocratic Oath taken by the new graduates of medical school, the first rule is to "do no harm." The UN project was a pilot project and therefore was bound to encounter numerous obstacles. These included low and fluctuating market prices, lack of credit, crop pests, poor transportation and packaging facilities, and a lack of an established market for the new crops. Despite these problems, progress was made under the project in encouraging hill tribe farmers to try new crops. Under the project a field crop development station was established plus two fruit and nut experimental centers.

I arrived in Thailand August 1978, just as the UNFDAC project was ending and just in time to become involved in the formulation of the successor project funded by UNDP. In 1979 the Thai/UN Highland Agricultural Marketing and Production Project (HAMP) was launched with initial UNDP funding of $3.7 million over a five-year period. In 1984, a non-governmental organization, Norwegian Church Aid, assumed the funding for the project which continued through 1992. In addition, UNDP collaborated with the governments of Sweden and Canada on other hill tribe projects that continued through 1994. The initial UNDP project operated in three major opium producing areas. The major substitute crops introduced during this five-year period were coffee, kidney beans, cabbage and cut flowers. Major project innovations included the establishment of a credit system and the issuance of land certificates by the government to hill tribe families in certain limited areas.

At the end of this first project in 1984 the good news was that the farmers had started growing alternative crops. The bad news was that they also continued to grow opium as a hedge and also because suppression (destruction of the opium fields) had not yet started.

On frequent trips to northern Thailand to monitor the project, I studied the seasonal phases of opium cultivation. In March, a haze covered parts of the golden triangle which was caused by the burning of the opium fields to return nutrients to the soil. When I was in the area in late August and September, I would see the farmers planting the new crop by depositing the seeds taken from the pods of the previous crop. In late December, many families moved into huts along the fields ready to harvest the crop. During the growing season (September–December), the opium poppy stalks would grow to a height of 3 to 5 feet (1 to 1.5 meters). Each had a bulb or pod on the top of the stalk about the size of a golf ball. The stalks had green leaves and around the pod were flowers that came in a mixture of white, pink, red and purple petals. If these poppies did not result in such diabolical consequences, they would be admired for their beauty. Two weeks after the flowers petals fall from the pods, the labor intensive harvest begins by cutting small vertical incisions in each pod. In the late afternoon a white substance begins to ooze from the incisions. The next morning the opium liquid has changed color to brown and now has a sticky tar like texture. Entire families, from small children to grandparents, descend upon the fields with crescent shaped knives to scrap the opium tar from each pod and deposit it in a cup attached to a waistband. In subsequent days they will return to the same pod as many as four times to scrap additional tar. The raw opium is dried in the sun and packed in banana leaves or plastic bags. Each portion is the weight of a standard "choi" (1.6 kilograms) and is ready for sale to the traders.

The factors necessary for success in the various highland projects over a thirty year period were:

- Participation of the people in the planning and execution of activities.
- Some form of citizenship for hill tribe people to bring them into the fold.
- Land certification and the elimination of the view of the government that these were untrustworthy aliens illegally occupying land.
- A more enlightened view of the Royal Forest Department by developing community forest areas.
- Increased attention to health and educational needs of the people.
- Improved roads, processing facilities and market development.
- Crop suppression once it was clear to government authorities that the hill tribe people had a viable alternative to opium.

Today Afghanistan, and not Thailand, is the world's major opium producer followed by Burma and Laos. Thailand still struggles with drug abuse and substantial quantities of heroin are smuggled into the country from its neighbors.

Some observers have tried to diminish the impact of the crop replacement efforts in Thailand by arguing that opium production simply shifted next door to Burma. If this were true, one would expect to see a steady increase in Burmese production as the production in Thailand decreased. But this was not the case. According to the UN Office on Drugs and Crime (UNODC) opium production in Burma peaked in 1996 at 1,760 tons and has been on the decline since. In 2008 production fell to 340 tons, an 80 percent decline. Twelve years ago Burma produced roughly one-third of the world's opium and now its production accounts for less than 5 percent. The explosion in opium production centers in

Afghanistan which produced 5,500 tons in 2008 accounting for more than 90 percent of the world's production. It is more than coincidental that we see a decline in opium production in Burma paralleling the decline in the career of the Burmese opium king, Khun Sa. He surrendered to Burmese authorities in 1996, the same year opium production peaked in Burma and there was a dramatic decline during the next decade. There certainly was not a shift in opium production from Thailand to Laos because there has been a 94 percent decrease in production in that country over the last decade.

For the past twenty years, the UN Office on Drugs and Crime has declared Thailand to be an opium free country. However, there has been an increase in opium production in the Golden Triangle in the past five years especially in Myanmar (Burma) and to a lesser extent in Laos. This production surge is due to a rapid increase in heroin users in China. The increased affluence in China plus ineffective drug control has led to an estimated 2.5 million Chinese injecting drug users.

4

Burma, Thailand and Cambodia: Political Turmoil Within the Region

Burma — Frozen in Time

In March 1980, Delores and I joined a group of Thais for a culture tour of Burma (in 1989 a military junta changed the English version of the country's name to Myanmar). As we drove from the airport to the hotel, we could imagine why Rangoon (now called Yangon) was once considered as one of the major tourist destinations in Asia. But thirty-five years after the end of World War II, the whole city seemed to be in need of paint and renovation. After our driver had passed a 1949 Nash (shaped like an inverted bathtub) and a World War II issue Jeep, I felt we were entering a country frozen in time. I soon learned that indeed it was. When the country gained independence from the British in 1948, everyone had high hopes for Burma. It had an educated and forward looking elite, an industrious population and a natural resource base which includes petroleum. Unfortunately, the country's most important leader, Aung San, was assassinated in 1947 (along with most of his proposed cabinet) and the country started sliding toward stagnation and instability. After fifteen years of lackluster civilian rule, a military coup in 1962 launched the country on a path of military rule. The leader of the new military junta was General Ne Win who was the dominant political force in Burma from 1962 to 1988 when he stepped down as Chairman of the Burma Socialist Programme Party. Like Deng Xiaoping in China, Ne Win still pulled the strings after his retirement until shortly before his death in 2002 at the age of 91.

Ne Win's new government instituted what was termed the "Burmese Way to Socialism" and all private enterprise became state-owned. Before long the new dictatorship shared many features with the Soviet Union: one party rule, centrally planned economy, abridgement of human rights, and absence of a private and non-governmental sector and the triumph of ideology over pragmatism. Yet the leadership made clear that the new political and economic system was not based on Marxist theory and, therefore, the country was not a communist state. Ne Win also reiterated on numerous occasions that Burma's foreign policy was based strictly on the principle of non-alignment. Hence, the country would be neither a part of the communist camp nor that of the West.

The policy of non-alignment was established under the civilian governments before the military coup in 1962. U Thant was a leader in the non-aligned movement and served as Burma's ambassador to the United Nations from 1957 to 1961. When UN Secretary General Dag Hammarskjöld (whom President John F. Kennedy once called "the greatest states-

83

man of our century") was killed in a plane crash in Africa in 1961, the Burmese policy of neutrality enabled U Thant to gain the support of both the United States and the Soviet Union in his bid to become the United Nations third Secretary General. U Thant then became one of the most famous Burmese in the modern history of the country.

Because of the misguided policies of the Ne Win government, the country's economy was virtually destroyed by the time we visited in 1980. Consumer goods were non-existent except for a thriving black market. The country's infrastructure (roads, buildings, communications, water and sewage, etc.) was antiquated and in a state of total disrepair. Except for sporadic clashes between government forces and minority group insurgents in northern Burma, the Burmese people had neither the organization nor the means to challenge Ne Win's government. In 1980, the cities and countryside were calm during our whirlwind visit. The people we met seemed to be resigned to the prospect of a military junta ruling their lives in perpetuity. But history shows that they could be lifted out of their lethargy if a charismatic political leader with the right pedigree arrived on the scene.

Burma: After the Rise of Aung San Sui Kyi

When I visited Burma in 1980, the whole country seemed to be a prehistoric fossil trapped in a bloc of amber. It was difficult to imagine that the political landscape of the country would ever change. But that was before the political rise of the daughter of the most revered leader in modern Burmese history. Today when people anywhere in the world discuss Myanmar, the conversation soon turns to the Nobel Laureate, Aung San Suu Kyi (pronounced Awng San Sue Chee). She is the sixty-seven-year-old daughter of Aung San, the father of Burmese independence who was assassinated in 1947. She spent several of her early years in India while her mother was serving as ambassador. She was schooled in England, married a British university professor and lived most of her life in the U.K. She returned to Burma in 1988 to care for her ailing mother and was soon caught in the maelstrom of groups opposing military rule and became Secretary of the National League for Democracy (NLD). She soon became known throughout the world as the major voice for freedom and democracy in Burma. In this position she was immediately viewed as a threat by the ruling military junta — the State Law and Order Restoration Council (SLORC). Therefore, she was put under house arrest in 1989.

In a surprise move, the SLORC allowed a multi-party election to be held in May 1990. The democratic opposition was surprised that the junta would allow an election and the SLORC was even more surprised with the results. There was an astounding 73 percent voter turnout and Aung San Suu Kyi's party, the NLD, received 60 percent of the vote and 80 percent of the parliamentary seats. The National Unity Party was backed by the SLORC and won a mere 10 seats. The junta could not allow the results to stand and, therefore, it refused to certify the results of the election. The NLD and numerous parties promoting democracy demanded the right to rule and, of course, were rebuffed by the SLORC. This started a "cold war" between military leaders and the democratic movement.

The NLD formed a government in exile called the National Coalition Government of the Union of Burma (NCGUB). This "government" has served as a lobbying group in Washington. The "Prime Minister" Dr. Sien Win is a cousin of Aung San Suu Kyi and a former professor. Until 2012, the main policy promoted by the NCGUB was a call for economic sanctions to be imposed on their country. Some members of the NCGUB recognized that sanctions could have an adverse effect on the impoverished people of Myanmar, but, as a matter of principle, they felt sanctions were necessary to weaken the military rulers. The lack of investment by the United States and some Western countries left an open field for the Chinese. In 2008 and 2009, Chinese investment in the mining sector alone exceeded $850 million. In addition to China, Malaysia and the United Arab Emirates have major investments in the oil and gas sector.

When I assumed the post of Director of the UNDP Office in Washington in 1995, I inherited a number of problems concerning the U.S. government contribution to UNDP. After the Republicans gained control of the Congress in 1992, they began reducing the overall U.S. contribution to UNDP year by year. When I reached the office at the end of 1995, the contribution had been reduced from $U.S. 100 million to $U.S. 85 million. A special problem I also inherited was a move on the part of Congress to restrict UNDP funding to the Burma program.

In March 1995, the "Prime Minister" of the NCGUB stated in a letter to the chairman of the House International Relations Committee, that his rump group was categorically opposed to any UNDP program for Burma in 1995. He went on to argue that even if UNDP funding was considered humanitarian aid, it would be controlled by the military junta. In addition he claimed it would give the SLORC a propaganda advantage. Most astounding was Sein Win's claim that $27.6 million would be going to Burma for the 1995 program when, in fact, the U.S. portion of funding for the 1995 program was only $1.12 million as certified by the U.S. Department of State. Mr. Win wanted $27.6 million cut from a total appropriation of $85 million for a reduction in the U.S. contribution of almost one-third. Fortunately the chairman of the House International Relations Committee realized the NCGUB was in error, but shared the view of the NCGUB that the U.S. portion of the funding for Burma should be deducted from the U.S. contribution.

As mentioned before, the congressional Republicans favored UNICEF over UNDP and UNICEF was exempt from the Myanmar funding restriction because it was considered a humanitarian program. The UNDP program was a grass roots level approach supporting primary health care, HIV/AIDS prevention, protecting the natural environment, food security and basic education. In fact, the UNDP program was just as humanitarian as the UNICEF program and, in addition, it was more carefully monitored and the U.S. State Department vouched for the fact that UNDP funding was not funneled to the SLORC. Each year between 1995 and 1999 that I directed the Washington office, the NCGUB kept pushing the Congress to tighten the noose around the neck of UNDP. Here sat this small group of self-declared representatives of the Burmese people, comfortably ensconced in Washington for the previous fifteen years, 8,400 miles (1,352 km) from Myanmar were dictating the terms of U.S. funding for UNDP.

The Director of the Regional Bureau for Asia and the Pacific at UNDP headquarters in New York just happened to be Burmese, Dr. Nay Htun. Out of exasperation, I gave Nay a call in the spring of 1988, relayed my frustrations, and suggested that I go to Myanmar to discuss the program with the UNDP resident representative so that I could gain first hand knowledge of the situation on the ground. He informed me that he was planning a trip to Burma in the near future and suggested we travel together. I gladly accepted his offer and asked whether or not we would be able to meet with Aung San Suu Kyi. I told him that I was anxious to meet her because she was reputed to be an intelligent and reasonable person and, therefore, I was hopeful that she would instruct the NCGUB to stop harassing UNDP. He was non-committal on my plan to persuade Aung San Suu Kyi and simply said,

Nobel Laureate Daw Aung San Suu Kyi at her home in Rangoon (Yangon) while she was under house arrest, with the author (center) and UNDP colleagues, 1999.

"Roy, we cannot arrange a meeting with her in advance. We must get permission from the SLORC to meet with her once we have arrived in the country."

I arrived in Myanmar several days before Nay to allow time to visit some projects and meet with the resident representative, a smart and capable Siba Das from India. I soon learned that Siba was an excellent choice for his post because of his nationality and Aung San Suu Kyi's positive impression of India gained during the years she lived there. The day after his arrival in Rangoon, Nay Thun and I had a meeting with General Khin Nyunt who was the senior member of the SLORC in charge of foreign affairs. Khin Nyunt was regarded as the more moderate member of the junta. He was responsible for initiating informal contacts with Aung San Suu Kyi and SLORC through a special representative of the UN Secretary General. Fortunately, Nay had previously met the general and since they shared the same nationality, the meeting was friendly and, more importantly, we were given permission (including Siba Das) to meet with Aung San Suu Kyi. Siba made all the arrangements and the three of us were invited for lunch and an informal discussion the next afternoon.

The following day we drove to her family home in Rangoon on the shores of Inya Lake. We were warmly welcomed and she was friendly, but a bit reserved. She was most comfortable with Siba Das and we allowed him to brief her on whom we had been meeting and the purpose of our visit. She had also invited to lunch four elderly gentlemen who were her democracy movement confidants. After lunch she readily agreed to my request for the two of us to discuss the situation in Washington. I was careful to note that I wished to avoid at all costs any appearance of an adversarial relationship between UNDP and the NCGUB. Rather, I said that there were a few misunderstandings I wished to resolve. Aung San Suu

Kyi asked, "And what would those misunderstandings be, Mr. Morey?" I replied, "For several years the NCGUB has been successful in encouraging the U.S. Congress to prohibit funding for the UNDP program in Burma." She simply replied, "Yes, I am aware of that." Finally I said, "I am in hopes you will ask the NCGUB to stop this practice." She calmly responded, "Mr. Morey, that is the policy that we follow — both the National League for Democracy and the National Coalition Government. We do not favor any foreign investment, any tourism, nor any development assistance — all of which we believe strengthens the hand of the SLORC." "Siba Das has told me," I replied, "that he has discussed the humanitarian nature of our program with you on several occasions. He has also told you that UNDP is prohibited by our Executive Board from channeling any funds through the national government." She answered, "Siba does a very good job and he keeps me well informed on UNDP activities." I retorted, "Don't you think it is important to have grass roots level projects that focus on primary health care, combating HIV/IDS, primary education and food security? That is precisely what UNDP is doing in Burma. Furthermore, isn't the UNDP the most useful life line you have with the outside world?" I maintained my equanimity, but I was visibly dumbfounded by her comments. She concluded by saying, "We know the UNDP projects are meant to alleviate problems in the areas you mentioned and we appreciate the work your country office does in keeping us in contact with the outside world. But, we will not change our policies concerning UNDP until Burma has a democratically elected government." I thanked her for her time and our afternoon discussion had come to an end.

Several months after my trip to Myanmar, the "Foreign Affairs and Reform and Reconstruction Act of 1998" was adopted by Congress. It contained a provision stating that UNDP assistance to Burma was required to be channeled through non-governmental organizations and only after "consultations with the leadership of the National League for Democracy (NLD) and the leadership of the National Coalition Government of the Union of Burma (NCGUB)." One questions the legality of this provision since a government in exile and foreign lobbying group (NCGUB) is given a direct role in determining U.S. foreign policy toward UNDP, the United Nations' largest development agency. It is astounding that this provision was never challenged in court. The legislation allowing the NLD and NCGUB to approve or disapprove the U.S. portion of the annual funding of the UNDP program in Burma has lapsed. Fortunately the practice of cutting the portion of the U.S. contribution earmarked for Myanmar will not be followed in the future because of an agreement former Secretary of State Hillary Clinton reached with Aung San Suu Kyi.

A Glimmer of Hope

A national election was held in November 2010. It was staged and manipulated by the military, but was designed to give the appearance of civilian rule. Those running for offices, who were members of the military dominated party, ran as civilians. Aung San Suu Kyi's party, the National League for Democracy (NLD) boycotted the election. In a surprise move that stunned the world, less than a week after the election, Aung San Suu Kyi was released from house arrest where she had spent fifteen of the previous twenty-one years. Shortly after her release, she was reunited with her youngest son after a separation of ten years.

After his inauguration as President in March 2011, Thein Sein took a number of steps to start moving the country forward — the archaic banking system is being overhauled; there will be less internet censorship; and labor unions have been legalized. More important, the new government released 300 political prisoners. However, there are still 1,500 who remain in their cells. In August 2011, Aung San Suu Kyi traveled 200 miles from Yangon to the new capital of Naypyidaw to meet with President Thein Sein.

The President has charted a new course for several reasons:

- Without the support of Aung San Sui Kyi, the U.S. economic embargo will not be lifted and the World Bank and the International Monetary Fund will not establish programs in the country.
- Myanmar wants and needs the respect and cooperation of the other nine members of the Association of Southeast Asian Nations (ASEAN). For years Myanmar's domestic and foreign policies have been out of step with the other members including the communist countries of Vietnam and Laos.
- The economy of Myanmar cannot grow without foreign direct investment which is now an area completely dominated by China. The Burmese leaders want more balance including an increased role for the U.S. as a new economic partner.

The most significant political event in Myanmar in 2011 was the visit of U.S. Secretary of State Hillary Clinton in December. This was the first visit by a U.S. Secretary of State in more than half a century. The Secretary had a cordial and productive meeting with the President and was warmly welcomed by Aung San Suu Kyi on two occasions. After gaining the approval of Aung San Suu Kyi, Secretary Clinton announced that the World Bank and the IMF will launch new programs in Burma and the U.S. will no longer deduct the Burma portion of its contribution to UNDP.

In April 2012, Aung San Suu Kyi's political party, the National League for Democracy (NLD), won 43 of 44 seats the party contested in a parliamentary bi-election. As a result she now holds a seat in the parliament and leads the opposition. In November 2012, President Barack Obama became the first American president to visit Myanmar. During his visit he announced that the U.S. would resume aid programs in the country. In the final analysis, the consent of Aung San Suu Kyi was required to restore full funding to the UNDP program in Myanmar, lift the sanctions on U.S. private investment, and resume the assistance programs of the World Bank, IMF and the U.S. Agency for International Development (USAID). In May 2013, President Thein Sein met with President Obama at the White House. It was the first time in forty-seven years a leader of Myanmar traveled to Washington to meet a president, and diplomatic relations between the two countries have now been fully restored.

Travel to Myanmar today is much easier than it was thirty years ago. Recognizing the value of increasing the country's foreign currency reserve through tourism, and gaining the support of Aung San Suu Kyi, in 2011 the country's tourism authority established a goal of attracting one-half million tourists per year. A visa can now be obtained on line and the length of stay has been extended from seven to twenty-eight days.

The United Nations and Cambodian Refugees

Few events in the past fifty years galvanized the world's attention like the mass movement of hundreds of thousands of Cambodians who started pouring across the border into Thailand in 1979. The terms Cambodians and Khmer will be used interchangeably. Today the country is called Cambodia, but the official language of Cambodia is Khmer. Most

Cambodians refer to themselves as Khmer and have done so since the ninth century when the powerful Khmer Empire was established with its iconic capital Angkor. Invariably politics is the cause of involuntary mass movements of people. Politics were behind the plight of the Cambodian refugees and politics made it difficult for the UN agencies and non-governmental organizations to deal with the refugee crisis.

The fluid political scene in Cambodia leading up to the crisis was filled with intrigue, deceit, violence, tragedy and occupation. For most Khmer refugees I talked with along the border starting in 1979, Norodom Sihanouk was still the most popular political figure, but it did him little good because at the time he was living in exile in the Democratic People's Republic of Korea (DPRK — otherwise known as North Korea). In 1955, Sihanouk abdicated the throne and formed a political movement called the People's Socialist Community. For the next fifteen years he ruled the country single-handedly. However, as the war next door in Vietnam continued to intensify, Sihanouk's hold on power started to slip.

In an attempt to keep his country out of a larger regional war in 1975, Sihanouk made a secret agreement with the Chinese and North Vietnamese which allowed the Chinese to use Cambodian ports to supply the North Vietnamese military and allowed the North Vietnamese to establish bases within Cambodia. It was one of several unholy alliances Sihanouk would come to regret in the years ahead. Sihanouk loved foreign travel and he was on one of his foreign jaunts when he was deposed. In March 1970, Cambodia's Prime Minister Lon Nol convened the National Assembly which voted to depose Sihanouk as Head of State and to grant Lon Nol emergency powers. Lon Nol was assisted in this takeover by Sihanouk's cousin who retained his post as Deputy Prime Minister. The new government called the Khmer Republic was immediately recognized by the United States.

Sihanouk went to China and announced the formation of a new government in exile — The Royal Government of the National Union of Kampuchea. He then made his second unholy alliance when he invited the Khmer Rouge to become a part of this new government. This arrangement could not have been more convenient for the Khmer Rouge because they used "King" Sihanouk as a front man to recruit tens of thousands of peasants to join their deadly cause. These peasants knew nothing of communism, but they were loyal to their King. During this period of the highly ineffectual and corrupt Lon Nol government (1970–1975), Sihanouk moved from China and lived in luxury in his sixty room palatial residence in Pyongyang as a guest of the North Korean government. Here he wiled away the hours hosting dinner parties and enjoying films in the indoor theater.

After five years of civil war, the capital Phnom Penh fell to the victorious Khmer Rouge troops in April 1975. As the troops approached the city, Lon Nol escaped by helicopter and eventually took up residence in Hawaii. When the troops first arrived, they were greeted with jubilation because the people believed the change of government would bring peace to their war torn country. Besides, their beloved King Sihanouk was the new Head of State. But joy soon turned to disbelief when the Khmer Rouge ordered everyone, young and old, to immediately evacuate the city and move to the countryside. The order to evacuate was made under the pretext that the Americans would soon be bombing the city. The peasants did not know any better. The educated elite knew there would be no American bombing and that was one of the reasons the Khmer Rouge already had plans to exterminate every one of them. The destination of the professional class was not the countryside — rather it was the Tuol Sleng prison known as S-21 in downtown Phnom Penh where prisoners were tortured with hot metal prods, electric shocks, knives and blunt objects. Before the Khmer Rouge were finally driven from the city four years later, more than 16,000 people were condemned to death in Tuol Sleng prison. After being sentenced, they were transported to a location just outside the city where they were brutally killed and thrown into a mass grave.

For the Khmer Rouge, the uneducated peasants were the "old people" who would become the backbone of the country living in a new communist agrarian state. While they were the favored class, they were still subject to strict rules and would be put to death for the slightest infraction. The new Democratic Kampuchea was a totalitarian state carried to the fourth decimal point in the sense that there was no part of a person's private life that was beyond the reach of the government.

City dwellers ("new people") by definition were regarded as traitors, closet capitalists and enemies. The Khmer Rouge hated cities and referred to Phnom Penh as the "whore of the Mekong." Paranoia ran so high in the inner circle of the Khmer Rouge that many of those sentenced to death in Tuol Sleng were Khmer Rouge supporters including Deputy Prime Minister Vorn Vet. Such fratricide among the Khmer Rouge is reminiscent of another period of communism. In 1937 in the Soviet Union, the Stalinists were killing off the Trotskyites for the sake of achieving a purer form of communist ideology. For a six year period (1975–1981) during the Khmer Rouge reign of terror, an astounding 1.4 million fellow citizens were executed out of a total population of 7.1 million thus accounting for nearly 20 percent of the entire population. The world had not seen such genocide since the days of the Third Reich.

As a fellow communist regime, the Khmer Rouge initially had the support of the Vietnamese. But one can never forget history in Southeast Asia, and the Khmer Rouge leaders remembered that 300 years ago the Khmer inhabited the Mekong Delta until they were driven out by the Vietnamese. Pol Pot and his gang envisaged the new idyllic agrarian state encompassing the Mekong Delta as well as all of Cambodia. Territory is more important than a shared communist ideology and the relationship soon soured and there were numerous skirmishes along the Vietnam-Cambodia border in which hundreds of Vietnamese civilians were brutally murdered. The border violations and the slaughter of innocent peasants prompted the Vietnamese army to make an incursion into Cambodia in December 1977. The Vietnamese Army withdrew a month later, returning with many captured soldiers and Khmer Rouge defectors. One of those defectors was Hun Sen who later returned under the protection of the Vietnamese army and has reappeared in Cambodian politics in various guises to this very day.

On Christmas Day 1979, Vietnamese forces invaded Cambodia and less than two weeks later they occupied Phnom Penh and forced the Khmer Rouge into the countryside toward the Thai border. Just as the Vietnamese were invading Cambodia, Sihanouk was sent by the Khmer Rouge to New York to address the United Nations General Assembly and protest the Vietnamese invasion. He was happy to take the assignment because when he finished his address, he boarded a direct flight to Beijing where he spent a brief period of time before returning to his Pyongyang palace. Even though the Khmer have had an antipathy toward the Vietnamese for centuries, for a brief period the Vietnamese were actually welcomed because the Cambodians felt nothing could be worse than the Khmer Rouge. However, soon the Cambodians began to resent the Vietnamese occupation and military resistance was organized to fight them.

The Vietnamese established a new national government known as the People's Republic of Kampuchea, and to no one's surprise, they selected as the puppet prime minister — none other than Hun Sen. Hundreds of thousands of families started the long trek back to Phnom Penh. Many found nothing was left of their homes nor any of their surviving relatives.

Eventually the Cambodians opposed to the Vietnamese occupation started to organize into groups which included the Khmer Peoples' National Liberation Front, a non-communist neutralist group led by Son Sen and the FUNCINPEC (French acronym for the National United Front for An Independent, Neutral, Peaceful and Cooperative Cambodia). This latter group was organized by the phoenix who once again was rising from the ashes — Norodom Sihanouk. He switched sides once again by publicly breaking with the communists and declared that his beloved Cambodia must be rid of the Vietnamese at any cost.

As a result of the Vietnamese invasion, the mass movement of Cambodians started once again and this time they went to the western portion of the country and eventually to the border with Thailand. This caused an enormous headache for the Thais because they were not equipped to handle hundreds of thousands of refugees. The Royal Thai Government is not a signatory to either the 1951 Convention on the Status of Refugees or the 1967 Protocol on Refugees. Hence, all refugees entering the country were classified as illegal immigrants. In April 1979, some thirty thousand Khmer refugees crossed the border into Thailand to avoid the fighting between Vietnamese troops, the Khmer Rouge and other resistance groups. As illegal immigrants, the Khmer were pushed back across the border by the Thai military. The surge of refugees occurred once again in June, but this time when they were forced back, many were killed by landmines and gunfire from the Thai military. The international community was outraged by this bloodshed and the inhumane treatment by the Thai military. There was also growing concern over the deteriorating food situation of all the people living under the control of the Khmer Rouge along the border. Because of mounting international pressure, the Thai government changed its policy in October 1979, and agreed to grant asylum to Khmer refugees with the proviso that the relief operations would also have to cover the resistance movements fighting against the Vietnamese including the Khmer Rouge.

The Thai government had a concern larger than the refugee problem which was the fear that the Vietnamese Army would push the Khmer Rouge across the border and then keep pushing on to Bangkok. Thailand's strongest ally, then as now, is the United States and the Americans not only shared Thailand's concern about a Vietnamese invasion, but were also willing to join the Thais in supplying the Khmer Rouge to create a buffer zone. Supplies were also given to the non-communist Khmer Peoples' Liberation Front (KPNLF) which was often more successful in resisting the Vietnamese than the Khmer Rouge. This group also called themselves the "Free Khmer."[1]

Today Vietnam and Thailand are members of the Association of Southeast Asian Nations (ASEAN) and they have a solid and friendly relationship. The government of Vietnam today is totally different from the one that invaded and occupied Cambodia. The earlier government was run by the all-powerful, arrogant, ruthless, and expansionist party chief, Le Duan. He and his cohorts had just directed the defeat of South Vietnam four years before the Cambodian invasion, and he was riding high. Le Duan and the Politburo were in the process of implementing an oppressive pro–Soviet regime which was uninterested in improving relations with the non-communist world. Relations with Thailand were especially negative because Le Duan and his Hanoi colleagues still remembered that the punishing air attacks by the U.S. Air Force during the Vietnam War were planes from airbases located within Thailand. Had Le Duan still been living at the end of 1989, he may not have agreed to a withdrawal from Cambodia.

In retrospect, the Vietnamese threat to Thailand might seem a bit far-fetched. But during the late 1970s and most of the 1980s it seemed very real to the Thai government and especially the one million Thais living in the border area. The Vietnamese controlled government in Phnom Penh and the Vietnamese military argued that their only objective was to root out the resistance groups inside Cambodia along the border. But they often diminished their own credibility by launching numerous incursions into Thai territory in which sizeable numbers of Thai soldiers and Thai civilians were killed. For example, in 1982, Vietnamese forces penetrated more than sixteen miles (twenty-six km) into Thai territory using tanks and armored personnel carriers in an area which was miles from any resistance camps. Eventually there were two holding camps established by the UN High Commissioner for Refugees on the Thai side of the border for those refugees being considered for third country reparation. Often these camps were associated with one of the resistance groups and were, therefore, considered fair game for Vietnamese attacks in which both resistance fighters and innocent women and children living in these camps were killed. For ten years (1970–1989), the physical landscape along the border was filled with land mines and the political landscape was filled with landmines as well.

Once the Thai government started allowing sanctuary for Cambodian refugees, the UN organizations — World Food Programme (WFP), UNICEF and the United Nations High Commission for Refugees (UNHCR) and a few non-governmental organizations (NGO's) established what became known as a "land bridge." Before building the refugee camps, food, blankets, plastic tarps and other supplies were deposited along the border (the land bridge) and the Khmer would cross the border, pick up the supplies and retreat back into the Cambodian wilderness. The United States and other major donors contributed a large volume of humanitarian supplies, but because of the political situation the contributions were funneled through the United Nations and a smaller amount through the NGOs.

The years 1979 and 1980 were busy for me in the border area. My involvement began with a phone call one afternoon in late October 1979 from my neighbor Farouk Abdel Nabi, the World Food Programme County Director. He informed me that Khun Xuchat (my Thai government counterpart for UN organizations) was organizing a clandestine mission to the border the following day and he wanted me to participate. I was told that we would travel to the border just south of Aranyaprathet, 156 miles (251 km) from Bangkok. I was further informed that we would travel in several unmarked Thai military vehicles and the group would also include two Thai military intelligence officers and a Cambodian working at the U.S. Embassy who would serve as our interpreter. On the ride to the border the next morning, Khun Xuchat gave us a briefing. He said now that supplies were being provided along the border, the purpose of the mission was to cross into Cambodia a short distance to determine if the supplies were reaching the intended recipients. He said that the plan was to visit a Khmer Rouge hideout in the morning and then go to an area in the afternoon occupied by the non-communist Free Khmer (KPNLF).

After arriving in Aranyaprathet, we took a dirt road south for a few miles and then headed east on a narrow road under a heavy jungle forest canopy. Of course the border was unmarked, but the two Thai officers knew exactly where it was. As we were climbing out of the vehicles, the two officers retrieved two American made M-16 rifles from the trunk and slung them over their shoulders. On seeing the rifles my first thought was, "My heavens, I didn't think weapons would be involved in this mission" and then I remembered, "Oh yeah, we are making an illegal entry into another country to visit an outpost controlled by the murderous Khmer Rouge — perhaps a couple of weapons would come in handy after all!" It was the first, but not the last, country I ever entered without being required to display my UN Laissez Passer or U.S. passport.

Khun Xuchat, left, Thai government counterpart, and Farouk Abdel Nabi, World Food Programme Country Director, with the author on the Thai/Cambodian Border distributing supplies to Cambodian refugees, 1979.

It was at the end of the rainy season and, therefore, we didn't worry about encountering Vietnamese soldiers because the Vietnamese always made their raids into the border area in the dry season beginning in late November–early December. The two armed officers and the Cambodian interpreter led the way as we walked along a muddy path with thick wet foliage on either side. We walked through several small streams which were also muddy from the run-off.

We had covered about two miles when we saw several weather-beaten thatched structures on a small hill. Soon we were greeted by two bare-chested teenagers in dirty khaki shorts and rubber sandals made from automobile tires — the signature footwear of the Khmer Rouge. Each youth had an AK-47 rifle slung over the shoulder and our interpreter approached them with a smile and started conversing with them in Khmer. He later said that he told them we had come as neutral parties and that there were United Nations officials in the group who wanted to check on the food supply because the food crossing the border from Thailand was coming through the United Nations. The boys with the guns replied that our intrusion would have to be explained to the commandant of the camp.

As we entered the camp a slender young woman emerged from one of the thatched huts. She was tall for a Khmer with coal black hair bobbed in the style one would have seen in photographs of Chinese girls carrying Mao's Little Red Book. She was wearing faded army fatigues. Her face was dark and radiant. All in all, she was quite a striking figure. The interpreter then repeated to her the same story told to the boys. She told him that she could identify him as Khmer and Farouk and I as UN officials, but asked why the Thais were in the group. The interpreter informed her that the Thais were helping to insure that food and other supplies were getting across the border. This explanation seemed to satisfy her.

At our request, the camp commandant showed us through the compound and it was like strolling through a morgue. The commandant seemed to be the only female out of approximately fifty. At least thirty of the men were lying in hammocks in a comatose state suffering from cerebral malaria. This is the worst form of malaria and occurs when the protozoan parasite in the bloodstream carries the infection into the brain. Cerebral malaria causes fever, convulsions and coma. It is almost always fatal especially if it is not treated properly in the first twenty-four to forty-eight hours. I asked the commandant how they treated it and she said, "Come with me and I will show you." We went to another dirty thatched structure where four or five men were lying in hammocks. Another was hunched over a small container filled with murky water. I was told that he had just crushed several aspirins and mixed the powder in the water. He then took a hypodermic needle, drew it full of the cloudy substance, injected himself in the arm and released the mixture into his bloodstream. The malaria would kill him in any event, but the injection would probably kill him first.

We then turned to the topic of food and I asked the commandant if her group had enough to eat. She replied to me in a stiff, shrill voice as though turning on a recording device, "Yes, we always have enough to eat because our great leader (Pol Pot) cares for all our needs." The scene was far too somber and macabre to laugh. I then asked her if we could see where the rice was stored and she reluctantly took us to a shed. When I opened the door, there sat six or eight gunny sacks filled with rice and stenciled on each bag was the clasped hands — the logo of the U.S. Agency for International Development (USAID) known throughout the world by those in need. When I asked the commandant about the origin of the rice, her voice went into robo tone again and she replied, "This rice comes from our great leader. As I have told you, the great leader takes care of all our needs." I certainly didn't want to enter into an argument, especially with the two boys standing nearby with their AK-47s, but I had had enough so I said in a well modulated voice (I was actually shaking in my boots), "Well, the great leader may care for all your needs but this particular rice comes from the United States of America and has been transported to the border by the World Food Programme, an agency of the United Nations."

As I walked along the trail back to the vehicles after leaving the Khmer Rouge compound, I had a most interesting conversation with the Cambodian interpreter. I said, "You know, the commandant is quite a beautiful woman in an eerie sort of way. By the way, did you notice a rather strange necklace she was wearing with odd shaped flat dark stones hanging from it?" He replied, "Those were not flat stones. They were solidified pieces of human liver she has taken from the victims she has killed. She wears them as a badge of honor." I exclaimed, "Oh. My God, I have never seen anything as hideous in my life." He retorted:

> That is because you have never seen the Khmer Rouge in action, I have. Fortunately I had heard stories about the Khmer Rouge before they captured Phnom Penh and therefore, I was one of the fortunate few to escape their terror. If it were possible to kill someone more than once, they would have killed me several times over because they would detest everything about me. I am considered an intellectual simply because I have a university degree. They would identify me as an intellectual merely because I wear glasses. Furthermore, I lived in a city and therefore, I was considered to be a traitor. Most importantly, I was an official in the Lon Nol government and friendly to the Americans. The commandant did us no harm today because she was not under orders to do so, but as a true believer she could have gunned us down in an instant without the slightest feeling of remorse. That, Mr. Morey, is just a small picture of the Khmer Rouge.

After reaching the vehicles, we drove back to Aranyaprathet and then took a dirt road north for several miles and turned east on a narrow road toward the border. We walked under a thick forest canopy for only two hundred meters before reaching a clearing filled with several thousand Free Khmer (KPLNF) Apparently the group had reached the clearing only an hour before our arrival. They were literally jumping for joy having found rice, blankets, tarps and other emergency supplies. We were probably less than thirty miles south of the Khmer Rouge camp we had just visited, but the atmosphere was 180 degrees different. There were no weapons on display and those in the group were taking turns to grab whatever they needed. There were lots of smiles and laughter and somehow they seemed to know that we had come in peace to help them. We were warmly welcomed, and our interpreter was inundated with questions from members of the group.

Finally I got my turn to use the interpreter's services and I was anxious to talk with an old woman sitting by herself. She told me that she had been walking toward the border for more than a month from her family farm in central Cambodia. For the first week she walked alone carrying only a cloth bag filled with some clothing and small prized family mementos such as photographs. She started with very little money and lived off the mercy of others for food and shelter. But often she was forced to sleep on the ground. She felt fortunate to join the group of Khmer of which she was now a part. At first she was wary of the group because she had no way of knowing if the members of the group would be friend or foe. They just happened to be associated with the Free Khmer and she was treated with kindness and respect by the others. She said that there is safety in numbers and while she felt more secure in the group, nonetheless, she still feared for her life. When I asked why she was not walking with her family, she suddenly looked grief stricken and her lips started to tremble. In a halting voice, she said:

> We were a poor peasant family raising enough rice and other crops to live. We did not interfere in anyone else's lives. We just wanted to be left alone and live in peace. But one day several Khmer Rouge came to our place and said that my two sons and my husband were enemies of the country. In front of my eyes, the Khmer Rouge shot each of them with a gun and threw them into a hole in the ground. One of my sons had not even died when they threw him in a hole and covered him with dirt. We were farmers and we used hoes for our crops. But what is a hoe when the Khmer Rouge have guns. The gun always wins. So now, the Khmer Rouge have killed my family and I must run for my life from the Vietnamese soldiers. I don't know what to do.

In early 1980, the UNDP office welcomed the new Resident Representative Winston Prattley. He also served as Representative of the World Food Programme. Prattley, a New Zealander, was the right man for the right job at the right time. He was smart, courageous and had excellent political skills. He had truly received a baptism of fire before his appointment to Thailand. He had been the UNDP Resident Representative and UN Resident Coordinator in Iran during the Khomeini revolution. If that weren't enough to test his mettle, he was then assigned to Afghanistan after the communist coup. But the straight-talking Prattley was not welcomed by that new communist regime and, therefore, he was available for the post in Bangkok. Within weeks, Prattley took charge of leading the UN agencies' efforts on the border and won the respect of the Thai military, the U.S. Ambassador and other key players.

During the remainder of 1980, periodically Prattley would ask me to go to the border area, check on the latest developments and report back to him. His new task was daunting. In early 1980, there were 700,000 Khmer living in the border area and most of them were trying to seek asylum. UNHCR was enlarging the main holding camp and there were new border camps under construction. Tens of thousands of refugees had to live in tents awaiting construction of the camps. During this time, the overwhelming health issue was cerebral malaria. There were numerous deaths from malaria each day and on one occasion when I was monitoring one of these temporary tent camps, an old woman collapsed and died right before my eyes.

A comparatively small number of refugees who had some hope of relocation in a third country were placed in holding centers within Thailand. The other camps were located just across the border in Cambodia, and most of these were associated with one of the three resistance groups — FUNCINPEC a non-communist group led by Prince Norodom Sihanouk, the KPNLF, a non-communist group led by Son Sen, and the Khmer Rouge.[2] In 1982, these three resistance groups created yet another unholy alliance by joining together for the common purpose of driving the Vietnamese out of Cambodia. The German philosopher, Friedrich Nietzsche, once said, "The best weapon against an enemy is another enemy." Following this principle, you had within FUNCINPEC, assailants and their victims joined together to form a non-existent government in exile called the Coalition Government of Democratic Kampuchea which was then given the Cambodian seat in the UN General Assembly. UN member states were strongly opposed to giving the seat to the Vietnamese puppet government sitting in Phnom Penh.

In 1981, UNICEF and the International Red Cross started reducing their roles in managing relief supplies on the border and UNHCR worked only with refugees in the holding centers located within Thailand. This meant that new arrangements were needed to care for refugees in the border camps associated with the resistance movement. To cover the needs of approximately 300,000 people living in these camps, in January 1982, the UN General Assembly created the United Nations Border Relief Operation (UMBRO) under the direction of Winston Prattley. UNBRO was designed as a temporary agency with no budget and, therefore, it relied on the support of the U.S., U.K., France, Australia, Canada, Japan and the European Commission. UNBRO worked under five guiding principles:

- The needs of full time residents would be met regardless of political affiliation.
- The camps would be managed by Khmer to the extent circumstances would permit.
- No one could be forced from a camp against one's will.
- Assistance was to go to civilians only.
- The camps were to be safe and secure havens for the residents.

There were several factors which made it very difficult for UNBRO to adhere strictly to the principles stated above:

- Insistence by the Thai government that the three resistance groups must receive assistance. Moreover, the major donor countries funding UNBRO supported this policy of the Thai government.
- When the border camps were established, it was virtually impossible to segregate combatants from non-combatants.
- The Khmer Rouge camps made it difficult for UNBRO staff to monitor the daily operations of their camps.
- The resistance groups continued to fight against the Vietnamese imposed government in Phnom Penh which meant that each dry season, Vietnamese forces returned to the border in an attempt to eliminate these resistance groups.

This conflict resulted in the shelling and attacks on the camps which resulted in the loss of lives among both combatants and non-combatants.

In 1983, Winston Prattley addressed the UNBRO donors at a meeting in New York. In his usual direct manner he told them that UNBRO officials had been "abused and held at gunpoint" and how the distribution of food and medicine had become "less efficient, more precarious and often dangerous." Because of the "polarization and militarization" of the camps, UNBRO was forced to operate in a situation "which stands in contradiction with the instructions of the Secretary General." Here was Winston Prattley, honest to a fault, describing the heroic efforts of UN officials operating under circumstances made virtually impossible by policies of the Royal Thai government, which in turn were supported by the donor countries.

The situation in the border camps continued to worsen and by the end of 1984, Vietnamese forces had destroyed five camps causing 90,000 Cambodians to flee across the border into Thailand. The bombardment intensified in 1985 and by the end of that year there were 240,000 displaced Cambodians on the Thai side of the border. The U.S. and other countries did not want to resettle these refugees because: a) Such a move would cause the border to become a magnet which would attract huge numbers of Khmer from the interior of the country who would be seeking placement in a third country; and b) If all the refugees were placed in third countries, there would be very little leadership talent to flow back into the country once peace was achieved. Until early 1992, UNBRO and fourteen NGOs continued to serve 300,000 Khmer refugees in fourteen camps.[3]

In 1986, the prospects for peace in Cambodia began to improve. This was not due to developments within Thailand; rather, it was because of major changes taking place in Hanoi. The aggressive and misguided Chairman of the Communist Party of Vietnam Le Duan died in July and by the end of the year the Sixth Party Congress adopted a new set of reforms. Among the key elements of the reform was the commitment of "opening up to the outside world combined with a great effort to improve relations with countries in the region and non-communist countries throughout the world."

In April 1989, Vietnam finally announced the withdrawal of its troops from Cambodia and the process was completed five months later. In May 1991, a cease-fire went into effect in Cambodia following an appeal by the UN Secretary General. In October 1991, the Paris Peace Treaty on Cambodia was adopted. The agreement called for the establishment of the United Nations Transitional Authority in Cambodia (UNTAC) to supervise the cease fire and the withdrawal of all foreign forces, take control of the administrative structure of the country including the police and finally, organize and conduct free and fair elections. Shortly after UNTAC was established in February 1992, the repatriation of Cambodians back into their country commenced under the supervision of the UN High Commissioner for Refugees. By the time this process was completed the following year, 360,000 Cambodians were resettled.

In September 1993, the indefatigable chameleon of Cambodian politics, Norodom Sihanouk, returned to Phnom Penh to assume the honorific title of King of Cambodia. Sihanouk was still a revered national figure, but gradually became a marginal player in politics due to old age, declining health and infighting within his political party. In the 1993 UN sponsored elections, his party won a plurality of the votes and his eldest son Prince Norodom Ranariddh became Prime Minister. But his position was overshadowed by the most crass opportunist in modern Cambodian politics — Hun Sen, who exerted enough pressure to gain a second Prime Minister position for himself. No one thought the dual prime minister system would last and it did not. In July 1997, Hun Sen led a bloody *coup d'état* and Prince Ranariddh was ousted and fled to France. Since the elections of 1998, Hun Sen continues to serve as Prime Minister —first as a Khmer Rouge commander, then a hand-picked Prime Minister under Vietnamese occupation and now the undisputed leader of his country — an opportunist indeed. In 2004, Norodom Sihanouk relinquished the ceremonial throne to his son Sihamoni. In October 2012, Sihanouk died in Beijing at the age of eighty-nine.

Today Cambodia is not a communist state, but it is far from a Jeffersonian style democracy. Cambodia was back in the news in July 2010 when a United Nations sponsored court convicted the first of five Khmer Rouge leaders for crimes against humanity. Kaing Guek Eav (68) "Duch," the former director of the Detention and Torture Center S-21 at Tuol Sleng in Phnom Penh, was sentenced to prison for thirty-five years, but the sentence will be reduced to nineteen years for time already served. It has taken thirty years to get this conviction. In September 2010, the UN backed genocide tribunal indicted the other four members of Pol Pot's inner circle. The four: Ieng Sary (80) former Foreign Minister, his wife Ieng Thirith (79) ex–Minister for Social Affairs, Nuon Chea (85) chief ideologist, and Khieu Samphan, former Head of State and the public face of the Pol Pot regime. A trial finally commenced in November 2011, but the Tribunal ruled that former Social Affairs Minister Ieng Thirith was unfit to stand trial due to memory loss and dementia and be released from prison. Some describe this war crimes trial as the most important since Nuremberg. The main reason for the delay in bringing these former Khmer Rouge leaders to justice has been the constant interference of Hun Sen and his government. In March 2013, a judge from Switzerland resigned in disgust from the Khmer Rouge tribunal. Most foreigners still involved believe the whole operation has become a farce.

Thailand Today

Since the end of World War II, the Thai economy has been noted for having strong export industries, a well-developed infrastructure, prudent monetary policy and a pro-market and investment orientation. Like most of the rest of the world, Thailand was affected by the contraction of global trade in late 2008 and the first quarter of 2009. The Thai economy was on a roller coaster in 2009. During that period Thailand's gross domestic product (GDP) fell 6.3 percent but rebounded 6.9 percent by the end of the year.

For the year 2010, the GDP growth rate for Thailand was 7.8 percent making it one of the fastest growing countries in Asia. In 2011, the rate dropped to a more normal 4.5 percent. According to the World Bank the financial sector is healthy, public debt is under control and foreign reserves are at a high level. Moreover, tourism has started to rebound after the violent political eruption on the streets of Bangkok between opponents of the government and the military earlier in the year. There are 14 million visitors to Thailand each year. The tourism industry accounts for 7 percent of the country's GDP. There are one million jobs which depend upon tourism and these are located mainly in the Bangkok area.

The economic resurgence of the Thai economy is music to the ears of the Bangkok elite, but is scarcely noticed by the poor and dispossessed in the northeastern region of the country. Like most countries in the world, including the United States of America, there is a serious gulf between wealth and poverty in Thailand. Less than one percent of the poor live in metropolitan Bangkok. But northeast Thailand, which is composed of 19 provinces and one-third of the country's population (21 million), contains 65 percent of the country's poor. The northeast, which is also known as Isan because of the name of the dialect spoken in the region (a mix of Lao and Thai), is the area that is along the border with Laos (the Mekong River) to the east and border of Cambodia to the south. It is predominantly an agricultural area with poor quality soil.

Because of the widespread poverty and the large number of ethnic Lao and Khmer, the people of the northeast have always been looked upon as the bottom rung of the socio-economic ladder. In most societies, those toward the bottom of the social order always need another class just below to reassure themselves that they are not the dregs of society. Such is the case in Thailand. Take for example, our wonderful housekeeper during our stay in Bangkok who comes from a dirt poor family in northern Thailand. Anytime the conversation turned to northeast Thailand, she would always say, in a dismissive tone of voice, "Those are Lao people."

During the last fifty years there has been enormous growth in the Thai economy and the quality of life has improved throughout the country especially in Bangkok. This improvement has also been true in the northeast. However, this has been accompanied by a growing recognition that people in the region still occupy the lowest rung on the socio-economic ladder and this has led to an increased feeling of discontent. It should be remembered that people do not rebel because they have an empty stomach. Rather, they do so because they feel the political system is loaded against them and lacks equal opportunity especially for their children. This is precisely the attitude of millions of downtrodden Thais from the northeast.

In the January 2001 national election, Thaksin Shinawatra and his Thai Rak Thai Party tapped into this discontent and mobilized the voters of the northeast and north to produce a landslide parliamentary victory. He also had strong appeal to the poor living in Bangkok. Thaksin became the most popular Prime Minister in Thai history and the only one to serve a full term and be reelected. As a billionaire telecommunications tycoon who wears impeccably tailored designer suits, it may seem odd that he became the hero of an aggregation of poor malcontents. Perhaps the poor farmers can identify with him because he was not always wealthy and he has always been seen as an interloper among the Bangkok elite. Moreover, his popularity was due to the populist programs he developed which for the first time sought to address the needs of the disaffected outside Bangkok. These programs included universal health care and microcredit.

Thaksin was born and raised in the north (Chiang Mai) and is the great grandson of a destitute Chinese immigrant. Unlike the Prime Minister who eventually replaced him and who attended Oxford, Thaksin went to a Thai police academy and received graduate degrees in criminal justice from minor universities in the United States. Typical of Thai politics, his government was ousted by a military coup in 2006. A subsequent government loyal to Thaksin was elected, but later dissolved due to a court's ruling based on the arcane language in a military imposed constitution. Meanwhile, Thailand's Supreme Court sentenced Thaksin in absentia to two years in prison on a conflict of interest charge. He now lives abroad as a fugitive from justice and many of his supporters have urged him to return because he was convicted on, what they believe to be, trumped up charges. In fact he offered to return to Thailand for a retrial, but his offer was not accepted by the government.

The seething anger of the rural poor boiled over in the spring of 2010 when thousands went to Bangkok, stormed the parliament building and eventually set up camp behind street barricades in an exclusive shopping area. After weeks of protests and disrupting street traffic, in May the army forcefully ended the protest. The protestors burned thirty buildings in downtown Bangkok including the Stock Exchange. The armed confrontation resulted in the death of six soldiers, eighty protestors and the injury of eighteen hundred others. There was also the torching of public buildings in the three major cities of the northeast. The protest leaders were jailed and the demonstrators were given train tickets to return to their homes in the northeast.

During the height of the confrontation, Prime Minister Abhistit offered to hold parliamentary elections in November 2010, but his offer was withdrawn after the protest leaders countered with a list of unacceptable conditions. The Prime Minister also offered a reconciliation plan, but it was rejected by protest leaders because they claimed it was vaguely worded and written without any opposition input.

The Bangkok elite believe Thaksin has created a monster by stirring the rural poor who someday may have the power to challenge their privileged position. Therefore, they have wrapped themselves in the cloak of the King and have tried to paint Thaksin's supporters as anti-monarchists. To emphasize the point when they are demonstrating, they wear yellow — the royal color to remind everyone that they are fighting to save the honor of the monarch. One is treading on sacred ground once the monarch has been injected into the fray and this makes reconciliation extremely difficult. Thaksin did not accuse the King of supporting the military coup which deposed his government in 2006. But he accused retired General Prem Tinsulalonda of plotting his overthrow. Prem is the King's close friend and directly reports to the King as President of the Privy Council. His Majesty refused to support military coups in 1981 (against his friend Prem) and in 1985. He did not openly oppose the coup against Thaksin in 2006.

A calm settled over Thailand after the conflagration of May 2010, but seasoned observers warned it should not be mistaken for acquiescence by the Thaksin supporters. Some observers of Thai politics were surprised when a member of Prime Minister Abhistit's cabinet, Finance Minister Korn Chatikabanij, admitted that social inequality was at the heart of the unrest and should be addressed. He said:

> There has been far too much focus through various governments — including, partly as a result of the economic crisis we faced last year, this government — on short term relief measures as opposed to measures which would genuinely address the issue of equal access to opportunity in the long term. All governments have been trying to create jobs through fiscal stimulus. Although these activities are important at the margin insuring things don't get out of hand in the short term, they cannot be expected to create job opportunities of the kind that people aspire to in the long term. There is a feeling in Thai society that access to opportunity and resources are not fair and transparent.[4]

Fragile but Hopeful

Perhaps Prime Minister Abhistit and other establishment leaders listened to cooler heads like Minister Korn, and parliamentary elections were announced in May 2011. In the July 3 elections, Thaksin's party (Puea Thai) won a landslide victory. It was not necessary for Thaksin to come out of exile from Dubai to lead the ticket. He had a very capable surrogate to direct the campaign — his sister, Yingluck Shinawatra. Relying on massive victories in the north and northeast, the Puea Thai party won 265 seats in the 500 member Parliament. The incumbent party won only 159 seats. In mid–July, the Thai Electoral Commission confirmed the results and the Thai military stayed in their barracks and quietly accepted the results. The beautiful forty-four-year-old Ms Yingluck is Thailand's new Prime Minister.

Recognizing the potential backlash from the army, there has been no move at this point to grant amnesty to her brother. Under Prime Minister Yingluck's leadership, political stability has been restored and the economy has improved.

Did the United Nations Make a Positive Difference?

The rubber replanting project made an enormous contribution to the Thai economy and saved the livelihoods of more than 50,000 Thai farmers. The World Bank/UNDP/FAO project was a textbook example of a well designed effort involving three United Nations organizations all in the same harness, pulling in the same direction with competence and coordination. Since all international organizations work through governments, it is not always easy to provide assistance which is of direct benefit to the private sector. The Thai farmers were the direct beneficiaries of both the World Bank loans and the technical assistance provided by UNDP and FAO. More importantly, the project helped preserve Thailand's position as the world's largest rubber exporter. No wonder World Bank President Robert McNamara described the Thai rubber replanting project as one of the most successful in the history of the Bank.

Conditions in southern Thailand were excellent for executing the project. A training center was already in place. The Office of Rubber Replanting Aid Fund (ORRAF) is a competent and well managed counterpart government agency. The Thai farmers were educated and eager to improve their technical skills. The project location was a safe and attractive place to live and, therefore, it was not difficult to recruit first rate foreign experts.

But the United Nations Office for Drugs and Crime (UNODC) and UNDP crop replacement projects were not nearly as straight forward as rubber replanting. The project setting in the Golden Triangle in the 1970s and 1980s was filled with obstacles. Any type of development work would be a challenge, especially projects designed to wean the hill tribes off opium production in favor of other cash producing crops. In retrospect, perhaps UNFDAC and UNDP should have taken a longer term and more holistic approach rather than leaping directly into crop replacement. Both projects had design flaws and there should have been a greater involvement of the hill tribe people in the project design and implementation. Of course, this would have been much easier said than done. When the UNDP project terminated, crop replacement was not successful until years later; therefore, these two UN projects cannot be considered an unqualified success. But the more telling question is — were the two projects a good investment? The answer is that they were both excellent investments. These were pioneer projects and they were undertaken long before conditions would allow successful crop substitution. As His Majesty the King always preached — there is considerable trial and error in doing development, but one must start somewhere. Like the accumulation of knowledge, these pioneer projects provided the shoulders on which subsequent and more successful projects were undertaken. National government approval is necessary to undertake a project and donor government approval is necessary to fund the project. When the UNDP project was launched in 1979, neither the Thai government nor the donor governments wanted a project that did not have as its prime objective the substitution of opium for other crops. This objective was not going to be achieved in 1979 or even ten years later. But eventually all concerned thanked their lucky stars that the project started when it did.

International development can be a frustrating business especially if one does not have a long term view. Years after my experience in Thailand, when I was doing similar work in China, I had high job satisfaction working with Chinese because most of them are taught to have a long perspective. For example, Deng Xioping once said that political reform would follow economic reform in China in a short period of time — 75 to 100 years. Western donor countries, especially the U.S. government, do not always share Deng's perspective For them, 75 to 100 years seems like an eternity especially while waiting for change to occur. It took 30 years to achieve success in the Golden Triangle and maintaining support over three decades was a difficult task. This point is beautifully illustrated by a conversation Giuseppe di Gennaro, Executive Director of UNFDAC had with His Majesty in 1982 on the subject of successful crop replacement. I quote from his notes:

> The King said that, according to his point of view, at least thirty years would be required to complete the task. I pointed out that thirty years was an unacceptable time frame. No serious planning could be so long term. Within such a time span, so many independent variables could hinder the productivity of any investment. I tried to let His Majesty understand that if I proposed such a long term time frame to my donors, they would disappear. The King listened in silence. I was sure I had changed His Majesty's mind. But when, after the audience, I mentioned this feeling to those accompanying me, they explained that it is a Thai custom not to react to such circumstances. Silence did not mean acceptance.[5]

The magnificent work done by the UN Border Relief Operation (UNBRO) for a decade (1982–1992) in caring for the Cambodian refugees will always be remembered as one of the UN's finest contributions in its history. Since 1945, there have been problems that must be addressed and the United Nations has been the only organization in the world which could take action. The monumental problem of caring for the Cambodian refugees is just such a case. The Thai government had neither the inclination nor the wherewithal to tackle the problem. The Vietnamese involvement in the equation made it impossible for the U.S., Japan or other western countries to take the lead. They were willing to help, but only though the UN. The UN General Assembly created UNBRO specifically to care for the refugees. At one point during the decade there were 400,000 people whose very lives depended on the good offices of the United Nations. Had the UN not been in existence, it would have been necessary to create a similar organization to meet the challenge on the border.

There has been plenty of adverse criticism of the policies of the Thai government and its supporters especially in keeping the Khmer Rouge supplied to fight the Vietnamese and thereby prolonging the conflict for years. Some have even argued that the Khmer Rouge should have been starved into submission. The problem with these arguments is that it was impossible to separate the Khmer Rouge combatants from the thousands of innocent people under their control. It is difficult to imagine that any country or organization would allow thousands to perish simply because they were under the control of a band of ruthless killers. Once again, the UNBRO experience illustrates the fact that UN organizations must operate at the behest of governments. These organizations have standards and principles that guide their work and they will not do things that violate these principles just because a government has ordered the organization to do so. There are numerous cases where UNDP resident representatives have been declared persona non grata and ordered out of the country (including Winston Prattley after he left Thailand and assumed a similar post in Sudan) because they would not compromise basic UN principles. In the case of the Cambodian border, UNBRO met a universally recognized humanitarian need. UNBRO officials carried out their duties literally under fire. They were brave, professional and effective.

5

Samoa and the Microdots

Introduction to Paradise

Shortly after arriving in Samoa in September 1981, I dictated a letter to my secretary, Fua Hazelman, to be sent to a friend in the Bangkok UNDP office. The letter was intended as a brief record of my first impressions. I said that I felt that we would enjoy living in Samoa despite its remoteness and removal from the rest of the world, especially Asia. When Fua finished typing the letter, she brought it to me and said, "Mr. Morey, do you mind if I make a comment on your letter?" While I was a bit taken aback by her question, nonetheless I told her I would be happy to receive her comments. She caught her breath and said, "You tell your friend that Samoa is isolated and removed from the rest of the world. But that is just your point of view because you are a palangi [foreigner]. If you were a Samoan, you would feel you were in the middle of the world. You are at least in the middle of the Pacific and it is the largest ocean in the world!"

I signed the letter and thanked Fua for her insightful comments. After she left the room, I chuckled to myself because I found her comments so amusing. Yet the more I thought about it, the more I realized that she actually made a good point. It brought to mind an adage used in Washington politics to explain why a person had a particular position on an issue—where you stand depends upon where you sit. Fua was right. If I were a Samoan, I would feel that this was my ancestral home and that it would always be my place and not at all isolated from anything I held dear. In addition to being a Samoan, Fua would see herself as a Polynesian and she learned as a child that Samoa is the epicenter of Polynesia. Samoa was the largest island country in which I served. But I was also UNDP Resident Representative in Tokelau, Niue and the Cook Islands which are also within Polynesia. These latter three are often referred to as territories, but I will simplify and refer to them as countries. They will be covered subsequently.

Polynesia is an oceanic triangle with the points being New Zealand, Hawaii and Easter Island which is off the west coast of South America. Those living within this vast expanse of water share the roots of a common language, history and culture. Samoans believe that Samoa is the cradle of Polynesia. However, other islanders believe the cradle of Polynesia is Raiatea located in French Polynesia.[1]

The Samoan islands were settled about 3,000 years ago by people originating from Southeast Asia. These were people who passed along amazing navigational skills from one generation to the next, which enabled them to sail thousands of miles in a sixty-foot double canoe guided by knowledge of the stars, the flight pattern of birds, clouds, winds and sea

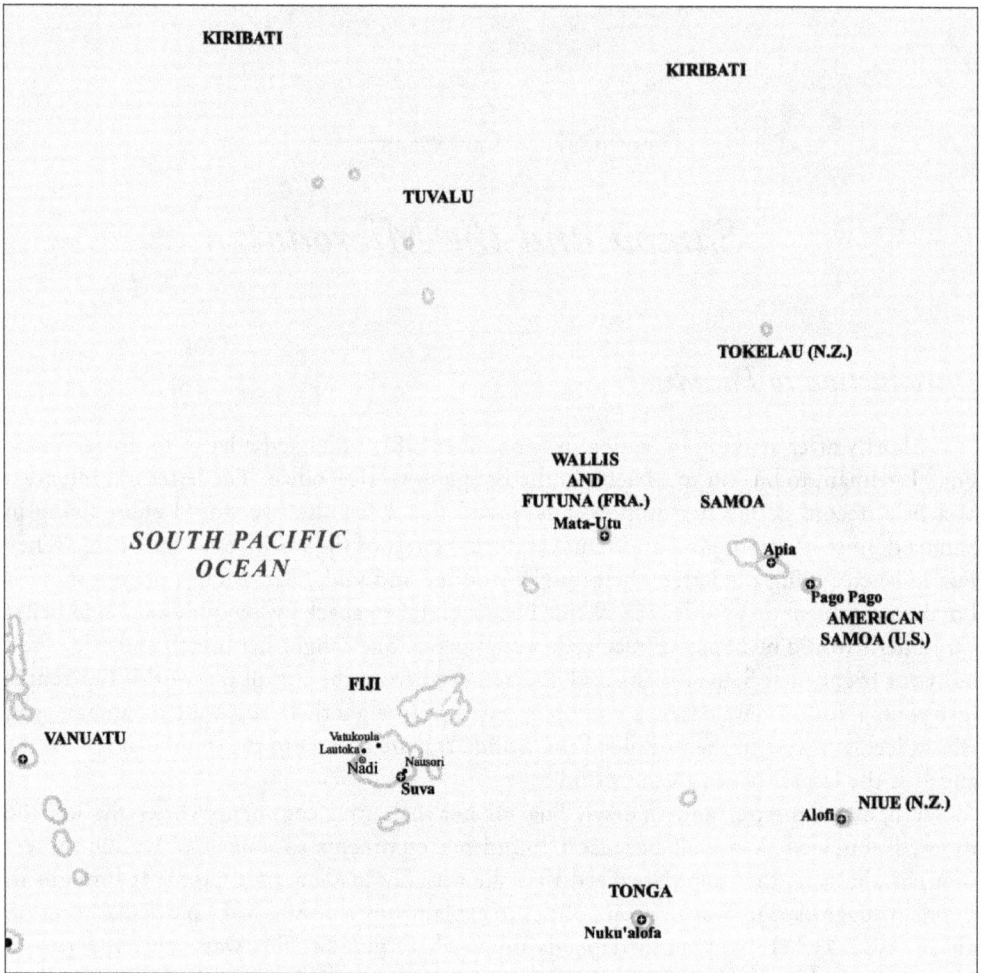

currents. In fact, in 1768 the Samoan islands were named the Navigation Islands by the famous French explorer, Louis-Antoine de Bougainville, after encountering Samoans in their ocean-going canoes.

While there was the occasional European who would land on one of the islands during the eighteenth century, the Samoans lived in splendid isolation from the western world until a fateful day in August 1830, when the famous John Williams of the London Missionary Society came ashore on the big island of Savaii. The London Missionary Society version of protestant Christianity spread so thoroughly that when Williams returned to Samoa in 1839 with his wife, he built a house with the intention of making Samoa his Pacific headquarters. But his plans never came to fruition because the following year, he was murdered by natives in what is now called Vanuatu.

The missionaries not only converted the Samoans to Christianity, but also had a major impact on the education system, and English was rapidly adopted as a second language. This in turn had an impact on the economy in general and agriculture in particular. In the latter part of the nineteenth century, as the production of copra (dried coconut meat) increased, Samoa soon emerged on the radar screens of major world powers. But it was not the fledgling economy that interested the British, American and German governments.

Rather, it was Samoa's strategic location in the middle of the Pacific which made the five small islands an attractive location as a refueling station for coal-fired naval vessels. All three countries wanted control of Samoa. Instead of going to war over this minute possession, each of the major powers supplied arms and training to warring Samoan groups which were engaged in a civil war to gain political control. This was a dark chapter in Samoan history which was chronicled by the country's most revered expatriate resident — the famous author Robert Louis Stevenson. His description of these events was published in 1900 entitled *A Footnote to History: Eight Years of Troubles in Samoa*.Stevenson moved to Samoa in 1889 with his family and purchased an estate called Vailima. His house still sits on Mt. Vaia, a few miles above Apia — the capital of Samoa.

The squabbling among the three major powers and their local surrogates finally came to a head in March 1889, when an event occurred which changed the islands of Samoa forever. The United States, Britain and Germany all had their warships anchored in Apia Harbor when one of the most catastrophic cyclones in the history of the country whirled in off the sea. The Americans and Germans each lost three ships. There were 54 American and 92 German sailors killed. The only warship to weather the storm and make it out of the harbor was the British ship Calliope. This disaster had a sobering effect on the three powers and they decided it was time to sit down and hammer out an agreement. The discussions led to the signing of the Berlin Treaty of 1889 which provided for an independent Samoa under the rule of a king, but with foreign strings attached. The king would be appointed by the three foreign powers and the consuls of the United States, Britain and Germany would have considerable advisory authority. Such an agreement was doomed to failure and sure enough it did. Internal conflict was not quelled and the king was constantly challenged. The spark that lit the fuse on the powder keg this time was the death of twelve foreign sailors. This second sobering event led to the drafting of a treaty ratified by the three powers which has affected the territory and the governing system of Samoa to this very day. Control of the western islands (including the big island of Savaii and the main island of Upolo where Apia is located) was given to Germany. The eastern islands including Tutuila and the main port of Pago Pago were given to the United States. The consolation prize for Britain was the Ellis Islands — tiny atolls located north of Samoa which is now the independent country of Tuvalu with a population of 12,000 and the highest elevation in the country of sixteen feet. If the sea truly does rise because of global warming, perhaps this will be the first country to be swallowed by the ocean.

Today there is the independent country of Samoa, which until recently was known as Western Samoa. Two hundred twenty-one nautical kilometers (one hundred thirty-seven miles) away from the main island of Upolu is American Samoa and the port of Pago Pago which is an unincorporated territory of the United States. German control of Samoa was short-lived (1900–1914), but important especially in agricultural development. The major German trading company established a large scale plantation system and introduced cocoa and rubber. The new crops and farming methods with all of the German advisors involved had an impact on the ethnic make-up of Samoa. In addition to German settlers, laborers were brought in from China and Malaysia to work the plantations. Like most places in the world today, there is a small Chinatown in Apia. Moreover, many prominent Samoan families have German names such as Schwenke, Wendt, Keil and Westerlund to name a few.

At the outbreak of World War I and at the behest of Britain, New Zealand forces landed in Samoa in 1914 and took control of the country without any resistance from the Germans. From the end of World War I until 1962, New Zealand administered Samoa as a Trust Territory. In 1962, Samoa signed a Friendship Treaty with New Zealand and thus became the first Pacific island country to gain independence.

The Samoans have a mixed feeling of resentment and admiration toward New Zealand which is similar to the feeling some Filipinos have toward the United States. In any event, the link between Samoa and New Zealand is very close and residency is the best indicator of this. The current population of Samoa is roughly 185,000, yet there are more than 131,000 Samoans living in New Zealand primarily in the Auckland area. In fact, the number of Samoans living outside of Samoa easily exceeds the combined population of Samoa and American Samoa. In addition to Auckland, there are sizeable Samoan populations in Honolulu, metropolitan Los Angeles, San Francisco and Salt Lake City.

First Week at Work

One of my first duties after arriving in Samoa was to arrange a meeting with the Prime Minister to present my credentials. A few days later I met Tupuola Efi who was serving at the time as P.M. Politics in Samoa is quite fluid. There were three Prime Ministers who served during my tenure in the country. When I was meeting with Tupuola, I had no idea that I would see him at the airport a few days later. During his tenure, he expected the diplomatic corps (all three of us!) to drive to the airport to see him off when he was traveling on official business. I thought this was ridiculous and I did it only once. Tupuola only stayed in office a few more months.

Next on my list was to make the rounds of the diplomatic community. Some years later, when I was in China, I had to be selective as to the number of ambassadors with whom I would meet, otherwise it would take at least a month to visit them all. In Samoa it could be done in less than half a day. There were only two — the New Zealand and Australian High Commissions. Samoa is a member of the British Commonwealth (as is New Zealand and Australia), therefore the embassy is called a High Commission and ambassadors are called High Commissioners. Australia is a much larger and powerful country than New Zealand and sometimes New Zealanders (most call themselves Kiwis) feel they are looked upon as the little brother, but not in Samoa. It is difficult to picture New Zealand as a metropolitan power, but Samoa was a Trust Territory of New Zealand for almost fifty years and as late as 1981, most Samoans would view New Zealand as a more important country than Australia. New Zealand has the largest Samoan oversees population. Scarcely a Samoan we met did not have at least one relative living in New Zealand. Most Samoans live in the Auckland area which is on the North Island and has a warm climate making it more appealing to an islander than the South Island. I became especially close to David Caffin, the New Zealand High Commissioner. At the time, New Zealand was by far the largest provider of official development assistance to Samoa. David and I collaborated in many activities since UNDP was a significant donor as well.

Lessons in Economics and Culture

Early in my stay I met with the country's top economist. As the conversation progressed it became clear that promoting economic and social development in Samoa and the other three island territories was not going to be easy. He started by saying that like many ancient non-monetary societies in the world, the ancient economy in Samoa operated on the principle of gift giving. A person would give a gift to someone with the expectation that a gift would be given in return. In the hidden economy of the country even today, gift giving is still the main principle of social and economic interaction especially at the village level. The building block of Samoan society is not the individual, but rather the extended family called the aiga (pronounced i ing ga). The aiga includes as many relatives as can be claimed — the bigger the better. The aiga gives a person dignity and purpose. The most crushing blow a Samoan could suffer would be estrangement from the aiga. Each village or town has numerous aiga which may be friends or rivals. The head of each aiga is a matai (chief). While some inherit the title of matai, most are elected by adult members of the aiga. There are also matais with the less prestigious title (junior matais) who serve the aiga in various ways including sitting on the Village Council.

In a traditional aiga, which you will still find at the village level, wealth and property is owned by the aiga and the decision-making authority on such matters is the matai. Each member's wages go to the matai and he in turn must care for the member's health, education, and spiritual and material needs. Older members of the aiga are in a better position to make demands on the matai which means that children are clearly at the bottom of the pecking order. Children must obey all adults within the aiga and are to be seen and not heard. As Samoans grow up, individual initiative must be subordinated to the aiga. To illustrate this point, there is an old Samoan tale about a young Samoan who was climbing a coconut palm with great speed and agility. Before he reached the top, other young Samoans climbing right behind him pulled him to the ground and told him that it was not a good image for the aiga to have such a show-off. Individual economic achievement might be fine in the outside world of the palangis, but a good Samoan serves the aiga.

It is possible for women to become matais, although most are men. Some titles command a great deal more respect than others. There is a small elite group of matais called the paramount chiefs. Anyone aspiring to become Head of State must be a paramount chief. Samoa's parliament is called the Fono and it is unicameral. There are 49 members elected by district to the Fono. With the exception of two seats reserved for citizens who are descendants of non–Samoans, the remaining 47 members must have a matai title. This is not as restrictive as it may appear because there are more than 25,000 titles registered out of a national population of 185,000.

Most of the population of Samoa still live in villages in rural areas and are engaged in subsistence agriculture. Taro (a starchy root vegetable) is the main crop. It has nutritional value, but is very high in carbohydrates which contribute to the large size of most adult Samoans. Many Samoans feel the preoccupation with weight in other countries is amusing. To be large in Samoa is the norm. If you want to be a big chief, you should play the part. The governance system for the village is the Village Council composed of matais from each of the aigas living in the village. The village is very important in a Samoan's life. Not only does one identify with an aiga, but also with the village. There is substantial devolution of decision-making authority to the Village Council. The Council sets the rules and adjudicates disputes. It operates mainly on tradition and not written rules, laws and regulations. The Council determines the punishment for crimes such as theft and violence. Most cases are settled by paying a fine, but in extreme cases the offender could have one's fale and possessions burned or even suffer ostracism from the village which would be the most dreaded punishment of all. While most cases do not go beyond the Village Council, those involved have access to a western style court system in Apia. But the decision of the Village Council is of paramount importance. Most Samoans would not take their case beyond the Village Council.

I learned a lot from my economist friend. It was clear to me that Samoan culture does not foster an entrepreneurial spirit to say the least and it is difficult to have economic development without it. This made sense to me because I noticed that most of the business community was made up of either afakasis (half castes) or palangis married to Samoans. What remained were a few state owned enterprises. Matais with well recognized titles and some level of higher education tended to go into national government service. As my meeting concluded, the economist said, "Mr. Morey, if you can make development work in Samoa, you can make it work anywhere."

Politics and Fa'a Samoa

We normally associate politics with official governmental institutions such as parliaments, presidents, prime ministers and courts. Wikipedia gives us a broader and more useful definition of politics as "a process by which groups of people make collective decisions." Note that the "political unit" can be a state, a sub-set of a state such as a province, city or school district. But it can also be a family, group of village elders, corporation, academic institution or a church. In Samoa, the most interesting politics is found in aigas and Village Councils rather than the national government. The basis of authority of the government is the national constitution. The basis of authority of the aiga, matais and Village Councils is 3,000 years of Samoan culture. Like most countries, the formal government in Samoa must be sensitive to Samoan culture and that is why one needs to be a matai to hold a seat in the national Fono.

In Samoa, you have official rule (the Fono) and traditional rule (aigas and Village Councils). Sometimes it is difficult to determine where traditional rule ends and official rule begins. This is especially true in settling disputes. The traditional approach to conflict resolution can be illustrated by an event that took place in a nearby village while we were living in Samoa. One afternoon young adults of the village were having their customary volleyball game when a dispute arose between two opponents over whether or not the ball had been hit out of bounds. A heated argument ensued and one of the players went to his fale, found a knife and upon his return he thrust the knife into the shoulder of his opponent. The volleyball game was promptly brought to a close and the matais who made up the Village Council went into session to determine a punishment. The unanimous decision of the Council was to burn to the ground the fale of the assailant's family. Most of the villagers agreed with the decision and felt it was in full accord with traditional Samoan justice. In the meantime, someone had called the fire station. When the fire truck arrived at the village entrance, the villagers blocked the road and started hurtling rocks at the fire truck. Soon one of the matais arrived, stopped the rock throwing and informed the driver of the Village Council's decision. The truck promptly turned around and returned to the station. The Council's decision was never challenged. It was a bitter experience for the family involved, but it could have been worse. The decision could have been to ostracize the family from the village. Traditional politics carried the day.

The Samoan Program

The comment made by the Samoan economist, "If you can make development work in Samoa, you can make it work anywhere," kept ringing in my ears as I went about the implementation of the Samoan UNDP country program. Island countries, like Samoa, share the same economic constraints. They have small land areas and are isolated from markets and trading partners. Transportation costs are high, especially commercial aviation. Often exports are low value agricultural commodities which fetch a small return once processing and transport costs are factored in. At least in the four small countries that I covered, the main stay of the economy was subsistence agriculture. Government and foreign assistance interventions could be made to improve peoples' lives, but it is still very difficult to grow the economy. In recent years, tourism has been important in growing the economies of Samoa and the Cook Islands, but such is not the case for Niue nor Tokelau.

Most UNDP projects are carried out in collaboration with a national or local governmental agency. UNDP projects in countries both large (China) or small (Tokelau) generally should adhere to the following principles:

- Projects should be identified in collaboration with the local government recipient. In other words, UNDP should not simply dream up project ideas and then foist them off on the government. If this were done, it would be difficult to ever get any local buy-in to the project.
- The bulk of the funding of the project invariably comes from UNDP. However, each project should have a cost sharing component where the government pays a variety of local costs.
- Projects should be sustainable. Once project assistance comes to an end, the government or community should continue project activities using their own resources. For example, if an agricultural extension agent funded by UNDP starts an aquaculture project which teaches farmers to raise fish, then the farmers and their offspring should continue the practice indefinitely. Or if the World Bank grants a loan to extend an electric power line, then there should be enough return on selling the power to pay off the loan.
- All projects must be reviewed periodically to determine if they are meeting their objectives and that proper accounting standards are used in the dispersal of funding. One can never anticipate all the problems in the initial formulation of a project and each time it is reviewed, the project will require adjustments to keep it on course.
- Most importantly, every project should build local human capacity. A UNDP funded adviser's job is not simply to drop into a country, do a piece of work and leave. The consultants and advisors must serve as mentors and pass on their skills and knowledge to enable their counterparts to continue the work after they leave the country. To paraphrase an old expression, UNDP helps those who help themselves.

Frankly, working in the four "microdots" under my charge, it was not easy meeting all the principles stated above, but we did the best we could. I could get government agreement to cost share projects in Samoa, but it simply was not possible to do so in Tokelau. We tried mightily to make our projects sustainable, but there were times when we invested in the training of someone only to find that a year or so after returning to the country, they would move to New Zealand or Australia. In these cases, we certainly enhanced human capacity, but the new found knowledge was not applied in the intended country. We conducted periodic reviews of our projects and would make the necessary adjustments, but the disbursement of funds was often very slow because of a weak government management structure. But I did not encounter any "hanky panky" in the way the funds were disbursed. In fact, we had a visit from the UNDP Internal Audit Office to check the office books and projects, and no serious problems were uncovered.

Samoa as a Least Developed Country (LDC)

Funding by UNDP to each recipient country is based on per capita gross national income and population size. To ensure that most of the assistance from the general fund goes to the most impoverished countries, a Least Developed Country category (LDC) was established so that these countries would be eligible for support from other special funds. Samoa is still included in this category. To qualify as a LDC, the per capita gross national income must be under $750. To put this in perspective, bear in mind that the highest per capita gross national income country is Luxembourg at $37,500 and the United States ranks fifth as $33,000. In addition, LDCs have low levels of health care, nutrition, education and adult literacy. The LDCs are also the most economically vulnerable countries because many (like Samoa) are small and isolated and some (like Nepal) are land-locked and are disadvantaged in international trade. I had roughly $1 million per year to spend on projects in Samoa. It was not a large sum, but considering the country had a population of 220,000, it amounted to more than $4.50 per person. There was a small amount allocated for the purchase of equipment, but most of the funding fell into three categories — training, advisors and consultants, OPAS officers and United Nations Volunteers.

Training, Advisors and Consultants

As one might expect, most projects were in the field of agriculture. The largest UNDP project was with the country's largest state owned enterprise — Western Samoa Trust Estates Corporation (WSTEC). The idea behind WSTEC was to establish plantations, especially on the largest island of Savaii, to raise crops (cocoa and copra) of sufficient volume to export. The World Bank, Australia and Japan provided funding to expand the plantations and UNDP funded advisors in coconut technology, crop diversification, short term consultants and training. While I was pleased with the quality of the UNDP inputs, I felt that WSTEC was only a mediocre operation. Just imagine the low level of efficiency of most state owned enterprises and then place this in the context of Samoa — I think you get the idea.

There were two excellent training projects that received UNDP funding. One involved training Samoan veterinarians in the Philippines to return to the country to instruct small farmers in livestock development. The other project provided fellowships to three technical officers to attend the Regional Telecommunications Training Center in Fiji to return and fill vacancies in the public service.

Officers in Operational Assistance (OPAS)

An OPAS officer is a UN euphemism for the direct hire of expatriates to fill local positions. On the surface, this doesn't appear to be a worthy expenditure of UNDP funding. It doesn't seem to square with the principle of advancing local capacity. On closer examination, in fact it is in line with the goal of self reliance as long as there is a training component included. In addition, an understanding must be reached with the government that there will be a finite period of service for the expatriate. During my tenure, there were four OPAS officers funded by the program. One ran the Electric Power Corporation, two ran the Telecommunications Authority and the fourth served as the Financial Secretary for the country. In the case of the Electric Power Corporation, a qualified Samoan was finally trained and replaced the OPAS officer a few years after my departure from the country. The Samoans being trained at the Regional Telecommunications Center in Fiji returned midway in my term and replaced the two OPAS officers in the Telecommunications Authority.

Replacing the OPAS officer serving as the Financial Secretary presented the greatest challenge. The officer was a competent and affable New Zealander who greatly enjoyed living in Samoa and was in no hurry to return home. The situation was further complicated by the fact that the officer was married to a Samoan who not only held a Chief's title, but was well connected in the government. She, too, was reluctant to move to New Zealand.

When I first arrived in Apia, I raised the issue with the Finance Minister. I was told that the Samoan deputy was not yet prepared to take over the job. The Minister went on to say that this was a key post in the government which involves negotiating agreements with financial institutions, overseeing the disbursement of funds and supervising budgetary preparations. It was clear that I would need to go to various sources to determine the readiness level of the deputy. My quiet investigation convinced me that he was prepared to take over. Hence, I kept up the pressure and when the Finance Minister was elevated to Prime Minister, he agreed to my request. Looking back on this case, it is clear that UNDP made a good investment. The OPAS officer was a good mentor and the deputy went on to become an excellent Financial Secretary. That same person now serves as the Prime Minister of the country.

United Nations Volunteers (UNV)

The United Nations Volunteers (UNV) is a sub-organization that operates under the aegis of the UNDP and is headquartered in Bonn, Germany.[2] It was established in 1971 and in the past four decades has fielded 30,000 volunteers. Each year UNV assigns 7,000 volunteers to work in 140 developing countries. It is similar to the U.S. Peace Corps, but it does not recruit volunteers straight out of university. UNV candidates must have a university degree or higher technical diploma, several years of professional work experience and a language fluency in English, Spanish or French. The normal tour of service is two years with a possibility to extend for a third year. UNVs receive a living allowance and medical coverage which is adjusted to the cost of living index in each country. In the 1980s in Samoa, the stipend was less than $14,000. Funding for the UNVs usually comes from the UNDP country program.

In Samoa and the other three countries covered by the office, UNVs were clearly the best value for money. They were not suitable for high level positions requiring an advanced level of training and experience such as directing the Electric Power Corporation or the Telecommunications Authority. For most other positions requiring the expertise of an expatriate, the UNVs worked out very well. The program funded UNVs serving in a coconut hybrid seed garden, as a trainer in auto mechanics, as an agricultural extension officer and as a trainer in office management. In addition there were UNV nurses in the national hospital.

The most popular physician in the national hospital was a UNV Filipino whose first name was Jesus. Of course, in the Philippines the Spanish pronunciation would be used (Hayzus). Not in Samoa. He was always paged over the intercom system in the hospital as Dr. Jesus. For the new patients, I can't imagine who they thought might be dropping by their room for a visit! Jesus was our family physician and he had our full trust and confidence.

Tokelau: Voyage to Another World

By anyone's standards, Tokelau is one of the most isolated countries in the world.[3] It lies 300 miles north of Samoa and there are no other populated islands within hundreds of miles. It consists of three atolls spread across 100 miles of ocean. There are roughly 500 inhabitants on each atoll. The combined land area of all three atolls is less than 13 square miles — a fraction of the size of Manhattan.

Tokelau is a dependent territory of New Zealand with a considerable measure of self government. Overall responsibility for the development of Tokelau rests with the Official Secretary for Tokelau who operates from an office in Apia. During our time in the Pacific, the Official Secretary was a New Zealand Foreign Service Officer by the name of John Larkindale who lived in Apia with family. Because none of the three atolls have enough land for an airstrip, all transport is by ship. As I had a responsibility to visit all projects funded by UNDP, I wondered how in the world I would ever travel to Tokelau. Then in early summer of 1983, I got a phone call from John Larkindale informing me that a New Zealand freighter was departing Auckland bound for Tokelau and would stop in Apia on the way. John said that the ship had several cabins and that he and his wife would occupy one and Delores and I were invited to occupy one of the others.

For centuries, the people of Tokelau lived in splendid isolation, but occasionally those from the outside world would arrive resulting in dire consequences. For example, in the late 1850s, Peruvian slave traders rounded up 250 natives (about half the population at the time) and shipped them off to South America never to be seen again. Also during the nineteenth century, a French missionary forcibly removed 500 islanders and sent them to another island where he thought they would be safe and have a better life. Two famous visitors from Britain also arrived on one or more of the atolls. The first European to discover Tokelau was Commodore John Bryon when he went ashore on Atafu in 1765. He claimed it for Britain and named it Prince of Wales Island. In the nineteenth century, John Williams of the London Missionary Society (LMS) visited Tokelau and the main church on Atafu is still called the LMS church. Also in the nineteenth century, Catholic and Protestant missionaries arrived from Samoa to convert the islanders to Christianity which they did with great success. Today Atafu is predominantly Protestant, Nukunono is almost 100 percent Catholic and Fakaofo has both Protestant and Catholic churches. Apparently there was a Portuguese ship that broke apart near Nukunono several hundred years ago. The surviving sailors swam ashore, eventually wed Tokelauan women, produced offspring and lived on the island for the remainder of their lives. This event helped establish Catholicism and there are several families on Nukunono who have Portuguese surnames.

Each atoll has numerous tiny islets. On the largest islet, the main village is located and is governed by a Council of Elders. There is also a small national parliament (Fono) composed of representatives from each atoll. Regardless of the intrusion of aliens from other parts of the world, in 1983 Tokelau was still one of the most unspoiled group of islands one could find anywhere in the world. Communication with the outside world was done on a two-way radio system. If someone from Nukunono wanted to visit a friend on Fakaofo, they would get in their outrigger canoe and paddle through 35 miles of open sea. The ship carrying fuel, food and other supplies made the round trip only once a month. There was no television. Most people lived in traditional housing much like Samoan fales with thatched roofs supported by poles without walls and only blinds to pull down in case of inclement weather. With a year round temperature of 80 degrees F, who needs walls! Most of the houses did not have electricity. The only motorized vehicle we saw on any of the three atolls was a motor bike used by the health worker at the clinic on Nukunono. A limited number of canned goods were available plus small quantities of pork, poultry, taro and breadfruit. For most people the diet had not changed for a 1000 years—fish and coconuts. The men use traditional fishing techniques that have been passed down for more than a millennium. Like most activities in Tokelau, fishing is a collective effort and the catch is shared among all families. Coconuts are plentiful. Some of the meat is eaten fresh and some dried as copra. In one form or another, adult Tokelauans consume half a dozen coconuts per day. Except for the diseases that have been brought to the islands from foreigners, such as dysentery, the islanders are healthy and live a long life.

On our voyage to Tokelau, we would arrive at the atoll in the evening, spend the night on the ship and visit the atoll the following morning. The first morning we went to the port side of the ship to view the atoll of Fakaofo. An atoll is a ring-shaped coral reef surrounding a lagoon around the top of an eroding volcano. The sea around the coral ring is dark blue because it is deep water around the sides of the submerged volcano. From the ship, we had a magnificent view of the dark blue sea, the coral reef and a narrow band of inhabited land and beyond the brilliant turquoise colored water of the lagoon. The lagoon was once the cone of a now extinct volcano. Since there are no ports on any of the atolls, sixteen-foot lighters with outboard motors leave a dock in the village, go through a passage way that has been blasted through the coral reef and travel the half-mile to the ship.

At each atoll, we were required to crawl down an eighteen foot rope ladder alongside the ship into the lighter. The routine was the same on each atoll. We were greeted by members of the Village Council and handed a green coconut with a straw stuck in the top so that we could refresh ourselves with fresh sweet coconut milk. We then proceeded to an activity hall for a meeting. Because of decades of New Zealand influence and English language instruction in the local schools, most of the Council members spoke English. John was thanked for New Zealand aid and I was thanked for UNDP assistance and, of course, we each had to make a brief presentation. I had not discussed Tokelauan pronunciation with anyone before arriving on Fakaofo and in my comments I pronounced it "Fookaofo." At the end of the meeting, I was informed by one of the Council members that the correct pronunciation was "Fuckaofo." I didn't want to offend nor did I want to break out laughing every time I mentioned the place. So, being a good diplomat, I resorted to mumbling the name. We then did a "walk about" on this densely populated narrow strip of land to view UNDP projects. We started our rounds by returning to the boat dock to view the passage way that had been blasted out of the coral reef. It seems that the year before, UNDP funded an explosives expert to go to Fakaofo and supervise the reef blasting. I told the Elders that I thought those involved did an excellent job on a project of vital interest to (mumble mumble) Fakaofo.

Our next stop was to visit several small areas planted in taro. UNDP sent an agronomist to Fakaofo to give instructions in taro cultivation. In several planting areas trenches were dug into the sand and filled with soil transported from other remote areas of the atoll — very basic and very ingenious. After lunch we paid a visit to the pastor of the Protestant church who, of course, was a highly respected member of the community. It was then time to be ferried back to the Frisna. During the night, the ship traveled the thirty miles to anchor off the next atoll — Nukunono.

Nukunono

We received the warmest welcome on the middle atoll — Nukunono. Perhaps it was due to a jovial and energetic nun who ran the school. She is a native Tokelauan who went to a New Zealand convent where she received her teacher training. She knew all about UNDP because the organization paid for a major shipment of English language books for her school library. We had to restrain her from showing us every book purchased by UNDP. She wanted to prove how they were being put to good use. The year before, UNDP funded her to attend a Conference on Women in Development held at UN headquarters in New York. Her eyes widened and her voice got louder as she told us what it was like for a woman from Tokelau to visit Manhattan. She started by saying that, of course, no one at the conference had ever heard of Tokelau, let alone knew its location on the globe. She said:

> So, I finally started telling everyone that I was just someone from an island visiting another island. I had to admit that Manhattan has a lot more people and a much bigger land area than my country. Since New York is such a big city, they could easily understand that it has many more people, but they found it hard to believe that the island of Manhattan is a much larger land area. One afternoon we were driving on the expressway to Long Island and I said to one of my new friends that this expressway is just about the width of much of Nukunono. I got my point across.

The nun was not far off. The widest strip of land in all of Tokelau is 200 meters (656 feet). The highest point incidentally is only 16 feet.

After visiting the Telecommunications Building to see a radio receiver that UNDP had co-funded with New Zealand, the Village Council members were anxious to show us the new piggery built with UNDP funding. As we waded around in pig manure inspecting every sty, I realized how a little money could brighten the lives of people living on a tiny bit of land completely removed from the rest of the world.

Atafu

Atafu is a more conservative and traditional atoll. The people are stricter in their religious practices which are reflected in a tighter regulation of alcoholic beverages. Moreover, the locals are prohibited from playing "a game for money with cards or with dice." As a result, our reception did not have the warmth and exuberance we found on Nukunono.

After being greeted at the dock, we were escorted by members of the Village Council to a small, but magnificent, meeting hall with large wooden pillars supporting the thatched roof. This was the only instance where the Council members had much more to say than their foreign guests. The highlight of our day on Atafu was a visit to the village elementary school which had received assistance from UNDP. As we entered the reception room, we noticed a faded photo poster of Prince Charles and Princess Diana two years after their gala wedding in London. (Keep in mind that "God Save the Queen" is one of two official national anthems of New Zealand.) At the school we met a young boy who spoke very good English. He had rarely seen a foreigner and had never been off the atoll. When we told him we lived in Apia, you would have thought that we said London or Wellington. He said, "I have been told that there are a lot of motor cars in Apia. Is that true?" Delores assured him that it was true and added that she drove one everyday. He continued his look of wonderment and said, "I know an older boy who is doing his studies in Apia and someday that is where I would like to do my studies." We bid a fond farewell to Atafu and took the lighter through the reef out to the ship. The trip back to Samoa took closer to thirty hours. On our return, we thought of the boy on Atafu as we climbed into our "motor car" and drove home.

Tokelau Today

Nothing stays the same anywhere in the world including Tokelau. In 1990 cyclone Ofa roared in from the sea and covered all three atolls with a wall of water that swept away most of the traditional housing. The charming open air fales have now been replaced with storm resistant closed structures build of imported lumber, concrete and corrugated iron with a few louvered glass windows. Fortunately floors are still covered with woven mats. Now most of Tokelau is electrified and telephone service is available. Small launches transport people among the atolls. Secondary education is available and an increased number of students attend university in New Zealand on scholarship. Many of these students do not return to Tokelau once they graduate. In short, it is not the quaint frozen-in-time place Delores and I visited in 1983. But we do not bemoan the changes because we are confident that there are few places in the world that have been more successful in preserving their culture and ancient way of life. An internet travel website says it all, "In Tokelau there is still no capital city, no airport, no seaports, no cars, no banks, no guns and no tourism."

Development Wisdom

Of all the senior leaders with whom I worked in the four program countries, Prime Minister Tofilau Eti Alesana was my favorite. He fit the perfect image of a Samoan chief. Tofilau had a wide girth and was always decked out in traditional Samoan garb — a solid color (usually beige) lavalava, a white shirt, tie and sandals. He was warm, witty and wise. He was always available when I needed to consult him. We simply enjoyed each others company. My first meeting with Tofilau was shortly after my arrival in Apia. At the time, he was serving as Minister of Finance. He said that he had an affinity for Americans because he was born in American Samoa. He moved with his family to a village in what was then called Western Samoa. He had decades of political experience dating back to a time before Samoan independence in 1962.

After a brief discussion of UNDP activities, Tofilau leaned back in his chair and said, "I have a high position in government, but I do not have much formal education. Mr. Morey, what do you think of a Minister of Finance, even in a small country like Samoa, who has only a seventh grade education?" Without hesitation, I replied, "Mr. Minister, a person can be highly intelligent and even wise without formal education. My father had only a seventh grade education and if you are half as good as he was, you will do a great

Author introducing UNDP Deputy Resident Representative Jan Wahlberg (right) to Samoa Prime Minister Tofilau Eti Alesana, Apia, 1983.

job." He rose from his chair, crossed the room, shook my hand, and said, "Mr. Morey, I think we will become friends." While Tofilau served as Prime Minister, I had numerous formal meetings with him. But we also had informal chats. At the time, the Prime Minister's office was located downtown on Beach Road in one of the remaining clapboard structures erected by the Germans. I would first check in with his assistant to make sure he was free and I was then allowed to take the back staircase to his office. I would enter his room unannounced and, without fail, he would invite me to sit and chat.

On one occasion, when I checked in with his assistant, I was told to sit and wait because the Prime Minister was meeting with two foreign guests. When I finally had my opportunity to sit down with Tofilau, I found him in a pensive mood and anxious to converse. He told me that the two guests who preceded me were anthropologists from the United States. They met with him to voice their concern over what they saw as the disappearance of Samoan culture. They especially saw the tourism industry as the greatest threat to a well-preserved traditional Samoa. He then asked me the following question: "Mr. Morey, do you think the current governmental policies promoting tourism and industrial projects like the new brewery [Vailima beer] will destroy the culture of this country?" I tried to add a little levity to my response by saying that no country can graduate into developed country status without a well functioning brewery and added that I did not share the fear of his two guests. Tofilau then went into a soliloquy that was more befitting a Ph.D. in anthropology than a man with a seventh grade education:

I am not an anthropologist, but I do know something about the culture of Samoa. I was born a Samoan, educated in this country, I speak the language and I have a well respected Chief's title. I know that over time more and more fales will be replaced by foreign style housing. I know that our youth speak more English than they do Samoan and they probably like pizza more than traditional Samoan food. But to me, a culture must grow and adapt to change or it really will start to disappear. These foreign anthropologists want us to turn this country into a museum so they can come and do their research and nothing will change from one year to another. In the meantime, I must worry about hundreds of young Samoans who need jobs to make a living and raise a family. Tourism is one of few options we have to expand our economy, increase opportunities and expand our tax base. Our country will change, but our culture will not die.

When the Prime Minister finished, I felt like cheering or at least applauding, but neither would have been appropriate. I simply told him that I was in full agreement with his views and added that I had never heard a case for development stated with such eloquence.

Niue: Coral Cliffs

Fortunately, travel to Niue (pronounced New-way) was not nearly as demanding as the voyage to Tokelau. Niue is almost equidistant between Samoa and Tonga. During my Pacific sojourn, Niue had scheduled flights on Polynesian Airways and had a airstrip long enough to accommodate Boeing 737s. The flight time was approximately one hour covering a distance of 380 air miles. There was one catch, however — one was required to spend three days on Niue before another scheduled flight arrived. For places to visit, events to attend and dinners to sup, spending three days in New York is one thing, but Niue is quite another. But I really couldn't complain because the whole idea was to explore the island and see UNDP projects in action.

Niue is a small island, only 260 square kilometers (162 square miles) — about one and one half times larger than Washington, D.C. The Polynesian population of Niue continues to drop from a peak of 5,200 in 1966 to an estimated 1,400 in 2009. During my visit to the island in the early 1980s, the estimated population was 1,800. But there was no official count and the issue was of political concern to the local government. Before my arrival, the UN Population Fund (UNFPA) helped the government organize a census which was undertaken, but the government never released the results. Most outside observers felt the results were not released because the figures indicated a population decline and the government feared that fewer people would result in a reduction of foreign assistance particularly from New Zealand. I was told in advance by the New Zealand High Commissioner to Samoa that it was a sensitive issue and there would be nothing gained by raising it. I accepted this sound advice.

The island was formed over a million years by the accumulation of coral. It is ringed by steep coral walls and the inhabitable land is a flat oval shaped table top sitting 100 feet above sea level. Below the cliffs are narrow white sand beaches. The cliffs are full of hidden caverns, buried grottoes and other natural fissures. It has the distinction of being the world's largest raised coral island. Like Tokelau, the Pacific is a deep blue with large waves crashing against the eastern cliffs of the island. The airport and seat of local government is located near the largest village of Alofi. Like Tokelau and the Cook Islands, Niue is a self-governing territory in free association with New Zealand. No doubt, New Zealand would be very happy if the three held a plebiscite and voted for complete independence (like Samoa). But the locals are not keen on the idea and why should they be? Each is self-governing, but has free immigration access to New Zealand. Furthermore, they can depend on New Zealand for protection and foreign assistance — not unlike the arrangement American Samoa has with the U.S. government. Most of the emigration from Niue has been to New Zealand, 2,400 kilometers (1,491 miles) to the southwest.

Like the other islands of the Pacific, Niue has an ancient past and a colorful history.[4] It was settled by Polynesians from Samoa 1,100 years ago. Because of its isolation, during the first 500 years the inhabitants established their own subculture of the larger Polynesian culture, lived in peace and were not threatened by the outside world. This changed in the sixteenth century when the island was invaded by Tonga. After the natives were defeated, a contingent of Tongans remained on the island. Peace and reconciliation was finally achieved 100 years after the Tongan invasion when a kingship was established patterned after the monarchal systems of Samoa and Tonga.

The famous British Captain James Cook arrived in 1774 and received a very hostile reception by the natives. After being repelled in his third attempt to land, he set sail never to return. Cook thought the bellicose inhabitants were painted with blood, but in fact, the substance on their teeth was from a native red banana. He cursed the natives and named their island, "Savage Island." The name stuck for those in the outside world until Niue started appearing on maps more than a century later. As was the case with Samoa, Tokelau and the Cook Islands, the Reverend John Williams of the London Missionary Society arrived in 1846 aboard his ship "Messenger of Peace." In view of the fact the island had an international reputation for being inhabited by savages, Williams did not attempt to convert the natives directly. Rather, he was clever enough to recruit a Niuean who was trained as a pastor at the Malua Theological College in Samoa. The Niuean pastor was allowed to return to the island, but only one village accepted him. After numerous setbacks, he was successful in spreading Christianity to the rest of the island. Today, Niue is predominantly Protestant with churches in all fourteen villages. Fearing colonization by a less benevolent power, Niue ceded sovereignty to Britain in 1900 and one year later, Britain passed the island on to New Zealand.

The 1974 Constitution established self-government with the creation of the Niue Legislative Assembly (Parliament) which consists of twenty democratically elected members. Executive authority is vested in the premier who selects another three members to form the Cabinet of Ministers. It is a system straight out of Whitehall via Wellington.

The purpose of my trip to Niue was to visit UNDP funded projects. The organization only provided $200,000 per year which wasn't much, but not bad for such a small country. The first project visited was also our largest — the headquarters of the Niue Development Board (NDB) a state owned commercial cash crop production and processing organization that functioned like a cooperative. The NDB focuses on export commodities and, at the time, UNDP was funding a senior advisor in production and marketing plus short term consultants in honey production and food technology. Developing exports in such an isolated place is an enormous challenge. But it is vitally needed to reduce the unfavorable trade balance, increase employment opportunities and encourage a greater retention of the population. Such efforts have had a modicum of success. Niue still exports passion fruit juice, lime oil, honey and coconut cream. But the volume is so small that it is not enough to correct the trade imbalance.

The other UNDP projects focused on agriculture with advisors (many of them UN Volunteers) working on citrus virus diseases, nursery production and grafting. For the next two days I drove the ring road around the island with the Secretary to Government and visited all fourteen villages. At one of our stops, I was introduced to a young woman from the Netherlands who was serving as a UNV horticulturist. After a brief chat, the Secretary to Government took me aside and asked that I speak to her. He said that she worked hard and her technical skills were excellent. Apparently she loved living on Niue and was well liked by her counterparts. He went on to say that she was far too intense and gave the impression that she cared more about the problems of Niue than the Niueans. That evening I sat down with the young lady and we had a beer before dinner. I knew I had to broach the subject with great care and so I began by telling her that when I was a new recruit in the development game in Thailand. I was indirectly informed by a colleague that I should relax a bit and stop pressing the Thais too hard with every "good idea" I had. I then tried to transfer my experience to her situation, but I failed miserably. The Secretary to Government was correct. She was too intense and she kept telling me that she had no idea in the world why I would deliver to her such a message. Her term expired six months later and she returned to the Netherlands after one year of service. It was a story I conveyed to the younger members of my staff for the remainder of my career. I told them that in keeping with the principles of UNDP, we are not in the country to solve the problems. We are in the country to help the locals solve their own problems.

Fly Me to the Moon (Scape)

In the fall of 1983 I was invited to attend the annual meeting of the South Pacific Conference (SPC), a regional organization of Pacific island countries. It was difficult finding flights out of Samoa to Saipan. After considerable effort, I found an Air Nauru flight that would take me the 1,500 miles to Nauru and after a brief layover would proceed to Saipan in the northern Marianas. The next week when I arrived at the air terminal, I noticed a Boeing 737 Air Nauru airplane parked near the runway. No one was waiting at the airline ticket counter and a young woman greeted me and said, "Mr. Morey, I am glad you arrived early so we can depart." It was 7:15 P.M. and the flight to Nauru was scheduled for 8:00 P.M. I said, "I thought the flight is scheduled to depart at 8:00 P.M." She replied, "It is, but we will leave sooner." I thought, my, this is strange. In most airports throughout the world, flights are often late, but I had never heard of one departing early. Shortly after fastening my seatbelt, the engines started to roar and the cabin door closed. I looked at my watch and it was only 7:30 P.M. I looked up from my seat and I was the only passenger on the entire aircraft.

After the plane reached cruising speed and the seatbelt light was switched off, the attendant came back to me and said, "Mr. Morey, we wanted you to occupy this seat for take-off, but now you can sit anywhere you like including our business class section. As the only passenger in the aircraft, there were three flight attendants caring for my every need. On the flight over, I didn't know much about Nauru. I knew it was the rare Pacific island country that was wealthy. But even so, how could such a minute speck in the ocean support an airline that could transport a single passenger 1,500 miles. For my return trip I was scheduled on a direct flight from Saipan to Samoa. But during the course of the conference I was informed by a member of the Nauru delegation that my flight was cancelled because the President decided to use the plane to take his family shopping in Sydney. I was rerouted on a flight to Nauru via Guam which required a twenty-four hour layover before proceeding to Samoa. During the layover I had a crash course on Nauru history and geology and was left feeling very sad.

Nauru is a tiny island located south of the Marshall Islands with a land area of only thirteen square miles. It is devoid of trees and has neither rivers nor streams. The water supply is dependent upon an aging desalination plant and rain water collected in large barrels. It has no arable land, no permanent crops and is subject to periodic droughts. It has a population of 14,000 which has been declining over the years with most of the emigration to Australia, the country with which Nauru has the closest ties. The people speak their own specific island language. However, English is a strong second language and is used in government and business. Nauru has a telephone system, radio and television service. The inhabitants live in non-traditional western style homes. There is an abundance of consumer goods available mainly imported from Australia ranging from food items to electronics. Given the volume of empty Foster's beer cans scattered around the island, there must be an insatiable thirst for that particular brew. It is a small but voracious consumer society with little regard for environmental degradation. Nauru is not a mecca for tourists. When I was there years ago, the guest house where I stayed was dark, dank and filthy. The food in the restaurant was even worse.

Nauru is classified as one of the great phosphate rock islands in the Pacific. For a century, the mined phosphate (used mainly in fertilizers) has been Nauru's source of wealth, but it will also spell its doom. In 1968, Nauru became the smallest independent republic in the world. Two years later, phosphate rights were acquired from Britain. During the 1970s, this little country no one had ever heard of, let alone be able to locate it on a map, was riding high and the sky was the limit. The mining was mainly done by a U.K., Australian and New Zealand consortium. The money just kept rolling in and the phosphate royalties gave the Nauruans the second highest gross domestic product (GDP) per capita — second only to the United Arab Emirates and one of the highest standards of living in the world. A portion of the royalties were distributed among the resident population and a family could get along quite well whether or not the breadwinner had a job. Among the youth, there was little incentive to hold a job and there would still be money for video games and beer.

During my visit, I found the place very depressing. Many of the inhabitants were too heavy, probably from lack of exercise and a diet high in carbohydrates and rich imported food items. The homes were ill kept with trash stacked in the back alley and, of course, the ubiquitous empty beer cans. I was taken to the main mining area in the middle of the island and it truly looked like the NASA photographs of the moonscape — nothing green, nothing growing, just great deep trenches of gray rock that had a volcanic appearance. I thought at the time, this little country is digging itself into the sea, and if one were to return to Nauru today, this observation would be very close to the truth

When Nauru joined the United Nations in 1999, the supply of phosphate was dwindling by the day and by 2006 the reserves were exhausted and the island has been reduced to an environmental waste land. Nauru appealed to the International Court of Justice located in The Hague to compensate the country for the damage done by foreign companies strip mining the landscape. The U.K., New Zealand and Australia consortium eventually agreed to settle out of court, but there would never be enough money to put the country back together again. Through massive financial mismanagement, including the operation of an airline that has lost tens of millions of dollars each year, the Government of Nauru is now on the brink of bankruptcy. The unemployment rate on the island is now 90 percent. For the people there are no more royalties and no more fun. It is now just a depressing place to live with a bleak future for the children. It is truly a tragedy of biblical proportions. In a number of developing and developed countries today, we still find that the misuse of a natural resource will lead to disaster.

The Cook Islands: A Colorful History

The Cook Islands are flanked to the west by Tonga and Samoa and to the east by Tahiti and French Polynesia. During my time in the Pacific, flights from Samoa to the main island of Rarotonga went via Niue. As was the case with Niue there were flights to the Cook Islands only a few times a week. It is a distance of 556 nautical miles from Niue to Rarotonga and the flight time is one hour twenty minutes. The Cooks (as we called them) are a collection of fifteen atolls and volcanic islands clustered in a southern group of nine (including the main island of Rarotanga) and a remote northern group of six with such colorful names as Puka Puka and Manihiki. The combined land area of the fifteen islands is only 240 square kilometers (92.7 square miles), but are scattered across an expanse of ocean of almost two million square kilometers and three times the size of Texas. Let's put this in perspective. In the 1980s the distance from Rarotonga to the northern islands was so great that islands like Puka Puka and Penryhn could only be reached from Rarotonga by ship which sailed only every six weeks. Today one can fly the 1,400 kilometers (870 miles) from Rarotonga to Penryhn, but it would be cheaper for Cook Islanders to fly to Paris! The distance from Puka Puka to Apia, Samoa is half the distance to Rarotonga. Perhaps this is the reason the residents of Puka Puka look and behave more like Samoans than they do Cook Islanders. During my tenure, I was able to visit two islands in addition to Rarotonga and they were both in the southern group.

Most students of the islands believe the original Polynesian settlers arrived from French Polynesia. It was not the British, but the Spanish who first spotted one of the Cook Islands — Puka Puka in 1595. The great British explorer, Captain James Cook, did not arrive for another 178 years in 1773. He named the islands the Hervey Islands. Captain Cook returned again in 1779 and was much luckier than he was on Niue because he went ashore on several islands and was welcomed by the natives. But his luck ran out a few months later when he returned to the big island of Hawaii (which he had previously named the Sandwich Island after the Earl of Sandwich) and was brutally murdered by the natives. Cook's name was legendary throughout Europe. He had mapped the Pacific, sailed the Antarctic Circle, explored Australia and New Zealand, and his name in New Zealand will be forever remembered because the sea passage between the north and south islands is called the Cook Strait. It was a Russian cartographer in 1824, who named the Cook Islands after the great British sea captain. As one would expect, the Reverend John Williams of the London Missionary Society first visited the Cook Islands in 1813, and the Islands today are predominantly Protestant.

Life and Politics in the Cooks

Since the Cook Islands had the second largest UNDP program ($1.2 million) under my charge, I went to Rarotonga often. At the time (and more so today) it had much more to offer visitors than Samoa. I am pleased we were involved in a more traditional lifestyle in Samoa, but Rarotonga was more fun — better accommodations, better restaurants, better organized recreation like fishing, diving, snorkeling and cycling. On the north coast, not far out of the main town of Avarua, is a spot considered sacred by the Cook Islanders called Marae Aroi-Te-Tonga. The remaining stones from a structure built more than 500 years ago can be seen. It was a royal court where the investiture of the high chiefs (Ariki) took place. On around to the east coast is the village of Ngatangila. According to Cook Island legend, it was from this spot that a large fleet of canoes left the beach in 1350, to travel the 1,500 kilometers (930 miles) of open sea to New Zealand where this group of Maoris settled the North Island. The Cook Islanders maintain this ethnic link through their language which is called Cook Island Maori.

The town of Avarua is also the seat of government. Much like Tokelau and Niue, the Cook Islands are a self-governing state in free association with New Zealand. Also like the other two, Cook Islanders receive New Zealand citizenship and the government receives New Zealand foreign assistance. All three have more of their population living abroad (mainly in New Zealand and Australia) than there are in the countries. Britain's Queen Elizabeth is also the Queen of New Zealand and the Head of State of the Cook Islands. In Avarua, she is represented by the Queen's Representative who is more than just a figure head and has the power to dissolve Parliament. The Parliament has twenty-four members representing all fifteen islands. The Prime Minister or Premier is leader of the majority party in Parliament and appoints the Cabinet.

Without question, the most colorful and controversial political leader in the Cook Islands in the last half century was Albert Henry. The Constitution established self-rule for the Cook Islands and was adopted in 1965. Albert Henry had returned from New Zealand to spearhead the self-government drive. His party (Cook Island Party) easily won a majority of seats in Parliament and Henry was elected the country's first Premier. He was then reelected consistently in 1968, 1972, 1974 and 1978. Like most Cook Islanders, Henry wanted his cake and eat it too, and he strongly favored self-rule with associated New Zealand nationality. Albert Henry knew that tourism would be the long term salvation of the economy and, therefore, he went about devising a financial scheme to enlarge Rarotonga's airport so it could accommodate Boeing 747 jumbo jets. He even persuaded Britain's Queen Elizabeth to preside over the grand opening of the airport. He established a National Tourism Authority and arranged for the construction of what is now called the Rarotonga Beach Resort & Spa.

Albert Henry was beloved by many Cook Islanders and was one of the Pacific's best known public figures. He was knighted by the Queen in 1974, shortly after the grand opening of the new airport. Everything was going swimmingly for Premier Henry until an investigation was held on the 1978 election. It seems that Henry and his close associates were flying in plane loads of overseas Cook Islanders to pack the vote at an expense to the government of over $300,000. After the fraud was uncovered, the 1978 election was given to the opposition Cook Island Democratic Party and Henry was stripped of his office. One must admit that this was a more audacious and imaginative vote rigging scheme than counting the names of gravestones in Chicago. At least Henry and his friends were counting live bodies! Later that year Albert Henry was convicted of electoral fraud and within months his knighthood was revoked. It is truly a sad tale. After his conviction, Henry's health began to decline and he died a disgraced and broken man on New Years Day 1981.

I arrived in the Cook Islands less than a year after Henry's death, but he was discussed in the bars of Rarotonga as though he were still among the living. My counterpart was Thomas Davis, the Premier who replaced Albert Henry. Davis wasn't nearly as flamboyant as Henry, but he was well respected and a man of great accomplishment. He was the first Cook Islander to gain a medical degree.[5]

The Program

Premier Davis was a man after my own heart because he stressed the role of private enterprise as crucial to the growth of the country's economy. He saw the role of the public sector in building the needed infrastructure especially in airport and harbor construction to better serve and integrate the outer islands. He also saw it as the public's responsibility to improve and expand educational opportunity and health care.

The new UNDP country program was designed to complement the national five-year plan promoted by Premier Davis and it was a good fit. We supported short term advisors in fruit processing and marketing, small-scale fisheries development, planning of airport networks and sea routes, harbor and airport planning and construction. We also co-funded, with the government, a large group of UN Volunteers (UNVs) who served as agricultural economists, public works engineers, equipment maintenance and repair specialists who would periodically visit the outer islands to work on electricity generators, water pumps, telecommunication equipment and the like. These were jobs for UN Volunteers and not highly paid consultants who would probably have objected to traveling to remote islands like Puka Puka and Manahiki. Without question, the most valued members of our UNV team were a married couple from Nepal working at the National Hospital on Rarotonga. He was a general surgeon (and the only surgeon in the country at the time) and she specialized in obstetrics and gynecology. As I recall, they served the maximum time allowed by the Organization — two terms for a total of four years. The government of the Cook Islands would have been pleased to have them stay forever.

Remaining Days in Samoa: Appropriate Technology and a Farewell Fiafia

The noted British development economist, E. F. Schumacher, put the cat among the pigeons in the global community of development theorists with the publication in 1963 of his internationally acclaimed book, *Small Is Beautiful.* The book popularized the concept of appropriate technology which Schumacher offered as an alternative to modern technology which he argues has helped contribute to the destruction of non-renewable and scarce resources. The transfer of modern technologies, he contends, has increased rather than lessened developing country dependence on the industrialized countries.

His critics countered by saying that this simplistic and highly romanticized philosophy would perpetuate the dominance of the industrialized countries by discouraging the modernization and industrialization in developing countries needed to enable them to become viable and competitive participants in the global economy. The debate continues to this very day. In recent years, international non-governmental organizations have extolled the virtues of appropriate technology and some have castigated the World Bank for promoting modern technologies from the industrialized world which they argue are totally inappropriate for many developing countries. In my twenty years of development experience I found that developing countries require a mix of technologies (some modern, some traditional) to meet different and sometimes competing development goals. Above all, success in applying a technology depends upon assuming a non-ideological approach.

If there were ever a group of countries Schumacher had in mind, surely it was the four microdots under my charge. Often in these small countries, a "small is beautiful" approach was appropriate. The best example was a UNV project UNDP supported that involved the construction of rainwater catchment tanks. Under this project, we hired a skilled and creative Filipino who transferred his experience from the Philippines first to the Cook Islands and later to Samoa. Using a low cost and basic approach, he and his local hire colleagues constructed pre-stressed concrete components which were then assembled to form the water tanks. The tanks were then sealed to prevent leaking. These were large tanks designed to catch the run off from the roofs of public buildings such as schools, clinics, churches and assembly halls. He also gave instruction to villagers on the fabrication of smaller household tanks. Most of the project work was done on the large under-developed island of Savaii.

The Four Countries Today and Their Economic Sustainability—The Economic Fate of Samoa

Delores and I returned to Samoa in 2007 and were greeted by Prime Minister Tuilaepa Aiono Sailele Malielegaoi. Tuilaepa was the Samoan who replaced the UNDP funded expatriate as Financial Secretary many years before. It was an excellent opportunity to meet old friends, many of whom are now senior government officials. Apia and the country had changed a great deal and mostly for the better. Health, education, transport facilities, public utilities and tourism infrastructure were substantially improved. There are now three commercial banks in Apia and a U.S. Embassy. For good or ill, Samoan youth can now gorge themselves at McDonald's and purchase a full range of video games. Everyone uses cell phones and ATMs, which didn't even exist when we lived there. Recreational activities are well organized and abundant. Restaurants are probably now more numerous and of better quality than those found in American Samoa.

Samoa is large enough with sufficient human and financial capital to enjoy a sustainable economy—but not without external help in the form of official development assistance (ODA) and remittances from overseas Samoans. There has been substantial growth in tourism and construction in recent years, but remittances from overseas Samoans still account for forty percent of GDP. Agriculture and fisheries still contribute to the economy. According to the World Bank, the government has demonstrated a commitment to sound economic management with the prospect of small but steady economic growth.

The biggest threat to Samoa's economy has been natural disasters. The country was struck by a destructive cyclone (Heta) in January 2004. In September 2009, an 8.0 magnitude earthquake occurred 20 miles below the ocean floor and the epicenter was 120 miles away from Samoa. The islands were badly shaken by the quake and soon a 20 foot tsunami wave of water hit the south coast of the main island of Upolu destroying entire villages, demolishing a tourist resort and claiming the lives of 200 people including several foreign tourists. With the help of the United Nations and generous bilateral assistance, Samoa is now well on the road to recovery, but the country will be forever vulnerable to natural disasters.

The Economic Future of the Cook Islands

The long term economic forecast for the Cook Islands isn't nearly as positive as that of Samoa. The Cooks have a much smaller population and resident talent pool. It has a minuscule combined land area. Its fifteen islands are spread over an immense expanse of ocean which results in huge transport and communications costs. There are now more than 100,000 tourists visiting the Cook Islands annually. But they are concentrated on Rarotonga and Aitutaki in the southern group. Tourism and services account for an estimated eighty percent of GDP. Black pearls from two of the outer northern islands are now the leading export.

During the 1980s and especially the 1990s, the government and the inhabitants lived way beyond their means. Government service became a bloated bureaucracy and the country accumulated an unsustainable foreign debt. More recently, the government has been successful in restructuring some of the foreign debt and economic management has improved. Nonetheless, there will be a large trade imbalance that will be virtually impossible for the country to correct. The economy may be sustained in the future, but not without remittances from Cook Islanders living abroad and generous foreign assistance primarily from New Zealand.

Niue's Future

The long term sustainability picture for Niue is even bleaker. Niue's land area is simply too small and its human resource base continues to shrink as Niueans continue to move off the island to New Zealand and elsewhere. The island continues to export, but the volume and value is so small that the country may net more money selling Niue postage stamps than its exports. Niue will always run an enormous trade imbalance because the country simply cannot maintain its standard of living and life style without a substantial volume of imported goods. The population of Niue will continue to decline, but it will continue as a political entity thanks to remittances and generous foreign assistance especially from New Zealand.

Tokelau: A Special Case

An assessment of the future of Tokelau should be done using an entirely different lens. Given the fact that the economy of Tokelau has not been internally sustainable for decades, the most important question is how will Tokelau as a political and cultural entity fare in the future? To answer this question, I start with the great eighteenth century French political philosopher, Jean-Jacques Rousseau, whose most enduring work is *The Social Contract or Principles of Political Right*, published in 1762.[6] The famous first sentence of the book reads, "Man is born free and everywhere he is in chains." This book quickly reached the American shores and probably had a greater impact than any other published work on Thomas Jefferson and his associates who signed the Declaration of Independence fourteen years later. One argument that especially appealed to Jefferson was the notion that a social contract is a sacred agreement among the people to protect rights, property and happiness. When these are abridged or denied by government, the populous has no choice but to replace the government by whatever means necessary.

I cite Rousseau for quite another purpose which is more relevant to Tokelau. He also argues that material progress can easily undermine the social contract and fray the fabric of traditional culture as man becomes more attached to material objects and greed starts replacing friendship and love. The development of agriculture and modern commerce, he contends, leads to economic inequality and conflict.

By the time *The Social Contract* was published, Tokelau had been a thriving entity for more than 500 years. I am not sure Rousseau could have found Tokelau on a map. But if there were ever a place I visited anywhere in the world where people live free and happy unencumbered by "chains" in Rousseau's idyllic state of nature, it would be Tokelau. The question is: Has its sacred social contract been destroyed by adjusting to modern life and experiencing the intrusion of the outside world? The answer is an emphatic "no." Once the three atolls united several hundred years ago, they devised a system of peacefully resolving conflict where the family unit is all important, but is balanced by certain collective chores and responsibilities. Tokelau has proven to the world that an ancient culture can endure in modern times with careful nurturing and a Tofilao Eti view of adapting and growing a culture.

Long term economic sustainability for Tokelau is another issue. Had a traditional life style been maintained along with the increased contact with the outside world in the last century, the primitive economy probably could have been sustained. But repelling the outside world would have been impossible — an exercise of shoveling sand against the tide. The economy of Tokelau has not been sustainable for half a century and it is not likely to be in the future. What keeps the economy going is foreign assistance especially support from New Zealand. But that isn't the most useful means of assessing Tokelau's future. Its future as a political entity, a people and a culture is bright.

Did the United Nations Make a Positive Difference?

Unlike other countries in which I served, there were no transformational projects in Samoa and the other three countries. After all, these are small countries and no one would expect such projects. Nonetheless, UNDP assistance made a substantial positive difference in each of these countries. Moreover, most of the projects were cost effective. As previously mentioned, projects supporting United Nations Volunteers were very good value indeed. Such projects provided life saving services of highly competent physicians in Cook Islands and Samoa. By following the KISS principle (keep it simple stupid), the UNDP programs delivered assistance at an appropriate level of technology and expertise. The agronomist in Niue and the rainwater catchment tank designer in Samoa are perfect examples of the KISS principle in action.

At the time, I resented paying the higher salaries to the OPAS (Officers in Operational Assistance) officers in Samoa. But in retrospect, I recognize that it was necessary and useful for the country. Eventually these expatriates were replaced by trained locals, but during the training period, development assistance was required.

As mentioned in another chapter, not all UN conferences are necessary and productive. However, some are very important and well worth the money. I have in mind the Catholic nun from Tokelau whom UNDP funded to participate in the Women in Development Conference in New York. The conference exposed her to ideas and experiences she could never have imagined living on the tiny atoll of Nukunonu. It was clear to me and everyone else in our group the afternoon we spent with her that UNDP had made an excellent investment.

In the final analysis, the best projects are those which enlarge the knowledge pool, enhance choices and opportunities, change behavior and change policy. In short, did the project enhance national capacity? Most of the projects in the South Pacific did just that.

6

China: The Dragon Stumbles

A First Glimpse

There we were with our faces pressed against a chain link fence peering into the land of the most ancient and mysterious civilization on the face of the earth — The People's Republic of China. Delores and I were standing on the border of the New Territory of Hong Kong and the mainland of China. It was July 1970, and the British still maintained political control of Hong Kong. We had just finished directing a one-year student abroad program at Waseda University in Tokyo and were on the first leg of an around the world tour. We had arrived in Hong Kong the previous day and our guide was a wise and gentle professor of Chinese history at the University of Hong Kong. As we drove back to our hotel on Victoria Island, I asked the professor, "Do you think we will ever be allowed to step foot on the mainland?" He replied in a soft and measured tone, "Dr. Morey, you and your wife are young, but I am ready for retirement in a few years. There is a chance the two of you will be able to visit China some day, but I don't think I will have the same chance."

In 1970, China was more inscrutable than ever because the Cultural Revolution was still raging. In Hong Kong the *de rigueur* tourist souvenirs were Mao buttons and the "little red book" of Mao's quotations which were on sale at a Hong Kong department store owned by the Chinese government.

Sometimes the world changes overnight. In April 1971, the U.S. table tennis team was competing in the World Table Tennis Championship in Nagoya, Japan. A member of the U.S. team mentioned to the captain of the Chinese team that the U.S. team would like to visit China. Word soon reached the highest levels of the government in Beijing and Chairman Mao personally issued an invitation. The U.S. team was soon hustled onto a plane bound for Hong Kong where they were ushered into the mainland not far from the spot where Delores and I had peered through the fence less than a year before.

Soon after the "ping pong diplomacy" started, my boss, President Richard Nixon, made his historic visit to China in February 1972. Two months later the Chinese table tennis team visited the United States. As a member of the White House staff, I had VIP seating with Delores to watch the U.S.-China table tennis match at Cole Field House on the campus of the University of Maryland, a few miles from the White House. In summary: only a few months after Delores and I wondered if we would step foot in the foreboding country, the Cultural Revolution had ended, the President of the United States had established a new relationship with China and it was clear that some day, indeed, we could visit the Middle Kingdom. Little did we know our visit would last four years.

Our First Visit

We now fast forward to January 1985. Delores, daughter Carolyn, and I were living in a Manhattan apartment and I had just taken an appointment at UNDP headquarters serving as the Chief of the Regional Programme Division for Asia and the Pacific. We had moved to New York from Samoa in 1983. While we only moved from one island to another, it seemed like we had moved to another planet!

Most people join the U.S. Foreign Service to serve in the field. The Foreign Service considers the "brass ring" to be appointed as ambassador. The same "brass ring" in UNDP is to be appointed UNDP Resident Representative and UN Resident Coordinator which is equivalent to an ambassadorial appointment. Years ago in the U.S. Foreign Service, the top appointments were probably the United Kingdom or France, and today it would likely be China or Russia. In UNDP, the top appointment is China. Despite the fact that Delores and I have always felt that New York is the most exciting place in the world to live, I was reluctant to take the New York headquarters assignment. I preferred another resident representative assignment in Asia. But Bureau Director Andrew Joseph made it clear that if I aspired to become a resident representative in a major country I would need to spend a few years at headquarters to establish the right connections. He knew that my unspoken goal was the China appointment and I knew that I would need to return to headquarters to queue up in line hoping to be tapped to go to Beijing.

After a year and a half of "proving" myself in New York, Andrew Joseph was pleased with my performance and made arrangements for Delores and me to visit China. Andrew insisted that this trip was not a boondoggle. Rather, it was to be a serious mission to assess the participation of China in various regional projects. I was more than willing to follow Andrew's admonition to refrain from sneaking around the incumbent resident representative's apartment measuring the drapes! I was also pleased to follow his advice to travel out of Beijing to other parts of the country. There were four events during that visit which made a lasting impression — three were inspirational and one was frightening.

On our flight to Shanghai the day after our arrival in Beijing, scenes from the 1966 Hollywood classic *The Sand Pebbles* kept flashing through my mind. In one scene Steve McQueen, as naval engineer Jake Holman, was arguing with his fellow swabbies on the gunboat USS *San Pablo* as it plied the waters of a Yangtze River tributary not far out of Shanghai. In another scene, McQueen was on leave strolling the Bund in central Shanghai with his duffel bag slung over his shoulder. Like the character played by McQueen, my father was also on a U.S. gunboat out of Shanghai only a few years after the Chinese Boxer Rebellion (1899–1901). He was so intent on escaping the mining camps of Colorado and seeing the world that he lied about his age and enlisted in the U.S. Navy when he was fifteen years old. By the time he reached China, he had already served in Japan and the Philippines. By the time he was twenty, he was a man of the world. The stories of his exploits I learned as a child sparked a desire in me to also see the world — especially China.

The Bund is a strip of land in central Shanghai on the western bank of the Huangpu River. For at least a century before the Chinese Revolution of 1949, the Bund was one of the most famous ribbons of real estate in the world. It was the foreigners' section of one of the most important international cities of Asia. The Bund housed the great banks and trading houses of the United Kingdom, France, the United States, Russia and Japan. The Bund was also home to the Cathay Hotel which hosted some of the world's most glamorous celebrities, political and business leaders. After the 1949 revolution, the hotel was renamed the Peace Hotel and became a property of the city of Shanghai. Like many state owned enterprises in China, the grand old hotel had slipped downhill by the time we registered in 1985. But it was still great fun wandering about trying to imagine the beauty and elegance of a bygone era.

After dinner Delores and I boarded a rickety elevator to the top floor where we were transported back in time by half a century as we listened to the music of a jazz band of octogenarians, all of whom seemed to be old enough to be our grandfathers. Fortunately one of the band members spoke English and informed us that he had been playing trombone in that faded art deco roof-top cabaret since 1945. He enthralled us with stories of the jazz greats who stayed at the Cathay and jammed the night away with his group. These included Benny Goodman, Jack Teagarden and none other than a very youthful Bhumibol Adulyadej, the current King of Thailand.

After a full jazz rush, we left the hotel in search of the ghost of Douglas Morey, the young sailor from Colorado. Dad had told me stories of taking shore leave and going to a small German-owned restaurant on the Bund where he would gorge himself on "a steak as big as a plate" and a half-dozen fried eggs. Of course, we never found the restaurant, but he was there that night in spirit as we searched for his old haunts.

The next item on the agenda in our exploration of Shanghai was to locate the mansion owned by the patriarch of the Soong family.[1] Charlie Soong was Hakka Chinese from Hainan Island and one of the most amazing men in the history of the last two centuries of his country. Sometime in the 1860s, without a cent in the world, and not speaking a word of English, he caught a freighter to Boston at the age of fifteen. He converted to Christianity, went to Durham, North Carolina, and was taken under the wing of Julian Carr, the father of "roll your own" Bull Durham Smoking Tobacco. Soong went to Vanderbilt University with the support of Carr and received a degree in theology in 1885. In 1886 he went to Shanghai as a missionary, but soon became a highly successful businessman selling bibles and other religious articles. Soong and Sun Yat-sen went to the same Methodist church in Shanghai and both became involved in the revolutionary movement to topple the Qing Dynasty.

Charlie Soong married and supported a family of three daughters and one son all of whom changed the course of modern Chinese history. Ai-ling Soong, the oldest daughter, married H.H. Kung who served as Minister of Finance in the Nationalist Government during World War II. He

Douglas E. Morey, U.S. sailor on the Yangtze River a few years after the end of the Boxer Rebellion, 1899–1901.

also amassed an immense fortune. The second daughter, Ching-ling married Sun Yat-sen who became the first president of the Chinese Republic in 1912 headquartered in Nanjing. After her husband's death, Ching-ling split with the family, supported the communists in 1949 and was appointed vice-president in the new communist government. The son, TV Soong, became Finance and Foreign Minister in the Nationalist Government and was considered to be one of the richest men in the world at the end of World War II. Many argue that all members of the Soong family became fabulously wealthy by diverting a portion of the three billion dollars of aid given to China by the United States during the war.

The youngest daughter, Mei-ling graduated from Wellesley College and married Chiang Kai-shek who became the head of the Nationalist Government throughout World War II. Madame Chiang Kai-shek fled to Taiwan with her husband in 1949 when the Nationalist forces were defeated by the communists and helped him establish the Republic of China. The Republic of China and the People's Republic of China both revere Sun Yat-sen and consider him the father of modern China. It is curious to note that Sun Yat-sen was a Christian educated in Hawaii, praised by Vladimir Lenin and served as President of the Republic of China for less than three months when his government was overthrown. It is doubly curious to note that while Chiang Kai-shek was serving as President of the Republic of China on Taiwan, one of his sisters-in-law was serving as the vice-president of the communist government in Beijing.

After many false starts, Delores and I finally found the Soong family mansion. Of course, today it does not appear quite as grand as it did a century ago. Some years ago the rooms were subdivided and it now serves as a care facility for seniors. It was in this home on December 1, 1927, that Mei-ling Soong married Generalissimo Chiang Kai-shek in a private religious ceremony. I doubt there will ever be another family quite like the Soongs.

The frightening experience during our first visit occurred on a train ride from Shanghai to Hang Zhou. An hour out of Shanghai the train pulled off on a siding to let another pass. A middle-aged man in ragged clothes approached the window of our railcar begging for cigarettes. A passenger across the aisle lowered the window, handed the beggar a few cigarettes, pulled out his camera and took a photo of him. I retrieved my camera and also took a photo of the beggar. I returned to my seat and put my camera away just as an armed security guard burst through the door and ran to the passenger with the camera in his hand. The guard grabbed the camera, opened it, ripped the film from the camera, deposited the exposed film in his pocket and flung the camera into an empty seat. When the guard left the railcar, I whispered to Delores, "By the grace of God that could have been me." When I related the incident a few days later to a UNDP local staff member, I was told that the government did not want any negative images of Chinese to be shown outside the country and it was standard operating procedure to rip film from a foreigner's camera. Days before the incident, Delores and I were reliving history and viewing the country through rose-colored glasses. The incident with the security guard brought us down to earth and reminded us that behind all of the magnificent history and culture of China, there still lurks the despotism of a communist totalitarian system.

Settling In

In April 1988, the office of the UN Secretary General sent my credentials to Beijing seeking the approval of the government for me to serve in the country as UN Resident Coordinator and UNDP Resident Representative. A month later the approval was received. We sold our house, packed our household goods, bid farewell to friends and family, and boarded a plane for Beijing in late September.

Our plan was to reach Beijing by October 1 to observe National Day. The date for National Day was set when Mao Zedong stood on a platform in front of the gates to the Forbidden City and announced the establishment of the People's Republic of China to an assemblage of 300,000 people standing in Tiananmen Square. Delores and I joined the diplomatic corps seated in the same area where Mao had spoken thirty-nine years earlier. The festivities were similar to what one would have seen in Red Square in Moscow — lots of speeches, a military parade and the display of four enormous portraits of Marx, Engels, Lenin and Stalin. After the collapse of the Soviet Union, there is now only a single portrait of Sun Yat-sen — the same portrait you would find in Taipei on a similar occasion.

Before 1949 there was an old diplomatic quarter in Beijing within walking distance of Tiananmen Square. But after the revolution, the government decided the area was far too small to accommodate a diplomatic community the government hoped to attract which would rival any other country in the world. During the 1950s, there was a race between Beijing and Taipei to attract as much diplomatic recognition as possible. Hence, the decision was made to designate three large areas of Beijing in which diplomatic compounds were built to house embassy offices and a spacious apartment for the ambassador's residence. The

Author presenting his diplomatic credentials to Chinese Premier Li Peng, Beijing, 1988.

compounds look like they all come out of a cookie cutter. They were all close together. They were painted a dull beige color and essentially they are all the same. Each compound is surrounded by a high wall. In more recent years, most of the large countries found their compounds too small and outdated and today these countries are occupying buildings of their own design.

The United Nations agencies are also provided a diplomatic compound. In addition to UNDP (which is the largest agency), the compound also housed the World Food Programme (WFP), the United Nations Population Fund (UNFPA), United Nations High Commissioner for Refugees (UNHCR), and the United Nations Industrial Organization (UNIDO). The apartment Delores and I occupied within the compound is large and serviceable, but certainly not luxurious. Below the apartment is a large meeting room which opens out onto a grass covered area suitable for hosting the annual UN Day reception on October 24. Having my residence and office in the same compound was a mixed blessing. I cut my commuting time to less than a minute, but ultimately I spent more time in the office.

When we arrived at the compound, I was pleased to find armed security guards at the gate, but I soon was advised that the guards were not there to protect the compound, but rather to keep unauthorized Chinese from entering. Non-Chinese could stroll into the compound at will. I learned about this lack of security the hard way a year later when a deranged Iranian entered the compound, went to the office of the representative of UNHCR and threatened his life by placing a knife against his throat. The Iranian was distraught because he was in China without a visa and had been informed the previous day that UNHCR was unable to find a third country of asylum for him. I was in a difficult position. I couldn't mobilize the other staff members and storm the UNHCR representative's office for fear his throat would be slit. The security guards at the gate, of course, would not lift a finger. I had to think twice about calling in the local police because I didn't want to violate the diplomatic immunity status of the compound. I quickly made a call to my friend, American Ambassador James Lilley, to seek his advice. He said that he had faced a similar situation while serving in Seoul as U.S. Ambassador to the Republic of Korea and in that case he was forced to call in the police. I made the same decision and mercifully the assailant was arrested without incident.

A Sharp Learning Curve

As the largest program in the UNDP system, China's UNDP office had a large staff (80) and two deputies — Herbert Behrstock (American) and David Lockwood (British). The office could command the best and brightest in the system and Herb and David were in the top rank of their professional level. After finishing the first day's obligatory address to the full office staff, I took the advice of Herb and David on how I should proceed. They had already scheduled a meeting two days hence with my counterpart in the Chinese government, Long Yongtu, Deputy Director of the China International Center for Economic and Technical Exchanges (CICET), in the Ministry of Foreign Trade and Economic Cooperation (MOFTEC). I looked forward to the meeting because Long was a friend. My friendship with him was a stroke of luck. When I returned from Samoa to New York to head the Regional Programme Division, I found that one member of my staff was a quiet, highly intelligent Chinese who had the air of a professor and called himself YT Long. He spoke impeccable English and had arrived in New York in 1978 as a member of the staff of the Chinese Mission to the UN. He was recruited into UNDP in 1980 and I first met him in January 1984. YT was one of the first Chinese (from the mainland) to join UNDP. I was his supervisor for a brief period before he was assigned to the Democratic People's Republic of Korea (North Korea) as UNDP Deputy Resident Representative in 1984. Fortunately, we established an excellent relationship and when I arrived in China in 1988, we simply picked up where we left off years before. Before I departed Beijing in 1992, YT had started his meteoric rise within the Chinese government. In 1992, he joined the negotiating team for China's ascension into the World Trade Organization (WTO) and rose to world prominence four years later when he became China's chief negotiator. His beaming face was seen on the front page of the *New York Times* when China was finally accepted into the WTO in 2001.

When I met with YT, he informed me that he had scheduled my first meeting at the Ministry of Foreign Affairs with Assistant Minister Li Daoyu. I was a bit disappointed and said, "Thank you for arranging the meeting, but I assumed my first meeting in the ministry would be with Foreign Minister Qian Qichen." I could sense YT was a bit put off by my comment, but maintained his smile and replied, "Roy, you will have plenty of opportunities to meet with Qian Qichen. But you should meet with Li Daoyu because he is in charge of international organizations and could become your most useful contact in the ministry." I quickly backtracked on my previous comment because I realized it revealed an arrogant attitude. I assured YT that I would be honored and pleased to meet with Li Daoyu. Fortunately this course correction warmed the atmosphere and encouraged YT to tell me more about Li Daoyu.

They first met while serving together at the Chinese Mission in New York. Despite his pleasing personality and high intelligence, Li Daoyu was not warmly embraced by some of his colleagues at the Mission because he was a direct descendant of the much reviled Li Hongzhang, a leading statesman and international negotiator during the waning days of the Qing Dynasty. Operating from a position of weakness, Li Hongzhang negotiated the highly unpopular Treaty of Shimonoseki which ended a disastrous war with Japan in 1895. Li Daoyu was grateful to YT for not harboring such a petty attitude and they became life long friends.

Before I left the meeting with YT, and perhaps inspired by my comment on Qian Qichen, YT gave me a brief tutorial on Chinese business culture which was of immense value for the rest of my stay in the country. His major points were: Do not be late for a meeting especially at the rank of minister. It is considered terribly rude; the host of a meeting should always be given the opportunity to speak first; look a person in the eye when you are addressing them; maintain a calm composure and never raise your voice; arrogance is a cardinal sin; never speak in a boastful manner; when a senior officer is accompanied by one or more of his staff members, address your comments and questions to the senior officer who will decide if one of his staff should speak; and most importantly, be yourself and be honest even if you are in disagreement but do so in a respectful manner.

Meeting with Li Daoyu

I was warmly greeted by Li Daoyu and it became clear immediately that he had a thorough knowledge of my background. He started by saying, "Mr. Morey, I know you served on the staff of President Nixon. I don't know what the reputation is of President Nixon in the United States, but in China he has a very good reputation and we consider him a friend of our country."

It was all sweetness and light from that point on. The two of us established an instant rapport. Among the topics we discussed was the U.S. presidential election which was then in full swing pitting George H. W. Bush against Michael Dukakis. Li Daoyu did not state his preference for either, but had high praise for Bush who had served as the Chief of the U.S. Liaison Office in Beijing in 1974 and 1975.

Before the meeting ended, Li Daoyu turned to the work of the UN and especially UNDP. He said that I was accredited to China, not only as UNDP Resident Representative, but also as UN Resident Coordinator. He recognized that coordinating the activities of all the UN organizations was a demanding task and added that he was willing to support me in that role. A few months after our meeting, Li Daoyu and his wife held a welcome dinner for us and invited all the heads of UN agencies and their spouses. In his remarks, he said that the Chinese government recognized my role as resident coordinator and would look to me to speak for the UN community as a whole. There were a few UN agency heads that were difficult to bring into the fold. But Li Daoyu had a positive impact on my success at "herding the cats."

Before I left Beijing for Hanoi, Li Daoyu rose to the highest levels of his profession. In 1990, he was Ambassador to the United Nations in New York and from 1993 to 1998, he was the Chinese Ambassador to the U.S. in Washington. When I became director of the UNDP office in Washington in January 1997, Delores and I reestablished our friendship with him and his wife. I was honored to be one of five invited to his farewell luncheon on the eve of his return to Beijing in 1998.

Nanjing Misadventure

Because of its historical significance, Nanjing is a city I had always wanted to visit. It became the capitol of the Republic of China for three months in 1912 during Sun Yat-sen's ill-fated tenure as president. In 1927 Chiang Kai-shek established it once again as the capitol (Nanjing means Southern Capitol) when the Kuomintang came into power. However, in 1937, Japanese forces were advancing so rapidly from Shanghai that Chiang was forced to move the military and the employees of the government, universities, libraries, laboratories and hospitals 700 miles up the Yangtze River by boat to the city of Chongqing. The move involved millions and remains one of the most incredible events in modern Chinese history. Unfortunately Nanjing was left unprotected. Japanese forces arrived in December, decimated the city and killed 350,000 of its residents. This event will forever be remembered throughout the world as "the rape of Nanjing."

Nanjing was our first foray out of Beijing and I made the mistake of allowing a staff member of the government's counterpart agency to arrange all the meetings. The trip soon turned into a fiasco. Forever after I never traveled out of Beijing without the accompaniment of one of my Chinese local staff members who was always in charge of arranging all meetings. Our trip was further complicated by a freak snow storm which paralyzed the city and closed the airport for several days.

Throughout a three-day stay in Nanjing I found that most of the visits were to state owned enterprises. The government staffer should have realized that UNDP would never provide funding directly to the budget of a state owned enterprise. Our visit slipped into the theater of the absurd one evening when Delores and I were taken to a meeting with senior executives of a company which produced ultralight aircraft. After suffering through a twenty minute presentation, I asked the CEO how he thought support for manufacturing ultralights related to the mission of UNDP. He has the audacity to reply, "I know that UNDP is interested in preserving China's forests and the ultralight aircraft would be useful in spotting forest fires." I tried to adhere to YT's Chinese business culture rules and perhaps I could have been a bit more subtle in rejecting the proposal out of hand. The banquet that followed (in China there is always a banquet following a meeting) was truly a frigid affair. The ultralight crew was dejected and peeved and did not utter a word. The restaurant was like a walk-in freezer because in those days in China there was no central heat south of the Huai River including Nanjing. Throughout the restaurant the diners' exhaled breath was visible as we minced our way through an eight course banquet wearing coats and mufflers. I seriously considered using chopsticks while wearing gloves. The scene did not improve the next day when we went to the airport. All planes were cancelled because of the weather. The snow began melting and the roof of the main terminal leaked like a sieve. We were in constant movement all day in search of a dry spot to sit. Luckily, the following day we caught a plane to Shenzhen.

The Special Economic Zone of Shenzhen

UNDP was involved in the economic reforms in China from the very start. At the request of the most senior level of government, UNDP was asked to fund an omnibus project which would assist in studying and establishing special economic zones (SEZs) attracting foreign investment and strengthening economic and trade ties with countries throughout the world. As a part of his effort to open China to the world, in 1979 Deng Xiaoping went to his friend Rong Yiren, a wealthy entrepreneur and former vice-president of China, and suggested that he establish a major firm to attract foreign capital and introduce new technologies and management practices in the reinvention of China's economy. The result was the creation of the China International Trust and Investment Corporation (CITIC). CITIC now has forty-four subsidiaries and is valued at $12 billion on the Hong Kong Stock Exchange.

The creation of CITIC went hand-in-hand with the establishment of the SEZs which were tasked to attract foreign capital, especially in manufacturing. Shenzhen was established as China's first major SEZ location in the mid–1970s. Studies leading to the creation of Shenzhen were funded by UNDP. It is located in the far south of the country and is adjacent to the new territory area of Hong Kong. Always looking ahead, Deng Xiaoping and his cohorts knew that some day the British colony of Hong Kong would revert to China (which happened in 1987). A highly developed area nearby was needed to assist in the economic absorption process. When Delores and I made our first visit to Shenzhen, it was still a fledgling, underdeveloped work in progress. It had a small airport, one hotel of international standard, dirt roads and a few manufacturing plants. I was there to co-chair a conference of international business leaders with the vice-president of CITIC. UNDP was also a co-sponsor of the conference. CITIC's purpose was to use existing ventures in Shenzhen to attract additional investment. On the last day of the conference, all participants were invited to tour a new plant built by the Pittsburgh Plate Glass Company to view a new and exciting "floating glass" technology. Seventy percent of the plant's product went to the domestic market and thirty percent was exported.

Those were heady days in China. We thought the sky was the limit and we were pleased to know that UNDP was playing an important role in making it happen. Shenzhen today is a sub-province of 15 million people and is China's third busiest container port after Shanghai and Hong Kong. There is now more than $30 billion invested in foreign owned and joint ventures. The city now has an international airport that rivals any in the world and is one of the world's fastest growing cities. Since our first visit in 1988, Delores and I have returned to Shenzhen several times. I never cease to be amazed by the progress made by China since the decade of chaos caused by Mao Zedong during the last years of his life.

A Cultural Revolution Vignette

The most satisfying days in the life of Mao Zedong were when he was leading the victorious forces in the 1949 Revolution. In the years after 1949, he became more and more dissatisfied because he felt the energy and commitment of the revolution were diminished. In his view, the government became unacceptably bureaucratic and the bureaucrats became too narcissistic. The Party became more hidebound. The intellectuals, he thought, were never fully a part of his cause. The heavy hand of Chinese history and culture was resistant to change especially Confucianism, and 800 million peasants were still living in poverty.

Thus he launched the Great Proletarian Cultural Revolution in 1966. Mao closed the schools and encouraged the youth to rid the country of all the trappings of the bourgeoisie. Red Guard units were formed to force millions of city dwellers to move to the countryside to "reeducate" them and learn from the peasants who were considered the real proletariat. Intellectuals, including religious leaders, were the prized target of the Red Guard and were tortured and slaughtered like cattle. Before the Cultural Revolution ended a decade later, more than one million people lost their lives and the country fell into a state of near anarchy.

The horror of the Cultural Revolution can be encapsulated in the experience of Tim Weber, a close friend living in New Mexico.[2] In September, 1967, Tim arrived in Shanghai as a member of a group of recent graduates of several American universities. The group was composed of devout members of a left-wing organization called Students for a Democratic Society (SDS). Tim was not a communist, but he found considerable value in Marxism. He was a starry-eyed idealist who went to China to help deliver the benefits of the 1949 Communist Revolution to the people. What a great time to be in China, he thought, as he camped with his friends under the benevolent gaze of two enormous posters of Mao and his wife Jiang Qing. Tim had a newly minted degree in psychology from the University of Chicago and was assigned to work with drug addicts at Wutaishan, a mountain located in Shanxi province considered sacred by Buddhists. Shanxi is in northern China adjacent to the Inner Mongolia Autonomous Region. Both areas are heavily populated by ethnic Mongols who have been living in this region of China for more than two millennia.

Years before moving to China, Tim was with his parents on a European ski vacation. By chance they met Dr. Bin Lee Liao and his wife and daughters. Dr. Liao's doctorate was from the Sorbonne in Paris. He was fluent in numerous languages including Mongol, Japanese, French, English and Mandarin. He was one of the most prominent figures in Chinese Buddhism and was the Chief Lama of the Pusading Temple built by Tibetan monks more than fifteen hundred years ago.

Tim's assignment to Wutaishan enabled him to reestablish his acquaintanceship with Dr. Liao and his family. Tim soon fell in love with Lia, one of the daughters and he proposed marriage. The year before Tim arrived at Wutaishan, Mao's wife Jiang Qing visited Dr. Liao and the Pusading Temple. She was truly evil incarnate and shared the belief of Marx and Lenin that religion is the opiate of the people. Therefore, she hated all established religions including Buddhism. She sized up Dr. Liao and decided she hated him as well because he represented all the Cultural Revolution was meant to destroy. He was a western educated intellectual who spoke foreign languages. He was a Mongol who occasionally wore western attire. Above all, he was one of China's most revered religious leaders. Without knowing it, Dr. Liao had become a marked man.

In 1969, Tim joined Dr. Liao and the family on a trip to the provincial city of Datong to buy a wedding dress for Lia. Dr. Liao was dressed in his finest Victorian style suit complete with starched collar and bib. They traveled in a Soviet built Zil limousine. Upon reaching Datong, a group of Red Guard stopped the vehicle by blocking the street. They opened the car door, grabbed Dr. Liao and marched him to a nearby park where they forced his daughters to line up and slap his face. The next day the Red Guard took Dr. Liao back to the park, stripped him naked and encouraged the bystanders to curse him and spit in his face. When his ordeal in the park ended, no one ever saw him again.

Tim and the rest of the family were released and returned home. Tim and Lia were married. They soon learned their fate when a group of Red Guard arrived at Wutaishan and went on a rampage. They set fire to numerous buildings. They looted the temples of their ancient art work and sacred objects, took them to a nearby road, spread them out and drove over them in trucks and a bulldozer. In a single afternoon, one of the most precious treasure troves of ancient Buddhist art in all of China was destroyed. The young Red Guard members were jubilant over the massive scale of their destruction and were convinced Mao and Jiang Qing would be proud of them. The Marquis de Sade could not have conceived of a more absurd and diabolical scene.

Sometime before the arrival of the Red Guard, Tim and Lia had become the proud parents of a baby girl, but Lia's new state of motherhood did not save her from being arrested by the Red Guard along with her aging mother and sisters. Tim was ordered to leave and fled for his life eventually reaching Hong Kong where he secured an air ticket to California. Lia joined a small group and was forced to walk each day with her daughter. Shortly after the harrowing journey began, Lia was separated from her child and continued on a forced march which ended months later at a reeducation camp near Guangzhou in southern China. She had walked a distance of more than 2000 miles (3218 km) and by some miraculous stroke of good fortune was reunited with her child.

Meanwhile, when Tim returned to the United States in 1969, he was immediately drafted into the army and assigned to Vietnam where he served as a medic. After his discharge, he returned to the United States and joined the faculty at the University of California, San Diego. Since his departure from China, Tim had lost all contact with his wife and daughter. There was an informal practice during the Cultural Revolution where loved ones outside of China would go to a wall near Victoria Station in Hong Kong and leave a note or scribble a message on the wall in hopes a refugee from the mainland would find the note and relay the message back to the intended recipient. Periodically Tim would visit Hong Kong and would leave and check for messages, but his efforts were in vain.

In 1974, Lia and her daughter escaped from the reeducation camp and walked to Guangzhou, the commercial capital of southern China located on the Pearl River 130 miles (209 km) from Hong Kong. Lia purchased a large inner tube and she and her daughter floated down the Pearl River and out into the South China Sea and eventually reached Hong Kong.

Completely unaware that his wife and daughter had escaped the camp and had launched their incredible nautical journey, Tim was on his periodic pilgrimage to Hong Kong. One morning he went to the wall and posted a message. To attract attention, he framed the top of the message in wood. That afternoon he went to the wall to check on his message. While he was viewing it, he felt a tap on his shoulder. When he turned around, there stood his wife and daughter. The three of them embraced and wept tears of joy. In 2003, Lia died of cancer at the age of forty-four in California. The daughter returned to China after university where she held a senior administrative position and has since returned to the United States with her daughter. Tim lived alone in New Mexico in a small house filled with rare Chinese antiques and a lifetime of memories. He passed away in October 2013.

The Transformation Begins

Most of the world did not know the name Deng Xiaoping until after the death of Mao in July 1977. In fact, he was one of China's most important leaders dating back to the legendary 6,000 mile Long March of 1937 and 1938 from the southern province of Jiangxi to Yanan in Shaanxi Province in central China. After the 1949 revolution, Deng became General Secretary of the Secretariat of the Chinese Communist Party and was elevated to the six-man Politburo Standing Committee in 1956. For decades Mao considered Deng one of the most intelligent and talented members of his team. But during the 1960s, Deng became alienated from Mao over policy differences. Three years after Mao launched the Cultural

Revolution in 1966 Deng was declared a "capitalist roader" and imprisoned on an army base. He was then exiled with his family to a rural area in Jiangxi province to undergo "re-education" and engage in manual labor.

Shortly after Mao's death, Deng made his political comeback. In an effort to destroy Mao's personality cult, Deng's first order of business was to organize a public trial of the notorious "Gang of Four" who were the most visible supporters of the Cultural Revolution and who were led by Mao's third wife, Jiang Qing. Deng's second order of business was to secure approval of the Central Committee to undertake reform policies in agriculture, industry, national defense and science and technology.[3] These reforms became known as the Four Modernizations. The goal was to quadruple the country's GDP by the year 2000. This was an incredibly ambitious goal which was actually realized. Deng proposed that this would be accomplished by opening China to the outside world through export oriented trade, foreign direct investment, technology transfer and enhancing knowledge via student abroad programs.

Communism is a combined political and economic system. Deng was a devout communist who wanted to change the economic side of the equation, but not the political. He was a pragmatist who recognized that continuing China's state-driven economic system would doom the country to lose ground to other market economies especially the "Four Tigers" (Taiwan, Hong Kong, Singapore and South Korea). What rankled Deng the most was the fact that the Hong Kong economy was the pride of Asia and this was also true of Taiwan just across the Strait from southern China. He knew that the Chinese in both of these locations could teach the mainland a major lesson on economic development. Deng was convinced that competition is necessary for a thriving economy. He also recognized that his market-oriented policies would lead to a wider gulf between wealth and poverty, but he nonetheless continued to push reform.

For millennia, China has been an agricultural country and it was, therefore, logical to focus the first reforms in the rural areas. The main benefit to farmers was the decision to de-collectivize agriculture and distribute land previously controlled by communes into private plots. Farmers were also allowed to keep a larger share of what they produced to sell on the open market. These steps resulted in an enormous increase in agricultural productivity which in turn provided new opportunities for rural industry. There was a veritable explosion of Township and Village Enterprises (TVEs) that received their name because of their location and not their ownership. Many were started by townships or villages. Others were essentially owned by the employees and some were privately held. They all operated on market principles and many gave bonuses to high performing managers. Employment in the TVEs grew from 28 million in 1978 to 135 million in 1996.

While Deng and his cohorts were busy stimulating the rural economy, they were also soliciting foreign direct investment from Asian and Western companies. A political decision was made to locate most of the enterprises receiving foreign direct investment in Special Economic Zones. The decision was also made to start the process of privatizing some of the state owned enterprises. Reforms were also undertaken in the financial sector and the role of the Central Bank in monetary policy was completely revamped.

In order to insure that the economic reforms received local support in such a large and diverse country, the Communist Party decided to turn over economic control to local authorities, especially provincial governors and Party secretaries. This decision led to spirited competition among the provinces in their quest to attract private investment. The provinces also wanted to attract UNDP projects. When I traveled to a new province, I always met with the governor and found them a most impressive group. Especially in the rapidly developing coastal provinces, the governors were reform-minded and had a good grasp of economics.

When I arrived in Beijing in September, 1988, there was a certain euphoria in the air. The reforms were going swimmingly. China was on its way to becoming a major world power. Thousands of students had returned with diplomas from U.S. universities and a new middle class was growing rapidly. There was an openness and press freedom that had not existed before. I remember an evening of conversation with researchers from the Chinese Academy of Social Sciences which has been described by *Foreign Policy* magazine as Asia's top think tank. The main topic we discussed was whether an open society is necessary for long term sustained economic growth. I felt like I was sitting in a coffee house in New York.

No wonder there was a sense of elation in Beijing in 1988 and early 1989. Zhao Ziyang was serving as General Secretary of the Communist Party of China and his vision and commitment to reform went far beyond that of his mentor, Deng Xiaoping. In addition to promoting market principles, including a stock exchange, Zhao saw flaws in the system which required attention including combating corruption, promoting a separation of the Party from the government, and eventually encouraging the growth of an open society and democratic institutions. Hu Yaobang preceded Zhao as General Secretary, but had to be eased out of office. Both were protégés of Deng and ultimately both were too reform minded for Deng's taste. The detractors of Zhao within the Politburo (who were numerous and jealous) started aligning against him because of rising inflation which was a result of reforms of the pricing structure promoted by Zhao.

An Encounter with the Best and the Brightest

China has always considered itself a developing country and has made extraordinary efforts to strengthen its outreach to other developing countries especially in Africa and Latin America. China's policy of cultivating these countries is now paying off enormously. In the next decade, China will lead the world in foreign investments in both of these continents. For more than a quarter century, UNDP has facilitated China's success in strengthening its relations with other developing countries. It has done so through a provision in successive UNDP country programs called Technical Cooperation among Developing Countries (TCDC). During my tenure in China, UNDP defrayed the costs of travel, food and lodging to facilitate the exchange of knowledge and experience in various field of technology and economic sectors.

In March 1989, a group of TCDC sponsored African economists visited Beijing and arrangements were made for a meeting with Zhao Ziyang. I accompanied the group and made the introductions. It was an event to remember. Zhao started with an overview of the major changes made in the Chinese economy during the previous decade. He said that the move to market principles enabled China to grow its economy by more than ten percent per annum and lifted tens of millions of Chinese out of poverty. He argued that price reforms were necessary despite the spike in inflation. He said that as a result of changes in economic policy, it is very important to take people and human behavior into account when making such policy. In the past he noted that the Chinese government did not need to worry about the behavior of people because they were not given a choice. Half in jest, he said that if people wanted rubber boots, there was only one kind and color. Now there are several kinds in various colors which is good for the people, but it makes planning more difficult. He mentioned that China was experiencing inflation and people were hoarding goods because they feared the prices would continue to increase. Zhao remarked that the leadership made some mistakes which needed to be corrected, but leaders must learn to put the people at the center of the economy. He concluded we must learn what the people are thinking so that goods are available at a fair price. This will require competition and rewarding those who make improvements.

Zhao was a warm and charismatic figure. The African economists sat in awe listening to his counsel. Moreover, they were delighted with his openness during the question and answer session. It was my first and last meeting with Zhao Ziyang. Three months later he was stripped of his position as General Secretary and placed under house arrest for the next sixteen years until his death in 2005. Like Icarus who flew too close to the sun, melted his wings and fell to his death; Zhao pushed the reform envelope a little too far and was punished by his colleagues including his mentor Deng.

Good Governance — Promoting Development and Alleviating Poverty

By the time I reached Beijing in October 1988, there was widespread agreement within the international development community that the ultimate purpose of development is the alleviation of poverty. There was also a growing recognition by some development scholars and practitioners that the best approach to attacking poverty is through the improvement of the country's governance system. This approach involves making public institutions more service oriented, effective, efficient, transparent, honest, and rule based. This approach also involves strengthening the non-governmental community including the business sector and non-governmental organizations (NGOs). Sound and sustainable development is not simply a state driven exercise. Rather it is promoted by a partnership between public institutions and non-governmental institutions. The governance approach to development has become more widely embraced after the collapse of the Soviet Union, declining appeal of communist ideology, and the growing appeal of market economics and democracy.

The governance approach was finally recognized by the full membership of the United Nations when the General Assembly unanimously adopted the United Nations Millennium Declaration in September 2000. The first and most important value affirmed in the document which is intended to guide national and international policymaking in the millennium states: "Men and women have the right to live their lives and raise their children in dignity, free from hunger and from the fear of violence, oppression or injustice. Democratic and participatory governance based on the will of the people best assures these rights." The Declaration goes on to state: "We [member states] resolve therefore to create an environment — at the national and global levels alike — which is conducive to development and the elimination of poverty. Success in meeting these objectives depends, *inter alia*, on good governance within each country." This wording would not have been adopted unanimously a decade earlier.

October 1988 was an excellent time to arrive in China with an agenda to promote good governance. Zhao Ziyang was General Secretary of the Party and many senior government officials were committed to reform. Within a few months after arriving, my UNDP colleagues and I were involved in discussions which eventually led to major projects on civil service, administrative and legal reform. But we were less successful on developing non-governmental organizations independent of the Communist Party control. After numerous meetings I became convince that leaders in the Women's Union were not willing to loosen Party control and become a truly independent NGO. Moreover, the All China Lawyers Association was also resistant to greater autonomy from the Party. Fortunately UNDP had much greater success encouraging the growth of independent NGOs in Vietnam.

Beijing Spring

In modern Chinese history, anniversaries, commemorative dates and the death of popular leaders have triggered public demonstrations. The death of Hu Yaobang on April 15, 1989, was the catalyst that caused thousands of students to pour into Tiananmen to express their grief. Two years prior to his death, Hu had been ousted as Party General Secretary. Among complaints made against him by his hard-line opponents was the charge that he had taken a soft-line toward student demonstrators in Shanghai. In addition to expressing their sorrow, the students of Beijing wanted to display their displeasure with the Party leadership for dismissing Hu unfairly.

During the first week of ever-increasing throngs of students on the Square, Zhao Ziyang was fully in charge and his advice to use patience and restraint in dealing with the protestors seemed to satisfy other members of the Politburo Standing Committee. But when he departed on a long-scheduled state visit to North Korea, Premier Li Peng and two other hard-liners went to Deng Xiaoping and convinced him that the demonstrators posed a grave threat to the Party and the country. Without informing Deng, Li Peng arranged for the major points of the meeting to be published as an editorial in all the major newspapers released on April 26. In addition to denouncing the demonstrators as "anti–Party" and "anti–Socialist" the editorial said, "All Comrades in the Party and the people throughout the country must soberly recognize the fact that our country will have no peaceful days if this disturbance is not checked resolutely." The students fully understood the Party's code words and from that point on the demonstration became a political confrontation. Clearly Li Peng and his cohorts were spoiling for a fight.[4]

As the weeks went on in late April and early May, there were major demonstrations in other cities including Shanghai, Guangzhou and Chengdu. In Beijing, demonstrators in various parts of the city organized marches to Tiananmen Square to show solidarity with the students. These marches included teachers, scholars, journalists, government employees and factory workers. In late April, I consented to holding a staff meeting to discuss the demonstrations. It was clear that virtually the entire local staff wanted to join one of the marches. I worried they might be identified and punished by state security, but they dismissed this concern by saying that there were too many people involved for state security to keep tabs. I agreed to their request to join one of the marches provided they did so as concerned citizens and not as representatives of UNDP. They were not to carry any UN banner and they were also required to use leave time. On the day the local staff marched, there were an estimated one million people on the streets of Beijing. The following morning when I was being debriefed on the previous day's activities, one local staffer said, "Yesterday many of us gave a personal donation to the students to help their cause." When I expressed concern that their transaction could be traced by state security, she nonchalantly replied, "Oh, don't worry, Mr. Morey, we got a receipt." The second week of May, the occupation of Tiananmen

Square became a hunger strike and sit-in. At this time the enormous "Goddess of Democracy" statue was put on display in the Square and miniature versions of the statue were being sold.

To complicate matters for the Party leaders, Mikhail Gorbachev arrived on May 15 for a state visit. The purpose of the visit, which had been planned for more than a year, was to restore full normalization of relations between the Soviet Union and China after a thirty-year chill. The students were delighted by the visit and especially the additional international media coverage that accompanied him. They greeted him on his arrival with one poster that read, "We Salute the Ambassador of Democracy." Another poster read, "In the Soviet Union, They Have Gorbachev, but What Do We Have in China?"

The day before his departure, Gorbachev traveled to the Great Hall of the People across the street from Tiananmen Square for his much anticipated meetings with Deng and Zhao. The demonstrators filled the Square as well as the streets and this necessitated ushering Gorbachev into the Hall through a side door. Deng was humiliated by the experience and was in a sour mood for his meeting with the Soviet leader. After his two hour meeting with Deng, Gorbachev then met with Zhao Ziyang and the atmosphere changed completely. He found Zhao charming, witty and a man after his own heart. Gorbachev said they both shared the same goals and concerns adding: Zhao Ziyang posed a seemingly rhetorical question stressing that we all had to answer it together: "Can a one-party system insure the development of democracy? Can it implement effective control over negative phenomena and fight the corruption in Party and government institutions? In this question I read all my own doubts."[5]

While Gorbachev was still in the city, Deng called a meeting of the old guard at his home in which a decision was made to impose martial law. Li Peng was in attendance, but Zhao Ziyang was excluded. After Zhao learned of the decision, he said that he could not issue the martial law order and submitted his resignation. But later he withdrew the resignation knowing that the confrontation with the demonstrators would become even more volatile if word leaked out that he had stepped down.

Zhao knew his days were numbered, but nonetheless in the early morning hours of May 19 (one day before martial law was declared), he went to Tiananmen Square and with the use of a megaphone delivered a speech to the students which electrified the country when it was broadcast through China Central Television. He opened his remarks by saying, "Students, we came too late. We are sorry. You talk about us, criticize us, it is all necessary. The reason I came here is not to ask for your forgiveness, but to ask you to stop your hunger strike." He went on to say, "If you stop your hunger strike, the government won't close the door for dialogue ever! The questions you have raised, we can continue to discuss." He concluded by saying that the students were young and full of hope but, "We are already old, it doesn't matter to us anymore." He laid his megaphone to the ground, bowed to the students — many of whom broke into tears. It was the last public appearance of a man who was perhaps the most inspiring Communist leader since the 1949 Revolution.

After martial law was declared, most of us in the diplomatic community felt that the use of weapons against the students was inevitable. In my capacity as Designated Official for Security, I called together the heads of all UN agencies including the World Bank. We reviewed the five phases of the UN Security Code:

- Phase One — all staff and dependents are to exercise caution.
- Phase Two — all staff and families are required to remain at home.

- Phase Three — staff and dependents are to be relocated temporarily.
- Phase Four — all international staff and dependents not directly concerned with the emergency are relocated outside the country.
- Phase Five — the UN offices must be closed and all staff are relocated outside the country.

Like the captain of the ship, the Designated Official for Security is to be the last UN officer to leave the country. Fortunately, we only reached Phase Four.

The view I shared with the agencies was that the People's Liberation Army (PLA) units that were arriving in the city were composed of young soldiers who were not equipped with weapons and did not pose an immediate threat. But I had the fear that if the marches and occupation of the Square continued, the next dispatch of troops would certainly be armed. I asked that the head of each agency appoint a security officer who could communicate periodically with one of my deputies. We agreed that Phase One of the security code should be put into effect and that we should go into Phase Two if weapons and heavy armaments arrived in the city. As anticipated, by the end of May, the PLA sent thousands of additional troops to the outskirts of Beijing along with tanks, armored personnel carriers and trucks.

While Delores and I were perfectly content to remain in the safe confines of our compound, we continued to attend receptions and dinner parties which provided excellent opportunities to exchange information with diplomatic colleagues. The three ambassadors who were most helpful to me were also the most impressive members of the corps — James Lilley (U.S.), Alan Donald (U.K.) and Earl Drake (Canada). I was on the phone with each of them almost daily to exchange information. Their embassies had much better intelligence to share with me than I had to share with them.

Blood in the Streets

On Saturday morning, June 3, I met with Song Jian, State Councilor for Science and Technology and Deng Nan, the daughter of Deng Xiaoping, who served as director of a major UNDP funded water study of northern China. At the end of the meeting Song Jian said:

> Mr. Morey, I am worried about the current turmoil in Beijing and I am also worried about the safety of your UN colleagues and their families. I have been informed that last night a truck carrying firearms was hijacked and the weapons were stolen. This means there could be an armed conflict between the protestors and the soldiers which now makes the situation explosive. I think you should stay off the streets.

I thanked him and mentioned that the previous evening a senior government official issued the same warning and added that I had already moved into a new phase of our security code and the entire UN community had been told to spend the weekend at home.

On Saturday night (June 3), a radio announcement was made by the government ordering everyone off the streets of Beijing. Delores and I promptly left a dinner party and returned to our apartment where I spent the next hour trying to get the latest news on BBC and VOA. At 2 A.M., we were awakened by the sound of gunfire. It was a horrifying experience to know that people were probably being killed less than five miles away. While the gunfire was still audible, the telephone started ringing. Friends and relatives of UN staff and families were calling to check on the safety of their loved ones. I also received several frantic calls from consultants who were staying in hotels near Tiananmen Square.

During the night of June 3, and the early morning hours of June 4, thousands of troops in armed personnel carriers, trucks and buses started down Chang'an Boulevard, the main route leading to Tiananmen Square. As the convoy approached the Square, it encountered thousands of demonstrators lining both sides of the street who used every means possible to stop the convoy from reaching the Square including hurling Molotov cocktails into the vehicles. A melee erupted in which a number of protestors and soldiers were killed and numerous vehicles burned. By the time the troops reached the Square, most of the protestors had fled to nearby streets. We will never know the exact number killed, but it was certainly several hundred. The protestors were gunned down in areas adjacent to the Square especially streets alongside and behind the Great Hall of the People. On that night, the PLA and a handful of communist leaders made a mockery of the name of this world famous edifice.

Most of the troops deployed to Beijing were young, raw and undisciplined recruits from rural areas. The recruits were chosen from out of town so that they would not be facing their own families and friends. In addition, they could be more easily brainwashed on the "hooligans" in the square. For a week after June 4, it was dangerous to be on the streets anywhere in central Beijing because flat bed trucks carrying these trigger happy neophytes were on patrol. Occasionally and without provocation, troops would fire randomly at buildings and pedestrians. One morning on her way to work, one of my local staff members witnessed a soldier on one of these trucks fire and kill an old woman walking down the street just for target practice.

Fortunately, most staff and dependents restricted to their homes followed the rules and did not venture outside. However, one UNDP international staff member ventured out of her apartment to purchase cat food. She was spotted by a PLA patrol truck. The truck stopped, several soldiers jumped to the sidewalk and pressed her against a wall with their rifles. Needless, to say, she never violated the security code again!

On the afternoon of June 4, while the sanitation workers were clearing the debris and scrubbing the blood off the streets, a young staffer from the UN Population Program entered my office and broke into tears. "My Chinese fiancée lives near Tiananmen Square and fears for her life because she is engaged to me, a foreigner," he sobbed. I patted his shoulder and asked how I could help. He replied, "Could you help her escape from the country and go to Switzerland?" I was taken aback by his request, but I felt I could not refuse to pursue it. "Has she been involved in the demonstrations and is there a chance she will be pursued by state security?" I asked. "No," he replied, "She would only be recognized in the fine arts community because she is an accomplished dancer." I then asked, "Do you think she can make it through security at the airport?" He responded, "Several people have told me that there is so much chaos at the airport, government security is almost non-existent." I finished our conversation by asking him to secure her Chinese passport and I promised to do my best to help.

I then called a friend and popular member of the diplomatic corps, Swiss Ambassador Erwin Schurtenberger. After briefing him on the case, he asked, "Do you consider her a political refugee?" I replied, "I consider any Chinese trying to get out of the country at this moment a political refugee." The ambassador instructed me to have the staffer go to the embassy the next afternoon with his fiancée's passport and she would be given a long-term visa for Switzerland — no questions asked. The following afternoon the staffer obtained the visa and brought his fiancé to the office so she could express her gratitude. As they were leaving to go to the airport, I said to her, "Take any flight out of Beijing you are allowed to board because you can always take another flight to Switzerland." Like most Western governments during the period of the crisis, Australia was pleased to accept political refugees and that afternoon she caught a flight to Sydney. After a stay of several months, she went on to Zurich. The staffer resigned his UN post, took a position with the Swiss government and they were soon married. As far as I know, they will live happily ever after in Switzerland.

On June 5, the normal work week started and I expected only three staffers to show up at work — my two deputies (Herb Behrstock and David Lockwood) and Ali Ensha, the chief administrative officer. To my surprise, several local staffers arrived and I was amazed by their bravery. There were guest quarters in the compound and I convinced the staff who insisted on working to stay in the compound and not return home until it was safe to do so. In our apartment we had plenty of food in the freezer and the pantry. For the remainder of the week, Delores was the cook and our dining room was the mess hall. We never left the compound and we were all amazed that services were not disrupted. Local television continued as usual. The telephone system never went down and most flights continued to arrive and depart at the airport. Despite the fact that we were confined to the compound, we received numerous reports of thousands of people being rounded up and taken off to incarceration facilities.

Television sets throughout the world displayed a photo of a cluster of tanks parked on an overpass between Jianguomenwai diplomatic housing complex and Tiananmen Square which is less than a mile away. This photo prompted me to make a phone call to U.S. Ambassador Lilley the morning of June 5, and he transferred my call to his Assistant Army Attaché Larry Wortzel. I said, "Major Wortzel, there are at least a dozen tanks parked on an overpass in front of the Jianguomenwai complex where most of the UN staff and families live. I assume the cannons on the tanks are loaded and if so, what would be the result if one of them lobbed a shell into the compound?" Without hesitation Wortzel replied, "A single shell could destroy an entire wall several stories high." He went on to add, "The Chinese military is very unpredictable at the moment and we simply can't gauge their behavior."

Throughout the crisis I was in close contact with two UN officials in New York — Andrew Joseph, Director of the UNDP Bureau for Asia and the Pacific, and Kofi Annan, serving at the time as Assistant Secretary General for Human Resources Management and Security Coordinator for the UN system. Because of the twelve-hour time difference with New York, I was compelled to call Annan at unseemly hours on several occasions. When we were chatting years later after he was elected Secretary General, he turned to his wife and said, "This is the man who kept waking us up at night by phoning from Beijing," and added with a wry smile, "but it was always for very important reasons."

I made one of those inconvenient calls to Annan on Monday and relayed to him the alarming report from Major Wortzel on the Jianguomenwai compound. Without hesitation he agreed that we should go to Phase Three and relocate the UN staff and dependents to a more secure location. I told him that in the event it was necessary to go to Phase Four and evacuate staff and dependents out of the country, I had been exploring options to charter an aircraft for a Beijing to Hong Kong round trip. The least expensive offer I had received to charter an aircraft was from Pakistan International Airlines at a cost of more than $400,000. The airline also specified the offer was good for only a three-day period. Annan said that he would agree to accept the offer if the security situation continued to deteriorate and if I could not find a better offer. I hung up the phone, called the two deputies into my office and told them to notify all UN security officers that everyone in the UN community living at Jianguomenwai would be relocated to the Kunlun Hotel starting the next morning

Secretary General Kofi Annan with the author, United Nations, New York, 1998.

(June 6). I told them to stress the fact that the compound was an unsafe location. I also told them to remind all security officers that under UN rules, there was only one suitcase and a carryon bag allowed per person. I then called in Ali Ensha, a smart and hard-bargaining Iranian, and told him to reserve the requisite number of rooms at the Kunlun at a good price. I knew there would be plenty of rooms available because all tourists had left the city. I chose the Kunlun because it was within sight of the UN compound.

By noon on June 6, all staff and dependents were safely ensconced in their rooms at the Kunlun. But I received reports that several staff spouses were unhappy because they thought the move was unnecessary. That afternoon I arranged a meeting at the hotel to fill them in on the details which led Kofi Annan and me to call for the relocation. Most fully understood the need for the UN security regulations and appreciated my concern for their safety. But there was still a rump group who continued to complain. At that moment I realized that a crisis brings out either the best or worst in people. It brought out the best in most of the UN community.

The following morning I received a frantic call from Ambassador Lilley urging me to get the UN staff and dependents out of Jianguomenwai as soon as possible. I assured him that I had done so the previous day on the strength of the conversation I had with Major Wortzel. When Lilley published his memoirs fifteen years later, I learned why he was so certain the diplomatic compound was in danger. The night before (June 6), Larry Wortzel had received an anonymous phone call. The voice identified himself as a young PLA officer. Wortzel was warned, "Please do not go to your apartment (in Jianguomenwai) between ten in the morning and two in the afternoon." The young officer concluded by adding, "Do not go above the second floor of your apartment building."[6]

Ambassador Lilley immediately arranged for all Americans to go to the embassy grounds for a meeting and only a few were left in the compound. Sure enough, on the afternoon of June 7, PLA troops fired numerous rounds into the compound smashing windows and piercing walls. Miraculously no one was killed. But I heard several stories of children having their heads pressed to the floor by their parents to keep them out of the line of fire. The PLA claimed that a sniper was on the roof, but machine guns sprayed bullets all over the building. It wasn't the trigger happy young recruits who were out of control, but rather it was clear that the attack was approved at a very high level in advance as the warning from the young officer the night before clearly showed.

The Jianguomenwai attack was the game changer. Within the international community, there was full agreement that a massive evacuation was required as soon as possible. The decision to evacuate is fraught with problems. The UN or an embassy would be damned if the evacuation were undertaken too early, but they would also be damned if it were done too late. Moreover, one must guard against the comparison blame game. Once one embassy decides to evacuate, the press runs to the other embassies asking why they are delinquent in protecting the lives of their nationals. One of the reasons I stayed in close contact with the ambassadors of the U.S., U.K. and Canada was to insure that there was a coordinated evacuation. Of course, these three country representatives had a much easier time lining up the aircraft required for the evacuation. As a result they commenced their operations two days before the UN. I was still dickering with Pakistan International Airways to lower the price for chartering a plane and the only response I received was a reminder the original offer would expire in two days.

I received a call from Jim Lilley who said, "Roy, I would like to accommodate more of your people, but we are evacuating only Americans. But I would be happy to include all your American staff and dependents." The following day I received a call from U.K. Ambassador Alan Donald with a similar offer, "I would be pleased to accommodate all British subjects and spouses plus those from the Commonwealth"—an inter-governmental organization composed of fifty-four member states of which all but two are former British colonies. There were thirteen from the UN group who accepted the British offer including David Lockwood's wife and Kenneth Stephens, an American with a British wife. Just before the Stephens' departed, I took Ken aside and said, "When you are at the airport this morning, check with the various airlines to see if any have a flight to Hong Kong with room for one hundred and ten passengers." Less than an hour after he arrived at the airport, I received a call from him. In an excited voice he exclaimed, "Cathay Pacific has a flight to Hong Kong this evening and one hundred and ten seats will be reserved for the next two hours, but you must respond by phone to hold them. They want a cash payment for the tickets and the cost will be approximately $33,000."

Under UNDP rules, a field office is not allowed to hold more than $10,000 in the safe at any one time. I simply assumed that such a rule would not apply in an emergency; therefore on June 5, I arranged for my driver to take Ali Ensha to the bank and withdraw U.S.$40,000. With the news from Ken, I was delighted to have violated UNDP rules! I called in Herb and David and asked them to notify everyone that buses would pick them up at the Kunlun and two other diplomatic compounds and depart for the airport promptly at 6 P.M. I confirmed the seats with Cathay Pacific and asked Ali to go out and find two buses to hire. Once again, I awakened Kofi Annan to inform him that the UN would save a bundle of money on the evacuation. He sounded pleased and groggy and told me to proceed. By 5:45 P.M. there were two buses parked in the compound. We fastened UN flags on the roofs of each bus and Ali climbed aboard one of them carrying a plastic Ziploc bag containing $33,000 in cash. During the afternoon, our efficient travel agent in Bangkok made all of the Hong Kong arrangements for hotel rooms and transport to the hotel from the airport. The few of us left in the office pumped the air with our fists when we received a call later that night informing us of the safe arrival of the group in Hong Kong.

The following morning David Lockwood entered my office grinning like a Cheshire cat, handed me a cable and said, "Boy, you are going to like this one." The cable was from the UNDP travel office reminding me that any travel of staff or dependents outside the country would require the approval of the travel office. I told David, "We won't answer it, but perhaps we should frame it!"

At UNDP headquarters, Andrew Joseph had been fully informed on the preparation and execution of the evacuation. He phoned me that morning to congratulate me on the success of the operation and then said, "Roy, it has come to my attention that Delores was not on the plane to Hong Kong, and some here in headquarters are wondering why she was not evacuated." I explained to him that unlike other spouses, Delores lived within the secure confines of the compound. Furthermore, she was doing yeoman duty cooking and looking after the needs of the staff staying in the compound. It was the first and last time the issue was raised.

The day after the blood bath, my government counterpart and friend, YT Long, came to my office. He entered the room, closed the door, embraced me and wept on my shoulder as he softly said, "My heart is broken." He regained his composure and we sat and chatted for an hour. He was immensely concerned about the safety of the UN community and wondered what my next steps would be. He said the most frequently discussed issue at the highest level of government is the question whether or not I planned to leave the country and order all the UN offices to be closed. I told him that would involve the final phase of our security procedures and the decision would require the approval of the Secretary General. I told him that it may be necessary to evacuate non-essential UN staff and dependents (which proved to be the case). But the security situation would have to deteriorate a great deal more to warrant a full evacuation. I informed him that the head of the World Bank office already had fled the country, but I was assured by his deputy there was no intention to close the office.

Before leaving, YT said, "In the next few days you will be requested to meet with the Vice Minister of Foreign Trade and Economic Cooperation. You will be given an official explanation of the cause of the turmoil and why force was required to stop it. Your meeting will appear on national television. Li Daoyu will do the same for the Ministry of Foreign Affairs." As soon as YT departed, I called Ambassadors Lilley, Donald and Drake. I told them they would be seeing me on television and I explained the reasons why. I didn't want anyone to be misled into thinking my appearance was an indication of my support of Party policy. Jim Lilley, an experienced "China hand" reassured me by saying, "Don't worry, Roy, we all know that it is textbook communist procedure." Ten days later film clips of my meetings appeared on national television.

After a week stay in Hong Kong, I secured Kofi Annan's agreement to return the evacuees to Beijing. By then the PLA patrols had ceased and it was sufficiently safe for UN families to reoccupy their apartments. Not all staff and dependents returned to Beijing immediately after the crisis ended — some went on from Hong Kong to take home leave and the office was not fully staffed for the remainder of the summer. We tried our best to return to normalcy, but there was a perceptible shift in the political climate and it took at least six months to regain momentum in the UN projects.

Postmortem

The Central Party School of the Communist Party of China is an elite institution located in one of Beijing's suburbs. The school offers courses on a variety of subjects including international economics, politics and culture. Any middle rank Party or government official who aspires to reach the senior ranks must undertake several months of course work at the school Top scholars in the country are on the faculty.

In line with the policy of opening up to the outside world, in the 1980s, the school established a program of inviting foreign scholars and political practitioners to lecture to the students. This practice received strong support from Zhao Ziyang during his term as General Secretary (1987–1989). One year before my arrival in Beijing, UNDP established a project with the school to defray travel and living expenses for some of the foreign visitors. One of the visitors funded by UNDP who was in Beijing during the Tiananmen crisis was Bradley Patterson, a former colleague of mine from the Nixon White House who gave lectures at the school on the function and operations of the White House and the American two-party system. It was an excellent project and fit perfectly into the mandate of UNDP. Our goal was to expose government and Party officials to the world of ideas outside China, but we never publicized the project for fear it would be misconstrued. I could just imagine the late Senator Jesse Helms taking the floor and announcing that UNDP was giving direct financial assistance to the Chinese Communist Party.

One week after Tiananmen, I received a call from YT Long who said that the Vice President of the Party School and the UNDP project director would like to meet with me for an off-the-record discussion of the Tiananmen crisis. He mentioned that he would serve as interpreter and also said that one of his colleagues would be attending the meeting. The colleague was the daughter of Chen Yun, one of the most senior members of the old guard and someone who strongly supported the crackdown. I agreed to the meeting and two days later we gathered in the private dining room of an obscure Chinese restaurant for lunch and discussion.

I had met the Vice President on a previous occasion and we had established a cordial and informal relationship. He started by saying that he felt it was important for senior leaders to receive the views of the events from a foreigner who witnessed them first-hand. He was then compelled to read to me the same Party line I had previously heard from the two ministry representatives. When he finished reading, he folded the paper, stuck it in his pocket and said, "Mr. Morey, what I would really like is to hear your views on the recent turmoil." He may have received more than anticipated because the session lasted another two hours.

I started by observing that the Party leaders seemed to consider the reaction of the outside world, and especially the United States, to be interference in an internal matter. In my view, the people of China should be grateful that millions throughout the world would mourn the loss of a single Chinese life, let alone several hundred. I said that I was proud of my fellow Americans who expressed such a high degree of interest, concern and grief over the events of Beijing. I argued that the bloodshed could have been avoided if the Party leaders had used patience and restraint rather than converting the protest into a confrontation. I added that I was aware of the fact that some of the protestors resorted to violence, but noted that military weapons encouraged the opposing side to use weapons. In addition, I said that no doubt there were state security *agent provocateurs* deliberately fanning the flames of the crisis. Finally, I explained why the use of lethal weapons was totally unnecessary:

In 1969, I was a visiting professor at Waseda University in Tokyo and I witnessed some of the most serious public disturbances in modern Japanese history. The U.S.-Japan Security Treaty was up for renewal that year and the demonstrations were triggered by the incursion into Cambodia by U.S. forces during the Vietnam War. One night there was an organized protest in Shinjuku district which I witnessed. There were an estimated one million protestors surging through the streets of Shinjuku breaking storefront windows and overturning vehicles. Before the following morning, the police had quelled the disturbance. No one was killed and the most serious injury was a broken arm,. The police were successful because they used a special riot unit trained in crowd control called the Kidotai. These highly disciplined units do not carry guns. The Kidotai are equipped with helmets and plexiglass visors, shields, clubs, gas masks and teargas. I suggest you tell your leaders to train a Chinese equivalent of the Kidotai and the next time there is a public disturbance, use them instead of poorly trained and undisciplined PLA troops packing lethal weapons. You will quell the disturbance and save the lives of your fellow countrymen.

As we concluded the meeting and the Vice President of the school seemed to be very receptive to the suggestions that I made. Unfortunately, the UNDP Party School project was soon terminated and I never saw the Vice President again. Since the Tiananmen crisis, there have been thousands of protests and demonstration each year. Most of these have occurred at a local level. Unlike Tiananmen, such disturbances have involved labor disputes and local issues including corruption, unsafe and polluted living conditions, and unfair treatment by authorities and employers. There are now local riot police who use tear gas rather than bullets in most cases. However, there is nothing at the professional level of the Kidotai.

The Tiananmen tragedy could have been prevented. But once the decision was made to use lethal force it would have been heresy for a senior leader to even hint at having second thoughts. In typical Communist Party fashion, an official report was eventually issued by Beijing mayor and politburo member, Chen Xitong. The report was a justification for the use of the People's Liberation Army to silence the protestors. In 1995, Mr. Chen was given a sixteen-year prison sentence on a corruption charge and was granted medical parole in 2006. In June 2012, a book was released in Hong Kong written by former senior Communist Party advisor Yao Jiangfu entitled *Conversations with Chen Xitong*. The book caused consternation among Beijing leaders because Mr. Chen is the first senior leader associated with the Tiananmen decision to break ranks with his former comrades. In the book he denies having written the official report on Tiananmen and says that he was ordered to read it out in public. In short, his colleagues used him as the fall guy. He also denies the corruption charge and contends that it was used to get rid of him in a party struggle. Most important, he expresses regrets about the Tiananmen massacre. The book quotes him as saying, "As the mayor, I felt sorry. I hoped we could have solved the case peacefully. Looking back, I consider [the massacre] a tragedy that could have been prevented, should have been prevented, but was not prevented."[7] Chen Xitong died at the age of eighty-three in June, 2013 only three days before the 24th anniversary of the Tiananmen massacre.

The Cause and Effects of Tiananmen

The sense of nationhood is created by the culture, and states are created by politics. As a nation-state during the past four thousand years, China has been a strong nation, but a weak state. This is not surprising given the size, diversity, complexity and history of the country. During the last century of the Qing dynasty and Manchu rule, the weakness of the political system became painfully apparent. Throughout the nineteenth century, the monarch, government and millions of Chinese felt their glorious country had been violated and humiliated by foreign powers. Russia and the Western countries (including the United States) wrested favorable trade agreements and forced the government to accept enclaves in the major cities which were virtually self-governing territories occupied by foreign nationals. In addition, foreign Christian missionaries were rapidly spreading an alien religion and gaining millions of converts. Most Chinese have a keen sense of history and to this day the leaders remember these decades of humiliation as though it were yesterday.

To make matters worse, during the past two centuries China was convulsed by two periods of virtual anarchy which almost brought the country to its knees. The first was the Taiping Rebellion (1850–1864) led by a messianic leader who claimed to be the younger brother of Jesus Christ. He succeeded in mobilizing millions of Christian converts to his cause. The goal of the rebellion was to replace the Qing dynasty with a new "Heavenly Kingdom of Great Peace." There were tens of millions killed during the rebellion, and at the height of the conflict, Taiping forces controlled most of southern and central China.

The second was the Cultural Revolution (1966–1976) inspired by Mao Zedong and his third wife, Jiang Qing. The purpose was to mobilize the Chinese youth to engage in class struggle to rid the country of all "bourgeois values." Like the dreaded Khmer Rouge of Cambodia a decade later, Mao thought most of the hated bourgeoisie were found in the cities and the true proletariat were the peasants residing in the countryside. The young Red Guard leading the revolt split into camps. Violence erupted and the country was thrust into chaos. There were mass relocations of people. Torture and incarceration were common and a million Chinese lost their lives. Unlike the distant memory of the Taiping Rebellion, most

Tiananmen Square, Beijing, 1989.

of the senior Party leaders in 1989 had lived through the horrors of the Cultural Revolution — especially Deng Xiaoping. True, the makeup of the Tiananmen protestors was quite different from the previous rebellions. Initially the protestors were the educated and privileged offspring of the new Chinese middle class. They were later joined by those of all walks of life. But there was the deep and abiding fear among most of the leaders that the prolonged and ever-increasing size of the civil disturbance in Beijing would lead to the mobilization of hysterical hordes who would rampage the country and destroy law, order and the Party.

Some months after Tiananmen, I had a chat with a senior Party official who likened China to a huge vessel filled to the brim with a liquid. "Only a slight tilt of the vessel," he said, "would disturb the liquid thus spilling a large quantity." A tendency toward "turmoil" has always been present in China, he contended, and any movement could tip the vessel and must be nipped in the bud with a resolute hand. In the foreseeable future, he maintained that the Communist Party must be preserved in order to hold the country together. He made a point, but I will never agree that lethal force was either wise or necessary.

There has been a recent revival of Confucius (551 B.C.–479 B.C.) and his teachings in China as evidenced at the spectacular opening ceremony of the 2008 Beijing Olympics. The genius of Confucius was not that he created Chinese culture, but rather that he was able to synthesize and distill the culture into rules and principles. The cardinal principle of Confucianism is to create and maintain harmony — harmony between spouses, a father and his children, a superior and subordinate in the work place, and, above all, the emperor and his subjects. Through the expansion of economic opportunities, the current communist leadership strives diligently to maintain harmony in the country. It is useful to have the teachings of Confucius on hand to confirm the value of their efforts.

Unfortunately, Tiananmen evolved into a Greek tragedy. When the students first occupied the Square, they were disciplined and voiced demands such as better student housing, more tolerance for free expression and transparency on the part of the government, and taking visible steps to stop government corruption. Party leaders were not surprised the students would seize the opportunity of Hu Yabang's death to stage a demonstration. Previous experience led them to believe it would blow over in a few days. But as the protests became an occupation of the Square and continued for weeks with no end in sight, the student leadership became restive, befuddled and indecisive. This in turn widened the gulf between the hard-liners led by Li Peng and the moderates led by Zhao Ziyang. As time went on, the voice of the protestors became more strident and their demands more unrealistic. Factions started to appear, the crowd was joined by outsiders who had their own axe to grind, and no one was empowered to speak for the group as a whole, thus making it difficult for the leaders to find a person or small group to sit down and hammer out a deal. The leadership role of the students was seriously weakened. Hence, after a month-long standoff, the hard-liners seized the opportunity to make their move during Zhao Ziyang's absence from the country, and, regrettably, the rest is history.

The most dramatic difference between Tiananmen and previous rebellions and civil disturbances is that it was converted from a domestic event into a global spectacle. The foreign press was limited and tightly controlled during the Cultural Revolution. This was not so for Tiananmen. Thanks to reporters like Nicholas Kristof and Sheryl WuDunn of the *New York Times*, Mike Chinoy of CNN Television, and Daniel Southerland of the *Washington Post*, millions throughout the world read their newspapers every day and sat glued to their television sets devouring every last morsel of news from Beijing.

As the Communist Party leaders became more clumsy and heavy-handed, the outside world's attitude toward the protestors evolved from sympathy to concern, to grief, and finally outrage. Chinese leaders, especially the old guard, saw this as foreign interference in an internal matter. For them, foreign reaction to Tiananmen brought to mind the humiliation of the country at the hands of foreigners a century before. In discussions Henry Kissinger had with Deng Xiaoping months after Tiananmen, Deng's recurring theme was that China will never knuckle under to "bullying" tactics by foreign governments, be it lectures on human rights, economic sanctions or even the threat of war.[8] Tiananmen had an enormous negative impact on China's foreign relations. Fortunately, the U.S. had a president at the time, George H.W. Bush, who had a thorough knowledge of China. Bush was compelled to impose economic sanctions, but he was careful to avoid any measures which would cause irreparable damage to the U.S. relationship with China. However, there are members of the U.S. Congress who still view China through a Tiananmen filter and harbor a deep dislike for the Communist Party and its leadership.

From the time of Mao's death in September 1976, until June 4, 1989, Deng Xiaoping was the most admired communist leader of all time, especially in Western Europe and North America. He saved his country. He was filled with wisdom and good cheer and loved to strike an appealing pose. Who can forget that photo of him wearing a cowboy hat at a Houston rodeo during his U.S. visit in 1979? This image was seriously tarnished after Tiananmen and only time will tell if it its luster will ever be restored outside China. Within China, it is a totally different story. One can still find billboards displaying his face and famous quotations. Most educated Chinese feel that some day Deng will emerge from the pages of history as a leader even more important than Mao. However, some Chinese will temper their admiration of Deng when they recall his ruthless approach to suppressing political dissent long before Tiananmen — the Anti-Rightist Campaign of 1957 and the Democracy Wall purge of 1976.

It is difficult to gauge the after shock and lingering effects of Tiananmen. There was domestic news coverage on events associated with Tiananmen, but there was no coverage of the fateful night of June 3. Therefore, those outside Beijing were left wondering how the "turmoil" was resolved. It does not seem to be a topic that preys on most people's minds. China has a huge population of youth and most of them know nothing about Tiananmen.

Tiananmen was an urban event which directly touched the lives of a small socioeconomic elite living in Beijing however it had a ripple effect in other cities including Chengdu, Xian and Wuhan where there were similar student protests. Within three years after Tiananmen, economic reforms were back in vogue and the spendable income and living conditions of those in the urban areas along the east coast improved dramatically during the next decade. The new prosperous middle class can spend its money as it pleases, travel abroad, buy a new home and send its children to universities anywhere in the world. The Party leaders have become convinced that continued economic improvements will tame the rebellious spirit of the city dwellers. So far the strategy seems to be working. As Earl Drake, former Canadian Ambassador to China, points out, either the death of Zhao Ziyang in 2005, or the twentieth anniversary of Tiananmen in 2009, would have provided a logical occasion for protestors to gather and express their grief and discontent — but this did not happen. True, there were police patrolling the Square on those dates, but no attempts were made to organize a rally.

My own thought is that there remains a hard-core group of intellectuals in the fine arts and social sciences who harbor strong feelings of discontent over corruption and the lack of the rule of law, human rights and transparency in the political system. They occasionally speak out and are arbitrarily incarcerated. Thus far their remarks have not sparked a larger public outcry.

Most Chinese may not be clamoring for more democracy, but they have a keen sense of justice and fair play. They will not stand by idly when they see their rights and those of others trampled by arbitrary and unfair actions taken against them by the government, the Party and employers. Even an uneducated peasant is aware of local government and Party officials who are engaged in corruption. This knowledge makes them sufficiently angry to band together and make their feelings known. For example, there have been several corrupt local officials assassinated by lynch mobs reminiscent of the old American West. In short, Tiananmen has moved to the rural areas and smaller cities with a decidedly violent twist. There are now more than 100,000 protests throughout the country each year. Often these protests focus on corrupt government officials colluding with private developers in selling public land for a pittance. Social unrest is on the rise and someday it will threaten the authority of the Communist Party.

Indeed, Tiananmen caused the dragon to stumble, but it did not fall. The next chapter will describe its slow recovery.

7

China—The Dragon Recovers

Starting Over

At the Fourth Plenum of the 13th Central Committee of the Communist Party of China in June 1989, Zhao Ziyang was excommunicated from the Party. At the same meeting Jiang Zemin replaced Zhao as Party General Secretary. Zhao was the biblical scapegoat for the Tiananmen debacle and his former friends and party comrades heaped their sins on him and sent him to the desert. The word desert in Spanish means a place of solitude. For Zhao this place was behind the high walls of his courtyard home where he remained under house arrest for the remainder of his life. For the foreseeable future, the Party will not allow the good name and reputation of Zhao Ziyang to be restored, but I predict some day Zhao will be regarded as one of the finest leaders in modern Chinese history.

Some historians of China believe Zhao had the potential to become a great political reformer, but during the Tiananmen crisis, he dithered instead of taking effective action and inexplicably allowed himself to be sent off to North Korea at the most critical juncture. Perhaps Zhao could have been more decisive, but first he had to win over his enemies on the Politburo and in the end, he could not do so because they were too numerous and well-placed. Relationships among members of the Politburo are not just political. They are intensely personal and some like Premier Li Peng took delight in engineering Zhao's down-fall.

I see Zhao as a political martyr who suffered the injustices of the Party he led. He was betrayed by his colleagues and mentor and was cut down during the prime of his leadership. As he commented to Mikhail Gorbachev (as noted in the previous chapter), he had serious doubts about the absolute power of the Communist Party and knew a one-party system could not have "effective control over negative phenomena and fight corruption." In addition, he felt that a one-party system would not "insure the development of democracy." In his secret journal, *Prisoner of the State,* published in Hong Kong in 2009, Zhao elaborates on these issues and concludes China should evolve into a parliamentary democracy. Finally, history shows that had Zhao's advice been followed in addressing the Tiananmen crisis, a major national calamity could have been averted. In this case Zhao the student demonstrated wisdom that the teacher Deng Xiaoping lacked.

Richard Nixon is also a tragic figure of history. He too was cut down in his prime, but it was done by his own hand. His flaws were personal and should be separated from his role as a visionary world leader. Many Chinese predict that some day the Nixon presidency will be reassessed and Richard Nixon will be admired as one of the great world leaders of the twentieth century. It's not likely that I will be around to witness these developments, but I am curious to know who will be rehabilitated first.

Jiang Zemin was an enigma when he assumed his leadership post. His Party record was spotless. He was a committed communist since the age of seventeen, but was much too young to prove his mettle as a revolutionary slogging along the road with Mao and Deng on the Long March. Jiang is a perfect example of a new type of technocrat who now runs the country. He holds a degree in electrical engineering and worked as a trainee at an auto plant in Moscow. He rose through the ranks in the Party holding industrial and technical jobs eventually becoming the mayor and Party secretary of Shanghai. These are two very important positions, but he was located some distance from Beijing which is the seat of power. He is still a respected member of the "Shanghai mafia." But in 1989, he lacked a power base in Beijing. It did not matter — he was hand-picked by Deng for the job.

In the foreign community, being close to Deng was normally viewed as a major plus. But in the aftermath of Tiananmen, China was ostracized by the rest of the world and Deng was viewed as a bitter old man who unleashed the troops on the defenseless students. Within the Party, however, Deng's endorsement was still of paramount importance. In any event, Jiang was seen by foreigners as a part of the clique of heartless hardliners led by Premier Li Peng who condemned Zhao Ziyang as a "party splitter" because they thought his economic and political views almost destroyed the Party. When divining tea leaves and attempting to understand the mysteries of the Communist Party, it is wise to look beneath the surface and attempt to determine how the party really works. There is an old adage popular in U.S. congressional circles which says: "To get along you must go along." This adage may not be embraced by the so-called Tea Party Republicans in the U.S. House of Representatives, but it is still fully applicable to the Communist Party of China. Jiang would have been a fool to buck the party leaders who put him in office. But this did not mean that he would forever be comfortable with his hard-line colleagues. Once Deng made his famous trip to the South to reset his policies of economic liberalization, Jiang became far less cautious, started to change his image, and became the new proponent of the "Socialist Market Economy."

Whatever one thought of Jiang's political and economic proclivities, he is unlike any of the leaders who preceded him. He is comfortable with foreigners and the media. He is jovial and possesses a rich sense of humor. He is a gifted story teller. He is fluent in English, Russian and Romanian. While in office, he was not shy about singing karaoke at informal international gatherings. Once Jiang's position within the party was secured, he proved to be a highly effective leader. My first meeting with him came a few months after he assumed office and the topic under discussion was the controversial Chinese population program.

The Truth About the UN Population Program

Without question the most controversial United Nations program in the annals of the U.S. government is the China program of the United Nations Population Fund. Many still refer to this organization by its original name — UN Fund for Population Activities (UNFPA), which was the name used when I served in China. During the last two years of the Reagan Administration (1986–1988), four years of the George H.W. Bush Administration and eight years of the George W. Bush Administration, the U.S. government withheld all contributions to UNFPA. This action was based on false reports that UNFPA was assisting the Chinese government in the implementation of draconian population policies including coerced abortion and forced sterilization. In truth, the Chinese government was certainly guilty, but not UNFPA.[1]

In 1979 the Chinese government started the so-called one child policy — limiting most Chinese couples to one child. During the next fifteen years there were numerous cases of coerced abortions and sterilization of impoverished Chinese with mental disabilities. In 1983 UNFPA made the unforgivable mistake of awarding the Population Gold Medal Award to Qian Xinzong, the head of the Chinese family planning program. UNFPA's mistake was compounded the following year when Qian was fired for alienating thousands of Chinese by his zealotry in the enforcement of his brutal policies. This costly and outrageous blunder by UNFPA caused members of Congress and the Reagan Administration to reassess U.S. funding to the organization. The new UNFPA Executive Director, Dr. Nafis Sadik of Pakistan, took office in 1987, and tried desperately to convince Washington that the harsh methods used by the Chinese were completely antithetical to the principles and policies of UNFPA. But it was too late. The Reagan Administration started the practice of withholding the contributions and this practice continued for fourteen years thereafter. The major donors in Western Europe and Japan continued to fund the work of UNFPA, but the absence of a $30 million annual contribution by the U.S. left a sizeable lacuna in the program.

In addition to my roles as UNDP Resident Representative and UN Resident Coordinator, I also served as the Representative of UNFPA, a demanding assignment to which I attached a high priority. In the summer of 1989, Executive Director Nafis Sadik requested that I arrange a meeting for her with General Secretary Jiang Zemin on her next visit to the country. Jiang's claim to fame in Shanghai was his recommendation to establish a special economic zone across the Huangpu River opposite the Bund. It is called Pudong and is now the wealthiest ($17,000 per capita GDP) and fastest growing area in metropolitan Shanghai. Cows were grazing on farmland in this same area when Delores and I made our first official visit to Shanghai after our arrival in 1988. In 2013, Pudong will attract millions of Chinese annually when the new Disney Theme Park is opened.

A day after Dr. Sadik's arrival, I picked her up at the hotel and we headed for the mysterious area of the city adjacent to the Forbidden City called Zhongnanhai for our meeting with the General Secretary. Zhongnanhai is a new Forbidden City and most of the office buildings and private residences in the area were built after the 1949 Revolution to house the senior leaders of the Communist Party. Like the Forbidden City, which served as the imperial compound for 500 years during the Ming and Qing Dynasties, Zhongnanhai is enclosed by a high wall. It is a tightly controlled security area and is off limits to the average Chinese.

Jiang was well-briefed and was especially aware of my American nationality. Shortly after we were seated, he asked me if I admired Abraham Lincoln. When I responded in the affirmative, he recited the entire Gettysburg Address by memory in flawless English! I literally applauded his effort and he then said, "Mr. Morey, I know you are here to discuss the population program, but I know you are also the UNDP Resident Representative. I am a member of the UNDP alumni because when I was Mayor of Shanghai, UNDP funded a series of visits I made to special economic zones in Asia and Europe. I will never forget your assistance." I replied, "Mr. General Secretary, perhaps your UNDP funded experience led you to recommend a new special economic zone in Shanghai." He retorted, "The funding was essential to my recommending the creation of Pudong which some day will be one of China's most important areas of commerce."

The General Secretary then turned his attention to Nafis Sadik and said, "Let's discuss

General Secretary of the Chinese Communist Party Jiang Zemin meeting with UNFPA Executive Director Nafis Sadik and the author, 1989.

population." He then went on to explain that it was necessary for China to make a strong effort to curb population growth to correct misguided policies of the past. He said that Mao believed that an ever-expanding population was required to provide a labor force to sustain his plans for industrial development. For many years birth control was condemned and the import of contraceptives was forbidden. He concluded by saying that the leaders now recognize that the country was becoming overpopulated with too many mouths to feed, too many babies to care for, and too many unemployed youth searching for work.

In her reply to the General Secretary, Sadik said that UNFPA was pleased to participate in China's population program, but she added that certain practices were being used to enforce the program which UNFPA opposed. She specifically mentioned the use of a cheap ($.04) but highly effective and uncomfortable steel-ring IUD (intrauterine device), coerced abortions, forced sterilization and the use of sonograms to determine the sex of a fetus resulting in the decision to abort females. She added that UNFPA is not only involved in population programs, but is the world's leading advocate for women's reproductive rights. Coercing abortions, sterilization or using any other means to overrule a woman's right to make reproductive decisions is a serious violation of her human rights. She concluded by noting that no funding from UNFPA could be used for such purposes in China or any other country. She was polite, but crystal clear in her message, and after the meeting I complimented her for having the courage to address such sensitive topics.

During my tenure in China, I visited women's sex education classes, prenatal care clinics, condom factories and a variety of other activities which were receiving UNFPA assistance. Never once did I find a case where there was even a hint of UNFPA support for practices condemned by Nafis Sadik in her message to President Jiang Zemin. Yet the detractors in Washington continued to destroy the positive image of the organization. A year after Sadik's first visit, I helped organize a visit to China by a group of congressional staff members concerned about the relationship between the government program and UNFPA. The staffers had free rein to visit any project they wished, examine UNFPA project expenditures and speak with both recipients and providers of the government program. The group returned to Washington and compiled a report which indicated that they found UNFPA funds were used to assist sex education courses, dissemination of prenatal care information and a national campaign to distribute condoms free of charge. But they found no evidence, whatever, of using UNFPA funds for coercing abortions, forced sterilization or any other unacceptable means of enforcing the government policy. Their report was ignored by the anti–UNFPA group on Capitol Hill and the misguided campaign against UNFPA continued unabated.

The UN Population Fund received a reprieve during the Clinton Administration until the Republicans gained control of the Congress in 1996. President George W. Bush announced his opposition to funding UNFPA as soon as he took office in 2001. In 1992, Secretary of State Colin Powell ordered an independent mission be sent to China to investigate UNFPA's involvement in the use of brutal methods of enforcing the country's population program. The report of this mission presented by retired Ambassador William Brown contained the following:

First Finding

We find no evidence that UNFPA has knowingly supported or participated in the management of a program of coercive abortion or involuntary sterilization in the PRC.

First Recommendation

We, therefore, recommend that not more than $34 million, which has already been appropriated, be released to UNFPA.

Apparently Secretary Powell was swayed by the report, but the Bush White House brushed it aside and continued to block UNFPA funding for the next seven years. In 2009 the Obama Administration voiced a desire to work with Congress to reinstate UNFPA funding. Fortunately, the President was successful and eventually secured an appropriation of $40 million as the U.S. contribution to UNFPA. However, in 2012, funding for UNFPA was eliminated by the Republican-controlled House of Representatives. The Republicans remain delusional about UNFPA. The 2012 national Republican Party platform states, "The United Nations Population Fund has a shameful record of collaboration with China's program of compulsory abortion."

In May 2011, the United Nations Population Division issued a sobering report indicating that the world's population will likely reach 10.1 billion by the end of the century representing an increase of more than three billion from the current level of seven billion. Obviously sound and sensible family planning efforts are required throughout the developing world now more than ever. This is especially true in India which will replace China as the world's most populous country by the end of the century. UNFPA will be needed more than ever. But this organization, which is the world's most respected advocate for women's rights and the most effective purveyor of humane, sound and sensible family planning methods, still does not receive the congressional support it deserves from the richest country on earth.

Getting Back in Gear

For the first six months after Tiananmen, a foreboding cloud of recrimination, intimidation and retrenchment hovered over Beijing. Some dissidents fled the country and others were incarcerated. Ceremonies were held to celebrate the PLA's victory over the "evil forces bent on destroying the country." A special medal was struck and awarded to the PLA soldiers who cleared Tiananmen Square. A number of government departments and agencies were in a state of near paralysis wondering which programs would be eliminated or de-emphasized. For the UNDP projects with a technical orientation such as the major water study of Northern China, it was business as usual and full speed ahead. But for our projects dealing with public policy including major projects on economic reform with the Chinese Academy of Social Science and the State Council, some of our Chinese project directors disappeared and we were told they were transferred or had taken ill. In the spring of 1992, after Deng's celebrated trip to the South, several former project directors resurfaced including one of the nation's leading economists who greeted me warmly and reported that he had recovered from his "heart ailment." As mentioned in a previous chapter, the exciting UNDP project with the Communist Party School was terminated after the Tiananmen crisis never to reappear.

Tiananmen placed a severe strain on China's relations with the rest of the world. Economic sanctions were imposed on China by the U.S. and other Western countries. For one year the country was shunned and ostracized. During these gloomy days, the government was searching for a project or event which would demonstrate that China was back in business and wished to mend its frayed ties with other countries. UNDP provided the perfect answer. We proposed sponsoring a senior level International Conference on Central Banking.

Chinese Foreign Minister Qian Qichen conferring with the author, Beijing, 1990.

Chinese President Yang Shangkun greets the author at the UN Day Reception, October 14, 1990.

We asked the International Monetary Fund (IMF) to collaborate with us. During the summer before the conference was held, I was in Washington and spent several hours at IMF headquarters plotting the strategy for the conference. We knew the Chinese were expecting a grand production and we knew that a star-studded group of current or former central bankers was required to attract international attention. We agreed immediately that the headliner should be Paul Volcker, former Chairman of the U.S. Federal Reserve (Fed). The idea was to approach Volcker first and if he accepted, we would allow him to choose two other prominent central bankers. We hit the jackpot. Volcker accepted and chose Miguel Mancera, Governor of the Bank of Mexico, who was the most respected central banker in the developing world, and Jean Godeaux, the most highly regarded central banker in Europe, who was former Governor of the National Bank of Belgium and former President of the Bank for International Settlements.

The Chinese government pulled out all stops in hosting the conference which was held in January 1990, at the Diaoyutai State Guesthouse which is normally reserved for heads of state. I co-chaired the conference along with the Deputy Managing Director of the IMF and the Governor of the People's Bank of China, the country's central bank. Volcker was clearly the star of the conference and the one most in demand for interviews with the Chinese and foreign press. In his comments, Volcker especially emphasized that any central bank must be independent within the government. The leadership and staff must be at the highest level of competence and professionalism and must not be involved in partisan politics. (This latter admonition no doubt is difficult for the People's Bank of China to follow.)

The conference was viewed by everyone involved as an enormous success. The IMF used the proceedings of the conference to publish a book entitled *Perspectives on the Role of a Central Bank* which is still available for sale on Amazon.com. The conference was used by the Chinese to announce that the country was back on track and welcomed foreign investment and improved economic relations with the rest of the world, especially the U.S. and Western Europe. Most important, the conference established a new relationship between the People's Bank of China and UNDP. It led to several projects in which UNDP provided funding for training and advisory services was which led to a strengthened Central Bank much along the lines recommended by Paul Volcker.

The Case of Mr. X

During my assignment in China, I was on the phone frequently with Kofi Annan. During Tiananmen, I contacted him in his capacity as Security Coordinator of the UN System. Otherwise, he contacted me as the head of the UN Personnel Office. It was in this latter capacity that he phoned me a few months after my arrival in Beijing. He said, "As you know, Mr. Morey, it is a flagrant violation of UN rules and practices for a member state to hold UN staff members against their will including their own nationals." He then proceeded to brief me on the situation. To preserve the privacy of the staff member, he will be referred to as Mr. X.

At the time, Mr. X was serving as a Chinese to English language interpreter and translator in the UN offices in Geneva. He met an Italian physician and they had a child out of wedlock. He returned to Shanghai with his Italian partner and child to be reunited with his parents and to become wed. Two weeks later, when the family attempted to board an aircraft for the return flight to Geneva, his new wife and child were allowed to board; but Mr. X was prevented from doing so by state security agents. Shortly thereafter, his wife, pregnant with a second child, decided to return to her home in Rome. Annan warned me that he had lodged a complaint with the Chinese Ambassador to the UN in New York and I should be prepared to be called to the Foreign Ministry to discuss the matter.

As anticipated, I was requested to meet with an assistant minister. I was in hopes I would be meeting with my counterpart, the kind and gentle Li Daoyu, but no such luck. Instead I was ushered into the office of a character straight out of Arthur Koestler's classic on totalitarianism, *Darkness at Noon*. The senior official was tall, slender and spoke English in a high pitched voice. He was aggressive and devoid of all social graces. Rather than a discussion, I was given a lecture which is exactly what drives the Chinese up the wall when it is delivered to them by a westerner. In a staccato style, the officer read a list of charges against Mr. X who was accused of being a liar and a bigamist. Most important, the officer said that Mr. X was a foreign service officer temporarily assigned to the UN and he had sullied the good name of the Chinese Foreign Service by his immoral behavior. He concluded this unpleasant experience by noting that as far as the Chinese government was concerned, Mr. X was still a foreign service officer and not a UN employee.

The contradictions and inconsistencies in any communist system are so numerous that it is difficult to know where to start. One of the most amusing and glaring incongruities is the issue of sexual morality. Mao Zedong lived in a veritable pleasure palace where he had access to girls and young women he used to satisfy his carnal desires. Yet here was Mr. X being held against his will because he had a child out of wedlock. I knew there had to be more to the story, and fortunately I had his telephone number.

Years ago there was a practice in all communist countries for the government to demand that their nationals working in the UN share a portion of their salary with the government. Therefore, the first question I asked Mr. X was whether he was sharing his salary with the government. When he replied that he had stopped the practice shortly after arriving in Geneva, I then asked him if he thought this was a major reason for his detention. He retorted, "I don't know if it is a major reason, but it is certainly a major irritant to the government." He informed me that the bigamy charge was a complete fabrication and concluded by saying that now that his wife and child were in Rome, he wanted to give up his position in Geneva and take a job with one of the UN organizations based in Rome.

After reporting back to Kofi Annan, I had a second meeting with "Mr. Personality" at the Foreign Ministry. When I informed him that Mr. X wanted to vacate his post in Geneva and find employment with a UN organization in Rome, he flew into a rage and proclaimed in a loud voice (very un–Chinese) that that would never happen. But Mr. X's wife, being a smart and determined woman, had a brilliant idea to break the deadlock. She went to the Chinese Embassy in Rome and announced that when her second child was due, she planned to rent an ambulance, park it in front of the embassy, and camp out until the baby was born. She then briefed the international press corps on her plans and her story was front page coverage in Italy's leading newspapers.

Fortunately, Mr. X had told me about his wife's scheme and I was not surprised to be summoned to the Foreign Ministry. My interlocutor was in a foul mood because he knew the government was forced to back down. His main message was, "Mr. Morey, Mr. X has forty-eight hours to leave this country and not a minute more. Furthermore, we do not want any press coverage of his arrival at the Rome airport." I replied that I would have him out of the country within the prescribed time frame, but I had no control over press arrangements at the Rome airport.

I quickly returned to my office, called Mr. X and told him to pack his bags and meet me at my office by 11 A.M. the following morning. I had kept the Italian Ambassador informed of every detail of the case and he assured me that he would open the embassy on a Saturday (the following day) and Mr. X would have a visa within an hour. He also promised to notify his Foreign Ministry so that proper arrangements could be made at the airport. The next day Mr. X had his visa by noon. We returned to my office for a champagne toast. My driver took him to the airport and he caught an Alitalia flight to Rome that afternoon. As expected, there was enormous press coverage of his arrival with his pregnant wife on hand to give press interviews to anyone who would listen. The game was over and I was not called into the Foreign Ministry for another lecture on the case.

When Mr. X's case came before the UN Human Rights Commission, the Chinese representative disguised the truth by engaging in a perfect example of "doublespeak." In his prepared statement the representative said:

> China has made it clear that Mr. X was free to leave China when the matter of his resignation from the United Nations was settled.... The problem of Mr. X is neither one of a political nature nor of a violation of human rights. China does not deprive any of the rights to which he is entitled. Now some people are going about and making appeals on his behalf.... This is evidently aimed at politicizing this question. If the practices of those of Mr. X's are to be protected as human rights, it will only be a mockery to human rights.

Shortly after Mr. X arrived in Rome, he joined the staff of the United Nations World Food Council and he is now serving in the United Nations Secretariat in New York.

Romancing the Hermit Kingdom

Perhaps the last great frontier in the world is Northeast Asia. This sub-region borders the Japan Sea and includes the east coast of South Korea (Republic of Korea, ROK), North Korea (Democratic People's Republic of Korea, DPRK), Siberia (Russian Federation), Northeast China (Manchuria) and Eastern Mongolia. It contains more than 114 million people (primarily in China) with a land area of 787,000 miles (1.27 million km). The epicenter of this sub-region is the Tumen River which flows out of China and forms the trilateral international border of China, Russia and North Korea.

For millennia, this frozen and remote area remained virtually untouched despite its endowment of some of the world's largest reserves of oil, natural gas, timber, minerals, seafood and farm land. During the seventeenth and eighteenth centuries, Qing emperors considered Manchuria (Northeast China) as a wilderness area suitable for hunting wild game. During most of the Qing Dynasty, China claimed all of the hinterland of Mongolia as well as most of the Siberian coastline along the Japan Sea. But the Qing emperors were incredibly weak when confronted by superior foreign military powers. A treaty was signed with Russia in 1858 (Treaty of Aihun), which allowed China navigation rights down the Tumen River to the sea, but ceded the entire Siberian coast to Russia. China was no longer a Japan Sea littoral state which is still the case today. One would think that China would have renegotiated this treaty during the past 150 years, but conditions were never favorable to do so. In the pre–World War II period, nationalist forces and the Red Army were preoccupied in a civil war. When World War II ended, Chiang Kai-shek's government was in charge and he did not press the USSR on the point because Mao and the Red Army controlled Manchuria. The Korean War then intervened and a decade later China and the USSR became bitter enemies. By 1991, Sino-Soviet relations were improved and China's navigation rights to the sea through the Tumen River were restored.

Among the three riparian countries on the Tumen River, China was most in need of a major port on the Japan Sea. China was very interested to find some type of collaborative arrangement to develop Northeast Asia. Therefore, it came as no surprise that my Chinese government counterpart, YT Long, scheduled a meeting with me in the fall of 1990, to report on a conference that had been held in Jilin province in Northeast China. The main conclusion of the conference was that China should take the lead in consulting with North Korea, the Soviet Union, Mongolia and South Korea to explore the feasibility of establishing an international initiative for developing the Tumen River area. The conference also felt that some time in the years ahead, Japan should be given observer status in any type of new arrangement. The conference further concluded that UNDP would be the logical international organization to assist these countries in such an effort. I expressed an immediate positive response to the proposal of formulating a UNDP regional project. I had just read a report indicating that the Far Eastern Region of the USSR (the Russian Federation since 1991) may hold 35 percent of the world's natural gas reserves. I was fully aware of the strategic economic importance of the region.

However, I curbed my enthusiasm slightly when I thought about the politically sensitive relationship among the countries involved. China did not have diplomatic relations at the time with South Korea and its icy relations with the USSR were just beginning to thaw. In 1990, South Korea did not have diplomatic relations with either the USSR or China and there was not yet a non-aggression pact between the two Koreas. North Korea (dubbed the Hermit Kingdom) was and still is a petulant and reclusive state with diplomatic relations with only China, Mongolia and the USSR at the time. I commented to YT Long that I thought something might work if the economic positives were strong enough to overcome the political negatives. We both agreed that North Korea was key to any type of arrangement.[2] We also agreed that romancing the Hermit Kingdom would be our highest priority. Long suggested that we visit Pyongyang before the end of the year. He assured me that Delores and I could travel to DPRK on my UN Laissez Passer which included Delores's name, photograph and marital status and suggested we leave our U.S. passports at home. The UNDP resident representative in Pyongyang, Henning Karcher, was most helpful in making our arrangements.

And so, in early December 1990, Delores and I boarded a North Korean train to commence our 870 mile (1400 km) journey to Pyongyang. Our rail car was clean and relatively new and was constructed in East Germany. The compartments had the same configuration as Chinese rail cars with four passengers sharing a compartment. We traveled with YT and his assistant and we all agreed it would be strictly non-smoking. A few hours out of Beijing the countryside was covered with snow as we started into the area formerly called Manchuria. During Japanese occupation (1932–1945), the area was called Manchukuo. Midway on the trip, we rounded a bend and could see the industrial city of Benxi in the distance. At the time Benxi was the most polluted city in China and, like the character "pig pen" out of the American comic strip *Peanuts*, there was a perpetual cloud of smog over the city. At mid-day, the sun was shining in a clear blue sky before entering the city. When we arrived at the Benxi station a few minutes later, it appeared that dusk had already started to settle. Ten minutes out of Benxi, it was bright and sunny once again as we traveled through pure white snow. Fortunately, if a visit were made to Benxi today, one would find the air relatively clean thanks to a major environmental initiative launched by UNDP and the government of China in 1994 called, Agenda 21. Since then, Benxi has spent nearly $50 million on air pollution abatement.

When we crossed the famous Yalu River into North Korea, we saw large chunks of ice floating in the river and I was reminded of photographs of the American advance into the north during the Korean War. No doubt, Delores and I were among the first Americans to be welcomed into North Korea since the end of the Korean War in 1953. We arrived in Pyongyang in the evening after an exhausting twenty-nine hours on the train. We were met at the station by Mr. Han, our counterpart from the Ministry of Foreign Affairs and taken to the Koryo Hotel in central Pyongyang. The Koryo was constructed in 1985 under the watchful eye of Kim Il-sung and was designed to impress foreigners. It is a twin tower building of forty-three stories. The hotel has 500 rooms and like other monstrous buildings in Pyongyang, it was woefully underutilized.

The streets of Pyongyang are wide and clean, but devoid of traffic because no one can afford a vehicle. There are no traffic lights and traffic is regulated by uniformed policewomen stationed on platforms in the center of the intersections directing traffic (mainly bicycles) in highly robotic-like motions. The first morning at the Koryo, Delores and I were awakened at sunrise by a strange murmuring sound. We opened the window and found it was a voice on a loud speaker broadcasting to large numbers of people trudging to work. We learned that the morning broadcast was used to encourage people to work hard and strengthen their love and devotion for the Great Leader Kim Il Sung. Each time Kim's name was mentioned, the voice quivered with reverence. The whole experience was quite weird and once again, Arthur Koestler's *Darkness at Noon* came to mind.

In North Korea, state security assigns all foreigners a "minder." Since we traveled as a couple, we had one minder for the two of us. He was with us at all times except when we were in a restroom or our hotel room. After the first couple of days we ignored his presence, but on our last day in Pyongyang, we decided to have a little fun. He followed us out of the hotel and Delores went in one direction and I walked in another. After walking 100 feet or so, we both turned around. There he was with a panicked expression on his face glancing in one direction and then the other. Each of us walked for twenty minutes and returned to the hotel from opposite directions. There he stood in a deep quandary waiting for our return. He stuck to us like glue for the remainder of our visit.

All foreigners are expected to start their visit at the birthplace of Kim Il Sung. The home is a peasant style house with a thatched roof located in a Pyongyang suburb. The building looked new and the place is considered a shrine. According to local lore, Kim was born in this house in 1912, and believe it or not, was raised as a Presbyterian. The Japanese gained control of the Korean peninsula in 1910, and their occupation lasted until 1945. When Kim was a child, he fled with his parents to Manchuria to avoid starvation and Japanese cruelty. He eventually joined the Chinese resistance movement against the Japanese, but was forced to flee to the Soviet Union in 1939. He received his political and military education in the USSR. He dressed as an army captain when he returned to Pyongyang in 1945, with the Soviet army to assume control from the Japanese. At the end of the war, Korea was divided at the 38th parallel into two military zones. The Soviet Union administered the north and the U.S. administered the south. Kim was selected by the Soviets to form a government in the north. With no provocation whatever, in June 1950, Kim decided to invade the south with the acquiescence and support of the Soviet Union.

The Korean War was brought to a close in 1953. The outcome was a stalemate and the demilitarized zone along the 38th parallel still separates the two Koreas. For the next forty-one years, Kim Il Sung developed an orthodox communist society and took extraordinary steps to seal off North Korea from any communication with the rest of the world. In addition, he perfected brainwashing as a whole new art form. He built a fantasy land on the backs of twenty-four million impoverished and starving people who still revere him as a demigod. They are convinced that the U.S. and South Korea were the aggressors in the Korean War and the Great Leader saved their country. To this day North Koreans believe their country is under constant threat by South Korea and the United States. For seventeen years, the people relied on the son and successor, Kim Jong-il (the Dear Leader), to protect the country even with the use of nuclear weapons if necessary. Periodically the North Korean government and military have created a military incident with the South to prove to the North Korean people that the government is ever vigilant in keeping the aggressors at bay.

In recent years, Kim Jong-il was in fragile health. He suffered a stroke in 2008, which caused government leaders and Korea observers to speculate on successor arrangements. In September 2010, the question was answered when his son, Kim Jong-un, was unveiled as the successor. In December 2011, Kim Jong-il died suddenly. After thirteen days of national mourning over his death, his young son, Kim Jong-un, believed to be in his mid-twenties, took the reins of leadership. The President of the North Korean Parliament declared, "Respected Comrade Kim Jong-un is now supreme leader of our party, military and people." Only time will tell if this dynastic transfer will endure. To this day most North Koreans are convinced that the South Korean "puppets" and their American master are constantly plotting to destroy their country. This distorted view first developed by Kim Il Sung has been inherited by his grandson Kim Jong-un as he attempts to solidify his position of power. Like his father and grandfather, Kim Jong-un periodically will test weapons and put his military forces on the alert to convince the people that he is ever vigilant to protect them.

In addition to our visit to the Kim Il Sung birthplace, we were taken to numerous other enormous and overwrought structures and monuments all designed to impress foreigners and locals alike that DPRK is an advanced and prosperous country. We were taken to a large ornate structure called The Children's Palace. Each day thousands of uniformed children go to the palace to learn about the Great Leader and his teachings. They also receive training in voice and musical instruments. After our visit to the palace, we were driven to the new (built in 1989) Rungrado May Day Stadium which seats 150,000—the largest stadium capacity in the world. Each year a festival is staged at the stadium over a two-month period to celebrate the birthday of the Great Leader. Some performances involve 100,000 participants and the performance is viewed by 150,000 spectators. The ancient political strategy of "bread and circus" has been carried to a whole new level in North Korea.

Still dominating the skyline of Pyongyang today is the empty shell of the Ryugyong Hotel. Construction started in 1987 and was halted in 1992. It is a three-sided structure of 105 stories and 3000 rooms and is the twenty-second largest skyscraper in the world. It is of such poor design and construction that it is unlikely to ever be completed. Given the minuscule number of tourists who visit North Korea, it was absurd to ever undertake such a project. But Kim Il Sung intended it to be one more impressive structure in his fantasy land. As the economy, particularly the agricultural sector, declined, military spending (25 percent of the national budget) and public works spending increased dramatically.

Next, we were taken to Mansu Hill to pay our respects to a sixty-five foot (twenty meters) bronze statue of the Great Leader. The statue was erected in 1972 to celebrate Kim's sixtieth birthday and tens of thousands still visit the statue on public holidays to honor their hero of heroes. No visit to Pyongyang is complete without a stop at the Tower of Juche erected in 1982. Of course, the tower would have to be constructed three feet taller than the Washington Monument! It contains 25,500 granite blocks, one for each day of Kim's first seventy years. Juche is the philosophy developed by Kim Il-Sung that stresses national autonomy and self reliance and calls for sacrifice, austerity and complete loyalty to the supreme leader. Juche will be found in the curriculum of all schools and universities. In commemoration of Kim's seventieth birthday, an Arch of Triumph was constructed which, of course, is taller than the original in Paris. The cult of personality surrounding Mao during the Cultural Revolution was ubiquitous, but Kim tops it in every respect. Kim's cult of personality is meant to last forever. The 1994 constitution declares Kim Il-Sung as President in Perpetuity thus depriving his son and successor, Kim Jong-il, the title of president. The son assumed many other titles including Supreme Commander of the Korean People's Army which has more than one million in uniform and is the fourth largest army on earth.

Of the five days we spent in Pyongyang, one was devoted to work and four to sightseeing. But our work day was highly successful. YT Long and I were driven to the Foreign Ministry in a government sedan and our minders were in a vehicle close behind. We were greeted in the lobby by our main contact, Mr. Han, who escorted us to a conference room. As in China, meetings are never conducted in a government official's office. Mr. Han was friendly, but apprehensive in meeting me and with good reason. I may have been the first American he had ever met. Long was greeted warmly and with good reason. China is one of the few friends North Korea has in the whole world

Mr. Han had received an advance copy of the UNDP Tumen River project proposal to allow him to discuss it at the highest levels of the government. It may not have been reviewed by President Kim Il Sung, but we knew we were pioneering a whole new course in North Korean foreign policy and we also knew we were treading on very sensitive ground. The involvement of YT Long was critical to DPRK's acceptance of the proposal. He had served in Pyongyang as the UNDP Deputy Resident Representative and he knew the North Koreans well. In addition, DPRK knew that China was strongly in favor of the proposal.

After Mr. Han's welcoming remarks, I started by noting that in addition to assisting countries with their development, another major function of UNDP was to promote inter-country cooperation and hence the reason why UNDP was willing to fund the project. I chose my words carefully in describing the role of the United Nations because I knew that North Korea had mixed feelings toward the organization. On one hand, it places enormous importance on its membership in the UN and the government expended a great effort to gain UN admission in tandem with their bitter enemy, the Republic of Korea. On the other hand, their foe (fourteen UN members led by the U.S.) during the Korean War fought under the authority of the United Nations, and the demilitarized zone is still monitored by the UN command. Years ago, UNDP was welcome to establish an office in Pyongyang, but for the first few years of its existence the resident representative was not allowed to fly the UN flag—the same banner used by the opposing forces in the Korean War.

Early in the discussion, Mr. Han indicated that his country was willing to sit with other countries in the sub-region to negotiate a UNDP project, but that it would reserve its position on the project until a final draft was negotiated. I told him this was a perfectly reasonable position and assured him that the other countries would take a similar stance. I reminded him in the most polite tone possible that the Republic of Korea was a likely signatory to the project and some day in the future Japan could well be invited to join as an observer. Without making reference to any other likely participants, Mr. Han simply restated the position of his government and the meetings came to a successful conclusion. Delores, YT Long and I were jubilant as we rode to the airport the following morning to catch a flight back to Beijing. Romancing the Hermit Kingdom was off to a rousing success, but we still had a long way to go.

Birth of a Much Celebrated Project

The government of China, and YT Long personally, had a major stake in the success of the UNDP regional project. But we agreed early on that the initial meeting needed to launch the project should be held in another participating country. Once we received the green light from DPRK, we brought the other countries on board through our network of UNDP country offices. Mongolia expressed an interest in the project from the very start and extended an invitation to have the first project formulation meeting held in Ulan Bator. In July 1991, UNDP organized the Northeast Asia Sub-Regional Conference. Delores joined me as we boarded a plane to Ulan Bator. The UNDP Resident Representative for Mongolia, Erick de Mul, was immensely helpful in organizing the conference.

The people of Mongolia are charming, friendly and confident. They harbor an intense pride in their history and culture. Unfortunately for them, this national pride has been severely bruised over several centuries. Every school child learns that when Genghis Khan established the Mongol empire in 1206, it covered all of Asia including China and stretched into central Europe. It was the largest land empire in the history of the world. It collapsed in 1368, and by 1700, the Qing Emperor claimed all of the remaining Mongol territory as a part of China. When the Qing Dynasty fell in 1911, the Mongols tried in vain to gain their independence. They went from a rock to a hard place in 1924, when the current state of Mongolia was absorbed into the Soviet Union. For more than six decades Mongolia suffered from a totalitarian political system and disastrous economic policies of the USSR and finally became an independent state when it broke away in 1990. China still retains a large chunk of former Mongol territory which is the Inner Mongolia Autonomous Region in northern China. Mongols comprise seventeen percent of the 24 million people living in Inner Mongolia and this constitutes a larger population than the 2.7 million Mongols living in the country of Mongolia.

The Mongolian government is pragmatic and fortunately does not dwell on the past. The government was pleased to invite China and the Soviet Union to the conference. Of even greater interest was the fact that both North and South Korea accepted their invitations. UNDP succeeded in bringing these competing parties to the same conference table for one of the first peaceful encounters since the end of the Korean War four decades before. UNDP is uniquely positioned to pull off such a coup and there are examples in other parts of the world where the organization has joined adversaries in peaceful pursuits. In short, it does what a UN organization was intended to do when the UN charter was adopted in 1945.

The conference achieved its main objectives and an institutional framework for regional dialogue and economic cooperation in the Tumen River area was established. It was further agreed that UNDP would fund a comprehensive study of the sub-region to be presented at the next meeting of the group of five scheduled to be held in Pyongyang a few months hence. In typical Asian fashion, a dinner was held after the conference to allow participants to mingle informally. The barriers of formality are best broken by an evening filled with drink, song, food and statements of appreciation. My former deputy, Herb Behrstock, had been transferred to New York headquarters and was representing the regional bureau at the conference. After an untold number of beers, Herb and I took our turn in the songfest with our rendition of "Take Me Out to the Ballgame." The highlight was when the Koreans, North and South, embraced, wept and sang traditional Korean folk songs. What a night and what a project!

To ensure all participants had the opportunity to learn about Mongolian history and culture, the Tumen meeting was scheduled to coincide with the national celebration of Naadam (July 11–13). Naadam is the most important festival of the year and is focused on the three traditional sports of wrestling, archery and horse racing. Mongolia has its own style of wrestling and it has been a favorite sporting activity for several thousand years. When we went to the National Sports Stadium to watch a few matches, we were introduced to several of the nation's top wrestlers. We were also invited to join them in sharing a bowl of fermented mare's milk as a part of their preparatory ritual. Mare's milk is definitely an acquired taste! We then traveled to the archery range and were amazed to find archers hitting targets from a distant of 75 meters (246 ft). But the *pièce de résistance* of Naadam is the horse race which is run over open country for 30 km (19 m). The jockeys are children from 5 to 13 years of age. We watched the last two kilometers of the race which was won by an eight-year-old boy. Life for the nomadic Mongols revolves around the horse; children often receive their first horse at three years of age.

In politics and life, timing is everything. When the Ulan Bator, Mongolia meeting was held in July 1991, the informal relations between North and South Korea were never better and a non-aggression pact was signed between the two eight months later; thus the second meeting of the Tumen project held in Pyongyang in October 1991 was filled with hope and goodwill. Unfortunately in 2013, North Korean/South Korean relations reached a nadir when North Korea abrogated the non-aggression pact. The experts hired by UNDP to undertake the comprehensive study presented their findings to the Pyongyang conference. We had encouraged the study team leader to think big and he did not disappoint. In fact, the delegates sat in wonderment as they listened to his report which envisaged an enormous infrastructure plan that would require a $30 billion investment over a twenty year period. It called for a trilateral international Tumen Economic Zone to be jointly administered by China, North Korea and Russia. The zone would service a larger triangular area of 602 miles (10,000 km) stretching from the lower part of northeast China to Chonjin on the eastern coast of North Korea and to Vladivostok, Russia. The UNDP project and the ambitious plan became a top economic news story in Asia and was the cover story of the *Far Eastern Economic Review* in January, 1992.

Enthusiasm for the project was at a peak and the next meeting of the newly created Tumen Program Management Committee (PMC) composed of China, DPRK, Russia, ROK and Mongolia was held in Seoul in February, 1992. The pieces were starting to come together very nicely. One month after the Pyongyang meeting, DPRK established the Rajin-Songbong Free Economic and Trade Zone near the mouth of the Tumen River. The newly established Russian Federation announced that Vladivostok was no longer a restricted military area and was open to outsiders. Hunchun, the main Chinese city on the Tumen River was opened to outsiders and discussions were underway on the establishment of rail and road links in the area.

The South Korean government was determined to make the Seoul meeting a grand event and a group of senior officials traveled the short distance to the demilitarized zone to greet one of the first (if not *the* first) official delegations of North Koreans to ever step foot on South Korean soil. UNDP had a large delegation for the meeting with officers from New York and resident representatives from all five participating countries. When the group of North and South Koreans arrived in Seoul, we all boarded a luxurious high speed train to travel the length of the country to the Port of Pusan which is the fourth largest container port in the world. The North Koreans had never been to the South and they were awe struck to put it mildly. From their birth, they were led to believe that South Korea was a shabby, undeveloped, unhappy place. Their jaws dropped when they saw Seoul. They were amazed by the high speed train. They were totally unprepared to view the Port of Pusan because it makes the main port for Pyongyang look like a relic out of the nineteenth century. Our last stop was Kyongju on the east coast not far from Pusan. It was the capital of the ancient Kingdom of Silla which ruled the Korean peninsula from 57 B.C. to A.D. 935. Kyongju is the most sacred place on the Korean peninsula and is considered the fount of Korean culture for North and South Koreans alike. Members of the DPRK delegation wept as they strolled through the ruins of the ancient capital.

The Tumen River project is still in existence, but much has changed since the glory days of its inception. It is now called the Greater Tumen Initiative (GTI) and the bulk of the funding is provided by the countries. The UNDP portion of the funding is now used mainly to support the participation of the private sector. The GTI is composed of a Consultative Commission, a Secretariat, five boards focusing on transport, tourism, energy and environment, and a Business Advisory Council co-chaired by an American from the private sector. Some years ago the five countries abandoned the idea of an international economic zone in favor of their own special economic zones. Through the years, billions of dollars have been invested in the area in port development, rail lines and roads. Recent surveys indicate that Mongolia has minerals worth $2.7 trillion ($2700 billion). There are vast quantities of uranium, coal, copper, gold and rare earths. Many of these reserves are located in the eastern part of the country. No doubt, a major rail line will be constructed in the years ahead to carry the ore or refined product to a port in the Tumen River area. Foreign investors are flocking to Ulan Bator in droves to invest in the world's last great mining frontier. For several years China contemplated dredging the Tumen to have a major port on Chinese soil, but the idea was scrapped when a feasibility study indicated the cost would be astronomical. Instead the Chinese are making a major investment in North Korea's Rajin-Songbong free port. Someday China and other flag carrier countries will use this port for their container ships and tankers to ply the waters of the Japan Sea. There is also a nearby port in Russia under development.

The major difference today is that the Consultative Commission and subsidiary bodies are composed of only four countries because DPRK withdrew from the project in November, 2009. No doubt it was for political reasons because six months earlier, North Korea withdrew from the Six Party Talks (DPRK, ROK, China, U.S., Russia and Japan) which were designed to encourage DPRK to abandon its nuclear weapons program. DPRK also announced that it was resuming its nuclear program. North Korea's love-hate attitude toward the UN swung to hate because their withdrawal from the Six Party Talks was precipitated by a UN Security Council condemnation of a failed satellite launch by North Korea. Fortunately DPRK's withdrawal from the GTI has not slackened the pace of international cooperation in the sub-region. Perhaps someday DPRK will forsake its self-defeating behavior and return to the Tumen fold.

A project is meant to be like a honey bee — once it strikes, it dies. In the case of the Tumen project, the participants don't want the bee to die, and continue to see the value of UNDP. When I was still serving in the U.S. State Department, I thought countries just wanted the money from UNDP. After joining the organization, I soon learned that the financial assistance was secondary. The major appeal of UNDP is that it is a part of the world's only truly global organization with universal membership. It is viewed as a neutral partner that can mobilize the latest knowledge and most competent advisory services to assist countries to solve problems and bring about change. UNDP is a minor financial contributor to the GTI, yet the governments want it to continue its involvement. It is a pity that some members of Congress who determine the U.S. annual contribution to UNDP are unaware of such an important and improbable project which is now twenty years old and continues to reap an excellent return on investment.

The Threat of AIDS—A Missed Opportunity

Social issues often do not receive world attention until a problem has been discovered in a major developed country. Such was the case with AIDS. There were several AIDS victims treated as early as 1969, but knowledge of the disease was sketchy and some cases took years to confirm. The first case of AIDS reported to the U.S. Center for Disease Control was a man from the San Francisco gay community reported in April, 1980. News of this report and his death a short time later spread instantly throughout the world. Most experts peg this case as the first person to die in the AIDS pandemic that still ravages the world especially in Africa and Asia. Since most early cases of AIDS in the U.S. involved gay men, many thought it was a homosexual disease that was not likely to affect the rest of the population. This assumption proved to be a fatal fallacy especially in China.

My first briefing on AIDS was in 1986 when I was on assignment at UNDP headquarters in New York. It was given by Dr. Jonathan Mann who had just established the World Health Organization's (WHO) Global Program on AIDS. The purpose of his New York visit was to elicit the help of UNDP in the global fight against AIDS. He received an immediate favorable response from our senior management. I was in a small group meeting with him where he gave a blunt and candid summary of how the problem should be approached:

- AIDS should not be treated as a medical issue, but rather as a multi-faceted social issue involving health, economics, politics, security and human rights.
- The UN AIDS program should not be a part of WHO, but rather a separate organization which would involve UNDP, UNICEF, WHO and other organizations.
- At the country level, the health ministry is often the most conservative of all ministries and should not lead a national AIDS program; rather the program should involve numerous ministries and agencies under the management of a senior leader.
- The behavior associated with the spread of AIDS should not be criminalized. If it is, the problem will be driven underground beyond the reach of those who want to help.
- Many government leaders and agencies will be in a state of denial and the UN must find effective and non-threatening ways to break this denial.

Given his views, it is not surprising that Jonathan Mann grew weary and frustrated by the World Health Organization straight-jacket and resigned his post in 1990. Five years later, UNAIDS was created and is the multi-disciplinary type of organization Mann had in mind. He will always be remembered as the founding father of global AIDS prevention. The world AIDS community mourned his death in the crash of a Swissair flight over Nova Scotia in 1998.

Often it takes a personal tragedy to motivate one into action. In the summer of 1990, Delores and I were staying in southern California with our life long friends when we received word that their oldest son had been rushed to the hospital and placed on a ventilator. He was a popular member of the gay community in Southern California and with good reason. He was a smart, witty and handsome young man with a sparkling personality and he was dying of AIDS. He was my godson and I loved him dearly. We bid him a final farewell while he was in his death throes at the hospital and took a flight home to Beijing the following day. He died two days later. As Delores and I flew over the Pacific dabbing the tears from our eyes while discussing Raymond, I vowed that I would not allow him to die in vain. I announced at a staff meeting the following week that I would make an all-out effort to start a new comprehensive project on AIDS.

I realized from the start that a project proposal on AIDS would be given a very cool reception by the Chinese national government. Based on my experience in other countries, I understood that Jonathan Mann was spot-on in his argument that ministries of health are the most conservative of all ministries and should not have the lead in a national AIDS program. Regrettably, in China the Communist Party gave the Ministry of Health the lead role concerning AIDS. Hence, I knew I would have a difficult task persuading the ministry to launch a national program. I decided to start off with a proposal to host a high-level AIDS awareness conference and have Khun Mechai Viravaidya of Thailand as the main speaker. I had heard Khun Mechai speak previously and I knew he and Jonathan Mann shared exactly the same view of the problem. Unlike most Thais, Mechai has a flamboyant colorful style. I wanted him to scare hell out of the Chinese and move them out of their lethargy. I asked the WHO representative to join me in a meeting with the vice chairman of health. In that meeting, my Mechai proposal went over like a lead balloon. The vice minister vetoed a Mechai appearance and the WHO representative did not utter a word. My WHO colleague was a pleasant person, but was cowed by the health ministry.

The week after that disappointing meeting, I was asked to meet with the vice minister of health and the WHO representative. I was told that the ministry accepted the idea of a UNDP sponsored conference on AIDS awareness, but it would be chaired by the vice minister and no outside speakers would be invited. I was unhappy by this counter offer, but I accepted it because I was willing to do most anything to get the ball rolling. The conference was a complete bust and before it was concluded, it was transformed into a theatre of the absurd. It provided a grim preview of the self-defeating policies the government of China would follow for the next decade. The vice minister advanced the following arguments:

- AIDS is primarily a foreigner's disease and that is the reason the government required AIDS testing of foreigners entering the country.
- AIDS cases reported thus far in China involved intravenous drug users and law enforcement agencies must be more vigilant in cracking down on drug trafficking. Moreover, drug trafficking is driven from outside the country especially in the golden triangle of Laos, Thailand and Burma.
- Aside from drug users, AIDS is primarily a disease spread among homosexuals and China does not have homosexuals.
- AIDS is associated with promiscuous sex which in turn is promoted by pornographic VHS tapes being smuggled into the country.

I had gone out of my way to invite the foreign press to the conference—a decision I learned to regret. After the meeting ended reporters quizzed me on reasons why UNDP would organize and support such an unbelievable event. During the remainder of my tenure in China, the government refused to undertake a national AIDS project. In 1993, the Chinese finally agreed to a UNDP project on AIDS awareness. But it had only a limited effect because the senior leadership refused to recognize the threat of AIDS and the problem was not given priority attention.

The Chinese violated every principle advocated by Jonathan Mann, Khun Mechai or any other expert in the international AIDS community. Based on recommendations from the Ministry of Health, the Communist Party adopted the absurd position that the AIDS pandemic would not seriously affect China because the country was devoid of homosexuals. Within the Chinese medical profession, homosexuality was listed as a psychiatric disorder until 2001. Homosexuality is still highly stigmatized in China and many homosexuals are married, thus increasing the risk of spreading AIDS. Sexual behavior associated with AIDS was criminalized in China and, as Mann predicted, the AIDS pandemic was driven underground insuring there would not be accurate reporting. Without a reliable reporting system, it is impossible to gain control of the problem.

Any communist country will have difficulty in establishing an effective AIDS program because of the absence of a strong and viable non-governmental sector. Countries such as the United States, Brazil and Thailand, which have been effective in combating AIDS, have relied heavily on community-based, non-governmental organizations (NGOs). In China, the few NGOs in existence have been harassed and hampered by government authorities because they have not been sanctioned by the Party. In fact, one of the most effective leaders of an NGO who focused on rural AIDS victims spent three and a half years in jail on subversion charges.

During the decade 1992–2002, it was clear that AIDS was spreading rapidly throughout the country — most of it through heterosexual contact. By 1998, AIDS had spread to all thirty-one provinces and was growing at an exponential rate with at least 700,000 infections. The country finally started to awaken to the pandemic when Hu Jintao was elected General Secretary of the Party in 2002. The alarm bell was sounded and a July 2002 editorial in the party controlled *People's Daily* warned that if an effective national AIDS program was not developed, the number of AIDS cases could reach 10 million with an economic loss to the country of $7.7 trillion ($7.7 thousand billion). In 2003, President Hu Jintao and Premier Wen Jiaboa instituted a major national program covering public education, testing, drug distribution and care for AIDS victims. In 2004, Premier Wen said, "We should be fully aware that HIV/AIDS prevention and control has great bearing on the strength of the Chinese nation and the fate of the country." China is still running hard to catch up with countries like Thailand and Vietnam which started national programs more than a decade earlier.[3]

Health data is notoriously unreliable in China, but most experts believe there are more than one million people carrying the AIDS virus. Since 2008, AIDS is China's leading cause of death among infectious diseases with more than 10,000 deaths in 2011. For the last several years, UNDP has been collaborating with the government on major AIDS interventions — better late than never. On one of my return visits to China several years ago, I met with Vice Premier Li Lanquing who told me that rejecting our UNDP proposal for a comprehensive AIDS national program was a serious mistake. Fortunately the government was much more receptive on the topic of AIDS in my next assignment in Vietnam.

Journey to the Top of the World

Tibet is the highest geographic region on earth with an average elevation of 16,000 feet (4,900 meters). Mt. Everest at 29,029 feet (8,848 meters) is the highest mountain in the world and is located on the Tibetan border with Nepal. Several other mountains in Tibet are among the world's ten highest mountains. Virtually every major river in Asia originates in Tibet and the Tibetan Plateau including the Yangtze, Yellow, Mekong, Indus, Ganges, Salween and the Brahmaputra. Therefore, more than sixty percent of the world's population depends upon the Tibetan region for water. No wonder the Chinese will fight to the death to keep Tibet a part of China. Water is the life blood of all existence and countries from Vietnam to Afghanistan share a fear that in the future China could divert the water of one of more of the great rivers which would impact 1.5 billion people. As mentioned in a subsequent chapter, in recent years China has constructed eight dams on the upper reaches of the Mekong River thus causing concern among the lower riparian countries, especially Vietnam. Throughout history there are numerous examples of water as the source of international conflict. Let's hope such a conflict over water can be avoided in Asia.

There was a day 1400 years ago when Tibet was one of the great independent and unified empires in the world. But it did not last long. Unity was eroded by dissension among sub-groups within Tibet. For a century (1270–1368), the Mongols ruled all of China including Tibet. It was during this period that Tibetan Buddhism was adopted by the Mongols. The Qing Dynasty (1644–1911) absorbed Tibet into China in the seventeenth century. But during the last sixty years of the Dynasty, the central authority was so weak that Tibet was essentially a self-governing area under the leadership of the Dalai Lama. The national government under Chiang Kai-shek tried to increase Chinese influence in Tibet but with little success.

For a decade after the Chinese Communists came to power in 1949, Tibet had a peaceful relationship with the national government. In 1950, the Seventeen Point Agreement was signed by the current exiled Dalai Lama. The agreement confirmed China's sovereignty over Tibet, but granted autonomy to the Tibetans. To strengthen the relationship, the Dalai Lama was elected Vice Chairman of the Standing Committee of China's National People's Congress. But tension gradually increased in the Tibetan capital of Lhasa where troops of the People's Liberation Army were garrisoned. In 1959, the inhabitants of Lhasa became convinced that the PLA planned to kidnap the Dalai Lama. A riot ensued which morphed into a rebellion. Scores of people were killed. The Dalai Lama fled for his life eventually settling in Dharamsala, India where he established a government in exile which still exists today. The Chinese government renounced the Seventeen Point Agreement and started a program to immigrate Han Chinese into Tibet. During the Cultural Revolution, Tibet was ravaged by the Red Guard. Buddhist monks were beaten, killed and imprisoned. All but a few of the 6,000 monasteries and nunneries were destroyed. Only the intervention of Premier Zhou Enlai saved the iconic Potala Palace (traditional residence of the Dalai Lama) from being destroyed. The most recent violent confrontation between Tibetans and Chinese occurred in Lhasa in 2008. There has been sporadic contact between representatives of the Dalai Lama and the Chinese government. But the results have not been encouraging. The Dalai Lama's chief negotiator recently described the conditions in Tibet as "very explosive" and this instability is a major hindrance to productive discourse.

During our time in China, a visit to Tibet was confined to air travel. Today one can travel to Tibet by air, train or road. In the last decade tourism has mushroomed. During the first six months of 2011, there were 1.2 million tourists visiting Tibet. In 1991, tourism was very small. Then, as well as now, foreigners are required to obtain a special visa for Tibet. These visas are much easier to obtain today than they were in 1991. We visited Tibet in the aftermath of the Tiananmen crisis and the Chinese government was reluctant to allow a large number of foreigners into Tibet. We got our visas with ease because of our United Nations affiliation. It was considerably more difficult for foreign journalists. Most visas were valid for only one week.

Before our trip, I called our Australian physician to ask his advice on keeping well while in Tibet. He reminded me that Lhasa has an elevation over 11,000 feet (3353 meters) and therefore, altitude sickness, which causes throbbing headaches, nausea and vomiting can be a problem. I was instructed that if these symptoms persisted more than two days, I should take the next flight out. To avoid altitude sickness, I was advised to avoid alcohol, drink plenty of water, keep physical exertion to a minimum and inhale oxygen if available. I was also told the sun is very penetrating at high altitudes and we should be equipped with a hat and plenty of sunscreen.

We followed the standard schedule by flying from Beijing to Chengdu, the capital of Sichuan Province. We spent the night and then took a two-hour flight the following morning to Lhasa. We were taken to the American owned Holiday Inn which was purchased in 1997 by a Chinese company and is now called the Lhasa Hotel. Our beds in the hotel room were equipped with a built-in oxygen supply. The restaurant on the ground floor served the much acclaimed yak burgers. Fortunately, neither Delores nor I suffered any ill effects from altitude sickness while in Lhasa.

The day after our arrival was devoted to visiting the major Buddhist temples in the Lhasa area. It was a sad experience because we saw a number of temples which were no more than a pile of rubble left in the destructive wake of the Red Guard. The most exciting visit was to the Jokhang Temple and Monastery on Barkhor Square in the center of Lhasa. The Jokhang is a four-story structure in a mélange of architectural styles from India, China and Nepal. It was built under the supervision of King Songsan Gampo in 642. It is on the register of the UNESCO World Heritage Sites and is considered by Tibetans as the most sacred site in Tibet.

An English-speaking monk gave us a special tour, and, when he learned that we were associated with the United Nations, he became very animated and spoke freely about conditions in Tibet. No doubt his observations would still hold true today. He was a young adult during the horror of the Cultural Revolution and it left him with an indelible image of the Chinese. He said as he matured he realized that not all Chinese are like the Red Guard. In fact, he felt the Chinese government was making a serious effort to placate the Tibetans by making major investments in development projects. He added, however, that the Tibetans were not asked to identify their own needs and as a result many of the projects were inappropriate and a waste of money. His main complaint against the Chinese was their lack of sensitivity and knowledge of Tibetan religion, culture and history. He said that most Chinese highly value their own history and culture, but failed to realize that religion is at the heart of Tibetan history and culture. He concluded by saying that most Tibetans are not interested in politics. They just want to be left alone to live their lives and practice their religion. I regret that this humble and articulate monk will never be asked to address the National People's Congress. His comments summarized the root cause of the deadlock of distrust that still grips Tibet today. Tibet is a volatile area and will remain so as long as the Chinese government continues its heavy-handed policies of brutal political repression. In the first six months of 2012, dozens of Tibetan Buddhists committed suicide by self-immolation. These acts of protests against the Chinese have occurred not only in Tibet, but also in the adjacent provinces of Szechuan and Qinghai.

Our last tour of the day was to the Potala Palace, another site in Lhasa on the UNESCO Register of World Heritage Sites. It sits atop the Red Hill and dominates the skyline of Lhasa. In 1649, the Fifth Dalai Lama moved into the Potala and it has remained the main residence of his successors until 1959, when the current Fourteenth Dalai Lama fled Tibet at the age of twenty-four. The Potala has thirteen stories as it descends down the Red Hill. It is 384 feet (117 meters) in height and 1181 feet (360 meters) in width. In addition to the Dalai Lama's living quarters and the numerous halls once used for official purposes, there are 10,000 shrines and a vast library containing Buddhist scriptures. Regrettably, a large number of scriptures were destroyed during the Cultural Revolution.

Like many high altitude areas, Tibet has an abundance of geothermal energy. There are more than sixty geothermal fields and one of the largest is located near Lhasa — the Yangbajing field. The first major UNDP project in Tibet started in 1981 and provided funding for a feasibility study on harnessing the geothermal energy by channeling it through a generating plant for electricity. When Delores and I visited the area in 1991, a small generating plant was in operation. Since then the installation has been enlarged and today Yangbajing is the largest geothermal power plant in China. It supplies seventy percent of the electric power demand for the city of Lhasa. Over two decades, UNDP provided $4 million in assistance in the establishment of Yangbajing and the local authorities assured me that it would never have been constructed with the help of UNDP.

The day after our visit to Yangbajing, Delores and I were taken on a day-long drive on a rough dirt road to Naqu in the northern part of the Tibetan Plateau. We ascended to an elevation of 15,000 feet (4572 meters). The purpose of the visit was to inspect the Naqu geothermal power plant. It was a hardship visit in every sense of the term. The small hotel had only kerosene lamps in the rooms and lots of soiled blankets, but no heat. We ate traditional Tibetan fare in the restaurant — yak meat and tea flavored with Yak butter. Altitude sickness hit Delores in the middle of the night. For more than an hour the following morning we sat in a frigid room listening to a lecture on the power plant and the generosity of UNDP. I informed the director of Delores's sickness and the best he could do was to provide a rubberized canvas bag of oxygen. For the drive back to Lhasa, she kept the bag in her lap and inhaled oxygen through a tube. Like magic, as soon as we descended to the elevation of Lhasa, the splitting headache vanished and so did the nausea. She felt fine for the flight back to Chengdu.

China Today

Mao will always be remembered as the father of modern China, but when history is written in the next several decades, Deng will eclipse Mao as China's greatest leader. Deng was able to escape the straight-jacket of communist orthodoxy and put China on the road to becoming the world's second super power. Nonetheless, Deng's image will remain tarnished because of his brutal suppression of political dissent.

There are now over one million millionaires ($U.S.) in China with 262,000 added in 2010 alone. China now ranks third behind the U.S. (5.22 million) and Japan (1.53 million). Singapore has the highest concentration of millionaires in the world —11.4 percent of a population of 4.7 million. The United States has 412 billionaires comprising 34 percent of the world's total number. China is second in the billionaires club with 115 excluding Hong Kong. Russia is third with 101.

A major problem for China is that it is facing an increasing income disparity between the rich and the poor. If one were to construct a topographic-economic map of China, it would show a high economic mountain chain along the seacoast. But in the center of the country running west toward the Gobi Desert, the vast rural area would be concave because this is the area where poverty is concentrated. While it is true that 400 million Chinese have been lifted from poverty in the last thirty years, there are still 650 million living on less than $2.00 per day. This problem is recognized by the top leadership and recently former Premier Wen Jiaboa said, "We will resolutely reverse the widening income gap." The map would also show two island jewels in the South China Sea — Hong Kong and Macau. Hong Kong reverted to China from the U.K. in 1997 and Macau was ceded by Portugal in 1999. Hong Kong is a free and open society and has been an economic dynamo for decades. In 2010, the Gross National Product (GNP) for Hong Kong was $224 billion. Thirty-six of the world's billionaires live in Hong Kong. Since reverting to China, Macau has become the world's gambling mecca and takes in almost six times the revenue of Las Vegas. Gaming revenues from its thirty-three casinos hit a record $34 billion in 2011, and by 2014, revenues could reach close to $50 billion. On a busy day, 120,000 tourists visit the Venetian Macau which is the world's largest casino with more than one-half million square feet of gaming space.

China is now the world's largest producer of numerous commodities including cotton, steel, gold and aluminum. It has the world's second fastest computer and is the largest automobile market. By 2015, an additional 36 million affordable homes will be constructed and by that time China will surpass Japan as the world's second largest consumer market including luxury goods. China now has the largest beer consumption and by the mid-twenty-first century it will be the world's top wine producer. Conspicuous consumption is the rage. For example, in 2011, a wealthy Chinese bidder set a world record by purchasing three bottles of a rare French wine. The cost of each bottle was $232,000. Who knows whether Mao would be pleased or dismayed by all of these world-shattering statistics.

Did the UN Make a Positive Difference?

When I served in China (1988–1992), the size of the UNDP country program was approximately $25 million per annum with UNDP providing most of the funding. Today the annual program is $35 million, but the Chinese government now provides $30 million and UNDP contributes $3 million to $4 million. For a small country like Samoa, funding from UNDP constitutes a significant source of foreign exchange. But money has never been the main reason why China places a high value on the work of UNDP as evidenced by the government's willingness to cost-share projects at a ratio of 10 to 1. Rather, it is because UNDP is a reliable and politically neutral partner capable of mobilizing first-rate foreign advisors and providing training opportunities in countries through the world. Most importantly, UNDP is a part of the only truly global organization in the world committed to strengthening international cooperation. Once Deng Xiaoping declared the policy of opening up to the world, UNDP became the country's logical international partner.

Even with $35 million for project funding per year, it is still only a few grains of sand in the ocean in a country of 1.3 billion people. I often told my staff that we could easily spend the annual allocation in a single afternoon simply by purchasing a few pieces of heavy equipment for a road construction job. Of course that would be an asinine decision because one should always strive for maximum leverage — the most bang for the buck. Fortunately, our government counterpart agency, the China International Center for Economic and Technical Exchanges under the Ministry of Commerce, was of the same mind. We agreed that we should have a long term vision in making our investments. Money should be used for human capacity building and not equipment. Our projects should be "upstream" by influencing policy formulation instead of policy application. For the past two decades, UNDP projects have been designed to promote sustainable development especially in the areas of governance, economic reform and the environment. Examples include:

Civil Service Reform: A major UNDP project laid the groundwork for a new approach in the management of China's civil service. Reforms include the separation of political cadres from career civil servants and the establishment of clear guidelines governing the appointment, promotion and tenure of civil servants. The project also provided training opportunities in modern personnel management techniques for thousands of senior and mid-level government officials. UNDP also played an important role in the establishment of the National School of Administration (NSA). The NSA is now the premier training center for all middle and senior government officials.

Administrative Reform: A project valued at more than $2 million was launched in 1991, to enhance the capacity of the State Organization and Establishments Committee (SOEC) to undertake the monumental task of streamlining the administrative structure of government through the country. The UNDP project started a process that led to the elimination of over 2 million redundant government positions and has helped improve the administrative structure of hundreds of government institutions and agencies at the national and provincial levels.

Social Security: For the past thirty years, China has been involved in the massive task of restructuring the social security system to bring it in line with a market oriented economy. Reforming the system, especially old age insurance, unemployment, health care and housing continues to be China's number one social policy priority. The government recognizes that a well-funded and managed social security system is crucial for maintaining social and political stability. UNDP in collaboration with the International Labor Organization (ILO) helped establish the foundation for social security reform through a series of projects designed to enhance the technical competence of planners and administrators. The projects provided internships for senior government officials to study social security and wage policies in a variety of market economy countries.

Legal Reform: The State Council is China's highest executive body and sets the policy for all ministries and agencies. It is headed by the premier. In 1991, UNDP launched a major project to assist the Legislative Bureau under the State Council to establish a new economic legal system. As a result of the project, Chinese legislation was computerized and 23 economic laws were drafted including the budget, foreign trade, banking, and securities laws.

Improving the Central Bank: In 1996, UNDP organized and funded a series of international study tours for the senior staff of the People's Bank of China. Knowledge gained through these visits to other central banks in the U.S. and Europe led to the implementation of monetary, prudential, supervision and treasury reforms.

Renewable Energy: Through the support of the Global Environment Facility, UNDP implemented a highly successful $26.5 million program to promote widespread adoption of renewable energy technologies. This project led to the development of a national capacity for the rapid commercialization of renewable energy systems in China including support for the establishment of the China Renewable Energy Association. The project led to the demonstration of successful models for hybrid power in rural households and developed national programs in solar water heating and wind energy. Moreover, it assisted with the formulation of China's new renewable energy law and the removal of bureaucratic barriers to promising renewable energy technologies.

Globalization and International Trade: Working in collaboration with the World Bank and other international organizations, UNDP was involved in a number of activities designed to enhance China's role in international trade. These activities made a significant contribution to the preparatory work required for membership in the World Trade Organization (WTO). After fifteen years of preparation and negotiation, China's admission to membership in the WTO was approved in 2001.

Launching Chinese Investment in Africa: In 2004, UNDP partnered with a Chinese private sector organization and the government to establish the China/Africa Business Council (CABC) with a $1 million contribution from UNDP. The CABC and UNDP organized numerous business missions, training sessions and investment fora in China and several African countries. Since 2004, the CABC has facilitated the creation of joint ventures in

Africa's ten fastest growing countries. China now leads the way among all foreign investors in Africa, and in 2010 Chinese investment topped $100 billion.

Safe Nuclear Power: China has the worst air pollution in the world. Much of this is caused by the burning of coal on a massive scale — three and one-half billion tons each year. The major consumers of coal are the electrical power generating plants. To reduce air pollution, the Chinese government decided years ago to replace coal fueled power plants with nuclear power plants. China is rapidly becoming the nuclear power leader in the world with thirty-two nuclear plants to be built by 2020, and perhaps another three hundred plants by 2050. UNDP has provided valuable assistance in this undertaking by collaborating with the International Atomic Energy Agency (IAEA) in supplying training and advisory services to ensure that construction and operation of the nuclear power plants conform to international standards

Iodine Deficiency Disorder (IDD): In a 2008 *New York Times* column entitled, "Raising the World's IQ," Nick Kristof identified iodized salt as one of his favorite forms of foreign aid to "make a difference." He noted, "When a pregnant woman doesn't have enough iodine in her body, her child may suffer irreversible brain damage and could have an IQ that is 1–15 points lower than it would otherwise be."[4] In 1990 UNDP collaborated with UNICEF, WHO and the government of China to launch a project to eliminate iodine deficiency disorder (IDD) by adding iodine to salt. At the time, over 300,000 Chinese were affected by the disorder. With inputs from this project, one decade later IDD was virtually eliminated from the country.

8

Vietnam: A Country, Not a War

The Lost Decade

When Saigon fell to the Communist forces on April 30, 1975, I received the news while representing the United States at a World Food Programme conference in Rome. That afternoon, an obnoxious representative of a West African country took the floor and made a comment to the effect that the mighty USA should learn a lesson on this day, that it is better to give assistance to developing countries like Vietnam rather than invading them.

I had no instructions for such occasions, but I could not let his comments stand. I grabbed the microphone and made two points: First, since the end of World War II, there has been no country in the history of humankind that has been more generous than the United States in helping countries both large and small. I had all the facts at hand to bolster my argument because President Gerald Ford had addressed this topic only a few days before. Second, I said that the fall of Saigon did not represent the defeat of U.S. military forces. Rather it meant the end of a way of life for millions of Vietnamese and that many in the South would face very harsh treatment by the Communist victors. The world soon learned that the triumph of the Communists would not only bode ill for the South Vietnamese, but would spell disaster for the entire country. Little did I know that I would arrive in Hanoi seventeen years later (June 1992), just in time to help a new crop of leaders put the country back together.

During the Vietnam War, UNDP had a program directed by a resident representative, but it was headquartered in Saigon and covered what was then called the Republic of Vietnam. In fact, the UNDP resident representative and the heads of other United Nations organizations departed Saigon from Tan Tsa Nut airport under rocket fire just before the city fell to the communist forces. Of course, most Vietnamese do not refer to the fall of Saigon, but rather, the liberation of Saigon. With the approval of the Governing Council, UNDP started negotiations with the newly reunited Vietnam to establish a program which was finally accomplished in 1978.

The new resident representative was a Swede by the name of Karl Englund. A Swedish national was a good choice because Sweden was one of the few non-communist countries that maintained diplomatic relations with the North during the war. Karl and his wife moved to Hanoi when the city was a dreary, rat-infested and impoverished place with few links to the outside world. Aside from the USSR and Eastern Europe, Vietnam had few friends in the world—with good reason. It was a troubled time for Vietnam in 1978 both within the country and with its neighbors.

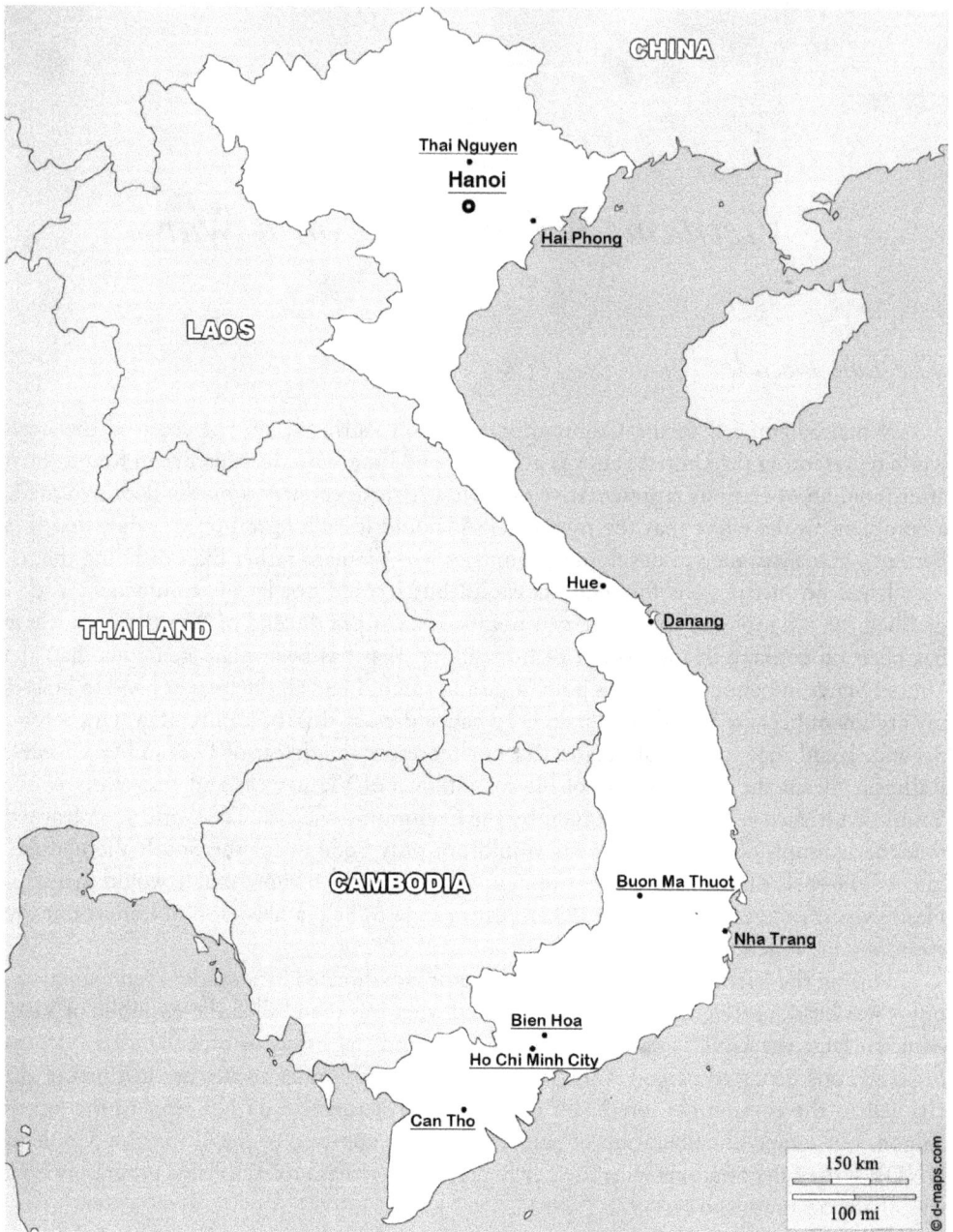

After the war, the Communist Party leadership in Hanoi, led by General Secretary Le Duan, was arrogant and overconfident. In the words of the Vietnamese they were "drunk with victory." During the last eighteen months of Ho Chi Minh's life, Le Duan found ways to sidetrack Ho. By the end of the war, there was an enormous concentration of power in the office of the General Secretary and, therefore, Le Duan was unchallenged as the most powerful figure in the country. He and his fellow members of the Politburo were riding high because in their view they had just defeated the mightiest military force on earth. The Party, which changed its name from Labor to Communist, took a hard line and emphasized orthodoxy. The name of the country was changed from the Democratic Republic of Vietnam to the Socialist Republic of Vietnam, and Saigon became Ho Chi Minh City.

With Le Duan leading the charge in December 1975, the Communist Party of Vietnam adopted various economic, social and foreign policy strategies intended to guide the country for the next several decades. But decisions made at the Fourth Party Congress were so disastrous and counter productive, that several years later the Party publicly admitted it had "committed serious errors."

On the social scene, a menacing black cloud descended over the entire country with the establishment of re-education camps on a massive scale. In reality, these re-education camps were gulags which imprisoned several hundred thousand Vietnamese who were associated (military and civilian) with the defunct regime in the South.

Instead of looking at the success of market economy practices previously found in the South, the Party sought guidance from the experience of the USSR and found a strictly planned economy model which they decided to apply (like a cookie cutter) throughout the reunified country. Le Duan described this as the "district as fortress" approach which was incorporated into a Five-Year Plan. It was forecast that production would double during the period 1976 through 1980. It was soon found that living standards were just as bad (if not worse), than the difficult conditions during the war. As an act of solidarity with their communist allies, in June 1978 Vietnam joined COMECON, the Eastern European Economic Community. But this move did little to help the country.

Just as ideology guided the thinking of the Party in domestic policy, the same was true in foreign policy. During the French colonial period, which started in the fourth quarter of the nineteenth century, Vietnam was always the most important entity among the Indochina colonies which today would be Cambodia, Laos and Vietnam. This was signified by the fact that the office of the French governor of the Indochina Union was located in Hanoi. Roughly 100 years later, the Communist Party leadership in Hanoi resurrected the ghost of Indochina and determined it would have a leadership role over the other two countries. In 1977, A Cooperation and Friendship Treaty was signed between Vietnam and Laos. In November 1978, Vietnam and the Soviet Union signed a friendship pact which the Chinese considered to be a threat to the peace of Southeast Asia.[1]

Because of the harsh treatment received by various groups in the South, especially ethnic Chinese and suspected "sympathizers" with the previous regime, hundreds of thousands of people began fleeing Vietnam. These refugees became known as the boat people. Most of them eventually found their way to the United States; but a large number of them were received back into China which the Chinese government felt was an enormous burden. The Chinese government was also angered over the treatment of their ethnic brethren.

The unraveling process continued with the Vietnamese invasion into Cambodia on Christmas Day 1978. The infamous Khmer Rouge government in Cambodia, led by equally infamous Pol Pot, had been making raids into Vietnam along the border and indiscriminately killing Vietnamese of all ages. This finally provoked the Vietnamese to invade Cambodia. To complicate matters further, the rise of the Khmer Rouge was supported by the Chinese and the invasion inflamed an already tense relationship between China and Vietnam. Hence, in January 1979, with the full support of Deng Xiaoping, 600,000 Chinese troops invaded the border region of Vietnam only 100 miles north of Hanoi. The attack was quickly repelled and the Chinese forces were driven back across the border leaving behind considerable destruction to life and property.

The score card for the first five years under the Vietnamese communist leadership revealed disaster across the board. The economy was in a shambles. Food was in short supply. Millions of Le Duan fellow countrymen hated him because of his draconian policies. Vietnam was considered an out-of-control menace by the rest of the countries in the region. Vietnam had no friends in the world, save Cuba, a few countries in Eastern Europe and the Soviet Union. The hubris of those heady days after the fall of Saigon started to fade.

The leadership was in trouble and they knew it. Despite the bungling and injurious policies, one must remember that most Vietnamese are practical, resourceful, industrious, self-reliant and smart. Without fuss or fanfare, the leadership began to change its tune. A Party resolution was adopted which indicated, for the first time, that the family as an economic unit should not be eliminated, but rather integrated into the system. In January 1981, the Politburo adopted a resolution which started the allocation of plots of land to farm households. By 1985, strong and open criticism of the government's policies was made on the floor of the National Assembly.

Significant change, however, did not emerge until after the death of General Secretary Le Duan in July 1986. At the end of the year, a significant about face was taken at the Sixth Congress of the Communist Party of Vietnam. A Party stalwart, with a distinguished record during the war, by the name of Nguyen Van Linh was elected General Secretary. Among the items included in the final document adopted by the Congress were:

- Admission of serious errors in public policy and the organization of the Party.
- Serious restructuring of the economy including the abolition of central planning in all sectors except defense; promotion of direct foreign investment and a gradual establishment of a market economy.
- Opening up to the outside world combined with a greater effort to improve relations with countries in the region and non-communist countries throughout the world.
- The all powerful role of the General Secretary was diminished in favor of a more collegial system in which the President, Prime Minister and General Secretary would share the most important roles and responsibilities.

The sum total of the socio-economic reform decisions made at the Congress became known as the policy of "doi moi," or renovation.

Obviously, the new line adopted by the Sixth Congress changed the political landscape considerably and in accordance with the Party's new posture, Nguyen Van Linh was elected General Secretary. His election started the era of reform (doi moi). Nguyen Van Linh is considered one of the founding fathers of the Communist Party of Vietnam. He was born in the North in 1915, but lived and worked in the South most of his life. He joined the Communist Youth League at the age of 14 and joined the underground against French rule. He was imprisoned by the French and sent to the infamous penal island of Poulo Condore at the age of sixteen in 1930. He became a full-fledged Party member in 1936. He was a free man for only a few years when the French caught him once again in "subversive activities" and imprisoned him from 1941 to 1945. Most of the founding fathers of the Party were imprisoned at one time or another by the French and they shared their experiences as a badge of honor in demonstrating their loyalty to the Party.

When Linh was released from prison in 1945, the Party leaders in Hanoi assigned him to the South where he spent most of the remainder of his life. He became a master in covert operations as he went about organizing popular resistance first against the French and, after the country was divided in 1954, against the South Vietnamese government and the Americans. He never had a public image until the war was over in 1975. He eluded detection by changing his name five times and conducting a disinformation campaign on himself so that his true identity was known only to a few top leaders in Hanoi and a few colleagues in his immediate circle. For a while Nguyen Van Linh was Party Secretary for all of South Vietnam in charge of organizing the resistance forces — The National Front for the Liberation of Vietnam commonly known as the Viet Cong. He directed propaganda campaigns and organized the training of agents to infiltrate the South Vietnamese government and military. During this time his deputy was Vo Van Kiet, who years later became Prime Minister and a personal friend after I arrived in Vietnam in 1992. In 1968, Linh directed all the non-military aspects of the Tet Offensive which was not a military success, but was skillfully used to start turning American public opinion against the war effort.

The Hidden Camp

After a thirteen year absence, Delores and I returned to Vietnam in May 2009. In Ho Chi Minh City (which most Vietnamese still refer to as Saigon) we rented a van and set off to find the secret headquarters used by Nguyen Van Linh and Vo Van Kiet and other top party officials who directed the guerrilla operations of the Viet Cong during the Vietnam War (which the Vietnamese will forever refer to as the American War). After bouncing over rutted roads for a distance of forty miles west of Ho Chi Minh City in Tay Ninh Province, we knew we were close when we spotted the major landmark in the area — Black Virgin Mountain. We ended our search less than two miles from the Cambodian border. We were in the irregular border area known as the Parrot's Beak where U.S. and South Vietnamese forces made a military incursion into Cambodia in 1969. The news of this incursion reverberated around the world because it was seen as extending the fighting into another country. This operation caused mass demonstrations in the United States including the tragic events at Kent State University where National Guard troops killed student demonstrators. A major purpose of the operation which was announced by President Richard Nixon was to destroy the headquarters known as the Central Office for South Vietnam or in U.S. military parlance, COSVN. During this operation Linh and his colleagues retreated across the border and were never apprehended nor was COSVN ever found.

Our sleuthing was much easier because COSVN is well marked and is now a memorial park. Our guide met us at the visitor's center and started the tour by describing the change in the forest cover of the jungle from the 1960s to today. The forest is still thick, but nothing like the double canopy of foliage that kept the camp virtually invisible from the air 45 years earlier. Today, COSVN consists of an open air meeting hall and several open air huts all with thatched roofs made of a forest fiber which has natural fire retardant properties. This roofing material was used to contain the fire from napalm and bombs. The two huts of most interest to me were those that had been occupied by Nguyen Van Linh and Vo Van Kiet. Each hut was equipped with bamboo shades which could be lowered during the rain. Each hut had a small bomb shelter which could be accessed through a hole in the floor. There were larger air raid bunkers for each area of the camp plus a network of slit trenches which connected the various structures to provide a modicum of protection for those required to move about during an air attack. There were numerous bombing attacks of the area by B-52s which dropped bombs from an altitude of 30,000 feet. There are B-52 bomb craters less than 10 yards from each of the huts. Because of the bombing, it was necessary to move

The hut occupied by Vietnamese Premier Vo Van Kiet during the Vietnam War in the secret Communist Party camp on the Vietnamese/Cambodian border.

the camp on several occasions into Cambodia. The guide told us that on one occasion, Linh scheduled a meeting at the meeting house for all senior staff, but for some reason (perhaps an alert from his intelligence network) he called off the meeting. Just at the time the meeting had been originally scheduled, a B-52 flew over and dropped a bomb which made a direct hit on the meeting house. Had the meeting taken place as scheduled, the entire Southern Communist leadership would have vanished. Would this have altered the course of the Vietnam War? We shall never know.

There were six layers of security in approaching the camp on foot or by vehicle and even the senior leaders were stopped and questioned each time they ventured beyond the perimeter of the camp. Communications were conducted over telephone lines (some buried), radio and telegraph using a type of Morse code. The telephone lines were patrolled to prevent tapping and radios were used less frequently because their signals were more easily intercepted. Many messages were also sent using runners. All in all, the communications system was quite rudimentary, but obviously effective.

Health problems in the camp were considerable. The water supply was primitive and many feared that it may have been contaminated by the defoliant Agent Orange. The jungle was always hot and humid and filled with mosquitoes. Inevitably, most occupants contracted malaria. When I asked the guide how the malaria was treated, I was informed that COSVN had infiltrated the medical corps of the South Vietnamese army and had established a clandestine pipeline of drugs and medications. Wouldn't you know!

On August 30, 1975, Saigon fell (or in the view of the Vietnamese was liberated) to the North Vietnamese forces and on May 1, Nguyen Van Linh ordered an evacuation of the camp and led a convoy east to the city. A few months later Linh was inducted into the

Delores, the author and Vietnamese Premier Vo Van Kiet, 1996.

Politburo (fourteen members) which generally meets in Hanoi, but he continued on in the South as Party Chief of the newly named Ho Chi Minh City.

Linh wanted to be a loyal Party member and could not ignore the decision of the Party to adopt a strict planned economy for the entire country. Nonetheless, he felt that the market economy previously found in South Vietnam should be retained in certain sectors on an experimental basis. In short, he was looking for practical results and not the application of an ideological plan adopted from the Soviet Union. As a Party leader in the South during this time, Vo Van Kiet shared Linh's point of view and they engaged in what became known as "fence breaking."[2] They would allow an enterprise or a farming area to continue to operate on market principles and then invite senior leaders from the North, including Prime Minister Pham Van Dong, to visit and observe first-hand the efficiency and effectiveness of these experiments. Through this approach, they started to win over their senior colleagues in Hanoi. However, General Secretary Le Duan found Linh's attitude and actions very disturbing and they had repeated arguments which eventually led to Linh's removal from the all powerful Politburo in 1982. The tension between Hanoi and the "fence breakers" continued as long as Le Duan was alive. Le Duan died in July 1986 and five months later the Sixth Party Congress elected Linh as the General Secretary to replace him.

Meeting with Nguyen Van Linh

Two years after my arrival in Vietnam, I met with Nguyen Van Linh in the spring of 1994 for two hours at a government office in Ho Chi Minh City. He was not wearing the war time black pajamas often seen on American television, but rather a shirt worn on the outside and a pair of dress slacks. He was trim, neat and well preserved for his age and the difficult life he had lived. He spoke in a deliberate manner and displayed a wry wit.

Linh opened his comments by saying he much appreciated the assistance provided by UNDP to the country. He said UNDP was providing assistance at a time when Vietnam had few friends in the world and this fact would not be forgotten. He especially appreciated the assistance UNDP provided to bring foreign economic consultants to the country and to send economists and lawyers to study abroad. He felt it was good for Vietnamese to be exposed to new ideas and systems found in other countries which had success in managing their economies.

A few months before our meeting, President Clinton lifted the U.S. economic embargo on Vietnam which had been in effect for thirty years. Linh welcomed this move and added that in reality the embargo harmed the interests of the U.S. more than Vietnam. Japan and Western European countries had a major advantage over the U.S. because they could export their goods and gain a share of the Vietnamese market while the U.S. sat on the sidelines with its embargo and watched it happen. He added that while he served as General Secretary, a policy was adopted which welcomed foreign investment and he hoped that American companies would take advantage of the policy. Such investment could benefit the economies of both countries and had the added advantage of fostering peaceful cooperation.

Linh said that Vietnam is predominantly an agricultural country and will remain so long into the future. Therefore, the most important and successful aspect of "doi moi" was to extend market principles to the pricing, distribution and production of agricultural commodities, especially rice. This was born out by the fact that the country emerged from a state of near starvation to the point that in 1989, for the first time, Vietnam was able to export 1.5 million tons of rice with plenty left over for the domestic market.

Nguyen Van Linh ended our meeting by discussing why it was so important to change government policy on the accumulation of foreign exchange. He said, "Surely you must know, Mr. Morey, that each year, the Viet Kue (overseas Vietnamese) send hundreds of millions of U.S. dollars to their families in Vietnam. Previously there were a lot of bureaucratic regulations and impediments that made this difficult; now we welcome every dollar that comes into this country."

Nguyen Van Linh, of course, was long retired by the time I interviewed him. He had relinquished his post as General Secretary in June 1991 "due to advanced age and declining health." He was 77 years old at the time and continued to live in Ho Chi Minh City with his wife, children and grandchildren until his death in 1998. With his support and blessing, his dear friend and like-minded colleague from the South, Mr. Vo Van Kiet, was elevated to the position of Prime Minister. With his election, a whole new era of economic and political reform commenced. Delores and I arrived in Hanoi one year after he became Prime Minister when I assumed the posts of UNDP resident representative and resident coordinator for all development operations in the country. I didn't know it at the time, but I soon learned that we could not have arrived at a better time to help the country accelerate its reform mission.

Settling In

The most difficult problem of the settling in process was securing a place to live which was affordable. The larger homes occupied by Vietnamese families who fled to the South when the communists took over the North after the country was partitioned in 1954, were appropriated by the Party and the government. The most suitable house we eventually found to rent was controlled by the army.

A couple of days after visiting the house, I went to the Ministry of Defense for a meeting with General Vinh who was in charge of all army properties. He was cordial and said that he knew UNDP was a valued organization, but he knew little more. I told him that I was not surprised that he did not know much about UNDP because in every country throughout the world, UNDP is prohibited by the Executive Board from undertaking projects which involve either the police or the military. When we finally got around to talking about the house, I was informed that there were several private companies which were interested in the property and were willing to pay at least $13,000 per month rent. When I was finally able to remove my jaw from the desk, I told the General that UNDP is a non-profit organization and that I would have to pay a part of the rent from my own pocket. We simply left the matter hanging in the air.

Shortly after my disappointing meeting with the army, I met with my counterpart in the Ministry of Foreign Affairs — a most impressive Assistant Minister by the name of Le Mai. He was highly articulate in English and was the main negotiator that led to the establishment of the American Missing in Action Office and Program in Vietnam. After covering other topics, I unloaded my tale of woe on Le Mai concerning the house. He informed me that he would take up the matter at the highest level. I was pleased to hear this and I left his office with a bit more optimism.

Introductory Meeting with
Prime Minister Vo Van Kiet

Two days after my session with Le Mai, I was formally received by Prime Minister Vo Van Kiet. I was immediately struck by the positive energy that filled the room and the warm and gracious manner in which he welcomed me. At the time, I knew little of the Prime Minister's important role during the war and I certainly did not know that he lost his first wife and two children in an American bombing raid. There are times when ignorance truly is bliss and had I known about his loss, I may have been uptight and defensive. Rather, I felt a connection between the two of us and by my second year in Hanoi, I became the Prime Minister's tennis partner on Sunday afternoons. We played on a court within the compound for senior officials. (In China, the equivalent restricted compound is called Zong Nan Hai next to the Forbidden City).

After an exchange of pleasantries, I told the PM that given the fact that I waited two months before my appointment was approved by the government, I didn't know whether or not such a delay was because of my nationality. He smiled and said that it was not at all due to the fact that I am an American, but rather it is because of bureaucracy. The PM ended the meeting by asking if Mrs. Morey and I were enjoying our new life in Hanoi. I answered by saying, "If you had asked that question two days ago, I am not sure my answer would have been an unqualified yes; but I have new hope that we will enjoy Hanoi very much." After my response was interpreted, he gave me a puzzled look and immediately started conferring with his staff. After a few minutes, he said, "You got the house, didn't you?" I replied, "Well, it seems I did and I deeply appreciate any role you may have played in this matter." His retort was, "Mr. Morey, we are pleased that you are now in Vietnam and we want you and your wife to enjoy Hanoi." The good news is that we got the house. The bad news is it took months to negotiate the lease and the renovation.

I had two other important meetings in the weeks after arriving in Hanoi. The first was with the outgoing Italian Ambassador. The second was with former Prime Minister Pham Van Dong. Although the Ambassador would be returning to Rome soon, I was encouraged to meet with him because he was one of the best informed members of the diplomatic corps. The Ambassador was well-briefed on my background and he said that I would start my assignment with three major advantages. First, I had just finished a four-year assignment in China. He said that the Vietnamese would never want to be seen aping the Chinese — heaven forbid! Nevertheless, there is no country on earth that they observe more closely and so would we all if we had the largest country in the world as our neighbor and had been occupied by that country over 800 years of the country's history. He added that the Vietnamese would be interested in my development experience in China and be keen to receive my observations on economic and governmental reform. His assumption proved to be well-founded.

He felt the second major advantage was the fact that I would be serving as the UNDP resident representative and the senior United Nations representative in the country. The Vietnamese place high value on their membership in the United Nations and the UNDP provides an excellent means of helping the country to improve its contacts and relations with the rest of the world — especially the West. He went on to say that the government sees UNDP as being neutral and objective and therefore, I would have better access to the senior leaders than anyone else in the diplomatic community. Once again, the Ambassador was "spot on" with his observations.

The third major advantage, and he added that I would be surprised with this one, is the fact that I am an American. He then shared with me a number of observations. He said, "Because of your country's involvement in the war, you may assume that the Vietnamese dislike Americans; but you would be wrong." He continued, "Despite party propaganda during the war, most people on the street never viewed the U.S. as having colonial designs on the country. If anything, most Vietnamese wonder why in the hell your country ever got involved in what they saw as a civil war," he confided. I interjected that as the war dragged on, most Americans started wondering the same thing. Even some of the strongest proponents of American engagement in the war, most notably Robert McNamara, years later had second thoughts.[3]

In the view of the Ambassador, the Vietnamese will try to maintain friendly relations with China, but they will never fully trust the Chinese. There is an amiable relationship between France and Vietnam, but the Vietnamese will not forget the haughty attitude and oppressive approach of the French during colonial days. Vietnam will be eternally grateful to Russia and the former Soviet Union for all the assistance provided during and after the war. For example, there were some 45,000 Vietnamese who received scholarships to study in Moscow. However, the thousands of Russian advisors and workers sent to Vietnam were not particularly well liked by the Vietnamese people. Like other Asian countries impacted by World War II, the Vietnamese appreciate the assistance, the sophisticated technology and business investments of Japan, but they cannot forget the cruel behavior of the Japanese occupying forces. "Hence, Mr. Morey, at the end of the day, the U.S. does not look bad at all to either the government or the people of Vietnam."

One of the highest items on the foreign policy agenda was to normalize diplomatic relations with the U.S. and establish a bilateral trade agreement. Both of these goals were eventually achieved. There are millions of Vietnamese who have a family connection with former refugees in the U.S. who send back to Vietnam each year at least a billion U.S. dollars in remittances. Today, there are more than 1.6 million Vietnamese living in America including an astronaut and a member of the U.S. Congress. During the remaining four years I spent in Vietnam, I found validation on every observation the Ambassador had made.

Meeting with Pham Van Dong

The first time I saw an image of Pham Van Dong was a television newscast in 1967 during the Vietnam War. He was the Prime Minister of the North Vietnamese government and therefore, he was the enemy. He was seen as leading the war effort in North Vietnam that frustrated the U.S. government so much that Dong and his ilk even got under the skin of calm and collected Henry Kissinger. At one of his high level briefings for Richard Nixon, Kissinger called the North Vietnamese "just a bunch of shits: tawdry, filthy shits."[4] No doubt Pham Van Dong got a kick out of the comment and probably told his colleagues not to worry that the Americans will give up the fight before we do. In fact, the PM was Mr. Cool in public statements and once said that when the Americans leave, "We will strew the path of your departure with flowers."

Here I was — a new arrival in Hanoi in June 1992, representing the United Nations. In this capacity I thought it would be wise to get acquainted with one of Vietnam's political icons. (Pham Van Dong died in 2000 at the age of ninety-four.) My first encounter with him was in 1992, when he was a clear and lucid eighty-six. If there is a correlation between longevity and a tough physical life, Pham Van Dong would be a prime example. He started his life in the underground against the French when he joined a student strike in Hanoi when he was just nineteen. When the French put down the strike, he fled across the northern border to China. This is where he first met Ho Chi Minh, who was organizing a resistance movement broadly based on Marxist principles. After returning to Vietnam, he was caught by the French and sent to the infamous prison island of Poulo Condore and was confined for seven years. He became a close friend of Nguyen Van Linh and other communist resistance fighters and they spent their time plotting their next moves after their release. In 1941, he became a founding member of the resistance group called the Viet Minh. He joined Ho Chi Minh at an encampment on the Chinese border in World War II during Japanese occupation. Pham Van Dong led the communist delegation to the Geneva Peace Talks that ended the French Indo China War in 1954. He then served as prime minister for three decades both before and after unification of the country. He retired in 1987.

Shortly after submitting my request to meet with Pham Van Dong through the Foreign Ministry, I was informed that he would receive me on a Saturday morning at the Presidential Palace. Without question, the Presidential Palace is the largest and most imposing structure in downtown Hanoi. Starting in 1906, it was the residence and office of the French Governor-General of Indochina. It is a perfect specimen of French colonial architecture transported directly to Southeast Asia from Europe. When Vietnam gained independence in 1954, President Ho Chi Minh would not live in the Presidential Palace because he felt it was too ostentatious and would send the wrong message to the people. Instead he lived in a traditional Vietnamese house on stilts with a fish pond on the grounds next to the grand structure.

Pham Van Dong wore a suit and seemed to be quite fit for a man of 86. I soon learned, however, that he was almost totally blind. I was seated next to him and he patted me on the leg and said, "Mr. Morey, I am pleased to meet with you today as the American representative." Needless to say, I was not prepared for this comment so I went into my professional UN mode and reminded Mr. Dong that all UN staff sign an oath that they will not serve the wishes of their home government. I went on to say that I am an American and proud of it. I noted that I served in the U.S. government at the White House and the State Department, but that was years before and now I am representing the United Nations. The former Prime Minister smiled and patiently listened to my pedantic recitation of the UN party line.

When I had finished, he patted me on the leg again and said, "Mr. Morey, you say what you have to say and I will say what I want to say. Now, where was I — oh, yes — as an American, I am pleased to welcome you to Vietnam and I would like to first talk about U.S.-Vietnam relations and then we can talk about the U.N." He went on to say that Vietnam wants to have friendly relations with the United States and the Western countries. The United States is the leader of the West and we will never have full relations with the West until we improve relations with the leader. He said he deeply regretted the involvement of America in the war, but the war is over and we must look ahead and not behind. He said the policy of the country was to improve relations with all countries regardless of their political and economic systems. He was especially pleased with improving relations with Vietnam's neighbors including China and those in Southeast Asia.

At this point in the conversation, Mr. Dong turned his attention to the historical relationship between Vietnam and the United States. He said that Ho Chi Minh was fluent in several languages and was a true scholar. He also traveled all over the world and was very well read in American history and government. Mr. Dong then asked me if I knew that Ho Chi Minh had lived in America. I replied in the affirmative and said that some years before I learned that Ho Chi Minh lived in Boston and served as a busboy and baker at the Parker House Hotel.

Premier Pham Van Dong with the author, Hanoi, 1996.

Pham Van Dong said that the period just after the end of World War II, when the Japanese occupation had ended and the French re-colonization had taken place, was a period when there was a chance that the United States and Vietnam could have become friends. He remarked that both he and Ho Chi Minh felt the United States would come to the aid of Vietnam against the French because the whole world knows of the successful American struggle against the British in the Revolutionary War. But instead the United States supported the French "much to our regret." He then put me on the spot by asking me why didn't American leaders heed the numerous pleas of Ho Chi Minh and side with the Vietnamese? I replied that despite Ho Chi Minh's attempts to present himself as a patriot fighting for the independence of his country unfettered by ideology, the policy makers in Washington saw him as a communist. The Cold War was just starting and the United States wanted France to be a part of the bulwark against the spread of communism in Western Europe. In fact, Washington was worried that the Communist Party might take control in France. I said that no doubt U.S. intelligence services were fully aware of Ho Chi Minh's attempts to establish links in both the USSR and China. In short, the United States was in the early stages of following a containment policy. I added that in retrospect perhaps it is unfortunate that the United States had a Cold War mentality, but when one looks at this period in history, it is easy to see why communism was seen as a global force which was clearly antithetical to the interests of the United States and its Western allies.

Pham Van Dong ended this excursion into history by commenting on the 1954 Geneva Accords which partitioned the country into North and South Vietnam. He didn't think it was a good agreement, but it got rid of the French and unfortunately the major powers either supported it (including the USSR and China) or stayed neutral and refused to sign the document which was the case with the United States. In Pham Van Dong's view, the most important provision in the document provided for an election to be held in 1956 to determine whether or not reunification should take place. But, the newly installed regime in the South (supported by the United States) never had any intention of abiding by this provision probably because they knew that Ho Chi Minh and his supporters (North and South) would win the election. We shall never know, but even Dwight Eisenhower (the President at the time) said in his memoirs, "I never talked or corresponded with a person knowledgeable in Indochinese affairs who did not agree that had elections been held at the time of the fighting, a possible eighty percent of the population would have voted for the communist Ho Chi Minh as their leader."[5]

Paying Tribute

During my first year in Vietnam, newly acquired friends in the diplomatic corps advised me that it was important to be in Hanoi on September 2 because I would be expected to participate in Independence Day events. September 2 is just as important to the Vietnamese as July Fourth is to Americans and July 14 is to the French. It was on this day in 1945 that Ho Chi Minh, President of the self-proclaimed Democratic Republic of Vietnam delivered his Declaration of Independence speech from a hastily constructed stand towering above a gathering that filled Ba Dinh Square in downtown Hanoi. He opened his speech with the line, "All men are created equal. They are endowed by their Creator with certain inalienable rights, among these are Life, Liberty, and the pursuit of Happiness." In his second line, he said, "This immortal statement was made in the Declaration of Independence of the United

States of America in 1776. In a broader sense, this means: All the peoples on the earth are equal from birth, all the peoples have a right to live, to be happy and free." He also quoted from the French Revolution Declaration on the Rights of Man and the Citizen which, of course, contains wording similar to that penned by Thomas Jefferson. He then went on to castigate the French for abusing the standard of Liberty, Equality and Fraternity in their oppressive control of colonial Vietnam. As a senior Vietnamese official once said to me, "Once independence was declared, just like the Americans, we had our own Revolutionary War; but even after the French were driven out in 1954, we still had more than twenty years of war to go."

Today on the spot where Ho Chi Minh delivered his speech stands a huge mausoleum which was inspired by Lenin's tomb on Red Square in Moscow. Inside the structure the preserved body of Ho Chi Minh is in a glass encased casket. Party General Secretary Le Duan, who publicly deified Ho Chi Minh more than anyone else, actually violated Ho Chi Minh's wishes by having the mausoleum built. In his will and in keeping with his public profile, Ho Chi Minh made it clear that he wanted to be cremated and have his ashes scattered in the hills of North, South and Central Vietnam.

On September 2, 1992, I lined up with the rest of the diplomatic corps and filed through the mausoleum and viewed the remains of Ho Chi Minh. Of course, in keeping with such a solemn occasion, I wore a dark suit, white shirt and tie. By the time I exited the mausoleum, I was wondering where I would be able to get my suit dry cleaned as the volume of perspiration it had absorbed by this point in the festivities, gave me the distinct feeling I had fallen into a swimming pool. But wait — I was told — there is more! The next stop was a military cemetery some distance from the city. On the heat and humidity index, this event was worse than the parade through the mausoleum because we were standing out in the sun in our heavy and overly moist suits listening to speeches in Vietnamese made by military and civilian leaders. After this half day ordeal, our cramped temporary apartment didn't look that bad. I stripped off my clothes, filled the bathtub with cold water and soaked for half an hour with beer in hand. Needless to say, this was the last time I participated in the Independence Day celebration.

The Donor Conference

The most important initiative undertaken by UNDP during my first year was organizing and staging a conference that would bring together Vietnam and its potential donor countries. Such conferences usually require the recipient country to describe national economic development goals projected over a two or three year period with some specificity on how the country would use the assistance if it were forthcoming. Each donor country then has an opportunity to outline the amount and type of assistance it would be willing to provide and the conditions under which it would be provided. Most development assistance falls into three categories: loans, grants and in-kind contributions. It would be very rare, especially in the case of Vietnam, for a donor country or international organization to simply hand the government a sum of money. Rather, the donors would make proposals in the form of projects which would specify the use of the funds for training (domestic and foreign), advisory services, equipment and capital improvements such as roads, power lines, schools, hospitals and so on.

For small countries, UNDP often organizes such donor conferences. For larger countries, the World Bank is usually in charge. For countries in conflict (Afghanistan), the United Nations often takes the lead. In previous years Vietnam had been the recipient of a large volume of assistance — especially military assistance from the Soviet Union and China. It had also received smaller amounts of aid from Cuba and other communist countries in Europe. Sweden was one of the few western countries that provided assistance during and after the war. During the reconstruction period after the war ended in 1975, the USSR was by far Vietnam's most important development partner. This came in the form of infrastructure improvement such as the Hoa Binh Dam and hydroelectric system north of Hanoi. The USSR also provided large amounts for education and training. For example, the Soviets were enormously generous in providing university education opportunities to more than 45,000 Vietnamese. Because so many Vietnamese studied in the Soviet Union, plus the large number of Soviet advisors in the country for a decade, Russian became the second language of the Vietnamese elite.

In the decade after the war, Vietnamese/Chinese relations were ruptured mainly because Vietnam signed a friendship treaty with the Soviet Union and invaded the China-backed Pol Pot government in Cambodia. Vietnam, however, remained the darling of the rest of the communist world, but was a pariah throughout the Western world. By the time I arrived in 1992, the Soviet Union had collapsed the year before and most of Eastern Europe had rejected communism. There were very few Russians roaming the streets in Hanoi. There were still some beautiful crystal stemware and chandeliers left over from the glory days of the presence of Czechoslovakia in Vietnam. But the bottom line was that the country was in very bad shape and it was looking for all the non-communist friends it could find.

When I first broached the prospects of UNDP organizing a donor conference to the Vietnamese senior leadership in late 1992, it was like the old ad on TV sponsored by the now defunct brokerage firm of EF Hutton — "When EF Hutton speaks, everyone listens." Well, I was EF Hutton and I had the undivided attention of the Vietnamese leaders when I mentioned the prospects of such a conference. Yes, they wanted a conference and, yes, the Vietnamese were quite sure they would have enough time to prepare their policy document.

My main government counterpart during my years in Vietnam was Do Quoc Sam, Minister of Planning and Investment. We became good friends and we were totally honest with each other. In my first meeting, he said, "Treat me with respect, but say anything you want to me," — what a great working relationship. He was enthusiastic about the conference, but had a slight reservation because he wanted the World Bank involved. This presented a problem because at the time the U.S. still maintained its objection to World Bank operations in Vietnam. We were between a rock and a hard place. Do Quoc Sam wanted the preparations to commence and he would settle for a UNDP-organized conference, but he still wanted Bank involvement. I was ambivalent. True, the Bank would add substantial weight to the effort. But in my mind, that was just the problem. I feared, with good reason, that the Bank would come in, push us aside and run the whole show.

The question was finally resolved after the visit of the Deputy Director of the Regional Bureau for Asia and the Pacific, a smart and beautiful Cuban by the name of Elena Martinez. I asked Elena to meet with Do Quoc Sam without my presence. In her debriefing on the meeting, she said, "Roy, you had better find an answer to this issue. Do Quoc Sam does not want to do something that will disappoint you, but it is clear he really wants the Bank involved."

The next week I went to Do Quoc Sam and proposed a solution — let's continue preparations in hopes the Bank will join the exercise and, if so, I would be willing to hold the meeting at the Bank facility in Paris. I told him that I would like him to convey this proposal to the Bank. Do Quoc Sam broke into a smile and said, "Mr. Morey, this is exactly what we should do." When we finished patting each other on the back, I said I had a personal message to share with him. I told him that I knew the Bank would like the proposal and they would insist that hereafter the conference should be a regular World Bank Consultative Group Meeting chaired by the Bank. I went on to say, "UNDP has always been one of your main development partners. When the World Bank finally returns to Vietnam with their big money bags swinging in the wind, will you simply push our face in the mud and forget about us?" True, we had an agreement to be honest with each other, but Mr. Sam was a bit shaken by my blunt outburst. He collected himself and then assured me that UNDP would always remain Vietnam's main development partner for technical assistance, but that the country desperately needed World Bank soft loans for major projects. He added that he thought the Bank conference facilities in Paris would be an excellent venue; however, he wanted both UNDP and the World Bank to co-chair the meeting. For the rest of my tenure in Vietnam, Do Quoc Sam was true to his word and UNDP and the World Bank each had an important role to play.

One week before departing the country, Do Quoc Sam hosted a farewell luncheon for me. In his toast he had lots of praise for UNDP and some nice words for me. He concluded by saying, "Mr. Morey, I do not see one bit of mud on your face!" I loved it, but there were only two of us in the room who could really appreciate the remark.

By any standard, the first donor conference in Paris in 1993 was an enormous success. The document on the table was the first ever macroeconomic analysis of Vietnam prepared by the government with assistance from the UNDP office. The conference was attended by senior representatives of twenty-two donor countries and seventeen international organizations. Commitments announced at the conference amounted to U.S. $1.86 billion in loans and grants. It was the first ever donor conference for Vietnam and established a mechanism for mobilizing assistance for the country that is still in use. Vietnam had not seen such assistance since the collapse of relations with China in 1978 and the disintegration of the Soviet Union a decade later. The World Bank has remained the leader in providing assistance, but UNDP has been the leader in helping the government become honest and responsible in the coordination of development assistance which is essential in avoiding duplication and waste.

The conference the following year (1994) was a regular Consultative Group Meeting chaired by the World Bank. But it was organized in consultation with UNDP as specified by Do Quoc Sam. There were the usual documents prepared by the government and World Bank, but the report that generated the most attention and discussion was the one prepared by UNDP entitled, "Vietnam: Technical Assistance in Transition." It was honest, blunt and not very well received by some of the remaining hardliners in the communist leadership. It described why development assistance in general, and technical assistance in particular, was often wasted and not utilized in an effective and efficient manner during the decade after the war when the country was following a Soviet economic model.

The report went on to argue that the picture improved remarkably after reforms (doi moi) were adopted by the Communist Party starting in 1987 with the move toward a market economy, a strengthened legal structure, an interest in renovating public institutions and an open door policy toward the rest of the world. The report maintained that even though technical assistance (the type of assistance provided by UNDP) constituted only thirty percent of overall development assistance, it remains important because its purpose is to build national capacity through the transfer of know how in the form of training and advisory services. Sound technical assistance recognizes the importance of individual initiative and equality of access to education. Technical assistance is nicely summarized in an aphorism popular in development circles which says, "*Give* a man a fish and you have fed him for a day. *Teach* a man to fish and he will eat for the rest of his life."

The Administrator's Visit

Until 1999, every Administrator of UNDP was an American starting with Paul Hoffman in 1966. This was because the U.S. was the largest donor to the organization. When William Clinton assumed the presidency in 1993, he recommended to the UN Secretary General that James Gustave (Gus) Speth be appointed Administrator. Gus Speth is one of America's leading environmentalists. He served at the White House as President Carter's Chairman of the Council on Environmental Quality.

Vietnam was chosen as Speth's first country to visit after becoming the Administrator. Much preparatory work was required by our office, but we were pleased to be the first UNDP country program to be reviewed by the boss. We were in the process of refocusing the program with more governance and environmental projects. There was a lot going on including the launching of a new major project on public administration reform. Besides the program, I had a couple of issues up my sleeve that required Speth's involvement. The first concerned the salaries of the local staff. Just as in China, and perhaps any other communist country, the Service Bureau of the Ministry of Foreign Affairs saw itself as the major recruiting office for UNDP local staff. After the staff member was placed in the UNDP office, the Service Bureau would take a certain percentage of the staff member's monthly salary. I was never able to stop this inequitable system in China, but I was bound and determined to do so in Vietnam. Once again, I got an opinion from the UNDP Legal Office in New York indicating such a practice by the government is both a violation of the basic agreement the government signed when the program was established, as well as the UN oath that all staff must take, both local and international, to serve only the United Nations and not a member state.

In working out the agenda for Speth's meeting with the deputy prime minister, I indicated that a requested change in government policy would be raised by Mr. Speth. The government argued that this was an inappropriate agenda item since it involved government policy and not UNDP policy. I countered by arguing that it was a government policy that impacted heavily on UNDP and was a violation of the basic agreement signed by the government in joining the UN. This standoff remained until the meeting was held. As soon as Gus Speth raised the issue with Phan Van Khai, the Deputy PM smiled and said, "Mr. Speth, it is not necessary to discuss this topic further because I have already sent a letter to the Service Bureau informing them that I want this practice stopped." After further delay, long after the visit of the Administrator, and with much prodding by the UNDP office, the practice of pilfering the pay envelopes of the local staff was finally brought to an end much to their delight.

The second issue I wanted to discuss with the Administrator concerned Jordan Ryan, an American staff member. While still in China, I hired Jordan as a consultant and I persuaded Bill Draper, who was then Administrator, to recruit Jordan into the organization as a full fledged staff member. The appointment was finally approved by the UNDP Human Resources Bureau. I found Jordan such a bright and valuable colleague that I asked headquarters to transfer him to Vietnam as soon as a position opened at his level. This was accomplished. After Jordan had spent a year in Hanoi, the position of deputy resident representative became open and I asked headquarters to elevate him to that position. However, this time I encountered a lot of flak from UNDP's Appointments Committee in New York because of his nationality. The Committee argued that a deputy and a res rep of the same nationality should not serve together. I did a little research on this issue and found that there were several cases in previous years where the two top spots were held by those of the same nationality. I brought my research findings to the attention of the Administrator and, of course, I arranged for Jordan to have plenty of face time with Gus Speth. This strategy worked and Jordan became my deputy. In fact, the strategy worked too well. Speth became so impressed with him that he was eventually transferred from Hanoi to New York as chief of staff in the Administrator's office. Jordan deserved the promotion and I was sorry to see him leave, but it was my own damned fault!

In Hanoi, Administrator Speth spent his time in meetings with senior government officials, program discussions with the staff and a formal dinner at our house. In addition to Hanoi, I planned a trip for him to visit Central and South Vietnam. As an American, I knew the first images of Vietnam to enter his mind would be a war-torn country. Therefore, I planned the trip to include project visits and visits to famous sites from the Vietnam War to give him a comparative picture of Vietnam today and Vietnam of yesteryear.

Project Visits and Reliving the War

The first leg of our journey was a one-hour flight to Danang where we were met and then driven for an hour to Dai Loc District, an impoverished rice farming area, where we spent the remainder of the day visiting a $15 million project funded by the UN Capital Development Fund (UNCDF). This Fund operates under the aegis of UNDP, but as the name indicates, capital improvement projects (equipment and infrastructure) are supported by the Fund instead of the more typical UNDP technical assistance projects that build human capacity through training and advisory services. The purpose of the project was to improve agricultural output by extending an irrigation system, improving the distribution of electricity and establishing a network of farm to market roads. The Administrator was sufficiently impressed with the progress of the project and he especially enjoyed the opportunity to speak directly with the farmers, more than half of whom were women. On the way back to the hotel, I had the driver go to a point where we could view Danang Bay. It was here in March, 1965 that a brigade of 3,500 U.S. Marines came ashore to secure the nearby U.S. airbase. For fear that the arrival of new troops would fan concerns in the American press, General William Westmoreland wanted this to be a quiet event. Instead it became a large public spectacle as the Marines were met by South Vietnamese officers, sight seers, Vietnamese girls with leis and four American soldiers with a huge sign stating "Welcome, Gallant Marines." Unfortunately for General Westmoreland, the event was widely publicized in the United States and many looked upon it as the first of a series of U.S. troop build-ups that eventually topped 540,000 in 1969. Speth and I both remember reading about this event and we discussed it all the way to the hotel.

The next stop was Ho Chi Minh City where we had meetings with city officials to discuss the UNDP public administration and legal reform projects that we were undertaking in cooperation with the city. Since the days of Nguyen Van Linh and Vo Van Kiet in Saigon, the city always has been the most progressive political unit in the country and eventually our reform projects were of considerable use in making the city administration and the local legal system more honest, transparent and private sector friendly.

Several weeks before the Administrator's arrival, I made an all out effort to gain permission for a visit to the old American Embassy building in Ho Chi Minh City. It was no easy task, and had it not involved the UNDP Administrator, I doubt permission would have been granted. After the war, the Vietnam government always made it clear that U.S. diplomatic property in Hanoi and Ho Chi Minh City would revert to the U.S. once diplomatic relations were established. Meanwhile, there was a state-owned petroleum exploration company occupying the building. The director greeted us and, of course, recognized that Gus and I are both Americans. Therefore, he went into a long explanation assuring us the property and building still belonged to the USA and that he looked forward to the day that it would be returned.

We began our tour in the outer courtyard with our guide showing us where the outer wall of the Embassy had been repaired. This is where the wall had been blown open on the morning of January 30, 1968, which allowed nineteen Viet Cong (VC) commandos to enter the grounds. A fire fight ensued between the VC and the U.S. marine guards. This was one of eighty attacks made that day as a part of the famous Tet offensive. The siege of the Embassy was quickly quelled leaving all nineteen VC and five American marines killed.

We then went inside the Embassy building which remained much the same as when it was evacuated 18 years earlier. On an upper floor we found the Ambassador's office which had been used by Ellsworth Bunker and the last American Ambassador, Graham Martin. We then ascended the stairs between the top floor and the helipad on the roof. Video footage of the stairway chock-full of screaming Vietnamese hoping to be evacuated on the next helicopter at the end of the war was viewed in horror by hundreds of millions of people throughout the world.

I had heard many stories about the evacuation of Saigon including some by UN colleagues who went through the ordeal. When Gus Speth and I reached the helipad on the roof, we looked east toward the coastal town of Vung Tau and the South China Sea. During the last evacuation of Saigon on April 29 and the early morning hours of April 30, 1975, 81 helicopters made round trips from carriers in the South China Sea which eventually picked up 1,373 U.S. nationals, 5,595 Vietnamese, international press and third country nationals. The chopper flew the 37 miles to the Vung Tau peninsula and then another 17 nautical miles to the carriers. There were additional helicopters, controlled by the South Vietnamese army, flying senior military and civilian Vietnamese to the carriers. In fact, at one point there were so many choppers making unauthorized landings, that some of them had to be pushed over the side of the carriers into the sea to make room for more.

With advancing communist forces shelling parts of Saigon including Tan Tsa Nut airport on April 29, the evacuation operation called "Frequent Wind" got under way. Americans and members of the international press were informed in advance that they should tune in to Armed Forces Radio and listen for the announcement that the temperature is rising followed by eight bars of the song, "White Christmas." This was the code signaling the start of the evacuation. According to one source, several Japanese journalists feared they would not recognize the tune and asked their American friends to sing the song for them. Of course, when the Vietnamese saw the Americans boarding busses headed for either Tan Tsa Nut or the American Embassy, they knew they had to make their move. Absolute chaos ensued with hundreds of Vietnamese scaling the ten foot outer wall of the Embassy. Those who were not repelled by the Marine guards barged their way into the building and up to the top floor stairs leading to the helipad. In the midst of the panic, a mother tossed her baby over the wall in hopes that some caring person would retrieve it and take it to America. Apparently it was retrieved unharmed and returned to the mother.

Ambassador Graham Martin, who had lost a son in the Vietnam War, was one of the last to leave. Before his departure he was driven to his residence under fire so that he could destroy the remaining top secret documents. The evacuation continued into the wee hours of April 30 and the last chopper left the roof with a contingent of marines at 5:15 A.M. After he returned to the State Department, Martin and I ate lunch together on several occasions in the senior staff dining room. He was a lonely and dejected man and I tried to raise his spirits by telling him what a hero I thought he was. I told him I would never forget the photo of him on that dreadful day boarding the helicopter and clutching the American flag that had proudly flown over the American Embassy.

Diplomatic relations between Vietnam and the U.S. were established in July 1995, during the term of President Clinton. The Embassy building was returned to the U.S., but it was in a dilapidated state and was leveled. On the same grounds the new U.S. Consulate was formally opened in August 1999 and is now the second most important U.S. diplomatic office in the country just behind the American Embassy in Hanoi. It is ironic to find that the name of the street on which the Consulate now stands was changed after the Communist takeover to Le Duan Street. The panicked Vietnamese, who were trying to scale the Embassy wall on 29 April 1975, knew they would be treated harshly if the communists won and they certainly were correct. It was Communist Party General Secretary Le Duan who ordered the incarceration of many of them in the so-called reeducation camps after the war.

Laying the Ground Work for Democracy

From the start, I knew that the importance of good governance would be an easier sell in Vietnam than in China. In our first meeting and without any prompting on my part, Prime Minister Vo Van Kiet suggested that UNDP should provide assistance to improve the performance of Vietnam's public institutions. Within weeks Vice Prime Minister Phan Van Kai (Vo Van Kiet's successor) arranged a meeting to discuss a major new UNDP project on public administration reform. This project resulted in a more professional civil service. Public institutions at all levels are now more transparent and service oriented.

After sufficient trust was established between UNDP and the senior leadership, my UNDP colleagues and I started pressing for projects directly related to laying the ground work for a democratic system. For example, I helped secure government approval for a UN Human Rights mission to visit prisoners in various parts of the country. More importantly, UNDP gained approval of a package of three major governance reform projects. One project was designed to enhance the role and responsibilities of the National Assembly. Today, the national budget must be approved by the National Assembly. The next project was intended to enhance the competence and independence of the judicial system starting with the Supreme Court. The third project was designed to improve the competence, organization and transparency of the public prosecutor's system.

The price tag for this cluster of projects was in excess of $10 million. Danida, Denmark's development cooperation agency, expressed a strong interest in executing the three projects. But the government (and Party) decided that a global and neutral organization like UNDP should oversee the projects rather than a bilateral donor. Danida provided $10 million to UNDP to fund the projects. Given the political sensitivity of the projects, the approval of the Politburo of the Communist Party was required. These projects in governance plus those in economic management and poverty reduction have now been taken over by the World Bank and other donors.

Progress was also made in strengthening the non-governmental sector. Essential to establishing a democratic governance system is an independent bar association to improve the competence, fairness, independence and ethical behavior of the legal profession. UNDP working in collaboration with a group of Vietnamese lawyers and the American Bar Association (ABA) created an independent Vietnam Lawyers' Association. As a result of this effort, the Vietnam Lawyers' Association and the ABA continue to maintain close and friendly collaboration with each other. Building on the collaborative efforts between the ABA and UNDP in Vietnam, there is now a formal project agreement between the two organizations. Within the framework of the ABA there is now an ABA-UNDP Legal Resources Unit to support and promote good governance, and rule of law through UNDP projects in countries throughout the world.

9

Vietnam: Mending Fences

The Mighty Mekong

No wonder the government of China is so intent on maintaining tight control of Tibet. Commonly known as the roof of the world, the Tibetan Plateau could well be the most environmentally strategic area in the world. The Tibetan Plateau is the largest plateau in the world. With more than 15,000 lakes and a large portion of the Himalayas in its territory, it is the source of most of the rivers in Asia. These rivers sustain the lives of almost half the world's population and 85 percent of the total population of Asia. From India in South Asia to Vietnam in Southeast Asia, all the countries in the region would be devastated without the life giving water that flows out of the Tibetan Plateau. The Mekong flows out of the Plateau down through Yunnan Province (the northern border of Vietnam), Burma, Thailand, Laos, Cambodia, and through the Mekong Delta of southern Vietnam into the South China Sea. It is 3,000 miles long. It starts at 17,000 feet and discharges an average of 57,000 cubic feet of water per second into the Sea. The Mekong River has a watershed of more than 300,000 square miles and is the life blood of all of Southeast Asia.

For decades there has been tension among the Mekong countries primarily over the issue of the volume of river water that would be diverted in each country and thereby jeopardizing how much would remain for the downstream countries. It has been of special concern for the Vietnamese because the Mekong Delta is the end of the line. Most of the 86 million Vietnamese who currently populate the country would have real difficulty surviving without the Mekong Delta. More than half of the country's agricultural product (especially rice) comes from the Delta and more than 75 percent of the farm raised fish and shrimp. One can easily see why Vietnam could not remain a divided country. The North would remain impoverished forever without the South and especially the Delta.

In 1955, under the auspices of what is now called the UN Economic and Social Commission for Asia and the Pacific (ESCAP), Vietnam, Thailand, Cambodia and Laos signed an agreement of cooperation to undertake scientific studies of various facets of the river including an analysis of how much water each of the countries was using. From the very beginning, UNDP supplied the bulk of the funding for such studies and started sending senior staff from UNDP to assume the key positions in the newly formed secretariat (including the CEO). It was essentially a committee of four countries run by UNDP staff and consultants. UN involvement in the Mekong Committee was symbolized by the participation of UN Secretary General Dag Hammarskjöld in the formal opening of the new Mekong Committee headquarters in Bangkok in 1959.

When the Communist Party of Kampuchea (commonly known as the Khmer Rouge) led by the infamous Pol Pot took over the government of Cambodia in 1975, all Cambodian participation in the Mekong Committee ceased. The remaining three governments and the secretariat were stunned by this move. It had a debilitating affect on the whole operation because the Mekong Committee was based on an agreement of all four countries. Finally, after much discussion and negotiations among Vietnam, Thailand and Laos, a new agreement was cobbled together in 1977 creating the Mekong Interim Committee. The three countries saw this as a stop-gap measure because it was simply impossible to have a sensible operation without the participation of one of the most important riparian countries. It was a period of ferment. The remaining three countries started squabbling and the UNDP Asia and Pacific Bureau strengthened its resolve to discontinue the practice of seconding senior staff and footing most of the bill for the secretariat. Tension among the countries increased when the government of Thailand started questioning the activities of the CEO — a friend and a UNDP staff member. Shortly before my arrival in Hanoi, the Thai government declared the CEO *person non grata* and ordered him out of the country without much attention to the concerns of the other two countries. The disagreement between the CEO and the Thai government came to a head in 1991. It centered on how the Mekong Committee should be restructured to allow the new government of Cambodia to regain its admission.

When I arrived in Hanoi in June 1992, I assumed my first few months would focus on the country program. I didn't know that the fallout of the UNDP Mekong regional project would start crowding my agenda. Within a week, the Minister of Water Resources requested an urgent meeting. When the head of a ministry requests a meeting, from whatever ministry, you jump to it. Soon I was in his office listening to a strongly worded tirade against the Thai government for booting the CEO out of the country without so much as a phone call to Hanoi in advance. The minister went on to say that the Mekong Committee had to be completely restructured to accommodate the reentrance of Cambodia. He also felt it would have to move beyond its research function to a decision making body. There had been several attempts by Thailand to call a meeting to discuss the situation, but Vietnam refused to attend.

In the following weeks, I consulted the UNDP resident representatives in the other three countries and the bureau director in New York. It was clear that nothing would happen if UNDP did not take the initiative to reduce tensions among the countries. We collectively decided to convene a meeting of the four parties in Hong Kong. Bangkok would have made more sense as a venue, but it was clear that Vietnam would boycott the meeting if it were held in Thailand. The purpose of the Hong Kong meeting was to let the countries air their grievances and outline what role they would see for a new Mekong Committee in the future. The meeting was chaired by the UNDP regional bureau director from New York. During the first day, the interaction between the Thai and Vietnamese representatives was stiff, overly formal and shallow. In good Asian fashion, UNDP hosted an open bar and dinner that evening. You guessed it — after everyone was sufficiently lubricated with alcohol, the whole tone of the gathering started to change. Everyone began to chat and joke and the tension of the afternoon evaporated. The meeting the next day was more friendly and conversational. I was greatly relieved because at each break in the meeting, I was no longer required to put on my happy face and dream up new ways of bringing together members of the Thai and Vietnamese delegations. The major decision of the second day was to meet again on neutral ground (this time Kuala Lumpur, Malaysia) to see if a consensus could be reached on a broad outline of the structure, role and responsibilities of a new Mekong Committee.

The dynamics of the interaction among the four delegations proved to be a guide for all the subsequent conferences and working group sessions. Vietnam and Thailand are two large and powerful animals which occasionally snarl at each other. Sandwiched between them are two much smaller and (except for the years of terror and bloodshed of the Khmer Rouge reign in Cambodia) much more gentle and powerless. Throughout long periods of history, Thailand coveted the two smaller animals and went to great lengths to extend its influence and control over them. Thailand was especially successful in extending its influence over Laos as one can easily see today in the similarity of the languages of the two.

Starting in 1887, Vietnam indirectly started to be the dominant power vis-à-vis Cambodia and Laos when the French Indochina Federation was established. Laos was added to the Federation in 1893. Vietnam was always the crown jewel of French Indochina, with Cambodia and Laos treated as appendages. After the first communist government took power in Laos in 1975, Vietnam's influence in the country was greatly increased and, at one time, Vietnam had 50,000 troops stationed in Laos. Vietnam invaded Cambodia in 1978, installed a puppet government to replace the Khmer Rouge in 1979 and occupied the country for the next decade. Hence, in one period of history or another, both Vietnam and Thailand asserted its dominance over the two countries and this was useful to keep in mind to sort out all the subtleties of these four countries. Cambodia received special attention because of its recent disastrous history and also it was seeking to rejoin the group. The other three were delighted Cambodia wanted to resume its membership, but as time went on, both the Thais and Vietnamese offered more gratuitous advice to Cambodia than it cared to receive. Cambodia and Laos, as the two small countries in between, agreed with each other on various points more often than either agreed with Thailand or Vietnam. Most disagreements involved Vietnam and Thailand and not the two smaller countries.

During the second meeting in Kuala Lumpur, it became clear that all countries wanted a whole new structure and role for the Mekong Committee. UNDP hired an outside independent senior advisor to guide the process of formulating a new agreement. An American professor by the name of George Radosevich from Colorado State University with a background in law and water management was chosen for the job. He had prior experience in Southeast Asia and his command of the subject and warm personality soon won over the key players in all four countries.

Working with a basic framework to which the four countries had agreed, Radosevich undertook a series of negotiations on a country by country basis. After each visit to Vietnam, I would follow up with my own meeting to put the weight of UNDP behind the efforts of Radosevich. Gaining an agreement on the structure of the new Mekong River Commission (as it became known) was challenging, but doable. Throughout the process, the sticking point was always the formula to be adopted on the diversion of water by each country.[1]

Radosevich and the UNDP resident representatives would prod their countries along in a common direction and when we thought there was a chance to get unanimous agreement on certain points, UNDP would quickly call a meeting and, in most cases, an agreement was reached on the issue at hand and we would then move on to the next key point. Eventually meetings were held in Vientiane, Laos, Bangkok and Hanoi. Progress was good and steady, but after each meeting the five hundred pound gorilla left sitting in the room which everyone avoided discussing, was the question of diversion of the water. It was agreed that the new commission would have a Council which meets once a year at the ministerial or cabinet level to set general policy. Below the Council is the Joint Committee which meets frequently to oversee implementation of general policies and to serve as an oversight board for the management of the Secretariat. From the very beginning UNDP made clear that it would no longer assign senior staff to manage the Secretariat.

Three years of prodding and cajoling were culminated on April 5, 1995, when the Deputy Prime Minister of Cambodia and the Foreign Ministers of Vietnam, Thailand and Laos formally signed the international agreement establishing the Mekong River Commission (MRC). The Secretariat is currently located in Vientiane, Laos. It was one of UNDP's finest hours. The senior government officials agreed that the accord would not have become a reality without the substantive involvement and financial assistance of UNDP. Yet when we all finished the champagne toasts that day in Chiang Rai, I still felt a sense of disappointment.

Persistent efforts by UNDP and George Radosevich were unsuccessful in convincing the four governments that the approval of the MRC Council should be required for any decisions by a member state to build dams on the river or construct new irrigation systems which would divert significant quantities of water. Under the agreement member states are to consult with each other through the MRC, but the organization lacks the authority to compel a member state to stop the construction of a dam even if it is opposed by other member states.

Since 1995, three of the countries (excluding Vietnam) have contemplated the construction of eleven new dams on the lower Mekong River. A panel of experts hired by the MRC issued a study recommending a ten-year moratorium on dam construction to allow time for studies to be undertaken to determine the environmental, social and economic impact of main-stream dams. Undeterred by the study, the government of Laos announced in November 2012 the start of construction on the massive Xayaburi Dam. This $3.5 billion project is strongly opposed by Cambodia and Vietnam which fear the dam's negative effects on fish stocks and the economies of the two downstream countries. Fifty million people in these two countries depend upon the Mekong as their primary source of protein. The river is the home of the giant Mekong Catfish which is the largest scaleless fresh water fish on earth which is an endangered species and is ten feet (three meters) in length and weighing 650 pounds. This behemoth has a migratory pattern covering hundreds of miles and experts fear that the Xayaburi Dam, regardless of the size and design of its fish ladders, will lead to its extinction.

Despite the efforts of the four countries and UNDP, China refused to sign the MRC agreement. In my view, China never had any intention of joining the MRC which in any way could restrict or influence its use of Mekong water. On the upper Mekong (known as the Lancang in China) the Chinese have completed construction of five megadams, eight are currently under construction and numerous others are planned along the river stretching into Tibet and Qinghai. These dams have already started to affect the migration of fish, the water level, and the flow of sediments. The MRC performs many useful functions of benefit to its four members, but its creation has not allayed the fears of the downstream countries.

Twelve Hundred Miles and a Cloud of Dust

After careful planning and lengthy discussions with selected staff members, Delores and I embarked on a twelve hundred mile road trip from Hanoi to Ho Chi Minh City in February 1994. The purpose of the trip was to visit several ongoing projects, explore the feasibility of some new projects, see what a large portion of the country looked like from the ground and visit some of the locations made famous by the Vietnam War. The trip took three weeks with many stops along the way. We traveled over dirt roads in a four wheel drive Toyota Land Cruiser with bottled water and an extra tire strapped on the top and two gerry cans of extra gasoline in the trunk. Of greatest importance were our two companions for the drive. Ban was our driver. He speaks very little English, but is a first-rate person and an excellent driver. Nguyen Xuan Thuan, Director of the UNDP sub-office in Ho Chi Minh City, was our guide and mentor. We would not have taken the trip without him. Thuan's English is as good as most native speakers and he is an impressive person — intelligent, wise, soft-spoken and has a vast knowledge of Vietnamese history, politics and development.

As one heads south out of Hanoi on Route 1, the first central Vietnam province is Nghe An. It is one of the poorest provinces, but also the best known because in a small village in this province, the father of modern Vietnam, Ho Chi Minh, was born. At birth his name was Nguyen Sinh Cung. He was a precocious boy and when he reached the age of ten, following Confucian tradition, his father gave him an additional name — Nguyen Tat Thanh (Nguyen the Accomplished). To make the picture even more confusing, after World War I, and after living in Paris, he changed his name to Nguyen Ai Quoc (Nguyen the Patriot). Around 1940 he started referring to himself as Ho Chi Minh (the Bringer of Light). For years as a young man, Ho Chi Minh was in the revolutionary underground and he found it useful to switch names to confuse the French security forces. The Vietnamese affectionately call him Uncle Ho. In the afternoon, after a brief stop in Vin, the provincial capital and port city, we drove a few miles out of our way to visit the simple five room farm house with a thatched roof in Kim Lien where Ho Chi Minh grew up. The house was dismantled in 1905 when Ho's father went to Hue for study. It was reconstructed in 1955, and the image of the house appears on the 500,000 Dong (Vietnamese currency) note. It is now a national shrine and there is a museum nearby.

Opium: All in the Family

After the stop at the Ho Chi Minh house, we got back on the road heading west into the mountain range that separates Laos from Vietnam. By nightfall we reached the Ky Son District and drove to a district guest house located almost within sight of the Laotian border where we spent the night. A few months before starting the trip, the United Nations Office on Drugs and Crime (UNODC) established an office within the UNDP compound in Hanoi. The first drug control project to be implemented by UNODC was under consideration and would be located in the Ky Son District. Hence, the purpose of the visit was to discuss the pending project with local authorities and to gain a first hand look at the proposed location. The location of the project was an easy decision to make. When we visited Ky Son in 1994, not only was the district one of the nine poorest in the entire country, but it was also the largest producer of opium. Hill tribe minority groups that migrated out of Yunnan Province in China over several hundred years located in the hill areas of Vietnam, Cambodia, Laos and Thailand. These minority groups have always been involved in raising opium poppies — especially the Hmong. A majority of the population of 55,000 in Ky Son District are ethnic minorities with the Hmong accounting for almost forty percent. The district is mountainous with steep inaccessible land. The district is bordered by Laos on three sides. We reached Ky Son from the coast at Vin on Highway 7A which continues across the border into Laos.

Most of the opium poppy fields in Ky Son were in remote areas not visible from the highway. However, after we finished meetings with local officials, we took Route 7A into Laos and there we found miles of poppy fields abutting the road and continuing as far as the eye could see. Like in northern Thailand years before, we saw Hmong families, from grandparents to small children, scraping the opium tar from the poppy bulbs and depositing it in sacks tied to their waists. Despite the fact that we were traveling through the poppy fields in a Ky Son police vehicle, the families were no more concerned with our presence than if they were harvesting strawberries. We learned that like Ky Son, the area we visited in Laos was the largest opium producing district in the country. Much of the opium produced in these two adjoining districts was sent down Route 7A to the Vietnamese port at Vin and shipped out across the South China Sea to various locations.

Shortly after our visit, UNODC started the project in Ky Son which introduced alternative agricultural crops, livestock and off-farm activities. As alternative income sources became available to the minority groups, suppression of the opium crop was increased and by 1999, poppy cultivation was eliminated. Moreover, interdiction of opium crossing the border from Laos was also enhanced with a larger and better trained border patrol.

The Coast of Central Vietnam

Whether it is highlands or lowlands, often the areas of enormous natural beauty throughout the world are also areas of enormous natural disasters. Such is the case with the narrow strip of land between the mountains and the South China Sea coast line. The beaches and rice paddies of central Vietnam are stunning. In fact, the beauty is such that it hides the fact that the central Vietnam provinces are among the most impoverished in the country. The national government has taken steps to improve the economy of central Vietnam including running the main north/south electric power line through the area. Moreover, the country's first petroleum refinery is located in a coastal province. This latter move is more a political than an economic decision.

One of the main reasons why the central provinces will remain poor is that they have forever been beset with natural disasters — mainly from flooding. When the annual typhoons roar across the South China Sea, they usually slam into the coast of central Vietnam. The loss of life is often quite high especially among the small boat fishermen from the villages along the coast. Every year there is extensive property damage caused by high winds and rain. Often there is massive agricultural damage especially caused by salt water intrusion into the rice paddies. Studies show that throughout the world, the most impoverished segment of society suffers the most by natural calamities. This is certainly true in Vietnam.

One of the UNDP projects most appreciated by those living in central Vietnam was one that helped the government establish the National Typhoon Center in Hanoi which is linked to an elaborate communications network in the central provinces, thus constituting an early warning system. As a part of the project, Norway financed a set of electronic buoys off the coast which record changes in the depth of coastal waters. While I served in Vietnam, the first American Peace Corps volunteer served with distinction on this project. But he was not there under the authority of the Peace Corps, but rather under the authority of UNDP as a Peace Corps volunteer transferred to the United Nations Volunteers. He was a computer whiz and helped the Typhoon Center computerize its operations.

Our main event before crossing the old demilitarized zone (DMZ) that separated North and South Vietnam during the war was in Quang Binh Province which is the last northern province before crossing the DMZ into Quang Tri (pronounced Quang Chi). Quang Ninh was a province that received heavy American bombing during the war and, frankly, Delores and I were a bit apprehensive about how we would be received by the local inhabitants. We should not have worried. We were received in the same gentle, friendly manner as was the case in the rest of the country. The purpose of our visit was to view the dykes built along the shoreline to prevent the seawater from inundating the rice paddies It was a joint UNDP/UN World Food Programme (WFP) project. UNDP funded training and provided consulting engineers. WFP provided food instead of money for the laborers constructing the dykes. A project much needed, practical and appreciated by the local farmers.

The Central Highlands

After traveling the coastal route for three days and spending the night in the fishing village of Qui Nhon, we took Route 19 to Pleiku in the central highlands. It is called the American highway because it was built by the U.S. military during the war. The distance from the coast to Pleiku is 83 miles and it was the first paved road we encountered after leaving Hanoi ten days before. The central highlands were always considered to be of strategic important to the North Vietnamese military. Therefore, the region was considered to be important to the South Vietnamese and U.S. armies. The United States had numerous military installations in the area including a large base An Khe, roughly half the distance up Route 19. Like most of the other stops on the trip, the purpose for visiting the highlands was to examine new project possibilities and visit the most famous battle sites. The highlands are heavily populated by ethnic minority groups. During colonial days the French established tea, coffee and rubber plantations in the highlands. The French called the collection of minority groups the Montagnard and actually treated them better than they were subsequently treated by the Vietnamese.

Since colonial days, the Montagnard lived in splendid isolation, and at one point had a population of three million. True, they were dirt poor and lived in very primitive conditions, but there were very few lowland Vietnamese living in the region to bother them. They were looked upon by the Vietnamese with disdain. Their fate began to change however, after the 1954 partitioning. The South Vietnamese government under President Ngo Dinh Diem started a program of moving lowland Vietnamese into the highlands who then started occupying land traditionally used by the Montagnard. During the war, the Viet Cong infiltrated the region and promised the Montagnard that life would be so much better for them under communism. But after 1975, the Montagnard developed an enormous antipathy toward the communist officials because they were deprived of their Christian religious practices and they lost control over most of their land.

Our first stop was at Kon Tom where we had a meeting with the director of the Provincial Office of Education. I outlined a UNDP project that I had in mind to improve the level of teacher training in the Montagnard teacher training institutions located in Pleiku and Buon Ma Thuot. Moreover, I wanted the Ministry of Education and the local authorities to allow the Montagnard teachers to do their instruction in the appropriate minority languages rather than being forced to teach everything in Vietnamese.

We returned to Pleiku where we had a meeting with the Provincial Governor to discuss the proposed teacher training project. The Governor hosted a dinner following the meeting.

During the course of the dinner, I told the Governor that the next morning we wanted to drive as close as possible to the site of the battle of the Ia Drang Valley. I told him my interest was peaked by reading about the battle in the *New York Times* best seller, *We Were Soldiers Once and Young*, by Lieutenant General Harold Moore and Joseph Galloway. The Governor smiled and said, "Mr. Morey, I just had a dinner recently, and General Moore was the guest of honor. Also at the dinner was the General of the Army of the People of Vietnam who led the forces against General Moore. They shook hands, became friends and talked about the battle for the remainder of the evening." The Governor got up, went to an adjacent room and returned with an autographed copy of Hal Moore's book which he proudly displayed for me. My, what time does to heal wounds!

The next morning we drove less than 20 miles to the edge of the Ia Drang Valley. The main battlefield, still thickly covered with brush and elephant grass, lies just below a mammoth rock formation called The Chu Pong Masif. The battle was memorable because it was the first encounter of U.S. and South Vietnamese army units with regular North Vietnamese forces. The battle started on November 14, 1965, when 450 soldiers led by Colonel Harold Moore were dropped by helicopter into the valley. There were 2,000 North Vietnamese troops hiding in the grass waiting for them. It was a three day fire storm fought in 100 degree heat and involved hand to hand combat. U.S. forces finally prevailed, but not without heavy casualties.

The battlefield is close to the Cambodian border. Despite road signs indicating that all traffic was prohibited, I asked Ban to drive a few kilometers down the road. I thought, what the hell, Thuan got us out of other scrapes, and if necessary, he could do so again. It was a foolish mistake. Within five minutes, the border police stopped us, took our passports and ordered us back to the police station. This time Thuan had to pull all stops — invoking the name of everyone from the UN Secretary General to his father — the famous general. Fortunately it worked and later Thuan had the courage to give me a good dressing down for acting so foolishly.

I should have remembered that it was a highly sensitive area because an excellent reporter for the *Far Eastern Economic Review*, Murray Hiebert, landed on the Cambodian side of the border by helicopter in 1992, and met with the leadership of the United Front for the Liberation of Oppressed People (FULRO). This was a Montagnard guerrilla army that took refuge in a remote and inhospitable province in Cambodia when the communists took over the Central Highlands in 1975. During the war, thousands of Montagnards were given small arms and training by the CIA and U.S. Special Forces and many were integrated into regular U.S. army fighting units. For seventeen years after the end of the war, this ragtag group of commandos was still fighting the war, crossing the border, making raids on hamlets and engaging the Vietnamese army in combat. Today these Montagnards have either been repatriated back to Vietnam or sent to third countries, especially the United States. When we reached Buon Ma Thuot (the third major town in the central highlands) later in the day, we had a meeting to discuss the Montagnard teaching project and went to the provincial guest house to spend the night.

As a result of meetings held at the teacher training institutions and with the Governor of Gia Lia Province, two UNDP projects were approved to strengthen teacher training capacity for the ethnic minority areas. A major objective of this joint UNDP-government effort was to make sure ethnic minority children could be taught in both Vietnamese and their minority languages.

From the beginning, the North viewed the central highlands as critical to their strategy for winning the war. In the spring of 1975, with U.S. troops long gone from the scene, the regular North Vietnamese forces easily took the highlands and used Buon Ma Tuot as the mobilization area for their final assault on Saigon. As we drove out of Buon Ma Tuot, headed for Ho Chi Minh City the next morning, we learned things about Thuan's life we had never known before. He is fluent in four languages (Vietnamese, Spanish, Czech and English). He received his undergraduate degree in Cuba before the war and a Ph.D. in electrical engineering in Czechoslovakia after the war. Just as the Vietnamese army started its final push through the central highlands and on to Saigon, Thuan joined an engineering team with instructions from the Hanoi government to assume control of the main television station in Saigon after the city was "liberated." He traveled day and night from Hanoi to Saigon just behind the advancing forces, arriving in Saigon the evening of its "liberation" (April 30, 1975).

On May 1, Thuan and his television team went to Independence Palace to record the ceremony when General Tran Van Tra (pronounced Cha), as head of the Military Management Committee in charge of Saigon, received the surrender from General Duong Van "Big" Minh, the President of South Vietnam who held that office for only two days. After the ceremony, Thuan started searching for his father who served at the rank of General under General Tsa's command. He was quite certain that his father had left the secret army jungle camp near the Cambodian border to accompany General Tra the forty-two mile distance (sixty-eight km) to Saigon. By nightfall father and son were reunited after a four-year separation.

Every few hours as we traveled from Buon Ma Thuot to Ho Chi Minh City, Thuan would point out a landmark he had remembered from twenty years before. When we finally reached Ho Chi Minh City, we drove to the building that had been occupied by the television station that Thuan and his colleagues had taken over. The next day Thuan, Delores and I flew back to Hanoi and the driver took a week returning the vehicle to Hanoi. During the return flight, I told Thuan that on several occasions I asked someone in the Ministry of Foreign Affairs, my official channel on such matters, to arrange a meeting for me with General Tra, but nothing ever happened. Thuan said he was not surprised because there was some controversy surrounding the General's background and therefore an officer in the Ministry would be reluctant to schedule such a meeting. Thuan said that his father was still a close friend of the General and he would use this connection to schedule a meeting. He added that the meeting would have to be held in Ho Chi Minh City because General Tra retired there many years before. Almost exactly one year later (March 1995), when I was in Ho Chi Minh City on other business, I spent three hours with the General at the headquarters office of the Veterans Association of Ho Chi Minh City. Best of all, Thuan served as my interpreter, which was a stroke of luck not only because of his language skills, but also because the General knew him and that made for a friendly and relaxed atmosphere.

An Afternoon with General Tran Van Tra

By way of background, it should be noted that when the war ended in 1975, there were only a few national war heroes and General Tra was one of them. The whole world recognized the name of General Vo Nguyen Giap, who was chief of the general staff of the Vietnam People's Army. Very few outside the armed forces and the Viet Cong fighting in the South would recognize the name Tran Van Tra. During the war, photos of General Giap were often seen in newspapers and television throughout the world. You would never see a photo of General Tra because he and his senior staff were hiding in a mosquito infested jungle camp about 70 miles out of Saigon near the Cambodian border. The site was called the B-2 Base. Like the nearby Communist Party camp described earlier, the military camp would also have to move back and forth across the border to avoid detection. The American and South Vietnamese knew of the base and the approximate area of its location, but despite repeated bombings and search and destroy missions, the camp was never captured nor destroyed. It was from this unlikely location that General Tra commanded all Vietnamese forces in the South. On the day Saigon fell to the communist forces, General Tra put on a clean uniform and traveled the short distance from his jungle base to receive the surrender of the Southern forces. A few days later, on May 7, the twenty-first anniversary of the communists' victory over the French at Dien Bien Phu, General Tra returned to the Presidential Palace in downtown Saigon and appeared before a mass rally of several thousand people. He introduced himself and ten other senior officers who were newly appointed members of the Military Management Committee that would serve as a provisional governing body for Saigon. Most importantly, in his address to the crowd, he promised leniency toward South Vietnamese who had worked for the South Vietnamese government or for the United States.

General Tra's comments were not received well by Party Secretary Le Duan and the Politburo back in Hanoi. The Party ideologues were already planning the establishment of reeducation camps where the South Vietnamese "traitors and puppets" would be incarcerated. Therefore, General Tra could not be fully trusted by communist senior leaders because it was clear that he would be too soft on the South Vietnamese. Not surprisingly, the General spent only a few months as head of the Military Management Committee before being reassigned to a do-nothing job in Hanoi. Tra was certainly a loyal communist — how else could he have risen to the rank of General? He joined the Communist Party in 1938 when he was still a student in Saigon. He fought the French and was a personal friend of Ho Chi Minh. Like Ho Chi Minh, the General's first priority was to liberate Vietnam from the French and then after 1954, his main objective was to reunite North and South Vietnam into a single country. He never felt at ease with the hard-line party ideologues in Hanoi. After a few years in that sterile atmosphere, General Tra happily retired and returned to Ho Chi Minh City to write his memoirs. In 1982, the fifth volume of his masterpiece was published. It caused immediate consternation of Party Chief Le Duan and his cohorts because Tra was very honest in describing how the Politburo interfered in military decisions by over estimating the capabilities of its own military and under estimating those of the South Vietnamese and the United States especially during the 1968 Tet offensive. He was purged from the Party and put under house arrest for three years. He was rehabilitated in 1985 just as Communist Party moderates started to gain more power.

General Tra's saga is typical of a dilemma faced by any Communist Party — the Soviet Union, China or Vietnam. The Party is always afraid of a hero. It is fine if the hero is walking in lockstep with the Party leaders, but if he or she steps out of line, they must be cast aside and ostracized. Otherwise such heroes may try to mobilize their admirers and supporters to challenge Party leaders. That simply will not be tolerated whether it is Premier Zhao Ziyang of China or General Tran Van Tra of Vietnam. The Party leaders became especially concerned when General Tra's comrades in arms organized the Vietnam Veterans Association with Tra as Vice President and the Ho Chi Minh Veterans Association with the General as President. During this time of strict communist rule, all so-called non-governmental organizations were initiated and supervised by the Communist Party. The organizers of these veterans' associations did not even consult the party when they were created.

When I was introduced to the General, I noticed he was a trim and very fit 77 year old. He was alert and, as far as I could tell, honest and forthright in what he had to say. He started by telling me how important it was for Vietnam to be an active member of the United Nations. He also praised UNDP for the useful work it does in the country. He said he was happy to be retired and living in the South. He had spent his whole life serving in the army and it was time for the next generation to run the military.

I told him that I wanted him to start at the beginning of his career and that he did. Like a typical Vietnamese he was not, in anyway, boastful in recounting his career. Rather, he told of his remarkable life in a matter of fact fashion. He spent most of his career in South Vietnam. After conducting a hit and run offensive against the French for nine years (1945–1954), he went to Hanoi and was appointed by Ho Chi Minh as Deputy Chief of the Armed Forces Staff for the Vietnam Peoples Army. In 1959, Ho Chi Minh asked General Tra to develop a trail from the North to the South. The General was in command of 500 soldiers who worked in secret to blaze a trail, parts of which traversed Laos and Cambodia, and terminated less than 50 miles from Saigon. The original trail was called the Truong Son Road and later became known throughout the world as the Ho Chi Minh Trail. The construction of the trail was done in three phases: clearing a narrow path for walking; widening the trail for bicycles, and further widening the trail and improvements in its quality for trucks and tanks.

In 1963, General Tra walked the 800 mile trail to take up his post in the South where he would stay until the end of the war in 1975. During this eleven-year period, the General returned to Hanoi four or five times via the Ho Chi Minh Trail. On three of these occasions he made the round trip journey (1600 miles — 2575 km) on foot. No wonder he looked so trim and fit at the age of 77!

From his secret jungle base near the Cambodian border, General Tra commanded all military forces (regular forces, local forces and guerrillas) in all of South Vietnam below the Central Highlands. Before understanding the full extent of the General's command, I naively asked him if he also had the Viet Cong under his command. With a baffled look on his face, he replied, "Of course, the National Liberation Front (Viet Cong) was under my command. It was necessary to coordinate the activities of the National Liberation Front with those of the People's Liberation Army of the South and the regular Vietnam People's Army. The National Liberation Front was critical in winning the war."

The General described life in the jungle base as difficult. It was always hot with high humidity. The area was infested with mosquitoes and most everyone had malaria at one time or another. The water supply was not always clean which resulted in gastric problems. The General said that the area around the base was bombed periodically by American B52s and, on several occasions, the base had to be moved on short notice to avoid being detected by American and South Vietnamese forces. Such moves were often across the Cambodian border.

The General made no comments about the Vietnamese "David" striking down the American "Goliath"—quite the contrary. He made it clear that the Vietnamese never had any illusions about the might of the American military. He said, "Vietnam knew American forces were stronger than Vietnamese forces in all aspects. Therefore, President Ho Chi Minh's war policy in fighting the Americans was not to destroy the American forces, but to let them know that they would never win the war and eventually they would leave the country." Of course, that is precisely what happened.

He explained, "The Tet offensive of 1968 was important because it showed the Vietnamese could fight against the Americans and the offensive had an impact on the attitude of the American public toward the war. However, the offensive was very costly because of the large number of Vietnamese lives lost." I agree with General Tra's observation. In my view, it is true the Tet offensive caused an American public opinion shift against the war, but this was an unintended consequence. In reality, the Tet offensive was a disaster. It was not a carefully planned military operation designed by Vietnam's most prominent commanders such as Generals Tran Van Tra and Vo Nguyen Giap. Rather it was a scheme dreamed up within the Communist Party, first at the party's headquarters camp in South Vietnam and later endorsed by the Politburo in Hanoi. In General Tra's view the Tet offensive underestimated the strength and mobility of American and South Vietnam forces. It never produced the popular uprising against the South Vietnamese government it was designed to create. Most importantly, during 1968 more than 180,000 Viet Cong and North Vietnamese Regular Army were killed. The ranks of the Viet Cong (under the command of General Tra) were cut by one third.

The General said, "The former Soviet Union and China provided much needed support in the form of equipment and supplies. They also gave Vietnam advice. They both advised that the Americans were too powerful to confront directly. They said the Vietnamese should use a guerrilla strategy and wear the Americans down over time. Support from the Soviet Union and China in the beginning was very little. It became greater only after they knew the Vietnamese could fight against the Americans. But their assistance was reduced when they knew that Vietnam would win the war."

Women in Development

U.S. Senator Jesse Helms of North Carolina once said that funding the UN was like pouring sand down a rat hole. He especially had a negative attitude toward UN sponsored conferences. Two years after serving in Vietnam, I had an opportunity to meet the Senator and as far as I could tell, I didn't change his views on the UN including the worth of international conferences. Frankly, I am not prepared to defend every UN conference, but there was one held in Beijing in September 1995 that had a major positive impact on the women's movement in numerous countries including Vietnam. It was the Fourth World Conference on Women.

As in China, the women's movement in Vietnam is led by the Women's Union. Also like in China, Vietnam's Women's Union was originally created by the Communist Party. What is especially interesting about the Women's Union in Vietnam is that over the years it has assumed the programs and functions one would associate with an independent, nongovernmental organization. Much of this change started with the Beijing Women's Conference in both the preparation and implementation of the resolutions adopted at the Conference. I am pleased to say that UNDP bore some of the cost of sending the delegation to Beijing.

The head of the delegation was Vietnam's Vice President Madame Nguyen Thi Binh (Win T Bing). Most will not recognize the name, but some may recall seeing a photograph of her after I have provided a little background. Nguyen Thi Binh joined the Vietnam Communist Party in 1948 and she was jailed by French authorities in the early 1950s. During the Vietnam War, she became a member of the Viet Cong's Central Committee and in 1969 she was appointed Foreign Minister of the Provisional Revolutionary Government of the Republic of South Vietnam which was a government created on paper by the Communist Party. As for recalling the photograph — Nguyen Thi Binh was the woman sitting across the table from Henry Kissinger at the Paris Peace Talks. She was one who signed the Paris Peace Accords on Vietnam in January 1973, ending the military involvement of the U.S. in Vietnam. Before becoming Vice President in 1992, she served as Minister of Education.

UNDP funded a number of projects in collaboration with the Women's Union, the most exciting of which was a training project to encourage more women to run for election to the National Assembly. As a result of our cooperation with the Women's Union, I had a chance to meet the leaders of the women's movement including Madam Nguyen Thi Binh. In the last meeting I had with her, she said, "Isn't life interesting. For years I fought against Americans in the war and now I am sitting and having a friendly chat with an American who has done so much to help the women of Vietnam through the UNDP." I was very touched by her comments and I replied, "Life is indeed interesting and we should never be held hostage by history." For our farewell meeting with the Women's Union, Delores donned her finest ao dai (ow zi) and she pleased the Vietnamese women to no end by doing so. The conclusion of the meeting became an award ceremony and I was given honorary membership in the Women's Union of Vietnam. To my knowledge, I was the first foreign male to receive this honor and I did so in my role as UNDP Resident Representative.

The Scourge of HIV/AIDS

Despite my best efforts, I was never able to persuade the Chinese government to establish a comprehensive HIV/AIDS awareness project. When I arrived in Vietnam in 1992, I vowed that I would not let it happen again in Vietnam. Fortunately, I did not meet the same governmental resistance in Vietnam that I had experienced in China. By 1992, it was clear that untold millions throughout the world would die from this virus. In the U.S. it affected primarily the homosexual male community, but in other countries health officials saw it primarily as a heterosexually transmitted virus.

Within a year after arriving in Vietnam, I organized a national conference on HIV/AIDS and I invited Khun Mechai Viravaidya as the keynote speaker. Michai, who was once named by *Asia Week* magazine as one of Asia's twenty most important leaders, is regarded as the father of family planning in Thailand. He gained enormous publicity in Thailand and throughout Asia by handing out free condoms on street corners and shops throughout Bangkok. He was also known to inflate condoms with helium and bounce them off the walls and ceilings of crowded restaurants. He is very proud of the fact that his antics brought a great deal of attention to the use of condoms. Early in his career, condoms were promoted for family planning and later in his career, they were promoted to reduce the risk of AIDS. In Thailand today, a condom is popularly known as a Mechai as a tribute to his work. By the time I invited Khun Mechai to the Hanoi AIDS conference, he was a member of the Thai Prime Minister's Cabinet with a portfolio to direct a national AIDS awareness and prevention program. By 1993, when Mechai spoke at the conference, AIDS had already spread over Thailand like a wild fire, especially among sex workers and those who injected drugs.

The introductory speaker at the conference was one of the Vice Prime Ministers of Vietnam. As is the practice at such gatherings, the high-level introductory speaker makes a few inane comments and departs immediately after speaking. I asked the Vice Prime Minister if that was his intention and he said, "Yes, because I have many important appointments." I pleaded with him to delay his departure until after Michai had given his address. He reluctantly agreed to do so. I was amused to find that the Vice Prime Minister was so stunned by Mechai's remarks that he cancelled his other appointments and spent the rest of the morning at the conference. Mechai described the 100 percent use of condoms program he had introduced in Thailand. Among other shocking statistics cited by Michai was the fact that if every AIDS victim was given a hospital bed in Thailand, no other type of patient would have access to a bed for several years.

I wanted Mechai to scare the hell out of the Vietnamese and that he did. For example, he talked about how devastating AIDS was in the Thai military, and on hearing this, the Vietnamese Vice Prime Minister sent his aide out to make a call to summon a general to attend the conference and talk to Mechai at the lunch break. Some months after the conference, the Vice Prime Minister became the head of Vietnam's National AIDS Task Force. The UNDP provided $1 million for a new information, prevention and control project on HIV/AIDS. Several years later, the World Bank funded a $25 million project for the same purpose. Today in Vietnam, AIDS is still a serious problem especially among sex workers, injecting drug users and gay men. Unlike Thailand, however, the spread of AIDS has been fairly well contained regarding the general population. The lesson is obvious. Unlike China, the Vietnamese government was quick to recognize the threat of AIDS and they wanted a UNDP project to be implemented as soon as possible. The Chinese government kept its head buried in the sand and paid a very high price. Did an early intervention by the United Nations (UNDP, UNAIDS, UNICEF, World Bank, UN Population Fund) make a difference in diverting a full scale AIDS catastrophe in Vietnam? The Vietnamese would be in the best position to answer that question. The last evening I spent in Hanoi with Vice Premier Phan Van Khai, he said, "Your intervention on AIDS was one of the UN community's most valuable achievements." Years after the Hanoi conference, I was reminded by the Vietnamese in attendance of my statement at the conference —"Vietnam has fought many wars in its history, but the war against HIV/AIDS could be the most challenging of all if the country does not develop a plan of action."

Tuesdays with Morey and the General

With the possible exception of Premier Pham Van Dong, no one was closer to Ho Chi Minh than Vo Nyugen Giap (Vo Win Ziap). Giap has an excellent university education, but it was not in military training. Rather, he received degrees in political economy and law from the University of Hanoi. During the 1930s he was a history teacher and journalist. Like other Vietnamese revolutionaries of his time, he was a member of the Communist Party and was imprisoned for thirteen months by the French. When the French undertook a massive crackdown on the communists in 1939, Giap fled to China with Phan Van Dong where they met up with Ho Chi Minh. During his exile in China, Giap's wife, father, sister and sister-in-law were arrested, tortured and executed by the French colonial authorities.

In February 1941, Ho Chi Minh reentered Vietnam from China and set up camp in Cao Bang Province in northern Vietnam on the border with China. Shortly thereafter Vo Nguyen Giap joined him and along with Pham Van Dong and others plotted their political strategy and eventually formed a resistance group against the Japanese. While both Ho Chi

Minh and Giap were communists, Ho Chi Minh formed a more inclusive group of resistance fighters of all political persuasions called the Vietnam Independence League (Viet Minh). In August 1945, Vo Nguyen Giap and a motley group of troops under his command marched to Hanoi with an American military unit commanded by an officer of the Office of Strategic Services (OSS). The OSS operated during World War II and was the precursor to the Central Intelligence Agency (CIA). Giap arrived in Hanoi in time to join Ho Chi Minh for his reading of the Declaration of Independence of Vietnam to the gathered masses on September 2, 1945, at Bao Dinh Square.[2]

The jubilation of "Independence Day" soon faded as the French started to regain their foothold in Vietnam. With the light arms supplied by the United States, Vo Nguyen Giap and Ho Chi Minh retreated back to the northern border area to mobilize and organize the Viet Minh Army to fight the French. After Mao Zedong and the communist forces defeated the National Forces of Chiang Kai-Shek in 1949, the fortunes of the ragtag Viet Minh Army changed dramatically when it started to receive large quantities of military equipment across the border from China.

After clearing the French forces out of the northern provinces, the Viet Minh Army under the command of Vo Nguyen Giap defeated the French at Dien Bien Phu on May 7, 1954 after 54 days of battle. Vo Nguyen Giap returned to Hanoi a national hero, but once again his jubilation was dampened later in the year when the Geneva Accords ending the conflict with the French did not provide for a united Vietnam. Instead it provided for a communist controlled North and a non-communist controlled South. Under the Accords there was to be an election of a president for all of Vietnam, but this was scuttled by the South Vietnamese with the advice of the United States.

By the end of 1956, the hard-lined ideologue, Le Duan, took over as Chairman of the Communist Party and he ordered supplies to start flowing to the Viet Cong in the South. Ho Chi Minh and Vo Nguyen Giap were considered moderates within the Communist Party hierarchy. Early on the moderates felt there might be a chance for a negotiated settlement with the South. But Le Duan and his intractable supporters in the Politburo were hell bent on an armed conflict to wrest the South from the grip of the "American puppet" South Vietnamese government.

Although Vo Nguyen Giap was the Commander of the People's Army of Vietnam and Minister of Defense, his advice on military affairs was often rejected by Party Chief Le Duan. President Ho Chi Minh was a staunch Giap supporter, but believe it or not, even his views did not always prevail once Le Duan and the hard-liners gained power. Because Vietnam is a communist state, we will never know for certain what went on behind closed doors in Hanoi during the decade before Ho Chi Minh's death in 1969.[3] If truth were known, Ho Chi Minh could have been likened to a frustrated father trying to lead a brood of unruly and belligerent children who were always squabbling. To make matters worse, Vietnam's two closest allies gave conflicting advice. The thinking of Giap and Ho Chi Minh and the moderates at one point envisaged a reunification of Vietnam through political negotiation. The moderates' point of view was in line with advice given by the Soviet Union.

Le Duan and the militants sided with Mao and the Chinese who argued that reunification should be achieved by military means and above all, the Vietnamese should not negotiate with the United States. At least this was the advice of the Chinese in 1963 and 1964. However, in subsequent years, as the enmity between China and the USSR continued to increase, the Chinese started viewing the United States as a useful counterweight to the Soviets. As a result, they did not want to see the United States humiliated. Hence, the

Chinese advised the Vietnamese to accept a military solution without overthrowing the Thieu government in the South. This position was the core of the eventual settlement between the U.S. and Vietnam.

Vo Nguyen Giap crossed swords with Le Duan on many occasions, but their differences were probably no greater than the period leading up to the Tet offensive. Le Duan was spoiling for a fight and felt it was time for a massive and direct military confrontation with the South Vietnamese and U.S. forces throughout the entire South including the major cities of Hue, Danang and Saigon. It was thought that the shock of such a move would be so great that it would cause an uprising of the people against the South Vietnamese government. Giap, on the other hand, supported more of a guerrilla military approach. Le Duan knew that he could not go to Giap with the plan he wanted so he went to General Nguyen Chi Thanh, Head of the Communist Headquarters in the jungle camp west of Saigon. General Thanh sketched a plan and in July 1967, traveled to Hanoi and presented his plan to the Politburo where it was well received. To celebrate his victory in winning over the Politburo, he went to a party that evening, probably overimbided and died of a heart attack.

After General Thant's death, General Van Tien Dung, Le Duan's sycophant, went behind the back of his boss, Vo Nguyen Giap, and volunteered to refine the plan. The decision to launch the plan during the Tet holidays (Chinese New Year) in January 1968 was a Communist Party decision made largely by civilians. Since Ho Chi Minh and Vo Nguyen Giap favored a guerrilla style approach to warfare in the South and were opposed to a major nationwide attack like the Tet Offensive, Le Duan had the votes in the Politburo to ignore their advice and do as he pleased. Before the Tet Offensive was launched, Ho Chi Minh and General Giap distanced themselves from the decision by leaving Hanoi. Ho went to Beijing and the General departed for Eastern Europe and stayed there for several months. Despite its failure to achieve its objectives, Giap defended the Tet Offensive to avoid breaking ranks with party leaders and to keep his positions in the government and in the Party. After the war, Giap continued to have differences with Chairman Le Duan and his party faction. As a result, he was stripped of most of his senior positions — in 1980 he was forced out of his position as Minister of Defense and in 1982 he lost his seat on the all powerful Politburo. As a consolation prize, he was demoted to the position of Chief of the Science and Technology Commission.

Like the case of General Tran Van Tra, Communist Party leaders in Vietnam have great difficulty in handling heroes especially when the hero bucks the party line. Gen Tra openly questioned party leaders in his memoirs after he retired and he paid a price for it.. General Giap did not want to retire and was willing to remain involved in government even at a much reduced level. It was a humbling experience, but he did not publicly break ranks and he maintained his dignity.

I had three meetings with General Giap during my tenure in Vietnam and frankly, I never found him as forthcoming with me as other senior leaders had been either of his generation or younger. At the time, I knew that he had fallen out of favor with party leaders some years before I arrived in Vietnam. But it was long after leaving Vietnam that I learned the reasons why. I can now understand the reasons he was so guarded sharing his views with me. He was eighty-one years old when I first met with him in 1993. Like General Tra, he held his age remarkably well and was trim and fit. In most of my meetings with him he wore his faded green army jacket with its four stars. He was warm and gracious in his opening remarks. He obviously had been briefed before the meeting. He said that Vietnam was happy to have an American representing the United Nations. He said, "Vietnam is proud of its membership in the United Nations and appreciates what it does to promote development and peace among nations."

During the first two meetings with the General, he reverted to the days when he was a history teacher and explained to me: "During its long history, Vietnam was forced to fight many wars of external aggression. But at the bottom of their hearts, Vietnamese people love peace and development. Hence, after Vietnam defeated Chinese invaders from the Han, Song, Yuan, Ming and Qing Dynasties, Vietnamese kings immediately sent their ambassadors to China to reestablish friendly relations with Chinese emperors, thus bringing peace to Vietnam and allowing the Vietnamese people to reconstruct and develop their country. More recently, the new Vietnamese government practices the same diplomatic policy with the French following its famous victory over the French at Dien Bien Phu in May 1954."

He then discussed more recent Vietnamese history, saying: "Vietnam and the USA were once allies in the fight against Japanese fascism. During the years immediately before Vietnam's successful revolution in 1945, several American pilots parachuted on to the revolutionary government's resistance base close to the Chinese border. We worked with these Americans and also with those under the command of General Claire Lee Chennault of the famous Flying Tigers. These Americans worked closely with Ho Chi Minh against the Japanese. As a close aide of Ho Chi Minh, I witnessed and I was deeply involved in many of the efforts made by the Flying Tigers and other Americans at that time."

General Giap then turned to the period just before the war. He said, "Vietnam was forced to fight a long, arduous, bloody war with Americans following the failure of the 1954 Geneva Agreement and the French departure from Vietnam. It was the U.S. government that installed Ngo Dinh Diem as its ally in Saigon. In turn, it was Ngo Dinh Diem who sabotaged the general elections envisaged by the Geneva Agreement to take place in July 1956 for fear that Ho Chi Minh would win such an election. However, Vietnam is ready to 'let bygones be bygones' and normalize its relations with the USA. Normalization would be for the common benefit of both countries and peoples."

In the third meeting with the General, he said that he was tired of talking about war and wondered if there wasn't something else we could discuss. I told him that I agreed and I thought we had covered the topic of war sufficiently in our previous conversations. Besides, I noted: "War is a topic where you look back and not forward." I had something in mind when I told him that I would like to hear his views on the youth of the country and on environmental degradation. On the first topic General Giap said, "Young people are very important for the development of all countries including Vietnam. I have full trust in the young generation of Vietnamese. They are patriotic, dynamic and bold. To shape the young generation, education is of particular importance and therefore it is critical to improve the quality of education."

On the second topic, the General went on to say, "The environment has become increasingly important for economic development. The environment in Vietnam has become polluted and eventually this will undermine the country's development. Therefore, it is important to raise the awareness of people, particularly of young people, in protecting the environment. Hence, environmental education at school is essential and urgent."

When he was finished stating his views, I said: "General, you have told me you were a teacher long before you were a general. If you would like to become a teacher again, I have a proposal to make." I told him that in a few weeks UNDP and the Ministry of Education would sign a new UNDP funded project which would introduce the various dimensions of the environment into the curriculum of secondary schools. In science classes students would work on projects and experiments related to the natural environment. In history classes they would study about the global environmental movement. In social studies they would study the role of government in making environmental policy. I then said, "What this project needs is an esteemed national leader like you to appear on television and public gatherings to speak about the importance of environmental awareness especially among youth." The General said he would be delighted to serve in such a role and added, "It will make me feel like a teacher again."

A few weeks after our meeting, the UNDP project organized a media event. General Giap and I drove a short distance to the United Nations International School in Hanoi and jointly planted a tree. We discussed with the press the new project and the importance of environmental awareness for the future development of the country. Subsequently the General appeared on television and at similar media events. After more than sixty years, General Vo Nguyen Giap was a teacher once again.In October 2013 General Giap died in Hanoi at the age of 102.

Normalizing Diplomatic Relations with the United States

Normalizing diplomatic relations with the United States was perhaps the single most important foreign policy objective of the Vietnamese government when I arrived in 1992. While no Vietnamese government official ever asked me to play a positive role in normalization, I knew the Vietnamese would be deeply grateful if I did. I was pleased to do so because once the government indicated its willingness to cooperate with the United States in the search for American servicemen missing-in-action, I thought normalization was good for both countries. Besides, it did not conflict with my UN role because the goal of any UN organization is to promote friendly and cooperative relations among nations. I doubt anyone in the U.S. State Department was aware of my role, but the Vietnamese at the highest level knew and appreciated my efforts.

The first opportunity I had to help was in the fall of 1993 when I arranged for senior level Vietnamese to travel the world in preparation for the first Paris Donor Conference. The visa arrangements were easy in all countries except the United States because the United States was the only country that did not have diplomatic relations with Vietnam. I worked with the U.S. Embassy in Bangkok and directly with the Department of State. I had in mind for the delegation to visit the Department of State, but in trying to secure the visas, I emphasized the importance of meetings that I had scheduled with the World Bank and the International Monetary Fund (IMF) in Washington and at UNDP headquarters in New York. Paris was the last stop before Washington on our whirlwind around-the-world trip. One day before departing Paris, I received word that the visas would be issued. The Vietnamese received their visas upon arrival at Dulles Airport. Our State Department visit was friendly, but a bit stiff. Nonetheless, it was the first face to face meeting of Vietnamese with State Department officials in Washington after the end of the Vietnam War.

I spent two days in Washington each year for consultations with the Department of State, the World Bank and the IMF. With the exception of 1992, when I met with junior officers, thereafter I met with someone at a senior level in the East Asia Bureau. In these meetings I described discussions I was having with senior Vietnamese officials and I stated my reasons why the U.S. economic boycott with Vietnam was not working and why the

General Vo Nguyen Giap, center, planting a tree in his capacity as Honorary Director of a UNDP environment project with the author, Hanoi, 1995.

United States should think about establishing diplomatic relations. No doubt these meetings were recorded.

During my tenure in Vietnam, Senator John McCain made several visits to Hanoi and I had the opportunity of conversing with him on the political and economic state of play of the country. The second occasion was especially memorable because it was a one-on-one conversation at a breakfast get together. I told him that while I was in graduate school at the University of Arizona, I became acquainted with Morris Udall who was my congressman. I knew this was a good opening because John McCain loved Mo Udall and held him in the highest esteem. McCain and Udall became friends when they were both serving in the House. Udall developed Parkinson's disease and for the last several years of his life, he was in Walter Reed Hospital. As McCain put it, "Mo was a prisoner in his own body." He could not speak nor could he move, but his mind was sharp and he could hear. At least once a week McCain would visit Mo and talk to him even though he knew that he would never get a response. McCain said that he knew Mo loved to hear Capitol Hill gossip so he would fill him in on the latest and juiciest stories involving members of Congress. McCain knew Mo enjoyed hearing the stories because he could see a twinkle in his eye.

Of course, one can not mention Mo Udall's name without marveling at his sense of humor. This led to a contest between the two of us to see who could come up with the best Mo story. In my story I recalled Mo speaking to a group of campaign workers and he told them there was a preacher who put a sign outside his church which said, "If you are tired of sin, come on in." Mo then added with great glee that below it, someone scribbled, "If you are not, call 822–2423." McCain topped my story because his actually happened. In 1970, Mo ran against Hale Boggs for the position of House Majority Leader. When the vote was over, Mo walked out the door of the majority caucus room and was immediately surrounded by the press. They all shouted, "Did you win?" and Mo said, "No, I lost." A reporter said, "How can that be, Mo? You told us that based on the promises of support made by your colleagues, you were certain you would win." Mo's response was, "Today I learned the difference between a cactus and a caucus. You see with a cactus, the pricks are on the outside!"

McCain's naval fighter jet was shot down as he flew over central Hanoi in October 1967. After parachuting from the plane, he landed in Truc Bach Lake less than two miles from the Hanoi Hilton (Hoa Lo Prison) where he was eventually tortured and incarcerated. Some years later the Vietnamese government erected a monument beside the lake with an inscription which states that on October 26, 1967, John McCain was shot down here. The monument shows a pilot falling in a parachute and the wing of a plane with "USAF" (United States Air Force) inscribed on it. Keep in mind that McCain graduated from the U.S. Naval Academy and is a Navy man through and through.

McCain was in rare form the morning we had breakfast. He said, "I have been out to take a look at my monument here in Hanoi and frankly I am unhappy. I know that the monument is not well maintained because for years the pigeons have been shitting all over the image of the pilot. But that doesn't bother me the most. What really bothers me is that my plane wing indicates U.S. Air Force and that is an indignity no Navy man should ever endure." Some of Mo Udall's humor obviously had rubbed off on John McCain. It is a shame that he did not use more humor in his race for the presidency in 2008.

In 1993, two-thirds of the Hanoi Hilton was demolished to make room for new high rise condominiums and office buildings. The French had built the prison at the end of the nineteenth century and called it Maison Centrale. After the demolition, I went to the site one evening and retrieved several of the original French made bricks. On one of these I attached a small bronze plate and gave it to my friend, Chuck Pilon. He returned to Phoenix and presented the brick to Senator McCain on my behalf. I am told that the brick can still be found on Senator McCain's desk in his Phoenix office.

The U.S.-Vietnam Trade Council, a non-governmental organization headquartered in Washington, also played a useful role in promoting normalization. On one occasion the Council organized a visit to Hanoi by Congressman Bill Richardson of New Mexico. While he was in the House, he had a penchant for traveling the world to negotiate the release of U.S. hostages and help improve diplomatic relations between various governments and the United States. I met with Richardson during his visit and I made my usual points on why diplomatic relations made sense for both governments. I did the same when former Secretary of State Edmund Muskie and his team was sent to Vietnam by President Clinton for the expressed purpose of discussing normalization.

Diplomatic relations were finally normalized in July 1995 and the congressional Republican leadership castigated President Clinton for taking this step. But the criticism was blunted by the support for the move strongly voiced by John McCain. In fact McCain stood beside the President when the formal announcement was made. McCain's support was critical because he gave the President protection from the MIA-POW group that strongly opposed normalization. McCain, after all, was America's most celebrated Vietnam War POW.

In January 1997, I assumed my new role as Director of the UNDP Office in Washington. Five months later, Le Van Bang became Vietnam's first ambassador to the U.S. I first met Le Bang when he was still serving in the Foreign Ministry in Hanoi. In 1993 he was appointed Vietnam's Ambassador to the United Nations and I met with him in New York on numerous occasions. After his arrival in Washington, we resumed our friendship and Delores and I were immediately added to the Embassy's social register. We attended most Embassy functions. Sometimes it was a bit embarrassing because as soon as we would enter the room, Ambassador Le Bang would announce that I was really America's first ambassador to Vietnam!

Farewell Meeting with Premier Pham Van Dong

Two months before leaving Vietnam, I had my last conversation with Premier Pham Van Dong. I told him that I would be leaving Vietnam to take a new assignment as Director of the UNDP office in Washington. He said that starting as a young man, he tried to learn as much as he could about the U.S. government and the city of Washington. He was almost wistful in telling me that Washington was a city he always wanted to visit but conditions were such that there was never an opportunity to do so.

I told Pham Van Dong that some months earlier Delores and I took a driving trip through the North that included stops at the Dien Bien Phu Battlefield and the cave on the Chinese border occupied by Ho Chi Minh during World War II. By mentioning these stops, it would encourage this frail and blind ninety-year-old to reminisce. It did just that.

He started his comments with the same theme as our first encounter four years before — there was a time during World War II when friendship between Vietnam and the U.S. could have been established and this would have averted a military conflict between the two countries. His story started with the time in 1941 that Ho Chi Minh ended his period of exile in China and crossed the border on foot to take up residence in Pak Bo Cave in Cao Bang Province. Eventually Pham Van Dong and Nguyen Vo Giap also crossed the border and established a camp near the cave. Soon other Vietnamese revolutionaries joined them. Ho Chi Minh periodically would call a meeting to discuss how the country would gain its independence. Out of such meetings the Viet Minh Party was formed for the expressed purpose of bringing together Vietnamese of all political persuasions who were willing to fight for independence. Dong said, "A common enemy can create a friendship. The Japanese were the enemy we had in common with the U.S. There were many examples of how the friendship grew between the two countries."

He went on to recount a story of an American pilot by the name of Shaw (Rudolph) whose plane experienced engine trouble and he was forced to parachute and landed near the Pac Bo camp. He was rescued by a group of Viet Minh and taken to Ho Chi Minh. At this point Pham Van Dong said, "Mr. Morey, I cannot see your face, but your voice sounds much like Lt. Shaw." Shaw spent several weeks at the camp and often he would have long conversations with Ho Chi Minh in English. Dong said that he regretted that he only learned French and not English and therefore he was not able to enter into the conversations. Ho Chi Minh and Pham Van Dong escorted Lt. Shaw to Kunming (the capital of Yunnan Province, China) and took him to the base of the American Flying Tigers under the command of General Claire Lee Chennault. Ho Chi Minh asked to have a meeting with General Chennault to discuss the rescue mission, but his request was denied. However, on a later visit to Kunming, Ho Chi Minh and Pham Van Dong met with the General and "it was a very friendly meeting." When the meeting ended, Ho Chi Minh requested an autographed photograph of General Chennault and the general was very pleased to give him one. Ho Chi Minh also requested a pearl handle pistol and he was given several. When they returned to Pac Bo camp, Ho Chi Minh prominently displayed the photo of the General in his cave and put one of the pistols on a shelf. Pham Van Dong said that when anyone would drop by the cave, Ho Chi Minh would show them the photo and the pistol and say, "These are gifts from my very good friend, General Claire Chennault."[4]

In early 1945, the American OSS (precursor of the CIA) office in Kunming supplied radios to the Viet Minh to report movements of Japanese forces in the area. Around the same time, the OSS sent to the camp small arms and several officers to provide military training to the fledgling Viet Minh army. After training there were volleyball games in the late afternoon. After the evening meal Ho Chi Minh could be found surrounded by a group of OSS officers deep in conversation. Pham Van Dong said that during those warm sunny days in Cao Bang, he felt certain that the American-Vietnamese friendship would last because more than one officer told Ho Chi Minh that President Roosevelt was opposed to colonialism and the President would object to France keeping its colonies after the war. There is plenty of evidence to support what Pham Van Dong had heard about President Roosevelt's views about France and its colonies. But when Pham Van Dong's spirits were so high that summer of 1945, he had no way of knowing how much the attitude of the U.S. government would change on the issue of France and its colonies after the death of Franklin Roosevelt in April 1945. What if Franklin Roosevelt had lived another year and insisted that the French be precluded from re-colonizing Vietnam? Would the U.S. have supported Ho Chi Minh and the Viet Minh and thus avoided the death of 58,000 American troops and several million Vietnamese civilians and combatants in the Vietnam War? We shall never know.

Farewell

In the summer of 1996 I came to an agreement with UNDP Administrator Gus Speth that I would relinquish my post in Vietnam at the end of the year and assume the position of Director of the UNDP Office in Washington starting in January 1997. It was not an easy decision for either of us. The annual congressional appropriation for UNDP had slipped well below the normal $100 million level and new leadership in the office was obviously needed. Delores and I preferred to stay in Hanoi for at least another year, but I knew that I had the best background for the job. In addition the Administrator convinced me that the move was in the best interest of the organization.

Wrapping up a four and one-half year assignment is a demanding task. There were a number of major projects under preparation which I wanted to approve before my departure. I had to break in a new Deputy Resident Representative (Nicholas Rosellini) who had taken Jordan Ryan's place. The annual Vietnam Consultative Group meeting (the major meeting with donors) was scheduled later in the year. I was required to travel, especially to the South, to make a final check on the progress of projects and bid farewell to project managers and government officials. Delores was responsible for supervising the packing of all our household belongings into a 40-foot container. In addition, there were numerous farewell receptions and dinners organized by our friends and the Vietnamese government. We were greatly relieved to finally board the plane at Noi Bai Airport Hanoi for our flight back home.

Vietnam Today

In the past twenty years, Vietnam has become a modern well functioning country. The most dramatic and positive changes in economic, political and social policies in modern Vietnamese history occurred as a result of the following events:

- The death of hard line Party Chairman Le Duan in July 1986.
- The historic Sixth Congress of the Communist Party in December 1986 when a policy of Doi Moi (renovation) was adopted which paved the way for a market economy and major reform of governmental, economic, political, financial, legal and social institutions.
- The election of Nguyen Van Linh as General Secretary of the Communist Party of Vietnam at the Sixth Congress in December 1986.
- The appointment of Vo Van Kiet as Prime Minister in 1991. He summarized his attitude in a 2007 BBC interview by wisely saying, "The Motherland of Vietnam does not belong to one person, one party or one group only."
- The warming of relations between the U.S. and Vietnam e.g., the establishment of the MIA office in Hanoi, the easing of U.S. economic sanctions, normalization of diplomatic relations and the bilateral trade agreement.

The most impressive progress report on Vietnam should start at the time the country was reunified in 1976. But, that is not possible because of the dearth of reliable data especially during the "lost decade" (1976–1986), the decade under strict communist rule. If the Communist Party had not made a radical course correction in 1986, figuratively speaking, the country would have simply slid off the map and sunk in the South China Sea. However, as a result of reforms starting in 1987, in just a few short years Vietnam was transformed from a country near starvation to the world's second largest exporter of rice after Thailand.

The progress Vietnam has made in development in the past twenty years is the envy of many countries in the world. As the most recent World Bank Brief indicates, the reduction of poverty and economic growth achieved by Vietnam during the last 15 years are tantamount to "one of the most spectacular success stories in economic development." According to the U.S. Department of Commerce, "Vietnam's economic growth rate has been among the highest in the world in recent years, expanding at an average 7.2 percent per year during the period 2001–2010, while industrial production grew at an average of 12 percent per year during the same period. Vietnam registered a GDP growth rate of 6.7 percent in 2010 and was one of only a handful of countries around the world to experience such levels of economic growth."

According to the Australian Agency for International Development, the poverty rate in Vietnam has been reduced from 58 percent in 1993 to 13 percent in 2008 and is now below 10 percent. In 2011, Vietnam had exports in excess of $93 billion and attracted more than $14 billion in foreign direct investment.

The most amazing story related to Vietnam's rise to middle income status is its evolving relationship with the U.S. It is especially noteworthy because the two countries were at war less than forty years ago and have had diplomatic relations only since 1995 — two decades after the fall of Saigon. The two countries signed a trade agreement in December 2001, and that really got the ball rolling. Between 2001 and 2007, trade between the two countries increased 900 percent! The United States is now Vietnam's largest export market followed by China and Japan. In 2010, U.S. exports to Vietnam grew by 19.8 percent to $3.7 billion. During this same period Vietnam's exports to the United States increased 21 percent to $14.9 billion.

In 2011, more than 300,000 American tourists visited Vietnam. Aside from trade, investment and tourism, the U.S. and Vietnamese governments cooperate in a host of sensitive areas including non-proliferation, narcotics control and terrorism. These and other topics are discussed in the annual bilateral defense consultations. If the truth were known, the Vietnamese are pleased that there is a strong U.S. military presence in Asia. The U.S. military serves as a counterweight to the massive expansion of Chinese military force.

Not only have there been dramatic changes in Vietnam's economy in the last twenty years, there have also been major changes in political and social institutions. Just like political parties in other countries, the Communist Party of Vietnam still plays an important role in macro policy making. Furthermore, Vietnam is a one-party state and it is difficult for a Vietnamese to reach the highest leadership levels in government without being a member of the Party. The Party still sets macro policy, but it no longer runs the day-to-day operations of the government.

- A modern civil service system has been established. It is still a work in progress, but the intent is to have recruitment and promotion based on merit. The second language required for promotion to senior levels is now English which is a change that took place during the time of UNDP's original project of civil service reform.
- The National Assembly is no longer a rubber stamp legislature. It has increased its staff in size and competence. It is developing a committee system similar to the U.S. Congress. Most importantly it now has the authority to review and approve the national budget and determine funding levels for the provinces.

- There has been a major devolution of decision making authority from Hanoi to the provinces, district and communes.
- There is a much higher level of transparency, availability of information and mechanisms for obtaining opinions and feedback from the citizenry at all levels of government. For example, Ho Chi Minh City recently conducted a major public opinion survey to get direct feedback from the residents on the services provided by the city.
- Judges and prosecutors throughout the country are better trained and are required to adhere to a code of conduct. The judicial system is more professional, efficient and transparent. A new independent National Bar Association has been established.
- Only a modicum of progress has been made in the field of human rights. Since the adoption of the Religious Freedom Act of 2005, the U.S. State Department no longer considers Vietnam as a serious violator of religious freedom. Nonetheless, there continues to be gross violations of human rights and substantial political repression. The Communist Party is still the ultimate arbiter and makes decisions which are arbitrary and lack the due process of law.

Vietnam is clearly on a path toward a more prosperous and open society, but reform and adjustments will always be required. In May 2009, Delores and I spent the afternoon talking to Nguyen Xuan Thanh, Director of the Masters Program in Public Policy at the Fulbright Economics Teaching Program in Ho Chi Minh City. I asked Thanh if he had to narrow his focus on the two or three most pressing problems in Vietnam today, what would they be? His immediate answer was corruption and increasing the quality and quantity of higher education institutions.

There has been a decrease in petty corruption such as policemen asking for a bribe to fix a traffic violation. But large scale corruption such as government and Party officials receiving kickbacks in contract bidding is still widespread. Thanh realizes that corruption is a corroding factor in economic development and undermines the trust people have in the government and the party. Thanh feels that China has had more vision than Vietnam in recognizing that quality higher education is the dynamo of economic growth. Fortunately, the World Bank is now making a substantial investment in Vietnam's higher education system.

For the first decade after economic reforms were instituted in Vietnam, economic growth flooded the country and raised the boats of virtually all the households. But in recent years the boats of the affluent, well-connected and well-educated households have risen at a rapid rate while most have risen at a much reduced rate or remained stagnant. The expanding gulf between wealth and poverty is not as great as is found in China. But the rate is accelerating and is causing the same increasing level of resentment between the "haves" and "have nots."

One also finds the same divide in both countries between the more affluent urban areas and the more impoverished rural areas. In 2013, *Forbes* magazine identified Vietnam's first billionaire. He is Pham Nhat Vuong who was born into a Hanoi family of limited means and has made most of his fortune through commercial real estate development. In his high-end shopping mall in Saigon, one can find the same luxury goods that are offered in New York or Paris.

Did the United Nations Make a Difference?

The best way to determine whether or not UNDP and the other UN agencies (including the World Bank which is a specialized agency of the UN) played an important role in the impressive improvements made in Vietnam during the last twenty years is to determine if behavior and performance has actually changed as a result of UN interventions. Here are a few examples of high impact projects and you can judge for yourself.

- Prior to 1986, most senior Vietnamese policymakers learned economics in the Soviet Union. But in 1986 the Communist Party decided to shift the country from a centrally planned to a market economy senior policymakers and most economists in the country at the time knew next to nothing about the principles of market economics. It was UNDP to the rescue when it launched a project in 1988 to provide training in market economics including 39 fellowships for study in the United States and the United Kingdom. Involved in this training program were two deputy prime ministers, twenty ministers and vice ministers and 260 senior policy makers at various levels of the government. It is this cadre of senior policymakers trained under this project who were responsible for implementing the new reform measures.
- In 1996, the UNDP in partnership with the Swiss government signed a $1.3 million project to provide training, research and advisory services needed to enable Vietnam to meet all the requirements to gain membership in the World Trade Organization (WTO). In January 2007, Vietnam was admitted membership in the WTO. In the intervening decade, Vietnam completely revamped its legal structure related to international trade, foreign investment and intellectual property. UNDP assistance played a direct and vital role in this lengthy and arduous process. Moreover, the project was of immense assistance enabling the Vietnamese to meet the same requirements for the U.S.-Vietnam Trade Agreement.
- One of the first major efforts to improve the governance system was a UNDP project launched shortly after my arrival in 1992 on public administration reform and the establishment of a professional civil service. This project, plus follow-up projects, helped separate governmental operations from the Communist Party.
- In 1996 there was a cluster of three major governance reform projects approved with a price tag in excess of $10 million with most of the funding provided by Denmark. These projects were so sensitive that approval by the Politburo of the Communist Party was required. One project was designed to enhance the role and responsibilities of the National Assembly. The next was intended to enhance the competence and independence of the judicial system starting with the Supreme Court. The third project was designed to improve the competence, organization and transparency of the public prosecutors system. (The impact of these projects has been described in the previous section.) Projects started by UNDP in governance, economic management and poverty reduction have now been taken over by the World Bank and other donors.
- UNDP started a project in 1996 to provide training for women in public management, to encourage a larger number of women to compete for senior government positions and to run for election for the National Assembly. There

Vietnamese Vice-Premier Phan Van Khai presenting the Friendship Medal to the author, 1996.

has been a significant increase in the number of women in both of these professional categories in the past 10 years.

- In 1997 a UNDP project was approved which provided training and advisory services in the integration of environmental concerns in the approval process for public investments. Today there is an environmental impact analysis done prior to the approval of all major capital investment projects.
- In 1999 the National Assembly approved the Enterprise Law which provides the legal framework for the private business sector. This law plus new regulations to streamline the licensing procedures for businesses were the direct output of a UNDP project entitled, "Improving the Regulatory Environment for Businesses."
- In 1997 a $12.6 million UNDP project established the Rural Infrastructure Development Fund focused on the 122 poorest districts and communes in the country. The project continues to operate and provides soft loans for projects (such as rural roads) that are identified and prioritized by the people living in communes and districts. These projects are then reviewed and approved by the local People's Councils. In short, this is grassroots democracy with a purpose.
- Vietnam is still fighting the battle against the spread of HIV/AIDS especially among intravenous drug abusers. Fortunately, the U.S. Agency for International Development (USAID) is providing significant assistance to the country in this struggle. The integrated United Nations HIV/AIDS project launched in 1995 did not eradicate the problem, but it at least helped the country avert a national pandemic.

On the last evening in Hanoi in December 1996, Deputy Prime Minister Phan Van Khai (subsequently Prime Minister) hosted a dinner where I was awarded the Vietnam Friendship Medal which is the highest honor given to a foreigner for assisting the country. I am the first American to receive this award after the reunification of the country in 1976. In my view, I did not receive the Friendship Medal in a personal capacity — not at all. I believe it was an expression of appreciation at the highest level of the government for the assistance provided by UNDP and the UN community in making Vietnam a more prosperous and well governed country.

10

Lessons Learned

Foreign Aid: What Works, What Doesn't and Why

Throughout most of world history, when a war ended, the prevailing attitude was "to the victor belongs the spoils" and the victorious tribe or country would plunder the defeated at will. Not so at the end of World War II. Presidents Roosevelt and Truman, George Marshall and Dean Acheson knew that the greatest threat to the peace after a hard-won victory would be to leave the axis powers in a stagnant and enfeebled position. Hence, the helping hand of the Marshall Plan was extended to Europe devastated by war. Through the use of loans and grants and working in close cooperation with three United Nations agencies (World Bank, UN Relief and Rehabilitation Administration and UNICEF), the Marshall Plan helped create a new prosperous and democratic Europe. The Marshall Plan was the first major effort in international development assistance and it was enormously successful. Some years later, international assistance was applied to developing countries, but the results in many cases were not nearly as successful. For the past half-century, the development assistance community debated why this was the case.

Fortunately, by the advent of the twenty-first century there is general agreement on what works and what doesn't. This new consensus on development assistance is recognized by UNDP, the other UN funds and programs, World Bank, IMF, regional development banks, bilateral assistance programs and international non-governmental organizations (NGOs). UNDP played a major role in building this consensus beginning with the publication of the *Human Development Report* in 1990. The concept of human development is extended beyond economic development to embrace social and political development. Before dissecting the new consensus, it is worth noting that development assistance is only one form of assistance under the rubric of foreign assistance. In fact, in monetary terms, it is one of the smallest forms. Much larger types of foreign assistance include: (1) humanitarian aid to refugees and those affected by natural and human caused disasters; (2) assistance for infrastructure such as World Bank loans for roads and power grids; and (3) security programs such as peacekeeping, military training and de-mining.

Beginning with Truman's Four Point Speech in 1949 and continuing through the next forty-two years of the Cold War, the United States was vying with the Soviet Union to win the hearts and minds of people living in developing countries. Most certainly there was a high degree of altruism in assistance provided by the U.S. and other bilateral donors. Nonetheless, there were also numerous questionable projects used to prop up corrupt and despotic regimes which were based on the hope that the country would not fall into the hands of the communists. During the Cold War period, most of the developing countries were run by an autocrat supported by a military junta or wealthy elite. Moreover, neo-socialism was in vogue in the developing world. Unfortunately, it took decades for leaders in these countries to recognize that socialism is neither effective nor efficient. Therefore, no matter how carefully crafted development projects were, policies and institutions in these countries suitable for sustaining sound development often did not exist. In many cases, funding was controlled by host governments which led to widespread misuse of funds. While we would like to think that this type of foreign assistance is a thing of the past, regrettably, it is not.

Currently there are indications that the waste of foreign aid has reached an unimaginable level. In September, 2011, a U.S. bi-partisan spending commission released a report indicating that the U.S. government wasted $30 billion in Afghanistan and Iraq in various aid projects over the last decade. One of the most egregious examples of waste in Afghanistan is the diversion of $360 million into the pockets of government officials, criminals, power brokers and even the Taliban.[1]

One should not assume that the American voter is opposed to all forms of foreign assistance. When Americans are asked if the government should assist in the improvement of health, sanitation, education and other vital services in poor countries, the vast majority say yes. Yet they are still skeptical about foreign aid and with good reason. Perhaps because of a Christian-Judeo conscience, Americans support foreign assistance but they grossly over-estimate the amount of money spent on foreign aid by the government. In 2010, World Public Opinion conducted a poll. When Americans were asked to estimate the portion of the federal budget devoted to foreign aid, the median response was a whopping twenty-five percent! When asked what an appropriate amount should be for foreign aid, the median response was ten percent which is still an enormous number given the size ($3.8 trillion) of the federal budget. In fact, just one percent goes to foreign aid. But since the beneficiaries of such aid are neither constituents of the U.S. Congress nor the President, foreign assistance is a highly vulnerable target in the budget cutting process.

Foreign Assistance That Does Not Work

There are several reasons why some foreign assistance efforts are failures:

- In the past there was a *noblesse oblige* attitude on the part of many donors which could be summarized as, "We are privileged and are, therefore, obligated to share some of what we have. Since we know how to accumulate wealth, we will also pass along our wisdom and knowledge." Despite the best of intentions, the project ideas which were hatched in Washington, New York, London and Stockholm and then transferred to developing countries often did not work because the recipients were not really involved in formulating the project and, therefore, never bought into it. Moreover, often it was the donor identifying the need and not the recipient. In short, there was more lecturing than listening on the part of the donors.
- There must be a modicum of stability for development to work. Money funneled into a country wracked by violence and unstable governance will often end up in the wrong hands and be spent on the wrong projects. As one document in the

commission's report on Iraq and Afghanistan says, "Funds begin as clean money, then either through direct payments or through the flow of funds in these subcontracting networks, the moneys became tainted."[2] While stability is essential for sustainable development, it should not be used as an excuse for maintaining the status quo by describing reforms as a threat to the social and political order. Dynamic stability is required to maintain equilibrium. It is the sustained stability of a bicycle rider and not someone standing in a fixed position. For months after the Tiananmen crisis, Premier Li Peng and other Chinese leaders put the brakes on reform for fear it would destabilize the country. Fortunately, Deng Xiaoping recognized that change and adjustment in a system is essential for long term stability and urged that reform be put back on track.

- In the past, good projects were formulated in collaboration with the recipients, but they failed because the country lacked the necessary policies and sound institutions to sustain the effort. For example, in the early days of the UNDP country program in Vietnam, misguided policies and weak institutions doomed such projects. In the decade after reunification, the communist leaders imposed a strict planned economic model adopted from the USSR. Within such a flawed policy framework, it was virtually impossible to have sound and sustainable development assistance projects.

- Often development assistance projects go off the track in countries with an autocratic and non-democratic regime such as Egypt under Mubarak. Problems often multiply if the funding is under the control of the government. However, with care and imagination, it is possible to have partial success in such countries. It requires strong, competent and honest project managers who are not tied to the political regime and an effective monitoring and accountability system. In short, the same standards UNDP requires in the rest of the world.[3]

Foreign Assistance That Does Work

Development assistance is the most difficult form of assistance because the concept of development in the words of Nobel Laureate economist Joseph Stiglitz, "represents a transformation of society, a movement from traditional relations and traditional ways of thinking ... to more 'modern ways.'"[4] Traditional cultural values may stay the same, but institutions and policies must adjust to a new globalized world and as the example of crop substitution projects in Thailand illustrate, development assistance projects take a long time to show results, and thereby test the patience of those who fund them.

It is clear from a review of failed development assistance projects that for the projects to succeed recipient country participants must play a strong role in identifying their own problems and fashioning solutions to address them. But the donor, be it UNDP or the U.S. Agency for International Development (USAID), must be honest and forthright in refusing to fund certain projects if the country has a weak institutional policy environment which will not produce project success. In such a case, UNDP or other development organizations should try to convince the government that certain policy and institutional reforms are necessary for sustainable development. Frankly, had I been in Vietnam before Nguyen Van Linh and Vo Van Kiet took office, I don't think the UNDP projects would have been nearly as successful as they were after the reformers took over. The good news is that starting in the 1990s and the collapse of the Soviet Union, political momentum in Vietnam and the rest of the developing world shifted toward market economics and democratic institutions.

Additional elements of the new consensus within the development assistance community on the basic goals of development include the following:

- the ultimate purpose of development is poverty alleviation
- development projects must help countries (not just governments) help themselves
- sustainable development rests on public institutions and practices which are democratic, transparent, just, participatory, honest, effective and efficient
- equitable distribution of land titles
- government plays an important role in development especially in social programs, education and health
- development works best when there is a strong and viable non-governmental sector (private foundations and NGOs)
- there is a crucial role in development for the private business sector and the larger civil society including the NGOs
- successful development is highly dependent on international economic cooperation through trade, foreign investment, education and technology transfer

Not only should development assistance projects be conceptually sound to achieve success, but must be executed in a professional and transparent manner. The time tested procedures followed by UNDP serve as a model. All projects are monitored and reviewed by the field office. Large expenditures must be approved in advance by UNDP. Projects are audited both by a special unit in UNDP headquarters and a UN audit group composed of member state experts. A final review of project performance is done by a team of outside experts.[5]

Is it Possible to Export Democracy?

In April 1917, American President Woodrow Wilson appeared before a joint session of Congress to seek a Declaration of War against Germany in order that "the world be made safe for democracy." Sixteen years later (March 1933) the Nazi Party in the German Federation gained the largest number of seats in the election to the Reichstag (parliament) and its leader, Adolph Hitler, became Chancellor. As Fareed Zakaria once quipped that instead of the pursuing the ill-advised quest by Woodrow Wilson to make the world safe for democracy, perhaps "democracy should be made safe for the world!"[6]

Following in the Wilsonian tradition, more than eighty years later the forty-third American President George W. Bush declared, "So it is the policy of the United States to seek and support the growth of democratic movements and institutions in every nation and culture, with the ultimate goal of ending tyranny in our world."[7] After the U.S. invasions of Iraq and Afghanistan, the Bush Administration worked mightily to install democracy in these two countries. But the jury is still out on the question of whether an honest, just, effective and lasting democratic system will evolve in either country. At the moment, the prospects look bleak especially in Afghanistan. The evidence gathered from various parts of the world indicates that the exportation of democracy is a highly unsuccessful enterprise. There are a number of reasons why this is so.

Defining Democracy

Before delving into the issue of exporting democracy, it is wise to pause for a definition of terms. The term democracy has been bandied about for centuries, but I am not certain everyone is reading off the same page. I do know it means one thing in the United States, something else in Europe and something quite different in China. Many have summarized the debate by describing democracy as the ability to throw the rascals out.

Democracy describes a decision-making process based on three principles: (1) Popular sovereignty — political authority rests with those who are governed (the people); (2) Political equality — one person, one vote regardless of gender, race, ethnicity, religion or wealth; and (3) Majority rule — fifty percent plus one in tabulating the votes.

Democracy prescribes a process, but not an outcome. One may believe that a certain decision is abhorrent, but if it was made according to the principles stated above and the vote tally was accurate, it would be a democratic decision. For example, in 2006 the radical Palestinian party Hamas, which is committed to the destruction of Israel, won a clear majority in the parliament. Independent international observers declared the election to be fair and free.

It should also be noted that democracy does not describe a particular structure of government. The U.S. structure is based on a separation of powers and checks and balances. But the most popular structure is a parliamentary democracy where the source of executive power is derived from the legislature or parliament. The American system of checks and balances contributed to the paralysis of the U.S. government in 2011 and 2012, and also the deadlock between the President and the House of Representatives. Newly emerging democracies favor the adoption of a parliamentary system and they are wise to do so.

Democracy as we know it today is not pure democracy where the governed are also the decision makers. True, there are a few examples of pure democracy such as the old town hall meetings in rural New England. Rather, the United States has representative democracy which is often called a republic and is an accurate description of the U.S. government. As contained in the U.S. Pledge of Allegiance, the United States is a republic which means that ultimate power rests with the people and is exercised by representatives chosen by them. All modern democracies are republics including the United Kingdom which is both a constitutional monarchy and a republic.

In order to preserve the principles of democracy, a number of requisites must be put into place to prevent governmental abuse and restrict the majority from running roughshod over the minority. A useful list of these requisites is found in the British Magna Carta drafted in 1215 and 576 years later in the first ten amendments of the U.S. Constitution called the Bill of Rights. These rights include freedom of speech, of the press, of assembly, the right to a jury trial, to petition the government, right to bear arms, and protection against unreasonable search and seizure. The first amendment also prohibits the establishment of religion by the government and preserves free religious practice. Such a provision would be of special importance in those countries which suffer from religious conflict.

Finally, there are several conditions necessary to sustain democracy which include the rule of law, an independent judiciary, and a strong and vibrant non-governmental sector. Moreover, the same conditions are required for both democracy and sustainable development, namely a set of public institutions and practices which are transparent, just, participatory and honest. When all of the above rights are protected and the required conditions are met, we have what most scholars call liberal democracy. Henceforth, when I speak of democracy, I am referring to liberal democracy.

Democracy Rests with the People in a Stable Society

The commitment to lasting democracy must come from the bottom and not imposed from the top at the insistence of an outside power such as the United States. It is particularly difficult to have sustained democracy in countries like Iraq and Afghanistan which are riven by ethnic, tribal and religious conflict. Elections in such countries exacerbate conflict and magnify divisions. The first order of business in a fledgling political system is not installing democracy. Rather, it is the imposition of law and order to achieve stability. After years of futile attempts by their national governments and billions of dollars of U.S. assistance, this first step has not been achieved in either Iraq or Afghanistan. We should heed the advice of James Madison, the father of the United States Constitution who warned in one of his famous *Federalist Papers*, that "in framing a government which is to be administered by men over men, the great difficulty lies in this: you must first enable the government to control the governed; and in the next place oblige it to control itself." Madison is correct, first achieve order and then work on a system that is fair and just.

Democracy Cannot Be Imposed with an M-16 or AK-47

It is counterproductive for an outside power to attempt to export democracy through the use of tanks and mortars. It is impossible to foster democracy within the chaos and destruction of war. In the aftermath of war, people are not worried about democracy. They are worried about where they will obtain potable water, how they will feed their children, how they will rid their homes and communities of sewage and rubble, and how long they will be required to wait until electric power is restored and their schools and hospitals are reopened. It is wise to first focus on the basic needs of the people and then turn to the task of building a democracy.

Development Leads to Democracy

In the first half-century after World War II, there was a "chicken and egg" debate over the question of which comes first—democracy or development? Now most development scholars agree that development is a necessary requisite to democracy. During the first half-century after the war, it became obvious that most developing countries which were dirt poor and underdeveloped were ruled by dictators and non-democratic regimes. In some of these countries policies were instituted to encourage economic growth and poverty allevi-ation, and, eventually open societies and democratic institutions started to emerge. In some countries there were enlightened despots who had the wisdom to establish policy frameworks which fostered sound development.

Such was the case of Park Chung Hee of South Korea. Park was an army general who led a military coup in 1961, and ruled the country with an iron fist for the next eighteen years until he was assassinated in 1979, by his security chief and director of the Korean Cen-tral Intelligence Agency. He was an autocrat who was brutal in suppressing political dissent. Yet his policies lifted millions of Koreans out of poverty and placed his country on a course to lead the "East Asian Miracle" countries. Whether he knew it or not, he sowed the seeds of his own destruction. South Korea today is a thriving democracy and is the first aid recipient country to become a foreign assistance donor with membership in the twenty-four member Development Assistance Committee (DAC) in the Organization for Economic Cooperation and Development (OECD). The OECD is an exclusive developed country assistance club established in 1961 with headquarters in Paris. In a penetrating article published in 2006, the highly respected Korean journalist Jae Hoon Shim wrote, "That makes you wonder what exactly do you mean by human rights — which comes first: the food or freedom of dissent. Much of the Korean society under Park had at least acquiesced in his iron rule because they placed economic progress ahead of democracy."[8] The Park name still has sufficiently strong appeal, especially among older voters, to enable Park Chung Hee's daughter, Park Geun-Hye, to be elected president and return to her childhood home — the presidential Blue House in December, 2012.

Evolution of Democracy

As was the case in South Korea and many other countries, development leads to democracy. But it takes many years and does not occur in a direct linear fashion. The culture that underpins any society constantly grows and evolves. Development impacts the culture which then causes changes in the social and economic milieu. This transformation in values and the belief structure occurs slowly in the early stages of development, and accelerates as the economy becomes more sophisticated especially with the emergence of a knowledge-based society. A knowledge-based society in the U.S., Western Europe, Japan or China is dependent on highly educated publics which are attuned to the mores and ideas of a globalized world. These knowledge workers communicate with each other throughout the globe on the internet. Social networking, for example, adds at least a million users a day and there were one billion Facebook users throughout the world by the end of 2012. This new generation is characterized by people who are ambitious, and independent thinkers who value personal freedom, social and professional engagement with others, and have opinions on how their society should be managed. This new generation of knowledge workers demands a more open society and democratic institutions. Democracy in turn depends on a civil society which is educated, well-informed and willing to join together to improve their community and country. Ultimately, development and democracy form a virtuous circle and reinforce each other.

Building Democracy

When one thinks of building democracy, holding elections and reforming political institutions come to mind. While both are important, it is certainly not the place to start.

First — social services must be put in place especially an educational system which assures equality of access and opportunity. Equal access to healthcare is also a requisite.

Second — a sound economic, financial and monetary system must be established to support a functioning democracy. All evidence indicates that development must precede democracy.

Third — instituting an electoral system and reforming the political structure involves a power shift. It is often seen as a zero sum game where some gain at the expense of others. Invariably, this leads to violence, dislocation and turmoil. This is exactly what has happened in the revolutions in Tunisia, Egypt, Libya and Syria.

Both China and Vietnam have faced political turmoil which has shaken each country to its roots. These two countries are also keen observers of their former communist comrades of the Soviet Union and their replacements in the new Russian Federation. Leaders in China and Vietnam recognize the mistakes of Boris Yeltsin and his friends in opting for instant democracy and a market economy. Through an opaque process driven by greed, collusion and corruption, the Russian state sold off its assets to a small group of cronies for a pittance — thus becoming a quintessential example of "Crony Capitalism." Today Russia has a government which is far from a democracy and an economic system which is not based on sound economic principles. The gulf between wealth and poverty in the new Russia is enormous and many Russians feel they are worse off under the new system than they were under communism. The Russian leaders truly put the cart before the horse.

What the Communist Party hardliners in China and Vietnam fear the most is the creeping threat called "peaceful evolution." When I was serving in Vietnam, a military newspaper accused me of promoting peaceful evolution which, of course, I was doing at the behest of Premier Vo Van Kiet and other reformers. The growth of a prosperous middle class is the biggest threat to the Communist Party and it is taking place through peaceful evolution. Much of this is being fueled by globalization and the revolution in information technology. As a researcher of social attitudes of youth at Beijing's China Youth University for Political Science told the *Financial Times* , "Students don't do sit-ins, they blog and use Twitter."[9]

In short, the best way to promote democracy is through the type of peaceful evolution employed by UNDP in China and Vietnam. Words are important in any political culture and it is not productive to sit down with government counterparts and launch into a diatribe on the evils of a one-party system and the virtues of democracy, human rights and capitalism. The wise approach is to sit down and say, "How can we work together to improve economic growth, promote equal opportunity, enlarge choices and give the poor a chance to lift themselves out of poverty through their own drive and imagination?" This requires transformational change in education, health, agriculture, industry, economic policies, environmental protection, public institutions which are honest, effective and efficient, and a strong transparent and fair legal and judicial system. These are precisely the major areas covered by UNDP in China and Vietnam. Focusing on the requisites and conditions for democracy is the place to start. Let the political reforms follow.

Will China Ever Become a Democracy?

Most economists feel that China is the most amazing case of development in world history and I tend to agree with them. Starting with Deng Xiaoping and accelerated by Jiang Zemin, Zhu Rongji, Wen Jiabao and Hu Jintao, China has adopted policies which have resulted in an economic growth rate and elimination of poverty at world shattering records. The question remains whether the Chinese leadership someday will show the same vision in instituting major political reforms. Of equal importance is the question of whether China can sustain its high level of development without adopting democracy; because if it can, it will prove to be the most conspicuous exception to a rule that has been established over several hundred years. To answer these questions, we need to examine several factors which are important in understanding the mentality of the Chinese leadership.

- As the most ancient civilization on earth, the Chinese have a concept of time which is quite different from the rest of the world. When Deng Xiaoping said that political reform would follow economic reform by seventy-five years, he saw this as a short period of time in his nation's history and he was correct. Given the short history of the United States by comparison, most Americans think a seventy-five year waiting period is an eternity.
- As a result of their concept of time, many Chinese are able to develop a long term vision of how the world and their country will evolve. For example, the Chinese are keen to gain the respect of the world as an emerging super power. Yet they still identify China as a developing country. Since the time of Mao, they have gone to extraordinary lengths to convince the rest of the developing world that China is a part of their camp. This vision is now paying off handsomely for China as it assumes the role of the world's largest investor in Africa and Latin America.
- In a nation-state, the state is a political entity with authority over a territorial area. A nation is a collection of people who share a common culture and, in some cases, also a common ethnicity. The concept of the nation-state originated in Europe and has been adopted throughout the world. In China the state is very new, dating back to 1949. The nation, however, is the oldest civilization on earth dating back five thousand years. There lies the problem. Throughout Chinese history the nation has been strong, but the state has been weak. That is still the case. Given the geographic and population size of the country, this fact should not be surprising. For Mao and his revolutionary cohorts, communism was the answer to bring discipline and order to a very fragmented country. Communism is an ideology which weds economics and politics, and is totalitarian because it destroys the separation between the public and the private. In a sense, communism allows the state to make deep intrusions into the nation with the attempt to mold the culture to suit its purposes. In the view of the "Long Marchers" the essential glue required to hold the whole thing together is the all-powerful Communist Party of China. The bonus for the Party is that the type of thinking I have just described fits perfectly with the deep seeded cultural value of maintaining harmony.
- Democracy will never come to China until the role and power of the Communist Party is altered. During the time Hu Yaobang served as Party secretary and Zhao Ziyang served as premier (1980–1987), attempts were made to create a more tolerant and transparent party. But Deng Xiaoping and his old guard cronies thwarted such efforts. Most Chinese agree that imposing democracy, even as recently as thirty years ago, would have been a mistake because the conditions required to support democracy were lacking. Some of those same Chinese contend that now an educated and prosperous middle class has emerged and, therefore, it is time to start changing the role of the Party and converting the People's Congress into a democratic parliament..
- Deng Xiaoping and Zhao Ziyang were not development economists, but they both recognized economic reform must precede political reform. They also both recognized that the ultimate goal of development was to lift people out of poverty; therefore, it was logical to start with agricultural reform in the rural areas where most of the poor were living.

- When the United States and Western European governments lecture the Chinese on human rights, the leaders always counter by saying, "The most basic human rights pertain to food, shelter and access to health care and education." When I first arrived in China, I thought this argument was simply an evasive smoke screen. I soon learned that their argument had validity. Once again, the lesson is: start with basic needs and the advantages of an open society will eventually be recognized.

- The most pivotal decision made by the leaders in modern Chinese history was the adoption of a market economy. The Party purists have gone through theoretical and verbal contortions to give the impression that the new economy conforms to communist ideology. But the pragmatist reformers have won the battle and have called their economic policies everything but capitalism. Not only is a market economy essential for economic growth, it is also favorable to the growth of democracy. In fact, the preeminent scholar of democracy, Robert Dahl, asserts that, "Polyarchal [dispersed power] democracy has endured only in countries with a predominantly market-capitalist economy; and it has never endured in a predominantly non-market economy."[10] The adoption of a market economy does not guarantee China will become a democracy, but the evidence is very compelling that market economics lays the groundwork for democratic systems.

- Given the background points that I have outlined, I feel it is safe to say that China will eventually evolve into a liberal democratic system. There are still several hundred million Chinese below the poverty line, but the government is taking steps to address this problem and basically the economy is on track to sustain democracy. There is a growing educated middle class which will eventually want a say in how its government is run and how its society is managed.

- A market economy has an enormous impact on society and culture. With tens of millions of workers traveling from rural areas seeking employment in the cities and special economic zones, the Chinese population has become mobile and restless. Labor unions are becoming more independent and there is a new sense of social justice within this mobile work force. Grievances are now being voiced, and so far, the party has done a poor job of handling the discontent. Most important is that some of the new generation of leaders recognizes that moving toward a more open society is not only the right thing to do, but also the smart thing to do. They recognize this is necessary to sustain economic growth in the future. They also recognize that their closed and non-transparent system will not be well-equipped to handle the social adjustments that must be made to achieve the coveted goal of maintaining harmony. They realize they must keep moving forward or they will lose control. Like Deng Xiaoping, they know that achieving stability in the social and political order is gained through the sustained stability of a bicycle rider moving forward and not the old guard trying to maintain stability by standing in a fixed position.

- The new crop of Chinese leaders led by President Xi Jinping and Premier Li Keqiang is smart, well-informed and has learned how to navigate in a world that increasingly embraces democracy. When the imprisoned Chinese pro-democracy advocate, Liu Xia, received the Nobel Peace Prize in October 2010, a group of retired senior Communist Party officials issued a letter denouncing the closed and non-transparent system and described the Party's Central Propaganda Department as an "invisible black hand" and called for an end to the Party's control of the media. These twenty-three former officials were especially incensed by the Party censorship of comments made by Premier Wen Jiabao a few weeks earlier. Yes, you read this correctly! The Party actually censored the sitting premier. While on a visit to the special economic zone of Shenzhen, Wen was censored for warning, "Without the safeguard of political reform, the fruits of economic reform would be lost and the goal of modernization would not materialize." In a subsequent interview with CNN in New York and, therefore beyond the reach of the Central Propaganda Department, Premier Wen said, "We need to gradually improve the democratic election system so that state power will truly belong to the people and state power will be used to serve the people."[11] Hopefully someday the People's Republic of China will truly be the *People's* Republic of China.

Women in Development and Gender Equality

World War II wrought enormous changes in American society. There was a labor shortage during the war, and women were recruited in the war industry to fill in for the fighting men who went into the military. It was pitched as a woman's patriotic duty to go to work. Posters were distributed throughout the country picturing a young woman wearing a red polka dot bandana and blue overalls. She had a determined look on her face as she proudly exposed her bicep and the caption read, "We can do it." She became known as Rosie the Riveter and will forever be a cultural icon in American history. There were plenty of "Rosies" in other allied western countries as well. When the war ended, most women returned to the role of housewives, but many decided to continue in the workforce. A social revolution was started and today a two-income family is the norm.

In developing countries, there was no such revolution because women have always been dominant in the workforce. It wasn't until I arrived in Thailand in 1978 that I learned the critical role women play in their national economy. While driving through the rice paddies in the central plain, who were up to their knees in water planting seedlings?—women. Who were carrying heavy loads of firewood on their backs walking along the road?—women. In small businesses, the workforce in Thailand and other developing countries is dominated by women. Unlike Rosie the Riveter, their contribution to the welfare of the community and nation was often unappreciated. Even worse, women were abused, discriminated against and gender equality was non-existent. If one were to review reasons why people fall into poverty (isolation, limited access to resources and lack of participation), one would find that impoverished women are more disadvantaged than men in every category.

Especially in the Muslim world, pushing for gender equality is very difficult and will be resisted for a long time to come at the local level. For example, while the Taliban were in control of Afghanistan, providing education for girls was prohibited. Nonetheless, UNDP, UNICEF and UNFPA could not ignore the UN Charter and the UN Declaration on Human Rights, and all three made gender equality a global policy goal to be followed in every country. UNDP took the lead and started advocating gender equality long before the publication of the *Human Development Report.* After publication of the report, which highlights the negative economic consequences stemming from sex discrimination, the UNDP resident representatives had a stronger base to argue the case.

In 1993, the World Bank published a major study entitled, *The East Asian Miracle*,[12] which complemented the Human Development Report and bolstered the argument for gender equality. It noted that a common feature of the eight fastest growing economies in Asia examined in the study was the need to invest in human capital to achieve economic success. The study also noted that economic success goes hand-in-hand with eliminating the gender gap by providing educational opportunities. One no longer had to make the argument for gender equality based only on moral grounds; there were now two major studies based on solid scholarship which made clear that the lack of equal opportunity for women is a serious deterrent to a country's effort to improve its economy. Now, it was not just the right thing to do; it was also the smart thing to do.

In 2010, the UN General Assembly established a new UN organization called UN Women to advocate gender equality and empowerment. The first executive director of the organization was Michelle Bachelet, the former President of Chile. The organization focuses on violence against women, economic empowerment, leadership and participation. With the creation of this new organization, hopefully the other organizations will not take the attitude, "there is now an organization exclusively devoted to addressing women's issues so let them do that and we will do something else." The creation of the UN Women is a positive step because women's issues require special and specific treatment. But addressing women's issues should be mainstreamed because rights for women are human rights and the promotion of gender equality is one more essential step in building democracy.

The Importance of Civil Society and Non-Governmental Organizations (NGOs)

Before joining the United Nations, I took NGOs for granted and paid little attention to them. I knew that professional organizations like the bar association and associations of certified public accountants had serious responsibilities they exercised on behalf of the public. I also recognized that organizations like the YMCA, Salvation Army, and local food banks were of vital importance in caring for community needs. It wasn't until I began serving in China that I realized the importance of NGOs because they encourage an open society and serve as an effective and efficient alternative to cumbersome government bureaucracy in meeting the needs of the people. I also learned that it is very difficult to eradicate poverty without the involvement of local level NGOs.

In countries like China and Vietnam, there are organizations which have the appearance of NGOs. But, in fact, they are neither independent nor private organizations because they are created by the Communist Party. In a communist state, authority derives from the Party; therefore, national and local organizations must, by definition, be creatures of the Party. In addition, the Party fears the growth of truly independent organizations because such organizations could become powerful and challenge the authority of the Party.

In China I represented both UNDP and UNFPA and I wanted to undertake projects for both organizations with the All-China Women's Federation. It is the largest organization of women in any communist country and has a local level presence in every province. UNDP was willing to provide assistance to help modernize the management structure of the Chinese Women's Federation and, frankly, enable it to become less dependent on the Party. But it became clear that a senior Party official would be involved in every step of project formulation and approval, and I concluded that it would not be worth the effort. UNFPA was more successful in partnering with the Women's Union to establish a training of trainers program on family planning and reproductive health. Such a program was welcomed by the Party because it had already established the one-child policy. UNDP had much better success with the Women's Union in Vietnam especially in launching a training program designed to encourage women to run for election to the National Assembly.

In China, professions like law and medicine are still tightly controlled by the state, and truly independent NGOs which even hint at social action are verboten. However, non-governmental philanthropic groups which focus on the poor, infirmed and those suffering from natural disasters are permitted but regulated. Beginning in 2004, the Communist Party finally recognized the value of philanthropic organizations and they were given legal status. Just as in the United States and Western Europe in an earlier period of history, the Chinese have become more involved in organized private charity as more people have amassed fortunes. There is now an umbrella organization located in Beijing called the China Foundation Center which receives contributions from Chinese families and corporations as well as from the Bill and Melinda Gates and Ford Foundations. There are 1,324 private foundations operating in China. In 2010, private foundation revenue was $1.6 billion and the figure will exceed $2 billion in 2012. The establishment of the China Foundation in 2010 led the list of the top ten events of Civil Society" and included on its board of directors is a former local staff member in the UNDP Beijing office.

Independent and professional associations are of vital importance to a country's ability to prosper. In the United States, if an attorney is guilty of illegal or unethical activities, the state bar association will take disciplinary action. In China, if an attorney takes a class action suit against an unsafe business which happens to have strong ties to a senior Party leader, the government will not only disbar the attorney, but file a criminal charge for good measure. This still happens in China. The rule of law is a principle strongly supported by UNDP and we always felt a good place to start was to encourage an independent bar association. During my years in China, we did not get very far in proposing changes to the lawyers' association, but UNDP had greater success in Vietnam. There, UNDP partnered with the American Bar Association to help the Vietnam Lawyers Association become a more independent, ethical and professional organization.

In both countries, UNDP also tried to reach out to the association of accountants. To reduce corruption in government and business, an independent, professional and honest association is required to introduce a system of certified public accountancy. This will not happen as long as the party holds sway over the accountancy profession. Accountancy is not mentioned in most development models, but perhaps it should be. Nothing reduces corruption like a good accountancy system coupled with sound corporate governance. Corruption retards economic growth especially when the ill-gotten gains are transferred outside the country. In recent years UNDP has developed a greater appreciation for the role of civil society in development and encourages partnerships at global and country levels with the private sector, foundations and civil society organizations.

An excellent description of the interdependence of government, the economy and civil society was made by former U.S. Secretary of State Hillary Clinton in her address to the World Economic Forum in 1998. She subsequently summarized this concept as follows: "A successful society is like a three-legged stool: You have an effective, functioning, accountable, responsible government; you have a dynamic, free-market economy creating wealth and opportunity; and you have civil society, which is an equal player in promoting what makes life worth living. Because it's in civil society that we have our families, that we exercise our faith, that we engage in volunteerism, that we try to make a contribution to help another person or improve our community."[13]

China versus Vietnam — Which Is Ahead?

Before making comparisons between China and Vietnam, it is necessary to keep things in perspective. The land area of Vietnam is very small — about the size of the U.S. state of New Mexico and has a population of approximately 88 million. China's land mass is enormous and has a population of 1.3 billion. There are several provinces in China with a larger population and land area than Vietnam.

In both China and Vietnam, the Communist Parties did not agree on significant reform until all-powerful leaders died. In China, Mao died in 1977, and in December, 1978 Deng Xiaoping convinced his comrades to adopt the Four Modernizations to reform agriculture, industry, national defense and science and technology. Eight years later in Hanoi, Secretary General of the Communist Party Le Duan, died in July 1986. In December of the same year, the Party adopted sweeping reforms and elected Nguyen Van Linh as the new reform-minded Party Secretary. China had an eight-year head start on Vietnam in economic development and has widened the gap between the two countries each year. But the same is not true in political and social reform. In recent years the Legatum Institute, a London-based public policy group has published an annual prosperity index which ranks the countries of the world according to eight factors: economy, entrepreneurship, opportunity, governance, education, health, safety and security, personal freedom and social capital. It is not surprising that the index for 2012 covering 142 countries indicates that China's economy is ranked eleventh. Vietnam's economy is ranked thirty-ninth, but it is still has a higher ranking than India and Indonesia. There is a gulf between China and Vietnam in per capita GDP. Moreover Vietnam imports more than it exports and China has not had this problem for seventeen years. In addition, Vietnam has a higher inflation rate.

But there are three sub-indices of the prosperity index which reveal that Vietnam has a higher rank than China — governance, safety and security, and personal freedom. Variables included in governance are rule of law and political rights. Safety and security includes the ability to express political opinions without fear. Personal freedom includes civil liberties and freedom of choice. On governance the spread between the two countries is close — Vietnam ranked sixty-first and China sixty-fifth. But on safety and security, the spread was much wider — Vietnam ranked fifty-fifth and China one hundred and first. On personal freedom Vietnam ranked ninety-ninth and China ranked one hundred twenty-eighth. The disparity between the two countries in their ranking squares with my own observations. Vietnam is further ahead in developing a representative political system. Vietnam's National Assembly is far less of a rubber-stamp parliament than China's People's Congress. For example, the Vietnamese National Assembly now has the authority to review and approve the national budget which is the most important power of any parliament. It is true that in the June 2011 parliamentary elections, communist candidates received 91 percent of the 500 seats. But there are now more self-nominated members and businessmen in the National Assembly than ever before. Entrepreneurs are now members of the Party and some are members of the policy-making Central Committee.

There is more democracy in elections within the Communist Party in Vietnam. More candidates than positions are offered to the Central Committee for election to the powerful

Politburo whose members are now ranked by the number of votes they receive. However, making the Party in Vietnam more open and transparent has been a process of taking two steps forward and one step back. For example, the Party Congress in 2006 was more open than the Congress in 2011. In 2006, the preliminary Party report was released to the public which resulted in a public discussion with opinions openly expressed on human rights, democracy and corruption. There is also more intra–Party democracy at the city, provincial and district levels where the local Party Congress elects the major local Party officials rather than having them appointed by Hanoi.

There is greater freedom of expression in Vietnam by the press and individuals. Perhaps this is because it has only a fraction of China's population and does not have China's history of popular movements spreading like a prairie fire with weak central control. In China, the Party clamps down immediately. Vietnamese authorities are more lenient until a popular movement starts to organize and then they bring the hammer down. It is not surprising that the Legatum Index indicates greater personal and religious freedom in Vietnam.

Vietnam receives a higher score than China on governance. In addition to the fact that Vietnam is a smaller and more manageable country to govern, there is also a better separation of Party and government functions. In Vietnam the hand of the Party is less involved in day-to-day governmental operations. They are both still one-party systems where the most important policy decisions are made in closed door Party meetings. Therefore, they both have major problems with corruption and lack an independent judiciary and rule of law. In building for the future, China is clearly ahead with better health care and a much better education system.

Vietnam will always have an uneasy peace with China. It was occupied by China for a thousand years and was invaded by China on its northern border as recently as 1979. China was an ally during the Vietnam War, but within the communist brotherhood, Vietnam received considerably more support from the Soviet Union. After quizzing me about my four years in China, a senior Vietnamese official said, "Mr. Morey, we have never pretended to be the Middle Kingdom. China does not want to rely on the rest of the world, but Vietnam is a poor country and we need as many friends as we can get." This is why the two major foreign policy goals when I arrived in Hanoi in 1992 were the normalization of relations with the United States and gaining membership in ASEAN (Association of Southeast Asian Nations). Vietnam now has much closer economic cooperation with the rest of the ASEAN members, and has a trade agreement with the U.S. Vietnam wants to increase military cooperation with the U.S. and was first in line among nine countries to sign the Declaration of the Trans-Pacific Partnership (TPP) at the November 2011 Asia-Pacific Economic Cooperation forum in Hawaii. By the end of 2012, eight other Asian and Pacific countries joined Vietnam in becoming members of the TPP, a new major trade agreement. Indeed Vietnam does need "as many friends as it can get" as it continues to cope with its gigantic neighbor to the north.

The United Nations in the Twenty-First Century

For American of my generation who were in elementary school in the decade after the end of World War II, the United Nations was the hope of the world. In those days there was a national news magazine designed to keep children informed on nature, science and current events called the *Weekly Reader*. The magazine is still published (print and digitalized) and distributed by subscription, but apparently not as widely read as it was fifty years ago. My teacher would quiz the class on topics covered in the magazine and that is when I first learned about the United Nations and how important it is to the United States and the rest of the world. To this day, the bulk of the members of support groups like the United Nations Association of the USA are over the age of sixty-five. Many members lived through the war and were taught the worth and importance of the United Nations. It was created by Franklin D. Roosevelt and Winston Churchill; came into being under Harry Truman; and was a pillar of foreign policy under Dwight Eisenhower who took the global leadership role in the creation of the International Atomic Energy Association and the World Food Programme. It has been used as an important tool in U.S. foreign policy by every U.S. president following Eisenhower.

Despite support for the UN by successive U.S. administrations, the UN has been under continuous attack by the extreme right wing of the Republican Party starting with the founding of the ultra-conservative John Birch Society in 1958. Even as a card-carrying Republican living in central Ohio in the mid–1960s, I was shocked when my eight-year-old daughter returned home frightened one Halloween night and informed me that she had been lectured in a loud voice by one of our neighbors who told her she should not collect 'trick or treat' funds for UNICEF because it was part of the United Nations and the UN was opposed to U.S. interests. Now the ultra-conservative wing of the Republican Party is under the influence of the so-called "Tea Party" which is a loosely organized backlash movement which gained prominence during the congressional elections of 2010. The leading Republican candidates running in the primaries for the presidential nomination for the 2012 election seem to be engaged in a rhetorical competition of UN bashing as they pandered to members of the Tea Party.

Why do these candidates and some voters have such a negative attitude toward the UN? There are several possible answers:

- In his farewell address in 1796, President George Washington advised his country to avoid entangling alliances with foreign countries. Isolationism has been a strong current in American political culture ever since. Isolation sentiment against a global organization reached its zenith in 1919 when a Republican-controlled Senate rejected U.S. membership in the League of Nations.
- Most members of the ultra-conservative Libertarian Party oppose the UN because they feel it restricts U.S. sovereignty.
- The John Birch Society was founded in 1958 when the fear of "godless communism" was running high in the United States. The organization's leadership claimed that the Soviet Union and disloyal Americans were colluding to create a "New World Order" antithetical to American values to be administered through the United Nations. Hence the John Birch Society calls for the United States to withdraw from the UN. The anti–UN, New World Order conspiracy is still perpetuated by extreme political conservatives and some fundamentalist Christians who view the UN Secretary General as the antichrist.
- Some still remember the troubled times described in Chapter 2 during the mid–1970s when the developing country bloc (Group of 77) joined the Soviet bloc in passing resolutions equating Zionism with racism. Today the Soviet bloc no longer exists and the identification of a developing country has become blurred since the Group of Twenty (G-20) Finance Ministers and Central Bank Gover-

nors was formed in 1999. The G-20 is composed of the European Union and the nine major developed countries plus ten countries from the Group of 77 including China, India, Brazil and South Africa. With the collapse of the Soviet Union and the trend throughout the world toward democracy and the market-economy, the stereotype image of "third world" countries using the UN to heap abuse on the U.S. simply no longer exists. Those UN detractors who still have this image are stuck in a time warp.

- The most heated dispute between the United States and other member states of the UN has not focused on the United States directly. Rather the discord has involved the Israeli-Palestinian conflict. This conflict resurfaced in October 2011 when Palestine was voted full membership in UNESCO. The United States and Israel opposed the vote, and both argued the Middle East conflict could only be resolved by direct negotiation. Under a 1990s U.S. law which prohibits funding to any UN organization which grants membership to Palestine until an agreement has been reached with Israel, the Obama Administration was forced to announce that UNESCO would lose an $80 million contribution which represents 22 percent of UNESCO's budget. No doubt, the Palestinian Authority will seek membership in additional UN organizations which will result in additional U.S. cuts. The process will continue until the President negotiates a new arrangement with Congress which doesn't seem likely in the near future.

- The UN is complicated and difficult to fathom. It is an organization composed of member states which make policy decisions that are carried out by international civil servants composing a secretariat. The UN is also a collection of organizations with their own professional staffs such as UNESCO, UNICEF and UNDP. When a disparaging remark is made by a politician against the UN, it is difficult to determine which part of the UN is being rebuked. Is it one or more of the member states? Is it the UN as an organization or one or more of the UN agencies? Is it the UN Secretariat? One of the 2012 Republican presidential candidates said that he would consider pulling the U.S. out of the UN; does he know that he may be including the World Food Programme which feeds millions of refugees everyday? Does he really want to pull out of the International Atomic Energy Agency which released a detailed report in November 2011 on nuclear weapons development in Iran? Does he really want to deprive the U.S. of its veto power on the Security Council? If he envisaged any of these steps, he certainly would not have the support of the American people.

Rather than harboring thoughts of a withdrawal from the UN, in reality 80 percent of the American electorate supports continued U.S. engagement in it. In a comprehensive bi-partisan public opinion poll conducted by Public Opinion Strategies and Hart Research Associates in October 2011, 65 percent of U.S. voters said they favor the United States paying its dues to the UN on time and in full. An even larger number of voters (71 percent) favor the United States paying its UN peacekeeping dues on time and in full. This attitude is shared by a majority of Republicans, Democrats and Independents. A majority of Americans (55 percent) oppose proposed legislation which would cut U.S. funding for the UN. More than two-thirds (68 percent) of American voters believe the UN is still needed in today's world. An overwhelming majority of Americans support the humanitarian and development work of UN programs and agencies. These include reversing the spread of

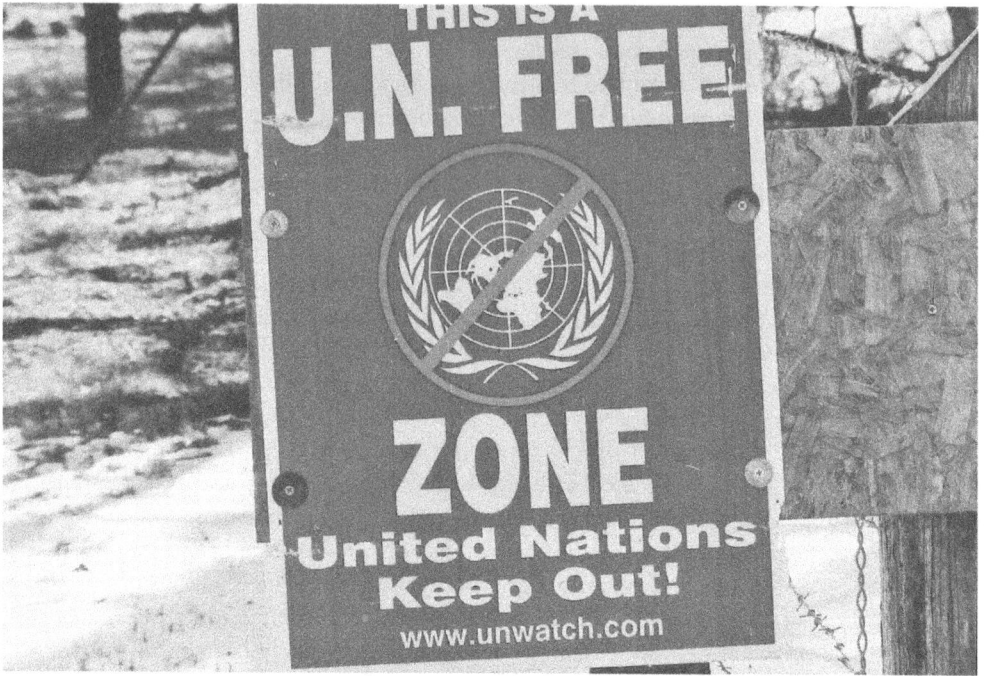

Sign on the front lawn of a UN opponent in rural New Mexico, 2012.

HIV/AIDS and malaria, safe drinking water, insuring girls are safe from violence and have access to quality education, and improving the health of mothers and children.

Myths versus Reality

In its winter 2011 newsletter, the UN Association of the United Kingdom published a list of misapprehensions and distortions of the role played by the United Nations. Included in the list are the following:

(1) Myth: The cost of the UN is too high.
Reality: The annual cost of the UN and all of its agencies is approximately $30 billion which is the equivalent of Wall Street bonuses in 2008. It is less than the cost of fifteen B2 bombers. It is a modest cost for humanitarian, development and peace-keeping operations in 140 countries throughout the world.

(2) Myth: The UN has a bloated bureaucracy.
Reality: The entire UN system, including all agencies, totals less than 85,000 employees. The total UN staff is smaller than the 93,000 permanent employees of the U.S. Internal Revenue Service or the 1.5 million world-wide employees of McDonald's.

(3) Myth: The UN is a world government and abridges the sovereignty of the United States and other states.
Reality: The UN Charter specifically safeguards the sovereignty of member states. The UN is a voluntary association of 193 sovereign states.

(4) Myth: U.S. staff members of the UN do not have to pay federal income tax.
Reality: A staff assessment is taken from the monthly salary of every UN staff member

to cover the payments of their national income tax. In the case of U.S. nationals, the staff assessment is the equivalent of the federal income tax.

Strengths and Weaknesses of the United Nations System

The following pages provide a summary analysis of both the strengths and the weaknesses of the United Nations. They are not intended to be a comprehensive treatment of any of the points, but rather to itemize the main thrust of the argument in each case.[14]

It should also be noted that they describe the United Nations system, which includes but is not confined to the UN Secretariat in New York. It includes a variety of funds, programs and specialized agencies, some of which even precede the establishment of the UN in 1945, but all of which are affiliated to the UN, while having their own intergovernmental governing bodies. In this regard, the most visible part of the UN — the Security Council — is only the tip of a much larger, and less controversial iceberg.

Intrinsic strengths of the UN, without which the world would be a poorer place — elements which would have to be reinvented, if the UN ceased to exist:

- World Parliament: The globalized world of the twenty-first century means that numerous issues are interconnected. This applies not only to the global climate, but also to the internet, trade, public health, animal and crop diseases and so on. The UN General Assembly provides a global parliament to discuss such issues. The effectiveness of this as a global forum for discussion should not be underestimated. Winston Churchill famously observed that, "Jaw Jaw is better than War War." As an old UN poster stated, "There wasn't a World War again yesterday."
- Universality of Membership: For such a world parliament to be fully effective, it should have universal membership, as the UN does. However problematic this may sometimes be, it ensures that all states are represented and remain within the loop of international diplomacy. Ostracism, which compromises this universality, can be counterproductive. The UN can thus be characterized as constituting a unique and indispensable mirror of the world as it is, with all its flaws and weaknesses.
- Forum for the Informal: Indeed, it is very often the corridors of the General Assembly rather than the main auditorium that yield the best results, as world leaders, who are not strictly on speaking terms, find it helpful to meet at the margins of the formal meetings. Such opportunities to break the ice in terms of bilateral relations may be more important than formal discussions in the main hall.
- "North-South" Cooperation: The UN promotes cooperation and collaboration between rich and poor countries. Just as foreign assistance is a critical part of a country's foreign policy, development assistance through organizations like UNDP promotes stability and friendly relations between major donor countries (north) like the U.S. and the developing world (south).
- Consensual Development of Normative Values: Partly because of the above characteristics, the United Nations has a unique role to play in defining and furthering normative values. The Universal Declaration of Human Rights

(UDHR), the Convention on the Rights of the Child (CRC) and the Convention on the Elimination of all forms of Discrimination against Women (CEDAW) are only the best-known examples of such normative values which have been adopted by consensus at the General Assembly, albeit after often extensive and intensive negotiation. These in themselves represent the best of U.S. ideals and values (compare, for example, the Preamble to the UN Charter with the U.S. Declaration of Independence).

- Granted, implementation of such universal values falls well short of the high aspirations that such conventions embody. However, it is surely better to aspire to such universal values than to dismiss them. There is a memorial to Eleanor Roosevelt in the UN gardens on the East River. Mrs. Roosevelt, FDR's widow, was a major force behind the Universal Declaration on Human Rights, which was adopted in 1948 and forms the basis for much of the global human rights legislation around the world. Her memorial states: "She would rather light a candle than curse the darkness, and her glow has warmed the world."

- Consensual Development of Normative Standards: No less important, and indeed of more practical impact on a day-to-day basis, is the steadily accumulating international technical standards which govern many of the routine transactions of the modern globalized world. Requiring a shelf or more of documentation to be fully elaborated, these range from civil aviation flight safety (overseen by ICAO), sharing of international weather and climate data (managed by the WMO), intellectual property rights, including patents and copyright, (managed by WIPO), and international maritime law (managed by IMO). This is just the tip of the iceberg in regard to such normative and operational standards, which are developed under the aegis of the UN system, and which guide the day-to-day work in so many sectors. Apart from being indispensable to day-to-day commerce and living, they gain value and credibility by virtue of the UN's universal membership and consensus decision-making in such matters. To a large extent (with some significant exceptions, of course) such normative standards are developed and adopted on a technical basis, without political rancor, but in the full understanding of a community of purpose.

- Global Public Goods: Just as there are some policy areas which are best dealt with at a local level (e.g. education and law enforcement in the U.S.), so there are some issues which can only be addressed at the global level. Economists call such items global public goods, i.e. issues which will go unaddressed unless they are addressed collectively. The classic example of a global public good is climate change, which everyone in the world shares; there can be no solution, unless everyone shares it. There are others, such as international war and peace (e.g. nuclear non-proliferation), management of international seas (e.g. the threat to international trade being posed by Somali pirates), international drugs and crime, and outer space. To be sure, there are sometimes regional versions of these, but they are best addressed regionally with a global framework. And, which other organization can provide such a credible global framework, if not the UN?

- International Rule of Law: One specific example of global public goods is the international rule of law. In UN terms, this started with legal disputes between member states and, since 1945, has been arbitrated by the International Court of Justice in the Hague. More recently, however, there has been an appreciation that a complete breakdown of law and order in a single member state can pose a threat to others in the region and beyond, if only in terms of an exodus of refugees. The UN, therefore, established a World Criminal Court (WCC), also in the Hague, to pursue individual perpetrators of "crimes against humanity," an institutionalization of the Nuremberg trials that followed World War II. International cross-border crime, drug and human trafficking are similarly global public goods which need to be addressed by the international community on a collective basis; efforts on this score are managed by the UN Office of Drugs and Crime (UNODC).

- International Economic Stability and Regulation: In the recent past and current times of economic uncertainty, the important of global economic and financial management is self-evident. Fortunately, the international mechanisms for this exist including those which operate under the aegis of the UN. The most important of these is the IMF and its sister, the World Bank. Their work is complemented by the World Trade Organization (WTO) which, though technically not a part of the UN system, operates according to the same principles. To be sure, these institutions are complemented by inter-governmental meetings of what is now termed the G20, the world's 20 largest economies, as well as by the regional institutions of varying capacities. The most notable of these is, of course, the European Union. However, there can surely be little doubt that economic affairs need a level of global management, however difficult this is to achieve.

- Power of Collective Political Action/Censure: The universality of membership means that, if the UN pronounces on a political matter, it has significant impact, even without an accompanying capacity to enforce. Sometimes, its pronouncements do carry with them some punitive measures, such as international sanctions. More often they do not because of the understandable difficulty in achieving a consensus among 193 member states, all of which have different and often competing national interests. However, UN global positions on Burma (Myanmar), North Korea (DPRK), Iran and others do have an impact.

- Value of Collective Humanitarian Response: In a world of frequent natural disasters and/or politically-caused civil disorder, either or both of which may have major humanitarian consequences, a collective response by the international community has many benefits. These include coordination among many actors (government, UN agencies and NGOs), prioritization between competing demands on humanitarian response capacity and linking the humanitarian response to political processes. The UN is uniquely placed to provide this central coordination role, which is performed by the United Nations Office for the Coordination of Humanitarian Affairs (UNOCHA), complemented by UNHCR, WFP, UNICEF and others. Collective assistance efforts in Haiti is just one recent example of this.

- Effectiveness of Collective Campaigns: Especially in the area of global public health, there is great value to be gained from worldwide campaigns led by the UN especially the WHO. The eradication of smallpox, the international response to SARS and Avian Influenza, HIV/AIDS (UNAIDS) and immunization programs (Global Alliance for Vaccines and Immunizations — GAVI) have proved their worth.

UN Weaknesses that are in principle amenable to change/improvement — however difficult/unlikely

Representative Deficit:

- One Nation One Vote: This principle effectively equates the U.S. (population 312,832,000) with Nauru (population 9.322). Although in a world which is still based first and foremost on nation states, this aspect of the UN's basic design is unlikely to change; it can be, and normally is, balanced by consensus decision-making on most issues.
- Security Council: The present membership structure of the Security Council, which provides a veto power to the five victors of World War II (U.S., Russia, China, France and the U.K.), is clearly unrepresentative of the world in the twenty-first century. While this is agreed by most member states, there are several alternative models, however with no agreement as to which to adopt. This is difficult to change, but not impossible and will probably happen some time in the future. Meanwhile, however, normal practice is for consensus decision-making even in the Security Council, with the veto being used very seldom.

Mechanism of International Accountability:

- Human Rights Council: The value added (rather than subtracted) of this organ of the UN has been questionable, as individual member states protect themselves from censure by resisting the justified censure of others. However, there is no reason in principle why this could not be strengthened as an instrument of human rights accountability. However, it probably is true to say that governments, individually or collectively, will never be as effective guardians of human rights as is the judiciary, a free press or the NGO community which often acts as the most effective conscience of all, e.g. Amnesty International, Human Rights Watch, et al.
- Numerous International Conferences: The steady development of the UN's normative standards discussed above is inter alia sustained by a succession of global conferences. While these certainly generate a great deal of hot air, they also provide a degree of pressure on member states to honor the commitments they have made and ratified, by requiring "state parties" to individual conventions to report to periodic meetings on the progress they are making to this end.

The UN's inherent weaknesses which are not amenable to change — the nature of the beast

It is also necessary to grasp the basic nature of the inter-governmental mechanism that is called the United Nations. This must be acknowledged, understood and accepted. In this respect, membership of the UN can be likened to that of the local golf club, some aspects of which may not always be wholly to the liking of an individual member, as a result of wholly understandable and appropriate collective decision-making. But that member will still want to be a member because of the many benefits that he/she has as a result — not the least of which is a regular round of golf.

The UN is an inter-governmental body, not a supra-governmental body. The UN derives whatever power it has from the member states, rather than transcending the powers of individual state members. The Secretary-General is a secretary, not a general. He commands no troops, cannot raise taxes and his little independent room for maneuver, being bound to carry out the wishes of the member states, acting collectively — when they agree, and often they don't.

The UN's basic architecture, founded on sovereign member states is difficult to change. The UN has changed a great deal in response to the challenges it faces since its founding in 1945, immediately after World War II. However, the fundamentals remain the same and are difficult to change. For example, the composition of the Security Council is very outdated in terms of the modern world, almost seventy years later. Everyone agrees with this, yet there is no consensus on how to change it, and any proposal can be vetoed by one of the five permanent members — including the United States.

No end in sight to the inefficiency of UN committees: In essence, the UN is a committee of 193 members. This is true of the General Assembly and countless other intergovernmental bodies which span the UN system. This is the price of universality and collective action in any context. Anyone who has ever been a member of a committee (e.g., the same golf club) knows how inefficient and tortuous such deliberations can be — and how ambiguous, unclear and individually unsatisfactory the resulting decision can be. Parliaments are little different (viz., the U.S. Congress.).

Beyond the control of a single member state, i.e., the U.S., or any other member state for that matter. In this respect, the golf club analogy works well. A club of any sort is a collective association, which no individual member can control or dominate. It requires give and take on the part of all members, and an acceptance of second-best at times. This is both a strength and a limitation of any collective action.

The political nature of the organization: Being made up of governments and led by politicians, it is not possible for the UN to transcend this characteristic. Most citizens have their frustrations with their own governments and with the politicians they elect to run them. It would be unfair to think that the UN — comprising 193 governments — would be any different.

Dysfunctional power of political symbols and totems: Moreover, such politicians have a penchant for grand gestures and symbolic posturing. If this is a characteristic of the U.S. Congress and all other parliaments, there is no reason to expect that the UN's intergovernmental processes — themselves parliaments of a sort — will be any different. Such symbolic gestures will not always be in agreement with U.S. policy, for example in the case of the Middle East, Israel and Palestine.

Political ambivalence and ambiguity: Partly because of the difficulty of achieving agreement among 193 member states, many UN resolutions are either vacuous or so ambiguous and ambivalent as to be ineffective. Constructive ambiguity has long been a hallmark of professional diplomacy but this characteristic, when translated into the UN context, means that many UN activities could be termed "ambidextrous," i.e., 'on the one hand, and on the other.' This does not make it easy for the international civil service which serves the member states in the UN Secretariat.

Inter-governmental bureaucracy: The secretariats of the UN exist to serve the intergovernmental processes described above, with all their weaknesses. It is impossible for this international civil service to transcend the political nature of the UN itself— or to avoid some of the politicization which characterizes most civil services. For example, the top positions throughout the secretariat, from the Secretary-General down, are filled by a political process which serves to ensure a balance among the 193 nations, and inevitably influences decisions and modus operandi. This is similar to the "spoils system" of the U.S. system whereby an incoming president appoints the senior positions in each federal department.

The UN or any other governmental organization will never be as fleet of foot as the private sector, nor produce as clear a bottom line.

Multicultural operating environment: It should always be remembered that the UN works in six languages, not just English. As for most staff and diplomats, even these six languages are their second or third. In this respect, language serves as a proxy for the multicultural nature of the UN, which underlines the difficulty of finding common ground and sometimes even agreement on apparently simple issues. In fact, rather than decrying its limitations and weaknesses, it is rather surprising that the UN works as well as it does.

Polycentric architecture: The UN system is actually a network of different organizations, each with its own different intergovernmental governing body. This reflects the way in which the system has evolved over the years, starting in the 1860s with the creation of the Universal Postal Union. Yet, this polycentric nature, while being the way things are, can also be seen as a strength not a weakness. Although it may appear to encourage inefficiencies and waste, it nonetheless is preferable as compared to a monolithic and sclerotic UN system.

In 2012, President Barack Obama was reelected and like all his predecessors, both Republicans and Democrats, he will continue to make use of the United Nations and its agencies as a useful and important component of American foreign policy. As the pace of economic globalization accelerates and the world becomes more interdependent and interconnected, the role of the UN and all of its agencies will be more important than ever. The oceans no longer buffer the United States from the rest of the world, and unilateralism simply does not square with global needs and realities.

Epilogue

The Global Race Between China and the United States

In the year 2013, Americans are gripped by fear. Most of these fears arise from domestic issues such as the national debt and unemployment. Many are wondering whether the position of the United States as the lone super power in the world will be lost to China. Whether or not the United States is eclipsed by China is dependent upon the will and ability of leaders in both countries to tackle enormous problems which could well derail each country's quest for dominance.

In analyzing the economic race between the two countries, there are several ways to measure the size, strength and wealth of a nation's economy:

(1) One way is to measure the gross domestic product (GDP) which is the market value of all goods and services produced in a given time period. By this measure, the current U.S. economy is $16 trillion and China's is $8 trillion. However, since China has a much higher economic growth rate, its economy may surpass that of the U.S.—perhaps by 2020.

(2) Another way to examine the comparative advantage of each country is to measure GDP per capita which provides a rough approximation of average income. By this measure, the United States is ranked ninth in the world at $49,800 (Qatar is first at $102,800) and China is ranked ninety-sixth at $9,100 (Singapore is fifth at $60,900, Hong Kong is tied for seventh at $50,760 and Taiwan is twentieth at $38,500).

(3) In 2011, Arvind Subramanian caused a stir among economists with the publication of his book, *Eclipse: Living in the Shadow of China's Economic Dominance*. He compares the two countries by measuring purchasing power parity (PPP). The price of a bag of rice or a haircut is much cheaper in China and, therefore, money goes much further. Thus, Subramanian argues that the PPP is a more accurate measure because it reflects purchasing power when the same value of money is used. He also takes into account that China has a large favorable trade balance (more exports than imports) and foreign exchange reserves of $3 trillion. The United States has an unfavorable trade balance and a national debt of $17 trillion. On this basis, he concludes that China eclipsed the United States in 2010.

Let's assume that Subramanian is correct. Conversely, we can use the GDP calculation and anticipate that the size of the Chinese economy will exceed the U.S. in several years.

By any calculation, China one day will have a larger economy than the United States This should not be the source of alarm for Americans or those living in any other country. In fact, we should be pleased with the growth and strength of the Chinese economy because it is good for China and the rest of the world. Above all, it is not necessarily a sign that the United States is in a state of decline. In addition it does not mean that China will become an adversary of the United States inevitably leading to a military confrontation. Just because China remains a communist state, it should not be viewed as an evil empire bent on destroying the United States. The United States has a host of problems, but they have been self-inflicted and not caused by China.[1]

Even if China develops the largest economy, it will not be able to repeat the role of the United States in the half-century after World War II when it bestrode the globe with an economic might that was even greater than that of the United Kingdom in the second-half of the nineteenth century. We now live in a globalized world where a country's territorial boundaries mean very little. We have already entered a new global knowledge economy. Knowledge is power which rests on an information base. The internet (invented by Americans) has leveled the global information playing field for billions of people living in countries large and small. The fact that in 2012 there were more than one billion people throughout the world (including China) communicating with each other just on Facebook alone, illustrates the point.

In the future it is unlikely that there will ever be a single super power amidst a field of lesser powers. The new world will be a multi-polar economic world. The U.S. and the European Union will be joined by the BRICS (Brazil, Russia, India, China and South Africa). For example, the UN Development Programme's Human Development Report predicts that by the end of the current decade, the economic output of Brazil, India and China will outstrip that of the United States, Germany, Britain, Canada, France and Italy combined. Economic power will be scattered throughout the world. Nonetheless, China and the United States will still be at the top of the heap. Global interdependence will continue to increase, and is a concept that fits comfortably in the political culture of China. This point is illustrated in a document released by the Chinese State Council in 2011 which states, "China cannot develop itself in isolation from the rest of the world, and global prosperity and stability cannot be maintained without China." Hence, it should not be assumed that China's ultimate goal is global domination. Rather, as David Gossett asserts, China's goal is to be the "necessary nation" and not necessarily the dominant nation.[2]

More Than a Strong Defense

A strong defense is important, but it may no longer be the key to global leadership. In the emerging world of the twenty-first century, military force will likely be confined to the defense of a country's territory and used in those cases when force is requested as was the case of the UN Security Council's decision to allow a NATO intervention in Libya at the request of the Arab League. This contention is supported by former Secretary Gates, who said on his retirement, "If we were about to be attacked or had been attacked or something happened that threatened vital U.S. interests, I would be the first in line to say, 'Let's go.' I will always be an advocate in terms of wars of necessity. I am just much more cautious on wars of choice."[3] In future U.S. military operations to counter terrorist organizations like al-Qaeda, there will be less reliance on nation-building and "boots on the ground."

There will be more reliance on "soft power" (diplomacy, public information and foreign assistance) and "grey power" which operates in the twilight worlds of Special Forces, drones and financial clearinghouses.[4]

The United States now has a national debt of $17 trillion. This amounts to more than $132,000 per U.S. taxpayer. The two wars of choice in Iraq and Afghanistan did not create the national debt, but it accounts for a sizeable portion. Neither the U.S. nor the rest of the world can afford the human and military costs of wars of choice. Some estimates indicate that more than 225,000 civilian and military deaths have occurred in Iraq and Afghanistan. The monetary cost to the United States of the two wars is a staggering $4 trillion including related operations in Pakistan, veterans' benefits associated with the two wars and the debt incurred.[5]

The United States spends more on defense than the combined spending of the next seventeen nations. Even if additional "sequestered" budgetary cuts are included, U.S. defense spending will still exceed the military budgets of the next ten countries combined. The current argument heard in the halls of the U.S. Congress is that the U.S. should continue to increase defense spending because of the rapid rise of Chinese defense spending. The Chinese are especially improving their navy. Most defense analysts believe that an enlarged Chinese navy will remain in the Pacific waters of Asia as a counterweight to current U.S. naval dominance in the region. President Obama and others have made it clear that the United States has no intention of diminishing its military profile in the Pacific and the Indian Ocean. In fact, if the United States contemplated reducing its force in the Pacific, it would be over the objection of South Korea, Japan and most member states of the Association of Southeast Asian Nations (ASEAN).

The ASEAN countries worry more about the rise of Chinese military might than the United States does. Much of this concern centers on the South China Sea where a quarter of the world's trade transits. Moreover, there is a territorial dispute between China and Vietnam and other countries in the area over two island chains believed to be rich in minerals and possibly oil. There have been several military confrontations between China and Vietnam over the disputed territory. The fear of Chinese dominance has led Vietnam to strengthen its military ties with its former enemy—the United States.

After spending several hundred million dollars of U.S. taxpayers' money in 1965, the U.S. Command in Vietnam held a formal ceremony to inaugurate the naval and air force base at Cam Ranh Bay. The base is a deep water sheltered harbor on the South China Sea, 180 miles (290 km) north of Ho Chi Minh City (Saigon). From 1965 to 1973, Cam Ranh Bay became one of the most important U.S. military installations during the Vietnam War. In 1978, the new communist government turned the base over to the Soviet Union on a 25-year lease. Cam Ranh Bay reverted to Vietnam in 2002 and in 2010, the Vietnamese Prime Minister announced that Cam Ranh Bay would be open for use by select foreign navies (including the U.S.) for rest, repair and refueling. With a touch of irony thick enough to cut with a knife, in August 2011, the USS *Richard Byrd* could be seen tranquilly anchored in port at Cam Ranh Bay. In 38 years, the clock came full circle. Now the only difference is that the base has a new proprietor friendly to a former enemy and worried about a 5000-year-old neighbor to the north. Regardless of how powerful the new Chinese navy becomes, the U.S. Navy will continue to make port calls in friendly countries throughout the Pacific. In addition, the United States maintains a significant military presence in Japan and South Korea.

In years past, the major trip-wire most experts saw which could cause a cataclysmic conflict between China and the U.S. is the military relationship the United States has maintained with Taiwan for the past 40 years. In the bilateral relationship between the two countries, the Chinese are more neuralgic about Taiwan than any other issue. Taiwan is seen as a part of China and the Beijing leadership will use any armed force necessary to keep Taiwan from becoming independent either with or without U.S. involvement in the conflict. The best hope is that someday Taiwan will be reintegrated into China with a special status agreement similar to Hong Kong. But the U.S. military relationship with Taiwan will need to be addressed before any special relationship between China and Taiwan is negotiated. Let's hope the Chinese continue their patience.

Today, a more likely scenario envisages the United States being dragged into a conflict as a third party. The most obvious example of this scenario is the increased tension between China and Japan due to the territorial dispute over the islands known to the Japanese as the Senkaku and to the Chinese as the Diaoyu. Because of the U.S.-Japan Security Treaty, which has endured for more than fifty years, if China were to attack the islands, the U.S. could well be obligated to enter the conflict. The crisis over the islands started in 2010 when a Chinese trawler captain confronted Japanese patrol-ships. Despite the fact there is an ancient animosity between China and Japan, if cooler heads from both countries are involved in negotiations, it is likely a conflict can be averted. But if the Chinese act out of a fear of encirclement and the Japanese act out of a perceived insult to their national honor, a dispute over these insignificant islands could lead to a major war.[6]

Obstacles to Chinese Dominance

There are several obstacles which will delay or prevent China's rise to supremacy. The first is environmental degradation. Historically, communist countries have had deplorable environmental records and China is no exception. The most alarming assessment of the problem was made by Jeff Schweitzer, a former Clinton White House science advisor. He notes that seventy percent of rivers, canals, lakes and streams throughout the country are heavily polluted. Of the twenty most heavily polluted cities in the world, sixteen are located in China. Almost 6,000 square miles of forests and grasslands are lost to desertification each year.[7]

China is now the world's largest auto market. More than 100 million vehicles are releasing tons of pollutants in the air especially in the cities. Most electric power generating plants burn coal, as do most Chinese households. One ton of coal is burned each year for every Chinese man, woman and child for a total of 1.3 billion tons. The World Health Organization estimates that 750,000 Chinese die each year from ailments directly attributable to air and water pollution. In recent years the Chinese authorities have taken steps to reduce environmental degradation because they know that China cannot have sustainable development without sound environmental policies. But the pollution beast escaped from the cage more than a half-century ago and the Chinese leaders will have a monumental task bringing it under control. Economists who follow the problem all agree that the government of China will be required to spend an enormous amount of money to clean up and restore its ecosystem which has been ravaged for the past half century.

Social Unrest, Rapid Development and Corruption

The Chinese have a strong sense of social justice. If treated unfairly, they will band together and organize a protest or demonstration to demand that a public official or business owner correct the injustice. There are more than 100,000 such protests each year throughout China. It is no surprise that most of these protests are unreported. In most countries, such protests occur in large cities, but in China most often they occur in a village, town or suburb. These disturbances are generally quelled by the heavy hand of the police without a proper hearing of the complaints being made. In many cases the confrontation leads to violence and the loss of life. Most protests focus on social and economic issues but usually have a political undertone because public officials become involved in suppressing the disturbance.

The Chinese are proud of their country's rapid economic rise, but there is a price to be paid for rapid economic growth which can easily be seen in the damage done to the environment. Another facet of rapid growth is found in the confiscation of farmland by local governments for developing housing or factories. The aggrieved farmers do not receive fair compensation and believe, with good reason, the local officials are in collusion with the developers who are constructing the factories and housing. In many cases insult is added to injury when an industrial plant is built on the confiscated land and then produces air and water pollution which threaten the health and natural beauty of the area. These types of conflicts involve both private owners and public officials. There have been thousands of cases of social unrest caused by factory owners who treat their employees like slave labor and force them to work in deplorable conditions. When the employees organize a protest, they are then charged with disturbing the peace and the protest is suppressed. Traditionally labor unions have been under the control of the Party, but in recent years there have been numerous cases of unauthorized strikes. Most of these are quickly thwarted; however, in several cases the local authorities have turned a blind eye to the strike if the factory has a foreign owner.

In December 2011 the residents of the small fishing village of Wukan, in the southern province of Guangdong, became so incensed over allegations of corrupt land deals between public officials and private individuals that they took control of the village and attacked the local police station. In typical fashion, security forces retaliated by using violence and arresting the leaders of the protest. In an effort to avert a mini–Tiananmen crisis, the provincial Party Secretary Wang Yang went to the village and agreed to changes demanded by the villagers. The residents of Wukan decided on a democratic process to select the new leadership for the village. An election was held and the corrupt village chiefs were replaced and punished. A brutal suppression was avoided and the public image of provincial Party boss Wang Yang was substantially enhanced. At least in the near future, it is unlikely that this democratic process will spread to Beijing despite the comments of former Premier Wen Jiabao, who reacted to the initial revolt by saying, "We can no longer sacrifice farmers' land rights to lower the cost of industrialization."[8]

Health and safety concerns rank high in the number of cases of social unrest. Since this is an area that involves the role of local and national government in the protection of health and safety, invariably grievances become politicized. A case that received global coverage occurred in 2009 and focused on the Sanlu Dairy which produced tainted milk that killed six infants and sickened 300,000. The outraged parents directed their scorn on public officials at all levels and charged them with neglect in oversight and collusion with senior executives in the company. A "show trial" was eventually held and three of the defendants received a death sentence and a score of others received prison sentences. The "show trial" did little to reduce the seething discontent of a half-million Chinese, many of whom remained convinced that the problem is endemic to the system.

A 2011 case which caused national consternation was a high speed train crash in which forty people were killed and two hundred injured. The Chinese internet was jammed with several million messages expressing outrage at the national government and especially the railway ministry. Familiar charges were voiced of incompetence, lack of oversight, rigged bidding and faulty construction. The incident caused the State Council to launch an investigation of public safety and the funding of major construction contracts. Fresh in the minds of most Chinese is the fact that a few months before the accident, the railway minister was dismissed for receiving $125 million in contract kick-backs. His case is still under investigation. Hence, it comes as no surprise that a Pew Research Center public opinion poll conducted in China in 2008, indicates that eighty percent of those polled see corruption of public officials as a major problem. It is a concern which seriously erodes public confidence in public institutions at all levels.

It is clear that China lacks an effective method of conflict resolution. In the years ahead, brutal suppression, "show trials," an enlarged security force and censorship of the press will not suffice. Social unrest will continue to increase to an unmanageable level until a transparent, impartial and honest mechanism is found. This can only be done through the adoption of the necessary accoutrements of democracy — the rule of law, an independent judiciary, freedom of speech and the press, a transparent legal system and a set of public institutions which operate under the law and are fair, honest, effective and efficient. This means that a transparent government must govern China and not the Communist Party of China.

Deng Xiaoping believed that harmony and stability could only be assured under the one-party system. His disciple, Zhao Ziyang, doubted that a one-party system would ever curb corruption and other "negative phenomena." Before his death Zhao concluded that a parliamentary democracy should be adopted to promote the continued prosperity and stability of the country. Former Premier Wen Jiabao is Zhao Ziyang's disciple. In a speech made in London in June 2011, Wen said, "Without freedom there is no real democracy and without the guarantee of economic and political rights, there is no real freedom." Wen then went on to address the cancer of corruption and said, "To be frank, corruption, unfair income distribution and other ills that harm the peoples' interests still exist in China." He added, "The best way to resolve these problems is to firmly advance the political structural reform and socialist democracy under the rule of law."[9]

Since the early days of communist rule, there has been a system of re-education-through-labor camps throughout China. For decades these camps, known as laojaio in Chinese have been used to incarcerate dissidents and "counter revolutionaries." Recently there has emerged a slight ray of hope in the struggle to improve human rights in China with the announcement in January 2013 that these "black jails" will be abolished within a year in the major southern province of Guangdong. Another southern province (Yunnan) followed suit by making a similar announcement in February, 2013. In light of the fact that there are an estimated 350 such facilities nationwide, these are small steps but nonetheless important.[10] This indicates that there are at least some senior leaders who recognize that they should seek the stability of a cyclist moving forward and not the stability of an unmovable object which is still the current thinking of the sclerotic Communist Party.

The Wealth-Poverty Gap

Analysts often dwell on the differences between China and the United States. But there is one glaring similarity which warrants closer scrutiny. It is the widening gap between wealth and poverty. According to data published by the IMF in 2010, among the ten largest economies in the world, the largest gap between wealth and poverty is found in the U.S. and China is second. According to the *Financial Times*, the top five countries with the largest number of millionaires per household plus the percentage of population this group represents within each country is as follows: United States — 5.9 m (2 percent), Japan —1.5 m (1 percent), China —1.3m (0.1 percent), U.K.—0.5m (1 percent), Switzerland —0.4m (5 percent). The sharpest rise of the super rich is found in Asia and the rate of increase of the super rich is highest in China.[11]

For most Chinese, eliminating the "iron rice bowl" (state guarantee of employment and benefits) in favor of a market economy has contributed to a significant improvement in living standards. Several hundred million have been lifted out of poverty and additional millions have a life style which would compare favorably with the U.S. and Western Europe. Unfortunately some have become enormously wealthy while many others are in the same poverty rut that existed at the time of the 1949 Revolution. As witnessed during the Industrial Revolution in the United Kingdom and United States, inequality is a by-product of development and capitalism.[12] Like the United Kingdom and United States, there has been a mass exodus of Chinese from rural areas to seek employment in the cities. But the major difference is that the enormous size of the Chinese population involved in this migration is simply unimaginable in either the United Kingdom or the United States.

Since the 1949 Revolution, the percentage of Chinese living in cities increased from thirteen percent to forty percent in 2005 and is envisaged to rise to sixty percent by 2030. Four of five of the world's most populous cities are in China. Since the beginning of the economic reforms, the urban areas along the coast have been the preferred areas of investment by the national government and have served as magnets for the rural dwellers. This hybrid planned-market economy has led to rapid economic growth, but has also created huge social problems which must be addressed to maintain the goal of harmony and stability.

There has been a household registration system in China that dates back to ancient times. As a means of social control, in 1958 the Communist Party continued the practice by adopting the household registration system called the hukou. The hukou was intended to reduce migration. Under the system, those eligible for receiving government benefits such as housing, education and health care are required to reside in their home area. If one moves to another area like a city, chances are that person will not receive the same benefits as the permanent residents of the area. The hukou may have made sense under a strict communist-style planned economy. But it is still in use in the new market economy and is causing discrimination, family hardship and social unrest.

In some cases workers go to the city and periodically return home to provide remittances and visit family. But in recent years the trend has been for families to move to the city and hope for the best. There are an estimated 230 million Chinese who make up this floating migrant worker population. The wealth-poverty gap is not an exact urban-rural split because there are large pockets of poverty in the cities. But a poverty analysis would show that those with a rural origin are mainly those in the poverty category.

Many Party officials recognize the hukou system as a ticking time bomb. But like most policies which have endured since the time of Mao, the hardliners are loath to change because it will overload the social services in the urban areas. Moderate leaders like Wen Jiabao know that standing pat is not the answer. In his keynote address to open the People's Congress session in March 2010, Wen said, "[We will] resolutely reverse the widening income gap." He said that part of this effort entails a reform of the household registration system because of the hardship placed on migrant workers and their families from the countryside. Thus he declared: "[We will] gradually ensure that they receive the same treatment as urban residents in areas such as pay, children's education, health care, housing and social security."[13] The operative word is "gradually." Judging from additional remarks in his speech, Wen went on to say that the reforms should start in the small and medium size cities which begs the question of when a new policy will also apply in the large cities like Shanghai and Beijing. Nonetheless, if this small step is taken, it is a start. Fortunately other senior officials share his concern. In March 2010 the Minister of Agriculture sent a letter to the *China Daily* in which he said that younger migrant workers are beginning to develop a strong sense of equality and democracy in an open society. He added: "They reject the rural-urban gap and demand equal treatment in employment, public services and political rights as cities' residents."[14] The vast majority of the Chinese public share this view, and regard the rich-poor gap as a major problem. In the 2008 Pew Research Center poll, 89 percent said this gap is one of China's most pressing problems — second only to their concern over rising prices.

The new Chinese leadership under Communist Party Chairman Xi Jinping recognizes that the inequality gap will ultimately lead to uncontrollable social unrest. As a result in February 2013, the State Council (the Cabinet) unveiled a new thirty-five point plan to reduce the wealth-poverty gap with the announced goal of lifting 80 million people out of poverty by 2015. Major features of the plan include increasing the minimum wage to 40 percent of average salaries, increasing the interest rate on savings, increase spending on public housing and education, and forcing state-owned enterprises to pay 15 percent of revenues in dividends to be used for social welfare programs.

A concern about the income gap and perhaps a guilty conscience over charges of unfair labor practices have led China's largest private manufacturing firm to establish the country's first truly independent and representative labor union. Foxconn Technology Group, a Taiwanese owned corporation, produces 40 percent of the world's electronics and employs 1.2 million workers in thirteen factories in nine Chinese cities. This new labor agreement could have a major ripple effect throughout the Chinese manufacturing sector and result in improved working conditions, increased benefits and higher wages.[15]

Economic inequality in the United States is also a major problem. But, unlike the Chinese, American opinion is split on the issue. On the question, "Is American society divided into two groups — the 'haves' and the 'have nots,'" a September 2011 Pew poll showed that 45 percent agreed and 52 percent disagreed. No doubt the 45 percent included many from the pool of 12 million workers unemployed. Some were also from the millions of people who hold mortgages larger than the value of their homes. In addition some were African Americans who have an unemployment rate more than twice the national average. The 45 percent also included Hispanics — an ethnic group that is falling into poverty at a faster rate than any other group. Those affirming the divide would probably be in the younger generation. The 45 percent would also include well-informed Americans who are aware of the fact that there has been an ever-widening gap between wealth and poverty which has accelerated in the past decade.

Regrettably, in both China and the United States there is truth in the adage, "The rich get richer and the poor get poorer." A study done by the Brookings Institution, an independent research organization shows that the number of Americans living in neighborhoods of extreme poverty increased by more than one-half in the last decade amounting to more than two million. These are areas of high crime and joblessness, failing schools, broken homes and despair. The most alarming trend in the past decade is the concentration of wealth among a few. The 400 richest Americans have a combined net worth greater than the worth of the lowest 150 million Americans. The U.S. Federal Reserve reports that the net worth of the wealthiest one percent of Americans is larger than the bottom 90 percent.[16]

The high degree of income inequality in America is reflected in a CIA Fact Book analysis comparing inequality in 140 countries. The U.S. ranks 40th in income inequality in the world and the wealth-poverty gap in the U.S. is not only greater than that of all Western countries, but is also greater than the BRICS not to mention Iran, Cambodia and Nigeria. The task of the Chinese government in reducing the wealth-poverty gap is monumental. The task in the United States is enormous too. The political environment has changed very little as a result of the 2012 U.S. election. But who knows, there may be more political will to tackle the wealth-poverty gap problem in the communist government of China than in the democratic government of the United States.

Before taking specific steps to reduce poverty and readdress the balance, the U.S. government must formulate an agreed plan to reduce the $17 trillion debt. Of course, such a plan will have a major impact on the wealth-poverty gap. If future savings are made by slashing programs like food stamps and Medicaid which benefit the poor, the number of Americans falling into poverty will increase. But if tax loopholes for individual and corporations are eliminated and the tax rate for the wealthy and middle class are readjusted to the level of the 1990s and adjustments are made to lower the funding flow for Medicare through means testing, funds will be available to put the United States back on a path where Americans are more competitive in the global knowledge economy. In 1993, the 400 wealthiest Americans paid 29.4 percent income tax. In 2008, it had dropped to 18.1 percent. The tax level of the 1990s is still lower than in the Western European countries.

It would be useful for U.S. policy makers to adopt an international development approach to the country's problems. They could start with the universally accepted proposition that the ultimate purpose of development is poverty alleviation and increasing life opportunities. The most pressing problem in America today is the growing gap between wealth and poverty. Poverty in the United States can be defined the same way a United Nations Development Programme report defined it in Vietnam as, "The absence of choice and the lack of ability to participate in national life, especially in the economic sphere." As in China or Vietnam, Americans fall into poverty for the following reasons: (1) they are isolated — physically, socially and linguistically; (2) they do not have sufficient access to resources — credit, skills, information and knowledge; (3) they do not know how to increase their participation — in the economy, in planning and in decision-making — in short, they do not know how to become empowered; (4) they have difficulty in managing risk — natural disaster, health problems, unwanted pregnancy and investments. Each factor can be broken down as follows:

1. In the United States today a large number of Hispanic children living in the country, legally or illegally, start their lives without English language skills. Without these skills, too often they spend the rest of their lives deprived of jobs where a high proficiency in English is a requisite. State and federal governments must place an emphasis on improving early childhood education and teaching English as a second language. However, more money for preschool, elementary, secondary or tertiary education does not provide the full solution. Teacher training must be improved. There must be a closer link between colleges of

education and other colleges on university campuses to ensure that both content and method are equally emphasized in teacher training. Moreover, the curriculum at every level needs to be improved so that there is a clear recognition on the part of students that developing certain skills will lead to more success and happiness in their lives. For some, education and training must be linked to job requirements and this will require a collaborative effort between the business sector and high schools and universities.

2. As President Obama noted, since the economic recession began in 2008, tuition has risen in public universities and colleges throughout the country. Without some form of financial aid, it has become impossible for children from working-class families to attend college. If they do not receive a scholarship, they can apply for student loans, but there are now students graduating from college with a student loan debt of $100,000. This situation is simply not sustainable. More state and federal assistance is required for students in need who meet the admission standards.

3. Nothing succeeds like success. Children born into a family whose parents are successful and have a high level of education have an enormous head start over children born into middle class and poverty families lacking the knowledge, education and connections to enable their children to compete. As socio-economic status decreases, so does voter and community participation. Those who fall into the lower socio-economic category are not empowered and lack skills to become empowered. Education is key to empowerment.

4. The more knowledge, education and financial resources one has, the ability to manage risk is increased. Unwanted pregnancies often push a family into poverty because the woman must drop out of school and the work force, and there is one more mouth to feed. As Charles Murray points out in *Coming Apart*, among white women who lack education and live on the margin, the rate of births out of wedlock have increased from six percent in 1970 to forty-four in 2008. But among college educated women, less than six percent of all births were out of wedlock in 2008, up from one percent in 1970. Among the more affluent and better educated, 83 percent of the marriages are intact. Among the less affluent with a lower level of education, a minority (just 48 percent) of the population lives in a two-parent family. Sex education and access to contraceptives is not the full answer to bridging this disparity because the problem is far more complex and involves differences in basic cultural values. Nonetheless, effective family planning, especially among those who live on the margin of society, is a necessary step in the right direction.

There are three public services in any country which are essential to alleviating poverty — education, health care and old age security. Regrettably, these are services in America which require repair, reform and adequate funding. The task of restoring America's balance is not simply the job of government. Americans must reexamine the social contract and reacquaint themselves with the rights and responsibilities in a well functioning society. Private enterprise, the health and legal communities, educational institutions and community-based organizations must all play their roles in putting the country back on track In today's world, the public sector is successful when it establishes strategic alliances and partnerships with the non-governmental sector in pursuit of the larger goal of good governance. This is an important area where the U.S. has an advantage over China. As a communist state, China has a weak private business sector. In addition, there is a lack of independent NGOs and private philanthropy is just beginning.

Which Will Be Number One?

If China has the world's largest economy by 2020, it will mean that the Chinese will be in a stronger position to withstand pressure from the rest of the world to alter its trade, economic and monetary policies. The U.S. will still be the world's largest developed country and China will be far behind. By 2020, China will still have several hundred million citizens near the poverty line. The Chinese leaders continue to describe their country as a developing country and they are correct in doing so. Perhaps it will remain a developing country for the remainder of the century.

In the Legatum Prosperity Index for 2012, as one would expect, the top ten countries in the index include the Nordics, Australia, New Zealand, Canada, Switzerland and the Netherlands. The "Asian Tigers" (Hong Kong, Singapore and Taiwan) all ranked in the top twenty and outranked France and Japan. In the 2012 global index, the U.S. slipped from the top ten countries for the first time with an overall ranking of twelve. The U.S. economy ranked twentieth.

In 2012, China's global index ranking was fifty-five — a slippage of three places from the year before. The Chinese economy had a ranking of eleven. In all, six of the top fifteen economies in the world are in Asia. The ranking of the Chinese economy seems appropriate for a country with a large and growing economy, also one plagued by various problems expected in a developing country. In summary, China may develop the world's largest economy, but in overall prosperity and economic well-being, it ranks well below the U.S. and Western countries. It will continue to lag the West assuming the U.S. President and Congress reach agreement on an effective approach to reducing the national debt and European leaders can agree on a plan to salvage the euro zone.

In the second half of the twentieth century, the United States reached a position of excellence because of an innovative business community, well-funded public education, and major federal government funding for infrastructure and research in science, technology and health. The country is now divided on the need to invest in the future because it is mired in personal and public debt, a widening gulf between wealth and poverty, and a political debate filled with misinformation and rancor. Unless U.S. leaders at both the national and local levels set a new course, it will be difficult for the United States to remain in the top echelon of countries in prosperity and well-being. Moreover, the United States could lose its coveted position as being the home of the largest number of Nobel Prize winners.

The Fate of America as a World Leader

Having the largest economy does not guarantee global leadership. As is true in all walks of life, a leader's ability to lead ultimately depends upon the willingness of the led to be led. This process works best when individual leaders and countries use influence and persuasion rather than power and violence. Moammar Gadhafi learned this lesson the hard way. In international relations it is now called "soft power." A country's ability to reign as global leader depends in part on a strong economy and defense force. But, of equal importance, this role also depends upon values and ideas. As long as China maintains a political system that abridges the freedom of expression, assembly, the press and religion, and ignores the rule of law, it will not be regarded as the leader of the world. The United States has all of these values and another that trumps them all — equality of opportunity, known throughout the world as the American dream. However, the United States may lose the high ground on equality unless the widening gap between wealth and poverty is addressed. The editors of the London-based *Economist* warned years before the 2008 recession that, "A growing body of evidence suggests that the meritocratic ideal is in trouble in America. Income inequality is growing to levels not seen since the Gilded Age. But social mobility is not increasing at anything like the same pace. The United States is on its way to becoming a European-style class-based society."[17]

U.S. leaders in both the public and private sectors should heed the advice of Jorge Castenada, the former Foreign Minister of Mexico. Referring to the expanding gulf between wealth and poverty in the U.S., Castenada poses two questions: "Does the United States really want to look like what Latin America was? And is there a lesson to be learned from its neighbors to the south — that once inequality becomes entrenched, reversing it becomes incredibly difficult?" He concludes his comments by asserting:

> Why would you [the United States] allow that to happen, when we in Latin America can show you how difficult it is to achieve the kind of exemplary middle class that you invented in the first place, and that gave you such economic power and social cohesion — at least since the 1920s? Especially when we all know its existence is crucial to preserving some of the best traits of your own national character.[18]

Recent scientific studies indicate that the human brain is hard-wired to have an optimist bias. The very foundation of American culture is built on optimism. If it were not for the optimism bias, the United States would still be a thinly populated country of small farmers scattered along the east coast. Large sections of the country are now covered by dark clouds of fear and loathing fueled by uninformed rhetoric from both ends of the political spectrum. But opinion poll data shows that this is not the country most Americans want. Someday a new course will be charted when hope triumphs over fear. A source of hope and inspiration for preserving the basic American value of equality of opportunity comes from Nobel Laureate Martin Luther King who mounted the steps of the Lincoln Memorial one sultry Washington day in August 1963, and proclaimed, "Even though we face the difficulties of today and tomorrow, I still have a dream. It is a dream deeply rooted in the American dream."

Chapter Notes

Chapter 1

1. The story of Roosevelt coining the term United Nations and trying it on Churchill is taken from David Wilton, *Word Myths: Debunking Urban Legends* (Oxford: Oxford University Press, 2004).

2. Lyndon Johnson was famous for his earthy expressions and used the same expression on more than one occasion. The story of Johnson and Wayne Morse was told to me by Senator Norris Cotton (R. N.H.) in 1965 while I was serving on his staff. Johnson also used the expression in explaining why he decided to retain the services of J. Edgar Hoover as Director of the FBI. See book review by David Halberstam in the *New York Times,* October 31, 1971.

3. See *The Journals of the Churchill Center Finest Hour,* p. m/31.

4. The definitive work on the United Nations Development Programme is: Craig N. Murphy, *The United Nations Development Programme: A Better Way?* (Cambridge: Cambridge University Press, 2006).

5. The background information on the UNDP Capacity Study is taken from Joan Anstee, *Never Learn to Type: A Woman at the United Nations* (Chichester, England: John Wiley and Sons, 2004), pp. 247–265.

6. For an entertaining account of Bill Draper's tenure as UNDP Administrator see William H. Draper III, *The Start Up Game: Inside the Partnership between Venture Capitalists and Entrepreneurs* (New York: Palgrave Macmillan, 2011), pp. 103–132.

7. My inspiration for the heading "Herding Cats" is from a delightful piece written by friend and former Bangkok colleague Robert England. *Corralling Cats: Management in the UN Environment.*

Chapter 2

1. The source of the quote of Caspar Weinberger commenting on the Domestic Council Staff presentation to President Richard Nixon is contained in Theodore H. White, *The Making of the President 1972* (New York: Atheneum, 1973), p. 63.

2. See John Erhlichman, *Witness to Power: The Nixon Years* (New York: Simon and Schuster, 1982), p. 343.

3. Randolph Jones, "Otto Passman and Foreign Aid: The Early Years" *Louisiana History* 26 (Winter 1985), pp. 53–62.

4. The definitive monograph of the World Food Conference is Edwin Martin, *Conference Diplomacy: A Case Study: The World Food Conference, Rome 1974* (Washington, D.C.: Institute for the Study of Diplomacy, 1979).

5. Doublespeak is when one deliberately distorts or reverses the meaning of words as found in George Orwell, *Nineteen Eighty-Four* (New York: A. Knopf, 1992).

6. Ambassador Moynihan's experience representing the U.S. at the UN is found in Daniel Patrick Moynihan and Susan Weaver, *A Dangerous Place* (Boston: Little, Brown, 1978).

Chapter 3

1. A history and analysis of three decades of development and crop replacement is found in Ronald D. Renard, *Thirty Years of Sustainable Alternative Development in Thailand Have Achieved Opium Reduction Goals (1970–2000)* (Bangkok: Regional Center, United Nations International Drug Control Programme, 2001).

Chapter 4

1. For a scathing political account of the plight of the Khmer refugees see William Shawcross, *The Quality of Mercy: Cambodia, Holocaust and Modern Conscience* (New York: Simon and Schuster, 1985).

2. An excellent review of the violence along the border is found in Cortland Robinson, "Refugee Warriors at the Thai-Cambodian Border," *Refugee Survey Quarterly,* Vol. 19, No. 1, 1993.

3. For a description of the valuable role of NGOs in the border operation, see Charlotte Benson, *The Changing Role of NGOs in the Provision of Relief and Rehabilitation Assistance: Case Study 2 — Cambodia and Thailand* (London: Overseas Development Institute, Regent's College, 1993).

4. Tim Johnson, "Thai Finance Minister Puts Focus on Inequality," *Financial Times,* June 28, 2010.

5. The quote is taken from Ronald D. Renard, *Thirty Years of Sustainable Alternative Development in*

Thailand Have Achieved Opium Reduction Goals (1970–2000) (Bangkok: Regional Center, United Nations International Drug Control Programme, 2001).

Chapter 5

1. The most enjoyable and readable books on Samoa are Fay Calkins Alailima, *Aggie Grey: A Samoan Saga* (Honolulu: Mutual, 1988), and Fay Calkins, *My Samoan Chief* (Honolulu: University of Hawaii Press, 1962). The most enjoyable and readable book on the various islands of the Pacific is Paul Theroux, *The Happy Isles of Oceania: Paddling the Pacific* (Boston and New York: Houghton Mifflin, 1992).

2. United Nations Volunteers publishes *UNV News*. Stories from this newsletter can be found on the website World Volunteer Web.

3. In 2010 Tokelau made world news. Three teenage boys were partying on the beach on the atoll of Atafu. When they went searching for additional vodka, their aluminum dingy started drifting and they spent the next fifty days lost at sea. They drifted 882 miles (1400 km) before their rescue and managed to stay alive by drinking rainwater and eating seagulls. *ABC Electronic News,* December 2010.

4. The early history of Niue can be found in Percy S. Smith, *Niue-fekai (or Savage) Island and Its History,* published in 1903; and republished by Stephenson Percy Smith (General Books, 2012).

5. Tom Davis, *Island Boy: An Autobiography* (Suva, Fiji: Institute of Pacific Studies, 1992).

6. Jean-Jacques Rousseau, *The Social Contract or Principles of Political Right.* First published in 1762 and republished New York: Dover, 2003.

Chapter 6

1. A fascinating account of the remarkable Soong family in the context of modern Chinese history is Sterling Seagrave, *The Soong Dynasty* (New York: Harper and Row, 1985).

2. The remarkable story of Tim Weber's harrowing experience during the Cultural Revolution was conveyed in an interview at his home, September 2011.

3. An excellent book on the reforms initiated by Deng Xiaoping is Harry Harding, *China's Second Revolution: Reform After Mao* (Washington, D.C.: Brookings Institution, 1987).

4. The infighting within the Communist Party during Zhao Ziyang's final days in office, his expulsion from the Communist Party, his observations of Deng Xiaoping and his musings on parliamentary democracy are found in *Prisoner of the State: The Secret Journal of Zhao Ziyang,* trans. and ed. by Bao Pu, Renee Chiang, and Adi Ignatius (New York: Simon and Schuster, 2009).

5. The conversation between Zhao Ziyang and Mikhail Gorbechev is found in *Mikhail Gorbachev: Memoirs* (London: Bantam, 1997), pp. 632–633.

6. The shelling of the diplomatic compound in Beijing is described by James Lilley, U.S. Ambassador to China 1989–1991, in his book *China Hands: Nine Decades of Adventure, Espionage and Diplomacy in Asia* (New York: Public Affairs Press, 2004), pp. 326–327.

7. The Chen Xitong quote appears in Jamil Anderlini and Enid Tsui, "Mayor Regrets Tiananmen Massacre," in the *Financial Times,* May 30, 2012.

8. For a book filled with insightful private discussions with China's top political leaders, see Henry Kissinger, *On China* (New York: Penguin, 2011).

Chapter 7

1. An excellent summary of UNFPA/U.S. funding difficulties can be found in chapter 8 of Nicholas D. Kristof and Sheryl WuDunn, *Half the Sky: Turning Oppression into Opportunity for Women Worldwide* (New York: Random House, 2009).

2. Background information on DPRK is taken from the definitive work on North Korea by Bradley K. Martin, *Under the Loving Care of the Fatherly Leader: North Korea and the Kim Dynasty* (New York: Thomas Dunn, 2006).

3. Much of the background information on AIDS in China is from Yangzhong Huant, "The Politics of HIV/AIDS in China," a paper prepared for the *Freeman Asia Studies Symposium China,* Lake Forest College, March 31, 2005.

4. Nicholas Kristof, "Raising the World's IQ," *New York Times,* March 31, 2005.

Chapter 8

1. "Vietnamese Foreign Policy: Multilateralism and the Threat of Peaceful Evolution" is an excellent account of changing Vietnamese foreign policy after the death of Le Duan and can be found in a book of readings edited by Carlyle Thayer and Ranses Amer, *Vietnamese Foreign Policy in Transition* (Singapore: Institute of Southeast Asian Studies, 1999).

2. The practice of "fence breaking" is described in Martin Rama, *Making Difficult Choices: Vietnam in Transition* (Washington: World Bank, 2008).

3. Robert S. McNamara and Brian Van De Mark, *In Retrospect: The Tragedy and Lessons of Vietnam* (New York: Times, 1995), pp. 321–323.

4. David Lamb, *Vietnam Now: A Reporter Returns* (New York: Doubleday, 1963), p. 176.

5. Dwight D. Eisenhower, *Mandate for Change, 1953–1956* (Garden City, NY: Doubleday, 1963), pp. 337–338.

Chapter 9

1. An outsider's account of the Mekong negotiations can be found in: Greg Browder, *An Analysis of the Negotiations for the 1995 Mekong Agreement* (Netherlands: International Negotiations, 2000). Another excellent source on the Mekong is Abigail Makin, *The Changing Face of Mekong Resource Politics in the Post-Cold War Era: Renegotiating Arrangements for Water Resource Management in the Lower Mekong River Basin (1991–1995)* (Sydney: Australian Mekong Resource Center, 2002).

2. The stories told to me by Premier Pham Van Dong and General Vo Nguyen Giap about the working relationship between the OSS and Ho Chi Minh

are verified in Dixee Barthomew-Feis, *The OSS and Ho Chi Minh: Unexpected Allies in the War Against Japan* (Lawrence: University of Kansas Press, 2006).

3. The best source of information and analysis on the political machinations within the Politburo during the war years is Lien-Hang T. Nguyen, *Hanoi's War: An International History of the War for Peace in Vietnam* (Chapel Hill: University of North Carolina Press, 2012), pp. 87–109.

4. Premier Pham Van Dong's stories about Ho Chi Minh meeting General Claire Chennault and the OSS officer Rudolph Shaw are described in Bartholomew-Feis, *The OSS and Ho Chi Minh*, pp. 151–157.

Chapter 10

1. See the U.S. government report "Transforming Wartime Contracting: Controlling Costs, Reducing Risks," U.S. Commission on Wartime Contracting in Iraq and Afghanistan (Arlington, VA: UNT Digital Library, 2011).

2. Ibid.

3. The best book on why development assistance does not work is William Easterly, *The White Man's Burden: Why the West's Efforts to Aid the Rest Have Done So Much Ill and So Little Good* (New York: Penguin, 2008).

4. Joseph E. Stiglitz, "Participation and Development: Perspectives from the Comprehensive Development Paradigm," *Review of Development Economics* 6(2), p. 164.

5. The best book on why development works is David Dollar and Lant Pritchett, *Assessing Aid: What Works, What Doesn't and Why* (Washington: World Bank Research Report and Oxford University Press, 1998).

6. Fareed Zakaria, *The Future of Freedom: Illiberal Democracy at Home and Abroad* (New York, London: W.W. Norton, 2004).

7. President George W. Bush, Second Inaugural Address, January, 2005.

8. Joe Hoon Shim, "Park Chun Hee: An Enigma," *IEKAS*, May 12, 2006.

9. Kathrin Hille, "China's Students Put Jobs over Democracy," *Financial Times*, May 21, 2009.

10. A compact and useful source of analysis is Robert A. Dahl, *On Democracy* (New Haven: Yale University Press, 2000).

11. The quotes of Premier Wen Jiabao on democracy are taken from Kent Ewing, "The Empty Talk of Wen Jiabao," *Asia Times* online, May 6, 201, and a Reuters article, June 27, 2011.

12. *The East Asian Miracle: Economic Growth and Public Policy*, A World Bank Policy Research Report (Washington: World Bank and Oxford University Press, 1993).

13. The quote by former Secretary of State Hillary Clinton is from an interview with Richard Wolf in *USA Today*, May 18–20, 2012.

14. The section on the strength and weakness of the UN system is the joint product of the author and Robert England, former UNDP colleague.

Epilogue

1. A penetrating account of the U.S. leadership role in the twenty-first century is Fareed Zakaria, *The Post-American World: Release 2.0* (New York: W. W. Norton, 2011).

2. "Chinese Centralities," Huffington Post blog, April 22, 2012.

3. "Looking Back, Gates Says He is Wary of 'Wars of Choice,'" *New York Times*, June 18, 2011.

4. "Grey power" is defined by Philip Zelikow in his article "Now Obama Must Act on His Asian Blueprint," *Financial Times*, January 10, 2012, p. 9.

5. Watson Institute for International Studies, Brown University (Eisenhower Research Project) press release, June 28, 2011.

6. For an excellent analysis of the island dispute between China and Japan, see Gideon Rachman, "The Shadow of 1914 Falls over the Pacific Ocean," *Financial Times*, February 5, 2013, p. 9.

7. Jeff Schwestzer, "The Ultimate Impact of Environmental Degradation," Huffington Post blog, January 16, 2009.

8. The remarks of Premier Wen Jiabao on the Wukan village revolt are taken from David Pilling, "Where Wukan Has Led, Beijing Will Not Follow," *Financial Times*, January 6, 2012, p. 9.

9. A full text of Wen Jiabao's address to Britain's Royal Society, June 28, 2011, is found on the Xinhau news website, March 16, 2010.

10. For a more complete description of the decisions made to eliminate the re-education-through-labor camps, see Brian Spegele, "China Region Halts Use of Work Camps," *Wall Street Journal*, February 7, 2013, p. A2.

11. David Oakley, "Rapid Growth in Asia Fuels Sharp Rise of the 'Super Rich,'" *Financial Times*, May 31, 2013.

12. Jerry Z. Muller, "Capitalism and Inequality: What the Right and Left Get Wrong," *Foreign Affairs*, March/April, 2013, Volume 92, No. 2, pp. 30–51.

13. World Bank Policy Research Report, *The East Asian Miracle: Economic Growth and Public Policy* (Washington D.C.: World Bank and Oxford University Press, 1993).

14. Found in the Chinadaily news website, March 2, 2010.

15. For a description of Foxconn's labor union decision, see David Pilling, "Foxconn's Union Is a Sign that Cheap China is No More," *Financial Times*, February 7, 2013, p. 9.

16. A comparison of the income tax paid by the four hundred wealthiest Americans in 1993 and 2008 is found in Steven Rattner, "Don't Just Blame Capitalism, Blame the Regulators," *Financial Times*, February 10, 2012, p. 9.

17. "Even Higher Society, Even Harder to Ascend," *The Economist*, December 29, 2004.

18. Jorge G. Casteneda, "What Latin America Can Teach U.S.," *New York Times Sunday Review*, December 20, 2011.

Bibliography

The Bibliography is divided into seven sections. Four focus on the three countries and one large region; the other three sections cover broad topics. The sections are China, Thailand, Vietnam, South Pacific, Democracy, Development Assistance, United Nations.

China

Ahn, Byung-joon. *Chinese Politics and the Cultural Revolution: Dynamics of Policy Processes.* Seattle: University of Washington Press, 1976.

Aiyar, Pallavi. *Smoke and Mirrors: An Experience of China.* India: HarperCollins, 2009.

Arkush, David, and Lee Ou-fan Lee, eds. *Land Without Ghosts: Chinese Impressions of America from the Mid-Nineteenth Century to the Present.* Berkeley: University of California Press, 1993.

Barme, Geremie R. *In the Red.* New York: Columbia University Press, 1999.

Baum, Richard. *Burying Mao: Chinese Politics in the Era of Deng Xiaoping.* Princeton: Princeton University Press, 1996.

Becker, Jaspar. *Mongolia: Travels in the Untamed Land.* London: Tauris Parke, 2008.

Bell, Daniel A. *China's New Confucianism.* Princeton: Princeton University Press, 2008.

Bergere, Claire. *Sun Yat-sen.* Stanford: Stanford University Press, 2000.

Black, George, and Robin Munro. *Black Hands of Beijing: Lines of Defiance in China's Democracy Movement.* New York: Wiley, 1993.

Brook, Timothy. *Quelling the People.* Stanford: Stanford University Press, 1998.

Calhoun, Craig. *Neither Gods nor Emperors: Students and the Struggle for Democracy in China.* Berkeley: University of California Press, 1997.

Carroll, John M. *A Concise History of Hong Kong.* New York: Rowman and Littlefield, 2007.

Chang, Iris. *The Rape of Nanjing.* New York: Basic, 1997.

Cheek, Timothy. *Living with Reform: China Since 1989.* London: Zed, 2007.

_____. *Mao Zedong and the Chinese Revolutions: A Brief History with Documents.* New York: Bedford/St. Martin's, 2002.

Chinoy, Mike. *China Live: Two Decades in the Heart of the Dragon.* Atlanta: Turner, 1987.

Cohen, Warren G. *America's Response to China: A History of Sino-American Relations.* New York: Columbia University Press, 2010.

Chun, Lin, and Gregor Benton, eds. *Was Mao Really a Monster?* New York: Routledge, 2009.

Des Forges, Roger, Luo Ning, and Wu Yen-Fo, eds. *Chinese Democracy and the Crisis of 1989: Chinese and American Reflections.* Albany: State University of New York Press, 1993.

Dreyer. June. *China's Forty Millions: Minority Nationalities and National Integration in the People's Republic of China.* Cambridge, MA: Harvard University Press, 1976.

Ebrey, Patricia. *The Cambridge Illustrated History of China.* Cambridge: Cambridge University Press, 1999.

Eckstein, Alexander. *China's Economic Revolution.* New York: Cambridge University Press, 1977.

Fairbank, John K. *The Great Chinese Revolution, 1800–1985.* New York: Harper and Row, 1986.

_____, *The Missionary Enterprise in China and America.* Cambridge, MA: Harvard University Press, 1974.

_____ and Merle Goldman. *China: A New History.* Cambridge, MA: Harvard University Press, 1998.

Fallows, James. *Postcards from Tiananmen Square: Reports from China.* New York: Vintage, 2008.

Fenby, Jonathan. *The Penguin History of Modern China: The Fall and Rise of a Great Power, 1850–2009.* New York: Penguin, 2008.

Gifford, Robert. *China Road: A Journey into the Future of a Rising Power.* New York: Random House, 2007.

Gilley, Bruce. *Tiger on the Brink: Jiang Zemin and China's New Elite.* Berkeley: University of California Press, 1998.

Gittings, John. *The Changing Face of China.* Oxford: Oxford University Press, 2006.

Glosser, Susan. *Chinese Visions of Family and State, 1915–1953.* Berkeley: University of California Press, 2003.

Goldman, Merle. *Sowing the Seeds of Democracy in China: Political Reform in the Deng Xiaoping Decade.* Cambridge, MA: Harvard University Press, 1994.

Gorbachev, Mikhail. *Memoirs*. London: Bantam, 1997.

Greenhalgh, Susan. *Just One Child: Science and Policy in Deng's China*. Berkeley: University of California Press, 2008.

Gries, Peter Hays, and Stanley Rosen, eds. *State and Society in 21st Century China*. New York: Routledge, 2001.

Harding, Harry. *China's Second Revolution: Reform after Mao*. Washington: Brookings Institution, 1987.

Harrison, Henrietta. *China: Inventing the Nation*. Oxford: Oxford University Press 2001.

Hessler, Peter, and Sang Ye. *Country Driving: A Journey through China from Farm to Factory*. New York: Harper's, 2010.

Hewitt, Duncan. *Getting Rich First: A Modern Social History*. Trenton, TX: Pegasus, 2008.

Hui, Wang. *China's New Order*. Cambridge, MA: Harvard University Press, 2003.

Iyer, Pico. *The Open Road: The Global Journey of the Fourteenth Dalai Lama*. New York: Knopf, 2008.

Jenson, Lionel M. *Manufacturing Confucianism: Chinese Traditions and Universal Civilization*. Durham, NC: Duke University Press, 1997.

Johnson, Ian. *Wild Grass: Three Stories of Change in Modern China*. New York: Pantheon, 2004.

Kissinger, Henry. *On China*. New York: Penguin, 2011.

Kristof, Nicholas, and Sheryl WuDunn. *China Wakes: The Struggle for the Soul of a Rising Power*. New York: Vintage, 1995.

_____. *Half the Sky: Turning Oppression into Opportunity for Women Worldwide*. New York: Random House, 2009.

_____. *Thunder from the East: Portrait of a Rising Asia*. New York: Vintage, 2001.

Lieberthal, Kenneth. *Governing China: from Revolution through Reform*. New York: W. W. Norton, 1995.

Lilley, James, with Jeffrey Lilley. *China Hands: Nine Decades of Adventure, Espionage and Diplomacy in Asia*. New York: Public Affairs, 2004.

Link, Perry. *Evening Chats in Beijing*. New York: W. W. Norton, 1993.

Ma, Jian. *Red Dust: A Path Through China*. New York: Random House/Anchor, 2002.

MacFarquhar, Roderick, and Michael Schoenhals. *Mao's Last Revolution*. Cambridge, MA: Harvard University Press, 2006.

Martin, Bradley K. *Under the Loving Care of the Fatherly Leader: North Korea and the Kim Dynasty*. New York: Thomas Dunne, 2004.

McGregor, Richard. *The Party: The Secret World of China's Communist Rulers*. New York: HarperCollins, 2010.

Mitter, Rana. *A Bitter Revolution: China's Struggle with the Modern World*. Oxford: Oxford University Press, 2005.

Morris, Jan. *Hong Kong*. New York: Vintage, 1997.

Nathan, Andrew J. *Chinese Democracy*. Berkeley: University of California Press, 1986.

Pan, Philip P. *Out of Mao's Shadow: The Struggle for the Soul of a New China*. New York: Simon and Schuster, 2008.

Perry, Elizabeth J., and Mark Selden, eds. *Chinese Society: Change, Conflict and Resistance*. New York: Routledge, 2003.

Saich, Tony. *Governance and Politics of China*. New York: Palgrave, 2002.

Salisbury, Harrison E. *The New Emperor: Mao and Deng, A Dual Biography*. New York: HarperCollins, 1992.

Seagrave, Sterling. *Dragon Lady: The Life and Legend of the Last Empress of China*. New York: Vintage, 1993.

_____. *Lords of the Rim*. New York: Putnam, 1995.

_____. *The Soong Dynasty*. New York: Harper and Row, 1985.

Shambaugh, David. *Beautiful Imperialist: China Perceives America, 1972–1990*. Princeton: Princeton University Press, 1991.

_____. *China's Communist Party: Atrophy and Adaptation*. Berkeley: University of California Press, 2008.

Scobell, Andrew. *China's Use of Military Force*. Cambridge: Cambridge University Press, 2003.

Selden, Mark. *The People's Republic of China: A Documentary History of Revolutionary Change*. New York: Monthly Review, 1979.

Shirk, Susan. *China: Fragile Superpower*. Oxford: Oxford University Press, 2007.

Short, Philip. *Mao: A Life*. New York: Holt, 2001.

Smil, Vaclav. *China's Environmental Crisis*. Armonk, NY: M. E. Sharpe, 1993.

Solinger, Dorothy. *Contesting Citizenship in Urban China*. Berkeley: University of California Press, 1999.

Spence, Jonathan D. *God's Chinese Son: The Taiping Heavenly Kingdom of Hong Xinquang*. New York: W. W. Norton, 1996.

_____. *The Search for Modern China*. New York: W. W. Norton, 1999.

_____. *To Change China: Western Advisers in China*. New York: Penguin, 2002.

Sun, Yan. *The Chinese Reassessment of Socialism, 1976–1992*. Princeton: Princeton University Press, 1995.

Svensson, Marina. *Debating Human Rights in China*. New York: Rowman and Littlefield, 2002.

Taylor, Jay. *The Generalissimo Chiang Kai-Shek and the Struggle for Modern China*. Cambridge, MA: Harvard University Press, 2009/

Tuchman, Barbara W. *Stilwell and the American Experience in China, 1911–45*. New York: Macmillan, 1971.

Tucker, Nancy Bernkopf. *Strait Talk: United States-Taiwan Relations and the Crisis with China*. Cambridge, MA: Harvard University Press, 2009.

Unger, Jonathan, ed. *The Chinese Democracy Movement: Reports from the Provinces*. Armonk, NY: M. E. Sharpe, 1991.

Van Ness, Peter. *Revolution and Chinese Foreign Policy: Peking's Support of Wars of National Liberation*. Berkeley: University of California Press, 1971.

Walder, Andrew G. *Fractured Rebellion: The Beijing Red Guard Movement*. Cambridge, MA: Harvard University Press, 2009.

Wakeman, Jr., Frederic E. *The Fall of Imperial China*. New York: Free, 1975.

Wasserstrom, Jeffrey N. *China in the 21st Century: What Everyone Needs to Know*. Oxford: Oxford University Press, 2010.

_____. *Student Protests in Twentieth Century China:*

The View from Shanghai. Stanford: Stanford University Press, 1991.

Ward, Peter Fay. *The Opium War, 1840–1842.* Chapel Hill: University of North Carolina Press, 1975.

Weston, Timothy, and Lionel Jensen. *China Beyond the Headlines.* New York: Rowman and Littlefield, 2000.

White, Lynn. *Policies of Chaos: The Organizational Causes of Violence in China's Cultural Revolution.* Princeton: Princeton University Press, 1989.

White, Theodore, and Annalee Jacoby. *Thunder Out of China.* Boston: Da Capo, 1980.

Yang, Guobin. *The Power of the Internet in China.* New York: Columbia University Press, 2009.

Yuan, Gao. *Born Red: A Chronicle of the Cultural Revolution.* Stanford: Stanford University Press, 1987.

Yunxiang, Yan. *Private Life Under Socialism.* Stanford: Stanford University Press, 2003.

Zagoria, Donald. *The Sino-Soviet Conflict: 1956–1961.* Princeton: Princeton University Press, 1962.

Zhisui, Li. *The Private Life of Chairman Mao.* New York: Random House, 1994.

Zhou, Kate Xian. *How the Farmers Changed China: Power of the People.* Boulder, CO: Westview, 1996.

Ziyang, Premier Zhao. *Prisoner of the State: The Secret Journal.* Trans. and ed. by Bao Pu, Renee Chiang, and Adi Ignatius. New York: Simon and Schuster, 2001.

Thailand

Arghiros, D. *Democracy, Development and Decentralization in Provincial Thailand.* Richmond, Surrey: Curzon, 2001.

Baker, Chris, and Pasuk Phongpaichit. *A History of Thailand.* Cambridge: Cambridge University Press, 2009.

Batson, Benjamin A. *The End of the Absolute Monarchy in Siam.* Singapore: Oxford University Press, 1984.

Benson, Charlotte. *The Changing Role of NGOs in the Provision of Relief and Rehabilitation Assistance: Case Study 2—Cambodia and Thailand.* London: Overseas Development Institute, Regent's College, 1993.

Bickerstaff, Bruce. *Your Investment Guide to Thailand.* Chiang Mai: Silkworm, 2010.

Brown, Andrew. *Labour Politics and the State in Industrializing Thailand.* London and New York: Routledge Curzon, 2004.

Boccuzzi, Ellen. *Bangkok Bound.* Chiang Mai: Silkworm, 2012.

Chandler, David. *Brother Number One: A Political Biography of Pol Pot.* Boulder, CO: Westview, 1992.

_____. *The Tragedy of Cambodian History: Politics, War, and Revolution Since 1945.* New Haven: Yale University Press, 1991.

Chandra, Nayan. *Brother Enemy: The War After the War.* New York: Free, 1988.

Connors, M. K. *Democracy and National Identity in Thailand.* New York and London: Routledge Curzon, 2003.

Diokno, Marie S. I., and Nguyen Van Chinh. *The Mekong Arranged and Rearranged.* Chiang Mai: Mekong, 2006.

Dixon, Chris. *The Thai Economy: Uneven Development and Internationalization.* London and New York: Routledge, 1999.

Dunlop, Nic. *The Lost Executioner: The Story of the Khmer Rouge.* New York: Walker, 2006.

Elliott, David L. *Thailand: Origins of Military Rule.* London: Zed, 1978.

Englehart, Neil A. *Culture and Power in Traditional Siamese Government.* Ithaca: Cornell Southeast Asia Program, 2001.

Fineman, D. *A Special Relationship: The United States and Military Government in Thailand, 1947–1956.* Honolulu: University of Hawaii Press, 1997.

Fordham, Graham. *A New Look at Thai AIDS: Perspectives from the Margin.* Oxford and New York: Berghahn, 2005.

Glassman, Jim. *Thailand at the Margins: Internationalization of the State and the Transformation of Labour.* Oxford: Oxford University Press, 2004.

Haas, David F. *Interaction in the Thai Bureaucracy: Structure, Culture, and Social Exchange.* Boulder, CO: Westview, 1979.

Handley, Paul. *The King Never Smiles: A Biography of Thailand's King Bhumibol Adulyadej.* New Haven: Yale University Press, 2006.

Hewison, Kevin, ed. *Bankers and Bureaucrats: Capital and the Role of the State in Thailand.* New Haven: Yale University Southeast Asian Studies, 1989.

_____. *Political Change in Thailand: Democracy and Participation.* London and New York: Routledge, 1997.

Hirsch. P. *Development Dilemmas in Rural Thailand.* Singapore: Oxford University Press, 1990.

Ingram, J. C. *Economic Change in Thailand, 1850–1970.* Kuala Lampur: Oxford University Press, 1971.

Kiernan, Ben. *The Pol Pot Regime: Race, Power and Genocide in Cambodia Under the Khmer Rouge.* New Haven: Yale University Press, 2008.

Kirk, Donald. *Wider War: The Struggle for Cambodia, Thailand and Laos.* New York: Praeger, 1971.

Lasswell, Harold. *Politics: Who Gets What, When, How.* Literary Licensing, 2011.

Lebel, Louis, Dore, John, Rajesh Daniel, and Yang Saing Koma. *Democratizing Water Governance in the Mekong Region.* Chiang Mai: Mekong, 2008.

Lintner, Bertil. *Aung San Suu Kyi and Burma's Struggle for Democracy.* Chiang Mai: Silkworm, 2011.

London, Bruce. *Metropolis and Nation in Thailand: The Political Economy of Uneven Development.* Boulder, CO: Westview, 1980.

Manickam, Mira Lee. *Just Enough: A Journey into Thailand's Troubled South.* Chiang Mai: Mekong, 2013.

McCaskill, Don, Prasit Leepreecha, and Kwanchewan Buadaeng, eds. *Challenging the Limits: Indigenous Peoples of the Mekong Region.* Chiang Mai: Mekong, 2008.

McCoy, Alfred W., Cathleen B. Reed, and Leonard P. Adams. *The Politics of Heroin in Southeast Asia.* New York: Harper and Row, 1972.

Missingham, Bruce D. *The Assembly of the Poor in Thailand: From Local Struggle to National Protest Movement.* Chiang Mai: Silkworm, 2003.

Morell, D., and Chai-Anan Samudavanija. *Political Conflict in Thailand: Reform, Reaction, Revolution.* Cambridge, MA: Oelgeschlager, Gunn and Hain, 1982.

Muscat, R. *The Fifth Tiger: A Study of Thai Development Policy.* New York: M. E. Sharpe and United Nations University Press, 1994.

Ockey, James. *Making Democracy: Leadership, Class, Gender and Political Participation in Thailand.* Honolulu: University of Hawaii Press, 2004.

Pasuk, Phongpaichit, and Chris Baker. *Thailand: Economy and Politics,* 2d ed. Kuala Lampur: Oxford University Press, 2002.

_____. *Thaksin: The Business of Politics in Thailand.* Chiang Mai: Silkworm, 2004.

Peleggi, Maurizio. *Thailand: The Worldly Kingdom.* London: Reaktion, 2007

Renard, Ronald D. *Thirty Years of Sustainable Alternative Development in Thailand Have Achieved Opium Reduction Goals (1970–2000).* Bangkok: Regional Center, United Nations International Drug Control Progamme, 2001.

Santasombat, Yos. *The River of Life: Changing Ecosystems of the Mekong River.* Chiang Mai: Mekong, 2013.

Shawcross, William. *Sideshow: Kissinger, Nixon and the Destruction of Cambodia.* New York: Simon and Schuster, 1987.

_____. *The Quality of Mercy: Cambodia, Holocaust and Modern Conscience.* New York: Simon and Schuster, 1985.

Siv, Sichuan. *Golden Bones: Journey from Hell in Cambodia to a New Life in America.* New York: HarperCollins, 2008.

Sopranzetti, Claudio. *Red Journeys: Inside the Thai Red-Shirt Movement.* Chiang Mai: Silkworm, 2012.

Steinberg, David I. *Burma/Myanmar: What Everyone Needs to Know.* Oxford: Oxford University Press, 2010.

Tanabe, Shigeharu, and Charles F. Keyes, eds. *Cultural Crisis and Social Memory: Modernity and Identity in Thailand and Laos.* Honolulu: University of Hawaii Press, 2002.

Taylor, R. H., ed. *The Politics of Elections in Southeast Asia.* Cambridge: Cambridge University Press, 1996.

Tejapira, Kasian. *Commodifying Marxism: The Formation of Modern Thai Radical Culture,* Melbourne: Trans Pacific, 2001.

Ung, Loung. *First They Killed My Father: A Daughter of Cambodia Remembers.* New York: HarperCollins, 2000.

Winichakul, Thongchai. *Siam Mapped: A History of the Geo-Body of a Nation.* Honolulu: University of Hawaii Press, 1994.

Wittayapak, Chusak, and Peter Vandergeest, eds. *The Politics of Decentralization: Natural Resource Management in Asia.* Chiang Mai: Mekong , 2010.

Wood, W. A. R. *Consul in Paradise: Sixty-Eight Years in Siam.* Chiang Mai: Silkworm, 2003.

Wyatt, David K. *Thailand: A Short History.* New Haven: Yale University Press, 2003.

Young, Gordon. *The Hill Tribes of Northern Thailand.* Bangkok: Siam Society, 1974.

Vietnam

Anderson, David. *Trapped by Success: The Eisenhower Administration and Vietnam, 1953–1961.* New York: Columbia University Press, 1991.

_____. *The Vietnam War.* New York: Palgrave Macmillan, 2005.

Asselin, Pierre. *A Bitter Peace: Washington, Hanoi, and the Making of the Paris Agreement.* Chapel Hill: University of North Carolina Press, 2002.

Bartholomew-Feis, Dixee. *The OSS and Ho Chi Minh: Unexpected Allies in the War Against Japan.* Lawrence: University of Kansas Press, 2006.

Berman, Larry. *Lyndon Johnson's War: The Road to Stalemate in Vietnam.* New York: W.W. Norton, 1989.

Bradley, Mark Philip. *Imagining Vietnam and America: The Making of Postcolonial Vietnam, 1919–1950.* Chapel Hill: University of North Carolina Press, 2009.

Browder, Greg. *An Analysis of the Negotiations for the Mekong Agreement.* Netherlands: International Negotiations, 2000.

Burchett, Wilfred. *The China Cambodian Vietnam Triangle.* London: Zed, 1981

Buttinger, Joseph. *The Smaller Dragon: A Political History of Vietnam.* New York: Frederick A. Praeger, 1961

_____. *Vietnam: A Political History.* New York: Praeger, 1968.

Colvin, John. *Giap: Volcano Under the Snow.* New York: Soho, 1996.

Conboy, Kenneth, and Dale Andrade. *Spies and Commandos: How America Lost the Secret War in Vietnam.* Lawrence: University of Kansas Press, 2001.

Currey, Cecil. *Victory at Any Cost: The Genius of Vietnam's Gen. Vo Nguyen Giap.* Westport, CT: Praeger, 1996.

Duiker, William J. *The Communist Road to Power in Vietnam,* 2d ed. Boulder, CO: Westview, 1996.

_____. *Ho Chi Minh: A Life.* New York: Hyperion, 2000.

_____. *The Rise of Nationalism in Vietnam.* Ithaca: Cornell University Press, 1976.

_____. *Sacred War: Nationalism and Revolution in a Divided Vietnam.* New York: McGraw-Hill, 1995.

Eisenhower, Dwight D. *Mandate for Change, 1953–1956.* Garden City, NY: Doubleday, 1963.

Ellsberg, Daniel. *Secrets: A Memoir of Vietnam and the Pentagon Papers.* New York: Penguin, 2002.

Fall, Bernard. *Last Reflections on a War.* New York: Doubleday, 1967.

Fitzgerald, Frances. *Fire in the Lake: The Vietnamese and the Americans in Vietnam.* New York: Vintage, 1973 [1972].

Ford, Ronnie. *Tet 1968: Understanding the Surprise.* London: Frank Cass, 1995.

Gaiduk, Ilya V. *Confronting Vietnam: Soviet Policy toward the Indochina Conflict, 1954–1963.* Stanford: Stanford University Press, 2003.

Gelb, Leslie H., and Richard K. Betts. *The Irony of Vietnam: The System Worked.* Washington: Brookings Institution Press, 1979.

Gilbert, Marc Jason, and William Head, eds. *The Tet Offensive*. Westport, CT: Greenwood, 1996.

Goodman, Allan E. *The Lost Peace: America's Search for a Negotiated Settlement of the Vietnam War*. Stanford: Stanford University Press, 1978.

Guan, Ang Chen. *Ending the Vietnam War: the Vietnamese Communists' Perspectives*. New York: RoutledgeCurzon, 2004.

_____. *The Vietnamese Communists' Perspective*. New York: Oxford, 2009.

Halberstam, David. *The Best and the Brightest*. New York: Random House, 1969.

Harrison, James Pinkney. *The Endless War: Vietnam's Struggle for Independence*. New York: McGraw-Hill, 1982.

Hayslip, Le Ly. *When Heaven and Earth Changed Places: A Vietnamese Woman's Journey from War to Peace*. New York: Penguin, 1990.

Hess, Gary. *Vietnam and the United States: Origins and Legacy of War*. Boston: Twayne, 1990.

Hiebert, Murray. *Vietnam Handbook*. Hong Kong: Far East Economic Review, 1993.

Herring, George. *America's Longest War: The United States and Vietnam, 1950–1975*. New York: McGraw Hill, 2002.

Hodgkins, Thomas. *Vietnam: The Revolutionary Path*. New York: St. Martin's, 1981.

Hung, Nguyen Tien, and Jerrold Schecter. *The Palace File*. New York: Harper and Row, 1986.

Jamison, Neil. *Understanding Vietnam*. Berkeley: University of California Press, 1993.

Joes, Anthony James. *The War for South Vietnam, 1954–1975*. Westport, CT: Praeger, 1990.

Jones, Howard. *Death of a Generation: How the Assassinations of Diem and JFK Prolonged Vietnam*. New York: Oxford University Press 2003.

Kahin, George McTurnan. *Intervention: How America Became Involved in Vietnam*. New York: Knopf, 1986.

Kaiser, David. *American Tragedy: Kennedy, Johnson and the Origins of the Vietnam War*. Cambridge, MA: Harvard University Press, 2000.

Kamm, Henry. *Dragon Ascending: Vietnam and the Vietnamese*. New York: Arcade, 1996.

Karnow, Stanley. *Vietnam: A History*. New York: Penguin, 1984.

Keikvliet, Benedict J. *The Power of Everyday Politics: How Vietnamese Peasants Transformed National Policy*. Ithaca: Cornell University Press, 2005.

Kimball, Jeffrey. *Nixon's Vietnam War*. Lawrence: University of Kansas Press, 1998.

Kirk, Donald. *Wider War: The Struggle for Cambodia, Thailand and Laos*. New York: Praeger, 1971.

Lamb, David D. *Vietnam, Now: A Reporter Returns*. New York: Public Affairs, 2002.

Lawrence, Mark A. *The Vietnam War: A Concise International History*. New York: Oxford University Press, 2008.

Lind, Michael. *Vietnam, A Necessary War: A Reinterpretation of America's Most Disastrous Military Conflict*. New York: Free, 1999.

Lockhart, Greg. *Nation in Arms: The Origins of the People's Army of Vietnam*. Sydney: Allen and Unwin, 1989.

Logan, William S. *Hanoi: Biography of a City*. Sydney: University of New South Wales Press, 2000.

Lowe, Peter, ed. *The Vietnam War*. London: Macmillan, 1998.

Makin, Abigail. *The Changing Face of Mekong Resource Politics in the Post-Cold War Era: Renegotiating Arrangements for Water Resource Management in the Lower Mekong River Basin, 1991–1995*. Sydney: Australian Mekong Resource Center, 2002.

Marr, David. *Vietnam, 1945: The Quest for Power*. Berkeley, University of California Press, 1995.

_____. *Vietnamese Anticolonialism, 1885–1925*. Berkeley: University of California Press, 1971.

_____. *Vietnamese Tradition on Trial, 1920–1945*. Berkeley, University of California Press, 1981.

McAlister, John T., and Paul Mus. *The Vietnamese and Their Revolution*. New York: Harper and Row, 1970.

McMahon, Robert. *The Limits of Empire: The United States and Southeast Asia since World War II*. New York: Columbia University Press, 1999.

McNamara, Robert S., and Brian Van De Mark. *In Retrospect: the Tragedy and Lessons of Vietnam*. New York: Times, 1995.

McNamara, Robert S., James G. Blight, and Robert Brigham. *Arguments Without End: In Search of Answers to the Vietnam Tragedy*. New York: Public Affairs, 1999.

Moore, Harold, and Joseph Galloway. *We Were Soldiers Once and Young*. New York: Random House, 1992.

Ninh, Kim N. B. *A World Transformed: The Politics of Culture in Revolutionary Vietnam, 1945–1965*. Ann Arbor: University of Michigan Press, 2002.

Nixon, Richard. *No More Vietnams*. New York: Avon, 1994.

Nguyen, Khac Vien. *Vietnam: A Long History*. Hanoi: Gioi, 1993.

Nguyen, Lien-Hang T. *Hanoi's War: An International History of the War for Peace in Vietnam*. Chapel Hill: University of North Carolina Press, 2012.

Oberdorfer, Don. *Tet!* New York: Doubleday, 1971.

Papp, Daniel S. *Vietnam: The View from Moscow, Peking and Washington*. Jefferson, NC: McFarland, 1981.

Pike, Douglas. *History of Vietnamese Communism, 1925–76*. Stanford, CA: Hoover Institution Press, 1978.

_____. *Viet Cong: The Organization and Techniques of the National Liberation Front of South Vietnam*. Cambridge: MIT Press, 1968.

_____. *War, Peace, and the Viet Cong*. Cambridge: MIT Press, 1969.

Pilon, Charles D. *Bridging the Gap: Twenty Years after the War in Vietnam*. Phoenix: Quail, 1996.

Porter, Gareth. *A Peace Denied: the United States, Vietnam and the Paris Agreement*. Bloomington: Indiana University Press, 1975.

Prados. John. *Vietnam: The History of an Unwinnable War, 1945–1975*. Lawrence: University Press of Kansas, 2009.

Quinn-Judge, Sophie. *Ho Chi Minh: The Missing Years, 1919–1941*. Berkeley: University of California Press, 2002.

Rama, Martin. *Making Difficult Choices: Vietnam in Transition*. Washington: World Bank, 2008.

Raskin, Marcus G., and Bernard B. Fall, eds. *The Vietnam Reader*. New York: Vintage, 1965.

Roberts, Priscilla, ed. *Behind the Bamboo Curtain: China, Vietnam, and the World Beyond Asia*. Washington: Woodrow Wilson Center Press, 2006.

Sanson, Robert L. *The Economics of Insurgency in the Mekong Delta of Vietnam*. Cambridge, MA: MIT Press, 1970.

SarDesai, D R. *Vietnam: Struggle for National Identity*, 2d ed. Boulder, CO: Westview, 1992.

Schlesinger, Arthur M., Jr. *The Bitter Heritage: Vietnam and American Democracy, 1941–1966*. Boston: Houghton Mifflin, 1966.

Schulzinger, Robert. *A Time for War: The United States and Vietnam, 1945–1975*. New York: Oxford University Press, 1999.

Sheehan, Neil. *A Bright Shining Lie: John Paul Vann and America in Vietnam*. New York: Random House, 1991.

_____. *After the War Was Over: Hanoi and Saigon*. New York: Random House, 1991.

Sidell, Mark. *Images of Asia: Old Hanoi*. Oxford: Oxford University Press, 1998.

Specter, Ronald M. *After Tet: The Bloodiest Year in Vietnam*. New York: Vintage, 1993.

Statler, Kathryn. *Replacing France: The Origins of American Intervention in Vietnam*. Lexington: University Press of Kentucky, 2007.

Tang, Troung Nhu. *A Viet Cong Memoir: An Inside Account of the Vietnam War and Its Aftermath*. New York: Random House, 1985.

Tanham, George K. *Communist Revolutionary Warfare: From the Vietminh to the Viet Cong*. New York: Praeger, 1967.

Templer, Robert. *Shadows and Wind: A View of Modern Vietnam*. New York: Penguin, 1999.

Thayer, Carlyle. *War by Other Means: National Liberation and Revolution in Vietnam, 1954–1960*. Sydney: Allen and Unwin, 1989.

Thayer, Carlyle, and Ramus Amer. *Vietnamese Foreign Policy in Transition*. Singapore: Institute of Southeast Asian Studies, 1999.

Tonnesson, Stein. *Vietnam, 1946: How the War Began*. Berkeley, University of California Press, 2009.

_____. *The Vietnamese Revolution of 1945: Roosevelt, Ho Chi Minh and de Gaulle in a World at War*. London: Sage, 1991.

Tucker, Spencer C. *Vietnam*. Lexington: University Press of Kentucky, 1999.

Vo, Thu-Huong Nguyen. *Khmer-Viet Relations and the Third Indochina Conflict*. Jefferson, NC: McFarland, 1992.

Vuong, G. Thui. *Getting to Know the Vietnamese and Their Culture*. New York: Unger, 1976.

Werner, Jayne S., and Luu Doan Huynh, eds. *The Vietnam War: Vietnamese and American Perspectives*. New York: M.E. Sharpe, 1993.

Westad, Odd Arne, and Sophie Quinn-Judge, eds. *The Third Indochina War: Conflict between China, Vietnam and Cambodia, 1972–1979*. New York: Routledge, 2006.

Wirtz, James. *The Tet Offensive: Intelligence Failure in War*. Ithaca: Cornell University Press, 1991.

Young, Marilyn. *The Vietnam Wars, 1945–1990*. New York: HarperCollins, 1999.

Zasloff, Joseph J., and MacAlister Brown. *Communism in Indochina: New Perspectives*. London: D. C. Heath, 1975.

Zinoman, Peter. *Colonial Bastille: A History of Imprisonment in Vietnam, 1862–1940*. Berkeley: University of California Press, 2001.

South Pacific

Alailima, Fay Calkins. *Aggie Grey: A Samoan Saga*. Honolulu: Mutual, 1988.

Calkins, Fay. *My Samoan Chief*. Honolulu: University of Hawaii Press, 1962.

Campbell, I. C. *A History of the Pacific Islands*. Christ Church, NZ: University of Canterbury Press, 1989.

Crocombe, Ron, and M. Meleisea, eds. *Land Issues in the Pacific*. Suva, Fiji: Institute of Pacific Studies, University of South Pacific, 1998.

_____. *The Pacific Islands and the USA*. Suva, Fiji: IPS, 1995.

_____. *The South Pacific: An Introduction*. Suva, Fiji: IPS, 1987

Davis, Tom. *Island Boy: An Autobiography*. Suva, Fiji: IPS, 1992.

Davis, Tom, et al. *Cook Island Politics: The Inside Story*. Suva, Fiji: IPS, 1979.

Faleomavaega, Neni F. H. *Navigating the Future: A Samoan Perspective in US–Pacific Relations*. Suva, Fiji: IPS, 1995.

Fanaafi, Le Tagaloa, et al. *Culture and Democracy in the South Pacific*. Suva, Fiji: IPS, 1992.

Freeman, Otis W. *Geography of the Pacific*. New York: John Wiley and Sons, 1951.

Ghai, Yash, and Jill Cottrell. *Heads of State in the Pacific: A Legal and Constitutional Analysis*. Suva, Fiji: IPS, 1990.

Gilson, Richard. *The Cook Islands, 1820–1950*. Suva, Fiji: IPS, 1991.

Hekau, Maihetoe, et al. *Niue: A History of the Island*. Suva, Fiji: IPS, 1992.

Hempenstall, Peter, and Noel Rutherford. *Protest and Dissent in the Colonial Pacific*. Suva, Fiji: IPS, 1984.

Hooper, Anthony, and Judith Huntsman. *Matagi Tokelau*. Suva, Fiji: IPS, 1991.

Huffer, Elise, and Asofou So'o. *Governance in Samoa*. Suva, Fiji: IPS, 2000.

Kamikamica, J. N., et al eds. *Law, Politics, and Government in the Pacific Island States*. Suva, Fiji: IPS, 1988.

Kamisese, Ratu Sir. *The Pacific Way: A Memoir*. Honolulu: University of Hawaii Press, 1997.

Kirby, Lawrence F. *Stories from the Pacific: The Island War 1942–1945*. Bloomington, IN: Authorhouse, 2004.

Mead, Margaret. *Coming of Age in Samoa*. New York: HarperCollins, 1961.

Meleisea, Malama. *The Making of Modern Samoa*. Suva, Fiji: IPS, 1987.

_____ and Penny Schoeffel Meleisea, eds. *Lagaga: A Short History of Western Samoa*. Suva, Fiji: IPS, 1989.

Michener, James. *Return to Paradise*. New York: Random House, 1984.

_____. *Tales of the South Pacific*. New York: Ballantine Books, 1974.

Oliver, Douglas L. *The Pacific Islands*. Honolulu: University Press of Hawaii, 1975.

Rabubu, Asesela. *Façade of Democracy: Fijian Struggles for Political Control, 1830–1987*. Suva, Fiji: IPS, 1995.

Rousseau, Jean-Jacques. *The Social Contract or Principles of Political Right*. New York: Dover, reprinted 2003.

Schumacher, E. F. *Small is Beautiful*. New York: Harper Perennial, 2010.

Stephenson, Percy Smith. *Niue-fefki (SavageIsland) and Its People*. General Books, 2012.

Tate, Sandra. *Japanese Aid Diplomacy in the Pacific Islands*. Suva, Fiji: IPS, 1998.

Theroux, Paul. *Happy Isles of Oceania: Paddling the Pacific*. New York: Houghton Mifflin, 1992.

Thomas, Larry, ed. *Musings on Niue*. Suva, Fiji: IPS, 1997.

Van Trease, Howard, ed. *Atoll Politics: The Republic of Kiribati*. Suva, Fiji: IPS, 1993.

Ward, R. Gerald, and Paul Ashcroft. *Samoa: Mapping the Diversity*. Suva, Fiji: IPS. 1998.

Democracy

Economics and Development Linkage

Ake, Claude. *Democracy and Development in Africa*. Washington: Brookings Institution Press, 1996.

Bellini, Eva. *Stalled Democracy: Capital, Labor and the Paradox of State-Sponsored Development*. Ithaca: Cornell University Press, 2002.

Berendsen, Bernard, ed. *Democracy and Development*. Amsterdam: Kit, 2008.

Bhardwarj, Rattan Chand, and Shri K. Vijayakhrishnan. *Democracy and Development: Allies or Adversaries*. Surrey, UK: Ashgate, 1998.

Greider, William. *One World Ready or Not*. New York: Simon and Schuster, 1997.

Hadenism, Axel. *Democracy and Development*. Cambridge: Cambridge University Press, 1992.

Hirst, Paul. *Associative Democracy: New Forms of Social and Economic Governance*. Cambridge: Polity Press, 1994.

Limongi, Fernando, Adam Przeworski, Michael E. Alvarez, and Jose Antonio Cheibub. *Democracy and Development: Political Institutions and Well-Being in the World, 1950–1990*. Cambridge: Cambridge University Press, 2000.

Midlarsky, Manus I., ed. *Inequality, Democracy and Economic Development*. Cambridge: Cambridge University Press, 1997.

Panizza, Francisco. *Contemporary Latin America Development and Democracy Beyond the Washington Consensus*. London: Z, 2009.

Ramaswamy, Sunder, and Jeffrey W. Cason, eds. *Development and Democracy: New Perspectives on an Old Debate*. Hanover and London: Middlebury College Press (published by University Press of New England), 2003.

Ruescheneyer, Dietrick, Evelyn Huber Stephens and John D. Stephens. *Capitalist Development and Democracy*. Chicago: University of Chicago Press, 1992.

Necessary Conditions

Archibugi, Daniele, and David Held, eds. *Cosmopolitan Democracy: An Agenda for a New World Order*. Cambridge: Polity, 1995.

Dahl, Robert A. *On Democracy*. New Haven: Yale University Press, 2000.

Gutmann, Amy, and Dennis Thompson. *Democracy and Disagreement*. Cambridge: Belknap Press of Harvard University Press, 1996.

Held, David, ed. *Prospects for Democracy: North, South, East, West*. Stanford: Stanford University Press, 1993.

Inglehart, Ronald. *Culture Shift in Advanced Industrial Society*. Princeton: Princeton University Press, 1990.

_____. *Modernization and Postmodernization: Cultural, Economic and Political Change in Forty-Three Societies*. Princeton: Princeton University Press, 1997.

Lindblom, Charles E. *Democracy and Market System*. Oslo, Norway: Norwegian Universities Press, 1988.

_____. *The Intelligence of Democracy: Decision Making Through Mutual Adjustment*. New York: Free Press, 1965.

_____. *Politics and Markets: The World's Political Economic Systems*. New York: Basic Books, 1997.

Linz, Juan J., and Alfred Stepan. *Problems of Democratic Transition and Consolidation: Southern Europe, South America, and Post-Communist Europe*. Baltimore: Johns Hopkins University Press, 1996.

Przeworski, Adam. *Democracy and the Market: Political and Economic Reforms in Eastern Europe and Latin America*. Cambridge: Cambridge University Press, 1991.

Sen, Amartya. *Inequality Reexamined*. New York: Russell Sage Foundation, and Cambridge, MA: Harvard University Press, 1992.

Von Hayek, Friedrich A. *The Road to Serfdom*. Chicago: University of Chicago Press, 1976.

Walzer, Michael. *On Toleration*. New Haven and London: Yale University Press, 1997.

Origins, Institutions, Benefits and Limitations

Barber, Benjamin R. *Strong Democracy: Participatory Politics for a New Age*. Berkeley: University of California Press, 1984.

Dahl, Robert. *Democracy and Its Critics*. New Haven: Yale University Press, 1989.

_____. *Democracy and Its Culture*. New Haven: Yale University Press, 1989.

Dewey, John. *Freedom and Culture*. Amherst, NY: Prometheus, 1989.

Diamond, Larry, et al., eds. *Consolidating the Third Wave Democracies*. Baltimore: Johns Hopkins University Press, 1997.

Fishkin, James. *Democracy and Deliberation: New Directions for Democratic Reform*. New Haven and London: Yale University Press, 1991.

Gutmann, Amy. *Liberal Equality*. Cambridge: Cambridge University Press, 1980.

Held, David. *Models of Democracy*, 2d ed. Stanford: Stanford University Press, 1996.

Huntington, Samuel P. *The Third Wave: Democratization in the Late Twentieth Century*. Norman: University of Oklahoma Press, 1991.

Keane, John. *The Life and Death of Democracy*. New York: Simon and Schuster, 2009.

Lijphart, Arend. *Democracies: Patterns of Majoritarian and Consensus Government in Twenty-One Countries*. New Haven: Yale University Press, 1984.

_____. *Democracy in Plural Societies: A Comparative Exploration*. New Haven: Yale University Press, 1977.

_____. *Parliamentary versus Presidential Government*. Oxford: Oxford University Press, 1992.

Linz, Juan J., and Arturo Valenzuela, eds. *The Failure of Presidential Democracy*. Baltimore: Johns Hopkins University Press, 1994.

Sartori, Giovanni. *Comparative Constitutional Engineering: An Inquiry into Structures, Incentives, and Outcomes*. London: Macmillan, 1994.

Vanhanen, Tatu. *The Process of Democratization: A Comparative Study of 147 States, 1980–88*. New York: Crane Russak, 1990.

Zakaria, Fareed. *The Future of Freedom: Illiberal Democracy at Home and Abroad*. New York: W. W. Norton, 2007.

Catalyzing Development: A New Vision for Aid. Washington, D.C.: Brookings Institution, 2011.

Kaul, Inge, Isabelle Grunberg, and Mark Stern. *Global Public Goods: International Cooperation in the 21st Century*. New York: Oxford University Press, 1999.

Martens, Bertin, Uwe Mummert, Peter Murrell, and Paul Seabright. *The Institutional Economics of Foreign Aid*. Cambridge: Cambridge University Press, 2002.

Moseley, Paul. *Foreign Aid: Its Defense and Reform*. Lexington: University Press of Kentucky, 1987.

Riddell, Roger C. *Does Foreign Aid Really Work?* New York: Oxford University Press, 2008.

_____. *Foreign Aid Reconsidered*. Suffolk, UK: James Currey, 1987.

Rostow, W. W. *The Stages of Economic Growth: A Non-Communist Manifesto*. Cambridge: Cambridge University Press, 1990.

Sachs, Jeffrey. *The Battle of Poverty*. New York: Penguin, 2005.

Sridhar, Devi. *The Battle Against Hunger: Choice, Circumstance and the World Bank*. New York: Oxford University Press, 2008.

Wood, Robert E. *From Marshall Plan to Debt Crisis: Foreign Aid and Development Choices in the World Economy*. Berkeley: University of California Press, 1986.

Development Assistance

Arvin, Mark. *New Perspectives on Foreign Aid and Economic Development*. New York: Praeger, 2002.

Addison, Tony, and George Mavrotas, eds. *Development Finance in the Global Economy*. Basingstoke, United Kingdom: Palgrave Macmillan, 2008.

Barder, Owen. *Beyond Planning: Markets and Networks for Better Aid*. Washington: Center for Global Development, 2009.

Banerjee, Abhijit Vinayuk, et al. *Making Aid Work*. Cambridge, MA.: MIT, 2007.

Birdsall, Nancy, and William D. Savedoff. *Cash on Delivery: A New Approach to Foreign Aid*. Washington: Center for Global Development, 2010.

Browne, Stephen. *Beyond Aid: From Patronage to Partnership*. Surrey, UK: Ashgate, 1999.

Collier, Paul. *The Bottom Billion*. New York: Oxford University Press, 2007.

Easterly, William, ed. *Reinventing Foreign Aid*. Cambridge MA: MIT Press, 2008.

_____. *The White Man's Burden: Why the West's Efforts to Aid the Rest Have Done So Much Ill and So Little Good*. New York: Penguin, 2006.

Eberstadt, Nicholas. *Foreign Aid and American Purpose*. Washington: American Enterprise Institute, 1989.

Fox, Jonathan, and David Brown, eds. *The Struggle for Accountability*. Cambridge, MA: MIT Press, 1998.

Germidis D. *Financial Systems and Development: What Role for Formal and Informal Financial Sectors*. Paris: OECD, 1991.

Herman, Barry, Jose Antonio Ocampo, and Shari Spiegel, eds. *Dealing Better with Developing Country Debt*. New York: Oxford University Press, 2009.

Karas, Homi, Kojo Makino, and Woojan Jung, eds.

United Nations

History and Evolution

Basic Facts about the United Nations. New York: United Nations, 1995.

Bennis, Phyllis. *Calling the Shots: How Washington Dominates Today's UN*. New York: Olive Branch, 1996.

Fasulo, Linda. *An Insider's Guide to the UN*. New Haven: Yale University Press, 2009.

Glassner, Martin Ira. *The United Nations at Work*. Westport, CT: Praeger, 1998

Gorman, R. F. *Great Debates at the United Nations: An Encyclopedia of Fifty Key Issues, 1945-2000*. Westport, CT: Greenwood, 2001.

Grey, Wilfred. *UN Jigsaw*. New York: Vantage, 2000.

Hanhimaki, Jussi M. *The United Nations: A Very Short Introduction*. New York: Oxford University Press, 2008.

Hoopes, T. *FDR and the Creation of the United Nations*. New Haven: Yale University Press, 2000.

Kennedy, Paul. *The Parliament of Man: The United Nations and the Quest for World Government*. London: Penguin/Allen Lane, 2006.

Luard, Evan. *A History of the United Nations*, vol. 1. New York: St. Martin's, 1982.

_____. *The United Nations: How It Works and What It Does*. New York: St. Martin's, 1994.

Malone, David M., and Y. F. Khong, eds. *Unilateralism and U.S. Foreign Policy: International Perspectives*. Boulder, CO: Lynne Reinner, 2003.

Meisler, Stanley. *United Nations: The First Fifty Years*. New York: Atlantic Monthly, 1995.

Mingst, Karen A., and Margaret Karns. *The United Nations in the Post-Cold War Era*. Boulder, CO: Westview, 2000.

Pines, Burton Yale, ed. *A World Without a U.N.* Washington: Heritage, 1992.

Riggs, Robert E. *US/UN: Foreign Policy and International Organizations.* New York: Appleton-Century-Crofts, 1971.

Righter, Rosemary. *Lost Utopia: The United Nations and World Order.* New York: Twentieth Century Fund, 1995.

Rivlin, Benjamin, and Leon Gordenker, eds. *The Challenging Role of the U.N. Secretary-General.* Westport, CT: Praeger, 1993.

Roberts, Adam, and Benedict Kingsbury, eds. *United Nations, Divided World.* Oxford: Clarendon, 1993.

Rosenau, James N. *The United Nations in a Turbulent World.* Boulder, CO: Lynne Rienner, 1992.

Sutterlin, James S. *The United Nations and the Maintenance of International Security: A Challenge To Be Met.* Westport, CT: Praeger, 1995.

Weiss, Thomas G., and Sam Davis, eds. *The Oxford Handbook on the United Nations.* New York: Oxford University Press, 2007.

_____, David P. Forsythe, and Robert A. Coate. *The United Nations and Changing World Politics,* 3d ed. Boulder, CO: Westview, 2001.

Leaders

Annan, Kofi. *Interventions: A Life in War and Peace.* New York: Penguin, 2012.

Boutros-Ghali, B. *Unvanquished: A US–UN Saga.* New York: Random House, 1999.

Brown, Mark Malloch. *The Unfinished Global Revolution: The Road to International Cooperation.* New York: Penguin, 2012.

Draper, III, William H. *The Startup Game: Inside the Partnership Between Venture Capitalists and Entrepreneurs.* New York: Palgrave Macmillan, 2011.

Glendon, M. A. A. *World Made New: Eleanor Roosevelt and the Universal Declaration of Human Rights.* New York: Random House, 2001.

Lie, Tryge. *In the Cause of Peace.* New York: Macmillan, 1954

Meisler, Stanley. *Kofi Annan: A Man of Peace in a World of War.* New York: John Wiley and Sons, 2007.

Moynihan, Daniel Patrick. *A Dangerous Place.* Boston: Little, Brown, 1978. Thant, U. *View from the UN.* New York: Doubleday, 1978.

Urquhart, Brian. *Ralph Bunche: An American Life.* New York: W. W. Norton, 1993

_____. *A Life in Peace and War.* New York: W. W. Norton, 1991.

_____. *Hammarskjold.* New York: Alfred A. Knopf, 1972.

Waldheim, Kurt. *In the Eye of the Storm.* Bethesda: Adler and Adler, 1986.

Social and Economic Development

Anstee, Margaret Joan. *Never Learn to Type: A Woman at the United Nations.* Chichester, UK: John Wiley, 2004.

Browne, Stephen. *The UN Development Programme and System.* New York: Routledge, 2011.

Emmerij, Louis, Richard Jolly, and Thomas G. Weiss. *Ahead of the Curve? UN Ideas and GlobalChallenges.* Bloomington: Indiana University Press, 2001

Frederick, Howard H. *Global Communication & International Relations.* Belmont, CA: Wadsworth, 1993.

Garcia, Adriano. *International Cooperation and Development: The United Nations Development Programme Resident Representative System.* Quezon City: University of Philippines Law Center, 1982.

Gardner, Richard N. *Sterling-Dollar Diplomacy: Anglo-American Collaboration in the Reconstruction of Multilateral Trade.* Oxford: Oxford University Press, 1956.

Helton, A. C. *The Price of Indifference: Refugees and Humanitarian Action in the New Century.* Oxford: Oxford University Press, 2002.

Heppling, Sixten. *UNDP: From Agency Shares to Country Programs.* Stockholm: Ministry of Foreign Affairs, 1995.

Hildebrand, Robert C. *The Beginnings: From Dumbarton Oaks to San Francisco.* Chapel Hill: University of North Carolina Press, 1990.

Jolly, Richard, Louis Emmerij, and Thomas G. Weiss. *UN Ideas That Changed the World.* Bloomington and Indianapolis: Indiana University Press, 2009.

Molle, William. *Global Economic Institutions.* London and New York: Routledge, 2003.

Murphy, Craig N. *The United Nations Development Programme: A Better Way.* Cambridge: Cambridge University Press, 2006.

Power, S., and G. Allison. *Realizing Human Rights: Moving from Inspiration to Impact.* New York: St. Martin's, 2000.

Russell, Ruth B. *A History of the United Nations Charter.* Washington: Brookings Institution, 1958.

Shaw, D. John. *The World's Largest Humanitarian Agency (World Food Programme).* New York: Palgrave Macmillan, 2011.

Speth, James Gustave. *The Red Sky at Morning: America and the Crisis of the Global Environment.* New Haven: Yale University Press, 2005.

Tesner, S. *The United Nations and Business: A Partnership Recovered.* New York: Palgrave Macmillan, 2000.

Ul Haq, Mabub. *Reflections on Human Development.* Oxford: Oxford University Press, 1995.

United Nations. *Human Rights Today: A United Nations Priority.* New York: United Nations, 1998.

Weiss, Thomas G., and Rorden Wilkens, eds. *The Global Institution Series.* London and New York: Routledge, 2005–2011. (Note: This is the most comprehensive series of books on various international organizations, primarily UN organizations.)

Index

Numbers in **bold italics** indicate pages with photographs.